AN ARCHAEOLOGICAL GUIDE TO
MEX   LA

4/94

WITHDRAWN

AN ARCHAEOLOGICAL GUIDE TO MEXICO'S YUCATÁN PENINSULA

By Joyce Kelly
Photographs by Jerry Kelly and the Author
Drawings and Maps by the Author

University of Oklahoma Press : Norman and London

By Joyce Kelly

The Poetic Realism of Alan Flattmann (Jackson, Miss., 1980)
The Complete Visitor's Guide to Mesoamerican Ruins (Norman, 1982)

Library of Congress Cataloging-in-Publication Data

Kelly, Joyce, 1933–
    An archaeological guide to Mexico's Yucatán Peninsula / Joyce Kelly.
      p. cm.
    ISBN 0-8061-2499-7 (alk. paper)
    1. Mayas—Antiquities—Guidebooks. 2. Yucatán Peninsula—Antiquities—Guidebooks.
    3. Mexico—Antiquities—Guidebooks. I. Title.
    F1435.K45   1993
    917.204'835—dc20   92-50715
                                                                 CIP

Text Design by Cathy Imboden.

The paper in this book meets the guidelines for permanence and durability of the Committee on Production Guidelines for Book Longevity of the Council on Library Resources, Inc.

1   2   3   4   5   6   7   8   9   10

This book is affectionately dedicated to the delightful people of the Yucatán Peninsula, who have made traveling in their land such a pleasure, and especially to those who have helped us reach the isolated sites. Their constant willingness, cheerfulness, and dedication are a joy.

CONTENTS

ILLUSTRATIONS

ALPHABETICAL LIST OF SITES AND MUSEUMS WITH SECTION AND MAP NUMBERS AND POINTS OF REFERENCE

Acancéh: 1—Mérida
Aké: 1—Mérida
Almuchil: 2—Uxmal, 2D
Balamku (Chunhabil): 5—Xpuhil
Balankanche (Cave): 1—Mérida
Balché: 2—Uxmal, 2D
Becan: 5—Xpuhil, 5A
Calakmul: 5—Xpuhil
Campeche Museum: 4—Campeche
Caracol (Tumba de Caracol): 6—San Miguel de Cozumel, 6B
Chac I (Gruta de Chac): 2—Uxmal, 2B
Chac II: 2—Uxmal, 2B
Chacbolay (Chacbolai): 2—Uxmal, 2C
Chacmultún: 2—Uxmal
Chakalal: 6—Cancún
Chicanná: 5—Xpuhil, 5A
Chichén Itzá and Chichén Itzá Museum: 1—Mérida
Chuncatzim I (Xcanelcruz): 2—Uxmal, 2B and 2B1
Chuncatzim II: 2—Uxmal, 2B and 2B1
Chunhuaymil I: 2—Uxmal, 2D
Chunhuhub: 2—Uxmal, 2D
Cobá: 6—Cancún
Cobá-Yaxuná Sacbé: 1—Mérida
Cozumel Museum: 6—San Miguel de Cozumel, 6B
Culucbalom: 5—Xpuhil, 5A
Dzibilchaltún and Dzibil-

chaltún Museum: 1—Mérida
Dzibilnocac: 3—Hopelchén
Dzulá (Tzulá): 2—Uxmal, 2C
Edzna (Etzna): 4—Campeche
Ek Balam: 1—Mérida
El Cedral: 6—San Miguel de Cozumel, 6B
El Meco: 6—Cancún, 6A
El Real (Temple 3): 6—San Miguel de Cozumel, 6B
El Rey: 6—Cancún, 6A
El Tabasqueño: 3—Hopelchén
Hecelchakán Museum: 4—Campeche
Hochob: 3—Hopelchén
Hormiguero: 5—Xpuhil, 5A
Huntichmul: 2—Uxmal, 2B
Ikil: 1—Mérida
Itzimté: 2—Uxmal, 2D
Izamal: 1—Mérida
Kabáh: 2—Uxmal, 2A
Kancabchén: 3—Hopelchén
Kiuic: 2—Uxmal, 2C
Kohunlich: 5—Xpuhil
Kom: 2—Uxmal, 2C
Labná: 2—Uxmal, 2B and 2B1
Limones: 5—Xpuhil
Loltún (Cave): 2—Uxmal, 2B
Manos Rojas: 5—Xpuhil, 5A
Mayapán: 1—Mérida
Mérida Museum: 1—Mérida

Miramar: 2—Uxmal, 2D
Mul-Chic: 2—Uxmal, 2A
Muyil (Chunyaxché): 6—Cancún
Ni Ku (Punta Cancún): 6—Cancún, 6A
Nohpat: 2—Uxmal, 2A
Oxkintok: 2—Uxmal
Payan: 5—Xpuhil, 5A
Pich Corralché: 2—Uxmal, 2B
Playa del Carmen: 6—Cancún
Pok-ta-Pok: 6—Cancún, 6A
Puerto Rico: 5—Xpuhil, 5A
Punta Laguna: 6—Cancún
Río Bec A: 5—Xpuhil, 5A and 5A1
Río Bec B: 5—Xpuhil, 5A and 5A1
Río Bec N: 5—Xpuhil, 5A and 5A1
Río Bec I: 5—Xpuhil, 5A and 5A1
Río Bec II: 5—Xpuhil, 5A and 5A1
Sabacché: 2—Uxmal, 2B and 2B1
Sacbé (Sacbé-Xhaxche): 2—Uxmal, 2A
San Gervasio: 6—San Miguel de Cozumel, 6B
Santa Rosa Xtampak: 2—Uxmal, 2D
Sayil: 2—Uxmal, 2B
Sodzil: 2—Uxmal, 2B
Tancah: 6—Cancún
Temple 1: 6—San Miguel de Cozumel, 6B
Temple 2: 6—San Miguel de Cozumel, 6B
Temple 3: *see* El Real

Temple 4: 6—San Miguel
de Cozumel, 6B
Tohcok (Tohkok): 3—
Hopelchén
Tulum: 6—Cancún
Uxmal and Uxmal
Museum: 2—Uxmal
Xcaret: 6—Cancún
Xcavil de Yaxché: 2—
Uxmal, 2D

Xcochkax: 2—Uxmal, 2D
Xelha: 6—Cancún
Xkampon: 2—Uxmal, 2A
Xkichmook: 2—Uxmal,
2C
Xlapak (Maler-Xlabpak):
2—Uxmal, 2B
Xpuhil: 5—Xpuhil, 5A
Xulhá: 5—Xpuhil
Yalku: 6—Cancún

Yamilum: 6—Cancún, 6A
Yaxché-Xlapak: 2—
Uxmal, 2D
Yaxcopoil Museum: 1—
Mérida

PREFACE

Some years ago when I wrote *The Complete Visitor's Guide to Mesoamerican Ruins,* I had to make a lot of decisions. Some turned out to be good, such as including only sites I had personally visited. I have never regretted that decision and have followed it also in this volume. Other decisions, such as not including area maps (which would have lengthened all already-long work), proved to be not the best, as has been pointed out frequently by readers and reviewers. That deficiency is corrected here.

Since the completion of my original book I have visited dozens of sites and museums that were not included in it, and another new decision had to be made. To incorporate these into the original format would have increased the size of the book considerably, making it more difficult to carry. For this reason I decided to concentrate on a single geographic area at a time.

A great deal of the new material I have collected is for the Mexican part of the Yucatán Peninsula, and that is covered in this volume.

There have been many changes since my first work appeared in 1982, such as significant advances in the decipherment of Maya hieroglyphic writing by a host of scholars, and architectural surveys that have allowed more precise dating of some of the structures. New excavations have been undertaken, and new theories have been proposed. In Mexico's Yucatán Peninsula many sites have been cleared and consolidated in the last few years, so visiting these sites is now worthwhile, and some new sites have been discovered and reported.

And, happily, some things have remained the same. The people of Yucatán are as delightful and gracious as ever and always happy to help you reach sites you could not get to on your own.

I believe another good decision I made originally was to include a rating system for the sites, to let the reader know at a glance how worthwhile a visit would be. That is retained in this work. Some sites and museums in my original volume have been upgraded because of improvements. There are no *new* four-star sites, however, or even three-star sites (with the exception of Hochob, which has been upgraded), though some come close.

Much of the new material involves isolated sites that you can reach only with the help of a local guide. When I am planning to visit a site of this type, there are certain questions I ask a guide. How far is it by paved road, rock road, and dirt road? What is the likely condition of the rock and dirt roads? How long a walk is involved? How long do you think it will take to get there, see the site, and return? Is there much standing architecture? Are there carved monuments? Is the site cleared or overgrown?

The reader will want answers to the same questions, which I have tried to anticipate. Driving times are listed for each part of a trip, and walking time is included. Road conditions—as far as it is possible to tell—are listed.

In *The Complete Visitor's Guide to Mesoamerican Ruins,* all of Mesoamerica was covered, and the capsule information at the beginning of each site included the heading "Culture," since sites pertaining to various cultures were included. In this volume all the sites are Maya, so the culture heading has been eliminated. In a few cases the original name of a site is known, and when it is, it is listed in the beginning capsule information. When the original name is unknown, then that heading is not included.

For ease of reference, the heading "Maps" has been added. The numbers following the heading indicate on which map, or maps, a site will be found.

My sincere hope is that the additions and changes incorporated here will make this work easier for the reader to use and less cumbersome to carry.

ACKNOWLEDGMENTS

During the preparation of this work several people have provided me with information, some of which would have been unavailable otherwise. To all of them I express my heartfelt thanks and sincere gratitude. My job was made easier because of their kindness, and this work is more thorough because of it. They are E. Wyllys Andrews V, Nicholas Dunning, Victoria Bricker, Walter R. T. Witschey, Bonnie and Jim Bade, Ruth Gubler, and Molly Mignon.

For digitizing my drawn maps and site plans into finished form and for cheerfully complying with many revisions, I would like to thank Phyllis and Robert O'Hair. Their work saved me countless hours.

I would also like to thank my husband, Jerry, for accompanying me to the sites, for taking and printing the black-and-white photographs used in this volume, and for offering constant and loving encouragement while this work was in progress.

PART ONE

• • • •

INTRODUCTION

THE PEOPLING OF THE NEW WORLD

Migrations from the Old to the New World took place across the Bering Strait at a time of glacial advance, when a land bridge formed, perhaps as early as 40,000 years ago. Migrations continued in several waves until around 8000 B.C. These early immigrants were hunters, who followed game across the land bridge. Once across, they followed the ice-free routes in present-day Alaska and Canada, heading south and eventually spreading through what are now the American continents. There is evidence that the Valley of Mexico was occupied by 20,000 B.C., coastal Belize perhaps as early as 9000, and the southern tip of South America at least by 7000.

The early inhabitants of the New World were a mobile population; in addition to hunting, they gathered wild plants to supplement their food supply. In the coastal areas, where some of the earliest evidence of settled villages occurs, the sea provided bountiful food resources, although agricultural products were consumed as well. Some of the wild plants that were originally gathered were later cultivated and domesticated, and as time went on, these agricultural products became an increasingly important part of the food consumed. This gradually resulted in semisedentary groups and, later, the formation of settled inland villages. These changes proceeded at an extremely slow pace, which varied in different regions.

Plants domesticated by the ancient Mesoamericans included maize (corn), beans, squash, chili peppers, and amaranth. Maize was the most important of these foodstuffs and remains so even today in the diet of the native populations. Pottery first appeared in coastal Guerrero around 2400 B.C., in the Tehuacán Valley around 2300, and in the Valley of Oaxaca between 2000 and 1400.

By 1150 B.C. the Olmecs on the southern Gulf Coast of Mexico had developed and were occupying San Lorenzo Tenochtitlán in southern Veracruz. According to Michael D. Coe, this site "has been established as one of the oldest civilized communities in Meso-america, if not *the* oldest." Most of the monuments at San Lorenzo Tenochtitlán were carved between 1150 and 900, including the famous colossal heads. Power then shifted to La Venta, which was the principal Olmec center from 900 to 400. This was during the Middle Preclassic period, when there were major developments in most of Mesoamerica. By the Late Preclassic period (300 B.C.– A.D. 250) ceremonial architecture is found throughout.

Various cultural groups were developing at different rates, but many proceeded to an eventual peak during the Classic period (A.D. 250–1000), when there was a proliferation of activity in architecture and sculpture.

For many years the Postclassic period (A.D. 1000 until the Spanish conquest) was seen as a time of decadence and decline in the Maya area. While many earlier centers collapsed (especially in the southern lowlands), other regions endured, and new centers arose. The view of the Postclassic has changed in recent years. Although a number of new interpretations have been suggested, no single view has been totally accepted. For now, perhaps this period is best thought of as one of reorientation, cut short by the arrival of the Spaniards.

Undoubtedly, tremendous accomplishments were realized in the New World by the native Americans, but the question of outside influence should be mentioned. Many scholars, while admitting *possible* trans-Pacific contacts (probably accidental), generally see no evidence that these contacts were more than incidental or that they had an important or lasting effect on the developments of the indigenous cultures.

The best information we have indicates that the pyramids, temples, sculpture, painting, and other arts we see today in Mesoamerica, as well as the advancements in calendrics, astronomy, and hieroglyphic writing, were products of the people whose ancestors migrated across the Bering Strait thousands of years ago.

THE ARCHAEOLOGY OF THE YUCATÁN PENINSULA

The earliest evidence of the presence of human beings on the Mexican part of the Yucatán Peninsula is found at Loltún Cave. A calibrated radiocarbon date of 2200 B.C. (with a range from 2456 to 2043) comes from a pre-ceramic-level deposit that contained stone tools (chert flakes) associated with animal remains (modern fauna). This is later than the earliest remains found elsewhere in the Maya area and other parts of Mesoamerica. It is possible, however, that earlier remains exist on the peninsula but are still undetected.

Loltún Cave also has some of the earliest ceramics on the peninsula, dating to around 700 to 650 B.C., in the Middle Preclassic period. There is also a platform at Loltún that dates to the same time. Other centers in northern Yucatán have ceramics dating to this period, including the cenote at Maní, Komchen (near Dzibilchaltún), and Chichén Itzá, but none from quite as early are known from Campeche or Quintana Roo as yet. Later in the Middle Preclassic, there is ceramic evidence from Campeche, at Dzibilnocac, Becan, and Edzna from 600 to 400 B.C. There is also evidence of the establishment of agricultural villages during the Middle Preclassic in Campeche.

The earliest known architecture on the peninsula is found at Dzibilchaltún (in the Mirador Group, 4.5 miles west of the site center) and at Komchen. According to E. Wyllys Andrews V, "Before 400 B.C. both Komchen and the Mirador Group provide sure evidence of public architecture in formal arrangements concentrated near the centers of villages or towns."

Beginning in the Late Preclassic, almost all parts of the Yucatán Peninsula were occupied, though the occupation in some areas seems to have been meager. The population growth that began in the Middle Preclassic period continued into the Late Preclassic. Later in the Late Preclassic, some earlier centers were depopulated, while others continued to thrive.

There were many ebbs and flows in the fortunes of individual areas of the Yucatán Peninsula (and their populations) from the Preclassic period onward, and many of these are far from being fully understood. Several causes (and combinations of causes) may have accounted for the shifts that occurred. Among them are population pressures due to rapid growth, partial deforestation of some areas, climatic changes that caused movements of populations to better agricultural lands, and changing trade routes (possibly because of outside influences).

A great deal is still to be learned about the Early Classic period (A.D. 250–600) in the Yucatán Peninsula, but some details of what was happening during this time are known. Dzibilchaltún and Komchen were then sparsely populated; Cobá (in the northeast), first inhabited in the Late Preclassic, continued to show urban continuity; in northern Yucatán, Oxkintok, Izamal, Aké, and Acancéh undertook major constructions.

At Becan, which had been an important Preclassic center in the south, there was a decline in population during the first part of the Early Classic period (A.D. 250–450), followed by an increase in the later part (450–600). Kohunlich, in the southeast, experienced a major period of occupation and construction during the Early Classic. After steady growth during most of the Late Preclassic period, Dzibilnocac suffered a drastic decline in population starting at the end of that period, and there is scant evidence of occupancy during Early Classic times. At Edzna, population also greatly decreased in the Early Classic from its peak during the Late Preclassic, but some architectural endeavors were undertaken.

The bulk of architectural remains seen today by the visitor to the Yucatán Peninsula date to the Late Classic (A.D. 600–830) and Terminal Classic (830–1000) periods, although there are substantial Late Postclassic (1200–1540) remains on the east coast. The

Late Classic period was a time of significant population growth everywhere in the Maya lowlands, including most of the Yucatán Peninsula. Some earlier centers that had been greatly depopulated (or abandoned) were reoccupied. Some of the existing buildings were enlarged and refurbished, and a great amount of new monumental architecture was constructed.

Three prominent architectural styles (named for the areas in which they are found) developed in neighboring regions of the central part of the peninsula during Late Classic and Terminal Classic times. These styles are Río Bec, Chenes, and Puuc (and a style called Chenes-Puuc in an intermediate area); see the Glossary for a brief description of these styles. There was some overlap in time among these styles, and influences flowed from one to the other. Various authorities propose different directions and dates for these flows. What follows is based on a "hybrid" model published in 1985, developed after a conference on the subject.

Briefly, the Río Bec style—the most southerly of the three—developed around A.D. 600, and influences proceeded from this area northward to the Chenes region shortly thereafter. On this, authorities are in general agreement. From the Chenes area, influences emanated to the intermediate Chenes-Puuc zone around 750, and from there to the Puuc area slightly later, again northward. When these influences reached the Puuc region around 770, there was already an architectural tradition in place. This dated back to as early as 550 at a few sites (Early Oxkintok style) and is well represented at a number of sites from around 610 to 770 (Proto-Puuc and Early Puuc styles). Some authorities believe that this earlier tradition was the main precursor of Classic Puuc architecture (770–1000), while others hold that the influences from the Río Bec and Chenes areas were more direct antecedents. Around A.D. 825, the direction of influence reversed, and the Classic Puuc architectural style began to influence Chenes-Puuc and Chenes sites. In the Terminal Classic Period, the Río Bec region felt some influence from the Puuc area. Classic Puuc architecture also spread to other areas during the Terminal Classic period: to Chichén Itzá and nearby sites in the northeast, to Dzibilchaltún to the north, and Edzna to the southwest.

During the Terminal Classic, the centers in the Puuc region developed trade relations with the people of the Gulf Coast of Campeche and Tabasco, as we know from the evidence of ceramics. These people are often called the Putun or Chontal Maya, but who they actually were is uncertain. There is also architectural evidence of influence from Oaxaca to the Puuc sites in the Terminal Classic, in the move to veneer masonry and mosaic decorations.

After the Terminal Classic, the Puuc centers were depopulated, as were some others in northwestern Yucatán. During the Early Postclassic period, Chichén Itzá was the dominant force in central Yucatán, until it, in turn, collapsed some time before A.D. 1200. While in its position of power, it controlled the region to the north, including the coastal area, and thereby controlled trade. Isla Cerritos, on the north coast of the peninsula, is believed to have been the main port of Chichén Itzá, and excavations there and in nearby areas have uncovered trade goods from central Mexico, the Gulf and Caribbean coasts, and both the lowlands and highlands of Guatemala.

In northern Quintana Roo (the northeastern part of the Yucatán Peninsula), Cobá—which had been the dominant regional center during the Classic period—went into decline toward the end of the Terminal Classic, when its main avenues of trade were cut off. Some east coast sites were occupied during the Early Postclassic period, but according to Anthony P. Andrews, "The Early Postclassic Period in northern Quintana Roo is at present poorly understood." The interior of northern Quintana Roo, north of Cobá, is almost unknown archaeologically.

After the fall of Chichén Itzá, the fortified site of Myapán became the dominant force in central Yucatán in the Late Postclassic period, but near the end of that period, it succumbed to waring factions. Also in the Late Postclassic, there was tremendous growth along the east coast of the peninsula and on the offshore islands. Almost all the sites known in this area of Quintana Roo were occupied during that time. Cobá experienced a resurgence, and the Tulum/ Tancah area was flourishing as a port of trade when the Spaniards arrived in the sixteenth century.

CHRONOLOGICAL CHART

The sites included in the chronological chart are large and important ones where significant ceramic studies and excavations have been undertaken. The thin lines in the chart indicate the time period during which a site was occupied; the thicker lines show the site's major period and the time when most of the visible architecture was constructed.

Three of the sites—Edzna, Dzibilnocac, and Becan—also had important peaks in their occupational and architectural histories during the Late Preclassic period, though structures from this period are seldom visible today. The early apogees of these sites were followed by declines (in some cases the sites were nearly abandoned) before peaks were reached in the Late and Terminal Classic periods, as indicated in the chart.

Cobá, after suffering a decline in the Early Postclassic period, experienced another peak in the Late Postclassic, and some of its architecture dates to that period. While there is ceramic evidence of some degree of occupancy at the Puuc sites in the Preclassic and Early Classic periods, it is generally very sparse. At Sayil it amounts to but a handful of potsherds.

The information used to compile this chart came from various sources and reflects the views of several authorities. Others use slightly different beginning and ending dates for some of the periods and for the major period at some of the individual sites. Some archaeologists divide the chronology into more periods, especially for certain areas, but for simplicity's sake these periods have not been included in the chart shown here. These periods are the Terminal Preclassic or Protoclassic (A.D. 50 or 75 to 250), the Middle Classic period (475 or 550 to 650 or 680), and the Middle Postclassic period (1200 to 1400). In any case, the chart should give the reader a fair idea of what was happening on the Yucatán Peninsula (at least at a few sites) during the times in question.

Notes on Dates Used in the Text

The hieroglyphic dates for inscribed Maya monuments given in the text have been converted to the Christian calendar using the Goodman-Martínez-Thompson (11.16.0.0.0) correlation.

In 1986 George F. Andrews published a work on Puuc architectural styles in which he explains his method of dating individual structures on a stylistic basis. This had been done in 1980 by H. E. D. Pollock, and Andrews's system differs somewhat from Pollock's. Andrews based his divisions on Pollock's work, his own earlier studies, and on work by Paul Gendrop.

Andrews breaks the architectural styles into six divisions with the following suggested dates: (1) Early Oxkintok (A.D. 550–610), (2) Proto-Puuc (610–670), (3) Early Puuc (670–770), (4) Classic Puuc Colonnette style (770–830), (5) Classic Puuc Mosaic style (830–1000), and (6) Late Uxmal—found only at Uxmal (1000–1050). (Not all authorities are in agreement with these dates, especially for Late Uxmal.) Andrews also lists structures at a few sites that are in a style he calls "atypical" or "intermediate." These structures seem to be clearly in the Classic Puuc tradition, but they do not correspond precisely to any of the three Classic Puuc styles.

For many Puuc structures covered in the text, Andrews's classification of styles and dates has been followed.

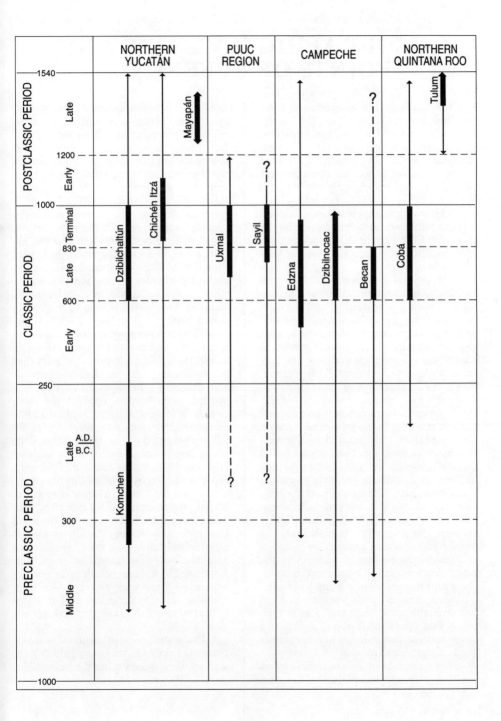

GEOGRAPHIC DIVISIONS AND POINTS OF REFERENCE

The Yucatán Peninsula is made up of three Mexican states: Yucatán on the north, Campeche on the west, and Quintana Roo on the east; geographically, the peninsula also includes the Department of Petén of northern Guatemala, and the entire country of Belize. In this volume only the Mexican portion of the peninsula is covered, and it is divided into six geographic sections. General information about each section precedes the coverage of the sites in that area. I recommend reading the general information for a section first.

The general information includes the availability of accommodations and restaurants, how to reach the area, and the location of nearby gas stations, along with any special points of interest about the area. It also indicates whether a guide is needed to reach sites in that section, and if so, who they are and where to find them. This will prevent excessive repetition of the information in the text for each site.

Each of the six sections is coordinated with an area map bearing the same number. The maps show mileages and the location and name of each site. For each section a point of reference is given. This is generally the best—or most likely—place to stay when visiting sites in that area. In the case of northeastern Quintana Roo, the general information is in two parts, and two points of reference are given: one for the mainland, and one for the island of Cozumel.

Possible stopovers, in addition to the point of reference, are listed, and these include information about lodging and food.

Some sections are so densely covered with ruins that the main area map is then subdivided into smaller areas, drawn at a larger scale, so that mileages and site names can be shown clearly.

The geographic divisions used here are based strictly on accessibility to the sites from the points of reference. These divisions sometimes overlap state borders, which are really unimportant in getting around. Different maps actually place state borders in somewhat different locations. In the case of the Yucatán-Campeche border along Highway 261, there is an arch over the highway, supposedly marking the frontier, but this is not where it is shown on most maps. The problem really is only for the writer who is trying to describe the location of a site. For instance, if the arch truly marks the border, then Yaxché-Xlapak is in northeastern Campeche. If the border is where most maps place it, then Yaxché-Xlapak is in west-central Yucatán. This is true of some other nearby sites as well.

The borders shown on the general map in this volume are those used on the 1: 1,000,000-scale topographic map published in Mexico in 1983 by the Secretaría de Programación y Presupuesto (SPP). These are the same borders used in the *Atlas Arqueológico del Estado de Yucatán* (1980) and on the *National Geographic* map (1989). All of these maps show the Yucatán-Campeche border to be south of the arch on Highway 261, and the location of the sites, given in the text, will follow these borders.

To aid the reader in locating a particular site, an alphabetical list of sites is included at the front of the book, following the list of illustrations. Following the site name is a number, indicating both the section and the area map where the site will be found. This is followed by a name, which is the point of reference for that area, and then—for some sites—an additional number and letter. This indicates on which detail maps the site will also be found.

Under the heading "Location" at the beginning of the coverage of each site, "Yucatán" refers to the state, not the peninsula.

GENERAL ADVICE AND MISCELLANEOUS NOTES

Maps

The maps included in this volume are intended to help the reader reach the archaeological sites and museums covered in the text. They do not show *all* the roads and towns on the Yucatán Peninsula. For this, and for connecting roads to other parts of Mexico, Belize, and Guatemala, you will want to have a good general road map—or several.

The American Automobile Association publishes a road map of Mexico, revised annually, available to their members through their offices in the United States. At a scale of 1:3,800,000, it is generally adequate to get you to and around the Yucatán Peninsula.

The same is true of the 1:3,000,000-scale road map by Shell, published by Prentice Hall and available at bookstores in the United States. You will need something with more detail, however, for the unpaved roads.

In 1989 the National Geographic Society published "Land of the Maya: A Traveler's Map" at a scale of 1:1,609,000. It covers the Yucatán Peninsula and includes some unpaved roads and many of the archaeological sites. It can be ordered from National Geographic Society, Washington, D.C., 20036.

Several maps are available at a scale of 1:1,000,000, which shows more detail. These include "Traveller's Reference Map of Yucatán Peninsula," which is sold through ITMB Publishing Ltd., 736A Granville Street, Vancouver, B.C., Canada, V6Z 1G3, and through some speciality map retailers. This map shows gas stations and many archaeological sites. It also includes plans for the major sites. Another map at this scale is "Mexico Road Atlas and Tourist Cities," published by Pemex (Petróleos Mexicanos), the national oil company of Mexico. It is in booklet form with 41 pages and has symbols indicating hotels, trailer parks, restaurants, points of interest, gas stations, and so forth. The Pemex atlas is sold at some bookstores, tourist shops, and hotel shops in Yucatán. Finally, Mexico's Secretaría de Programación y Presupuesto produces individual folding tourist maps of all parts of Mexico. The one of interest here is "Mexico, Sureste (Península)," which covers the entire Yucatán Peninsula. It has extensive text on the back (in Spanish), describing the various points of interest, and these are cross-referenced to numbers on the map. It can be purchased at the same kind of places as the Pemex Atlas.

If you need maps with even more detail, see "General Information for Section 1" for where to buy them in Mérida.

Guides—The Paper Kind

For your travels around the Yucatán Peninsula, you will want to have a general guide that has more detailed listings of hotels and restaurants than it is possible to give in this volume. Though the guides listed below are recommended, they are far from being the only ones available. Check at your bookstore for others.

A good general guide, and an old favorite, is *Fodor's Mexico* (Fodor's Travel Publications, New York and London). It has information on deluxe to modest hotels (although it does not list them all), restaurants, sights, and so forth. It is revised annually.

Bantam Books (New York) recently began publishing travel guides to various countries, including Mexico. The title is *Mexico,* followed by the year of that issue, and it is updated annually. This guide has become popular, with good reason. It is well arranged and has the usual listings of better hotels and some of the more modest ones, restaurants, shopping, and points of interest. It also gives road connections.

The American Automobile Association (AAA) publishes a *Mexico Travel Guide* annually, and it is available to members. Only AAA-rated hotels and restaurants are listed. While all of these facilities are good to excellent, it excludes other more modest but perfectly acceptable places.

A useful guide for the region is Chicki

Mallan's *Guide to the Yucatán Peninsula,* published in 1986 and revised in 1989 to include Belize. It is available from Moon Publications, 722 Wall Street, Chico, CA 95928. It is also available at some bookstores and hotel shops on the peninsula. It has good informataion for budget travelers, including listings of youth hostels, trailer parks, budget hotels (as well as better hotels), and bus schedules.

Aimed almost exclusively at the budget traveler is *Let's Go Mexico,* (Harvard Student Agencies, Inc., St. Martin's Press, New York), updated annually. It lists *only* budget accommodations and restaurants and has detailed bus information.

A variety of regional guides for the Yucatán Peninsula or for parts of it are sold in bookstores and hotel shops in the larger cities and resort areas on the peninsula.

The Mexican government's National Institute of Anthropology and History (Instituto Nacional de Antropología e Historia, INAH—pronounced *"een*-ah") publishes excellent small guides to the major archaeological sites. These guides are not always available, as certain issues may be out of print at any given time. If you see one for a site you plan to visit, do not pass up the chance to buy it. The guides are not always available at the sites themselves. Look for them at museums and bookstores.

Guides—The Human Kind

Whether to hire a guide to take you on a conducted tour of the larger sites is strictly a matter of personal preference. I am speaking here of sites such as Chichén Itzá and Uxmal and others that are easy to reach on your own. If you have an INAH guidebook or a site plan (see below), you can really get around by yourself, and you will not be hurried through. However, some of these sites have bilingual guides who are generally pleasant and conscientious. They are also bonded by the Mexican government and have identification to that effect. Rates for a tour of the site are sometimes set by the government and should be discussed beforehand. When bilingual guides are available at a site, it is mentioned in the text.

Note: I recommend copying the site plans for the places you intend to visit. Mark any special points of interest and carry the plans with you. The site plans included in this volume are intended to help the reader reach the structures that are of interest to the visitor. They do not show all the structures at the sites.

For some ruins that you can reach on your own, a local guide can be of assistance in visiting the site itself, especially if you do not have a site plan. Examples are Muyil and Chicanná. Often the caretaker or one of his children will offer to show you around, and this will save some time. These guides generally do not speak English, and price is not generally discussed beforehand, though there is nothing wrong with doing so. The price of a couple of beers is normally sufficient for a tour of the site; more, if they have had to do a lot of clearing.

For some isolated sites you *must* have a guide just to get there. Not all of these sites are terribly remote; some, in fact, are only a few minutes from a paved road, but you will not be able to find them without assistance, and it would be foolhardy to try.

It is often possible to locate a guide, make arrangements for a trip, and leave immediately. If time permits, however, try to make arrangements the day before, especially if it is going to be a long trip.

In the "Getting There" section for a site, if the heading *Guide* is included, it means you *must* have one even to reach the site in question. These sites are found in Sections 2, 3, and 5 of this book. The name of the guide recommended for that site is given, as well as where you can find him. More details are provided at the end of "General Information" for that section, under *Guides.* All of the guides listed are reliable and trustworthy and are highly recommended, but this does not indicate that they are the only ones.

It should be understood that while these guides can get you to a site and can point out features of interest that you might miss without them, they do not take you on a conducted tour. These guides do not speak English, and generally price is not discussed beforehand, but you certainly may if you wish. The difference between these guides and the ones who show you around a site you have reached on your own is that you will be spending a lot more time with them. Getting there generally takes longer—sometimes much longer—than visiting a site. Sometimes the trails to and around an isolated site and the site itself are partly overgrown. Your guide will always have a machete along to do the needed clearing. He should be properly compensated.

While I try to avoid gross overpaying, I feel it is better to err in that direction when in doubt.

Language

If your goal is only the four-star sites, lack of Spanish will not be much of a hindrance because guides and key hotel personnel generally speak some English. If, however, you plan to visit some of the isolated sites, a little Spanish will help considerably. You will have to use whatever Spanish you know both in making arrangements and in traveling to and from the site. This really does not take a lot, and sign language will also help.

I recommend carrying one of the small Spanish-English phrase books and dictionaries. Berlitz's is the best known. If you are driving, you will want to know the Spanish for the parts of the car in case you should need a mechanic.

Visiting the Isolated Sites

An isolated site, as the term is used here, is one that can be reached *only* with the assistance of a guide, as described above. By far the best way to reach these sites is in your own vehicle. The availability of car rentals is discussed in the general information for each section. Buses do not go to these sites, but in some cases, where there is a town nearby that can be reached by bus, there is another possibility. You may be able to find someone there with a vehicle, invariably some kind of truck, who will be willing to take you. If they also know how to reach the site of your choice, that is a bonus. If not, you will still have to locate a guide. In any case, this method of reaching isolated sites cannot be guaranteed, but for those who may wish to try, the closest bus connection is mentioned when it is reasonably near, and when the site in question is worth the effort.

Some of the isolated sites can be reached in a standard vehicle, while roads to other sites will require a high-clearance vehicle or one with four-wheel drive. When a standard vehicle is adequate, no mention of vehicle type is made in the text, but when a special type is needed, it is specified in "Getting There." An example of a high-clearance vehicle would be a Combi (a Volkswagen minivan), or even a Volkswagen Beetle. Sometimes four-wheel drive is needed if a dirt road is wet, but not if it is dry, in which case a high-clearance vehicle would suffice. (See "Climate and Travel in the Rainy Season.")

When visiting isolated sites, it should be noted that no food or drink is available, and you should take whatever you will need with you. These sites generally do not even have a resident caretaker.

In traveling to some of these sites, you will be on seldom-used roads that will probably have trees or other vegetation lying across them. Your guide will have his machete, as pointed out above, but having your own to help clear the road is a good idea. In some cases an ax will be better, in which case it would be best to have your own. When you are likely to encounter this type of situation, such as going to Calakmul or the Río Bec sites, it is mentioned in the text.

A few of the dirt roads going to isolated sites are not shown on even the most detailed published maps. In these cases I have had to approximate the routes and have mentioned this in the text. Although the *path* of the road may be approximate in such cases, the *distance* is accurate.

When you are traveling to isolated sites, you will invariably come across unmarked branch roads. Your guide will be able to direct you, and this is the main reason that you must have one along. The maps included here give the distances, but even if you carefully check your odometer reading, you could easily miss an unmarked cutoff by a couple of hundred feet. The cutoffs for some dirt roads are barely discernible, and for some foot trails, impossible to spot. Another reason for having a guide is that if you should have car trouble, someone will have to go for help, and your guide will be better able to do this than you. A third and very important reason is that, because of the looting of the ancient sites, unescorted visitors who go wandering around sites where there is no resident caretaker are not looked upon too kindly by authorities, no matter how honorable the visitor's intentions.

See "What to Take" for additional information.

A Note on "Connection(s)" and "Getting There"

The headings "Connection(s)" and "Getting There" are at the end of the coverage of each site. Generally the first connection given is from the point of reference for that section.

In the case of some isolated sites, an intermediate point is listed, and this is where you can find a guide for the site in question. From the intermediate point, mileages and times to the site itself follow. In some cases, following these directions will entail some backtracking. However, this will give the reader a more accurate idea of the distance and time involved, since a guide is necessary to reach the site. In case you already have a knowledgeable guide with you, distances and times *directly* to the site from the "Connection" are given.

The times listed for driving—and sometimes walking—*are when the roads and trails are in fair condition.* If a dirt road is very muddy or if it or the trail is overgrown and vegetation has to be cut back, it will of course take longer. The distances listed for foot trails are approximate, but the time given should be fairly accurate unless the trail has become terribly overgrown.

The times listed in the text do not include the time needed to find and make arrangements with a guide or to drive him to his home afterward.

Is It Dangerous?

Two questions we are often asked are, first, "Is it dangerous to travel alone in the remote areas?" I assume the questioner wants to know whether one is in any physical danger

from the people. The answer is emphatically no. Maybe we have been inordinately lucky, but we have never felt the least bit threatened or even uncomfortable, and other frequent visitors report the same thing. In fact, the more remote the area, the nicer the people. The people of the Yucatán Peninsula have a well-deserved reputation for their friendliness.

You should use common sense, however, and not invite trouble. Do not leave luggage or camera gear visible, even in a locked car. Keep the items out of sight in the trunk, and keep the trunk locked, especially in the more touristed areas.

The second question is, "What about snakes?" Yes, there are snakes, but we have encountered few, and never in a threatening situation. When you walk through the jungle, you will be making lots of noise and will normally scare off any snakes that may be around. You will find insects to be much more of a problem. Nevertheless, it is advisable to look where you are stepping when you walk on jungle trails.

What to Take

FOOTGEAR: Comfortable footgear is a must. If your only goal is the larger, cleared sites, tennis shoes or the equivalent will suffice. If, however, you plan to visit some of the isolated sites, you will need something more serious, like good hiking boots. When you are climbing over loose rubble and walking over muddy trails, boots are better than tennis shoes. I was once accused (jokingly I hoped) of having a foot fetish. Maybe so, but my sense of adventure dwindles rapidly in direct proportion to the increase in discomfort of my feet. If boots are recommended for a particular site, it is mentioned in the text; otherwise, tennis shoes may be considered adequate.

CLOTHING: For visiting the ruins the most comfortable clothing is lightweight but fairly sturdy cotton. Denim jeans or khaki work pants are fine. For the major cleared sites, ladies will find split skirts (culottes) more comfortable for climbing. Shorts for both men and women are now considered acceptable attire at the major sites, but for overgrown, isolated sites, pants are better for the protection they afford.

I recommend pants (or shorts) with belt loops whether or not you use a belt (see the section "Camera Gear" for why). Cotton or cotton-synthetic blends are best for shirts. Those that are 100 percent synthetic are hot as Hades and cling to you uncomfortably when you get wet, which is always. Long sleeves offer more protection from the sun, insects, and thorny bushes, while short sleeves are cooler. I use one or the other, depending on the trip. Make sure your shirts have pockets—the more the better.

Guayaberas (shirts worn outside the pants) are available throughout the Yucatán Peninsula. They come with long and short sleeves, in cotton and blends, in sizes for men, women, and children, in various colors, with or without decorations, and generally with four pockets. They are ideal. (See "General Information for Section 1" for the best places to buy them.)

You will find a few large handkerchiefs or bandanas useful to wipe the sweat from your brow. Facial tissue just won't do.

Other items you should have are sunglasses (preferably glare free) and a sun hat (lightweight and with good ventilation) for the larger cleared sites and hikes across open country.

MISCELLANEOUS GEAR: If you are traveling by car (yours or a rented one), by all means take or buy an ice chest. It will repay you a thousandfold. Inexpensive, plastic-foam chests are now available in the cities and larger towns of the Yucatán Peninsula. Icehouses are found throughout most of the peninsula, and their locations are listed in the general information for each section. Ice, water, and cold drinks whenever you want them can extend your endurance considerably.

Take one or two terry-cloth towels. When dipped in the cold water in your ice chest and applied to the face and back of the neck, they can be incredibly refreshing, especially when you return to your car after climbing around ruins or from a long hike.

To get rid of the bugs on your windshield, take along a pot cleaner, the sponge kind with a plastic mesh covering. The sponge holds enough water to make the job easier, and the plastic mesh won't scratch the glass.

You will also want a plastic bottle for carrying drinking water with you in your vehicle. These are available in *tiendas* ("shops") in even the smallest towns. The water in the Yucatán Peninsula is very alkaline. Add the juice of a lime to the water to make it more palatable, or carry bottled water. There are times when beer or *refrescos* ("soft drinks") just won't do.

When you are walking to a site and will be away from your vehicle for more than an hour or so, you should have a canteen of water with you. When this is needed, it is mentioned in the text.

For long trips to isolated sites you should have some food along. Canned tuna, deviled ham, and crackers or bread are available almost everywhere (don't forget a can opener), or order something from your hotel restaurant the night before. Box lunches, in general, are not recommended. They consist of two dry sandwiches, a hard-boiled egg, an orange, and a banana. I personally prefer club sandwiches, even if they get a little soggy.

You should have insect repellent with you for all the sites, since even the cleared ones can have insects. Repellent is crucial for sites that are overgrown. We generally carry a spray can in the car and have an extra small bottle in our camera bag for use on the trail.

You will often need matches (or a butane lighter) and paper at isolated sites or on the trails going there. This is to smoke out wasps from their nests. Your guide will carefully do this. He may have some paper with him, but he will never have matches.

CAMERA GEAR: Since all photographers will have their own favorite equipment (preferably already well tested), only general recommendations are made here. You will have a normal lens, of course, and a telephoto will sometimes be useful. Absolutely essential, however, is a wide-angle lens (the wider the better, short of a fish-eye), especially for sites that have not been cleared. Often it is impossible to back off far enough from a struc-

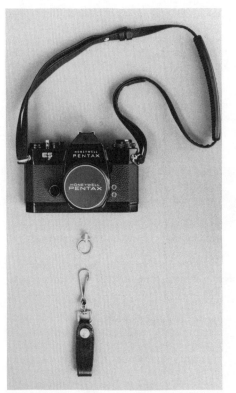

to screws that fit into the bottom of the camera (the case may have to be removed). A machinist can make it for you. To our belts (or belt loops) we attached a leather loop with a snap. To this is attached a spring-type clip. The clip can be hooked through the loop hanging from the camera. It is easy to engage and disengage (see illustrations). It is extremely helpful, especially if you are carrying more than one camera. Lens caps should be kept in place, except while actually shooting.

Your gear will get dirty, and you should have lens-cleaning liquid, tissue, and a brush. Sunshades are a help, and a flash unit can be useful.

Bring your film from home. It is available in the cities and larger towns and at some sites, but it is more expensive, and often the selection is limited. Keep exposed film in its original container and in a plastic bag. Store it in a cool place—which may be hard to find—and have the film processed as soon as possible. Mailing your film home immediately in prepaid mailers is a possibility,

Top to bottom: Camera; screw that fits into camera bottom with attached metal loop; snap clip attached to leather loop, to be connected to belt or belt loop. Unless otherwise noted, black-and-white photographs by Jerry Kelly.

ture to get an overall shot with a normal lens. My favorite lens is a wide-angle zoom that goes from 24 mm to 35 mm. The only improvement I can think of would be if it went to 20 mm on the wide end.

If you are visiting a site that requires a long hike and you have a lot of camera gear, carry it in a waterproof backpack. This is more comfortable than a shoulder-strap bag on long hauls.

While we are at a site, we wear the cameras around our necks and attach them to our belts or belt loops, which leaves our hands free for climbing. This way you don't have to worry about an expensive new lens banging against a stone. We attached metal loops

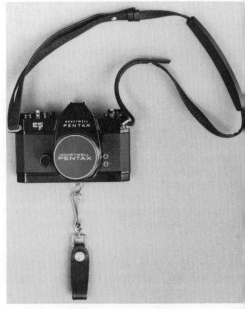

Camera, screw and metal loop, and snap clip and leather loop, as they should be assembled.

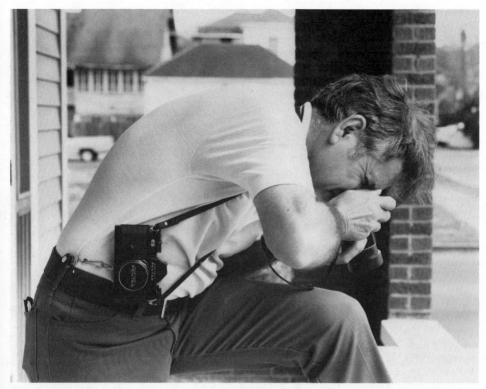

Camera, screw and metal loop, and snap clip and leather loop, attached to belt. Shown as used. Photograph by author.

but I'd hesitate to trust the mails with valuable film.

Photography is freely permitted at the archaeological sites and museums, but tripods and video cameras are generally prohibited at both places. (Exceptions are noted in the text.) Most museums also prohibit flash equipment. Ask before using it.

If you are carrying camera, lenses, tape recorders, or other equipment of other than United States manufacture, you should have it registered with United States Customs *before* you leave home. You will be given a certified list that you can present upon your return. Otherwise, you may be required to pay duty on them.

Entry Requirements and Departure Tax

Citizens of the United States and Canada are not required to have passports to enter Mexico. They must, however, have proof of citizenship and a tourist card. A birth certificate or a passport can be used as proof of citizenship. Naturalized citizens of the United States can use their naturalization papers, but naturalized citizens of Canada must have a passport. Tourist cards can be obtained at the border when you enter Mexico upon presentation of proof of citizenship. If you fly to Mexico, you can get a tourist card through your airline, with proper proof of citizenship.

Requirements vary for citizens of other countries; check with the nearest Mexican consulate for particulars. In general, however, a valid passport with a visa for Mexico will probably be required.

You should have your tourist card with you at all times, since officials at certain checkpoints will want to see it. See "Immigration and *Aduana* (Customs) Stations" for the location of these stations on the Yucatán Peninsula.

If you are driving your own car into Mexico, *please note* that new regulations went into effect in January 1992 and were changed again three months later. As of April 1992, the requirements were as follows: Tourists must sign a declaration promising to return their vehicle to the United States and must pay a $10.00 fee using an international credit card (Visa, MasterCard, or American Express). Cash and checks are not acceptable. (The purpose is to prevent cars from being illegally sold in Mexico.) This fee entitles a tourist to a six-month multiple-entry visa. You must also have your original car title, in the driver's name, and the original current registration.

If the car is registered under another person's name or is in the name of a company, you must have a notarized letter from the owner, giving you permission to bring the car into Mexico for a specified period of time. If the car is not fully paid for, you must have a notarized letter from the lienholder to the same effect. You must also have, of course, a valid driver's license. You will be issued a car permit at the border (as part of your tourist card) to bring your vehicle into Mexico, upon presentation of the above documents.

Since regulations tend to change, it would be best to check with your nearest Mexican consulate beforehand for current requirements.

Mexico has a departure tax on flights, both domestic and international. The tax on international flights is the equivalent of about $13.00 in United States currency; it is lower for domestic flights.

Note: Some airports require that the tax be paid in pesos. Save some for this purpose when you are leaving.

Auto Insurance

If you are driving your own car into Mexico, you must buy auto insurance; your United States or Canadian policy is not valid.

Sanborn's, one of the best-known agents, has several offices in the United States near the Mexican border. If you want your policy ahead of time, write to Sanborn's Mexican Insurance Service, P. O. Box 310, McAllen, TX 78502. They will also give you excellent road logs for your trip. Other agents can be found near the border as well.

The American Automobile Association will provide coverage for its members through some of its offices in the United States. These offices are in the states that border Mexico, and in Louisiana. Check with your nearest AAA office for more details.

If you fly to Mexico and rent a car, you can get insurance through your rental agent.

You should drive carefully, of course, and avoid night·driving on the highways. The hazards include people walking along the edge of the road, cattle occupying the center of the road, and slow-moving vehicles without taillights.

Gas Stations and Car Repairs

All gas stations in Mexico are operated by Pemex (Petróleos Mexicanos), the national oil company. Stations are not as numerous as they are in the United States, but with a little planning you should have no trouble. The location of stations is listed in the general information for each section of the peninsula.

There are two grades of gasoline: Nova (leaded), dispensed from a blue pump, and Magna Sin (unleaded), from a green pump. Diesel fuel is also sold and comes from a red pump. Nova and diesel are sold at all stations. Magna Sin is available at many, but not all stations. If you need Magna Sin, keep an eye out for the green pump and fill up once your tank reaches half full.

If you rent a car, you will be able to use the more widely available Nova in many cases. Check with your rental agent.

Sometimes stations or individual pumps run dry. This is signaled by putting the pump hose across the top of the pump. Stations that often have this problem are mentioned in the text.

There are mechanics even in the small towns—look for a sign saying Taller Mecánico. They can handle minor repairs on the spot with only a minimum of equipment. If your problems are major, of course, you will have to get to the nearest large town or city.

If you need a tire repaired, look for a sign saying Vulcanizadora, or keep an eye out for a tire propped up near the road or hung from a pole. This indicates the same thing.

Immigration and **Aduana** (Customs) Stations

There are a few Immigration and *Aduana* stations on the Yucatán Peninsula. Have your tourist cards (both driver's and passengers') ready for inspection. Depending on which direction you are traveling, you may be waved on.

These stations are at the following locations: (1) On Highway 180, 50.9 miles west of Cancún, near Nuevo Xcan and the cutoff for Cobá. (2) On Highway 186 at the east edge of Escárcega. Be prepared to stop if you are traveling west into Escárcega from Chetumal and the station is in operation. (3) On Highway 186, 19.9 miles east of Xpuhil, and (4) 17.1 miles farther east (near Francisco Villa and the cutoff for Kohunlich). These stations are 25.4 miles and 42.5 miles west of the junction of Highways 186 and 307. Stop if you are traveling west toward Xpuhil in the last two cases. (5) On Highway 307, 0.9 mile north of the north end of the Bacalar bypass (and 13.7 miles north of the junctions of Highways 186 and 307). Stop if you are traveling north, toward Tulum.

Climate and Travel in the Rainy Season

It is warm to hot all year on the Yucatán Peninsula, except for a few chilly mornings in the winter. Highest temperatures, which can be searing, occur at the end of the dry season in April and May, before the rains start. June through October are also hot, and then it cools off a bit from December through March.

The rainy season is June through October, with a slackening of precipitation in July and August. Generally it rains hard, but for short periods, in the afternoon or evening, and this does not interfere with travel plans in most cases. If you plan to travel on dirt roads, however, you should check locally about their condition. General road conditions for reaching each site are given in the text, and mention is made if a high-clearance vehicle (see "Visiting the Isolated Sites" above for a description) or one with four-wheel drive is needed. Nevertheless, extremely wet weather can render some dirt roads impassable, even for vehicles *with* four-wheel drive.

Note: You should not try to travel a seriously muddy road in a four-wheel drive vehicle *unless you also have a winch.* If you do get stuck, you will have a difficult time getting unstuck. At least with a standard vehicle, you will not get in as deeply and can more easily get out.

Dress Code

One of the delights of the Yucatán Peninsula is its casual dress code, which is due in great part to its tropical climate. Men wearing *guayaberas* or sport shirts with slacks will be properly attired no matter where they go or what time of day it is, except for a couple of places on Cancún. See "General Information for Section 1" for the best places to buy *guayaberas.* Ladies may wear skirts or slacks with blouses, or casual dresses to the best places on the peninsula.

If you want to dress up—ladies especially—no one will object, but it is nice to know you have a choice.

Even though casual dress is acceptable, neither men nor women should wear beach attire in the cities and towns. Please save that for the beaches.

Shorts are acceptable attire for everyone for climbing around the major archaeological sites. See "What to Take" for more details.

Archaeological Sites and Artifacts

There are fees to enter the larger archaeological sites and museums, but they are reasonable and vary with the site or museum; Sundays are generally free. Isolated sites where there is no guardian are free. Sites are generally open every day, from 8:00 A.M. to 5:00 P.M. Check locally if in doubt.

Mexico has laws prohibiting the removal of pre-Columbian artifacts. These items are considered part of the national patrimony, and United States Customs is cooperating in preventing the entry of such items into the United States.

Looting of the ancient sites has reached alarming proportions, and the Mexican government is enforcing its regulations more stringently than ever to halt this illegal traffic. An incredible amount of information is lost to the world of archaeology because of this illicit digging and thievery.

High-quality reproductions of Maya polychrome pots, sold as reproductions, are available in Muna. See "General Information for Section 2" for where to find them. Careful looking will also turn up good reproductions in shops in Mérida and Cancún and in the town of Ticul, known for its pottery industry.

Museum Names

In each museum section the formal name of the museum is listed first, followed by the popular name. The popular name indicates the city or site of the museum.

The popular name is used in the Contents, in the "List of Sites and Museums by Ratings," in the photographic captions, in the text, and in the "Alphabetical List of Sites and Museums."

Glossary

Many specialized words, foreign words, anagrams, and names of deities are used in the text. Those that occur frequently are explained in the Glossary at the end of the book. Those used infrequently are explained in the text.

THE RATING SYSTEM

The rating system was devised to help the reader see at a glance how worthwhile a visit to a particular site would be. The rating does not necessarily indicate the relative importance of a site in ancient times but reflects a combination of factors, of which relative importance is one. Other considerations are the degree of preservation or restoration and ease of access compared with the visual rewards received. For instance, Nohpat is rated one star, even though it is a very large site and was obviously an important one in ancient times. It is on a *sacbé* that connects Uxmal to Kabáh, and it has an abundance of architectural remains. However, Nohpat is overgrown, much of the architecture has fallen, and there has been no restoration. In addition, getting around the site is difficult, so it offers little to the visitor.

Other examples are Hormiguero and Río Bec B, both rated two stars. These sites have been consolidated and partly restored, and the structures are very exciting visually, but access is rather difficult. If they were on a paved road, both would rate three stars.

Finally, there is the special case of Calakmul, which is unrated. Because of uncertainties of access (which can range from difficult to impossible), I am unable to give a fair rating for this site. I can only suggest reading the text before even considering a visit. Calakmul is *by far* the most difficult site to reach that is covered here.

Ratings

★★★★ A site of major importance and a must for all visitors.

★★★ A very important site and a must for the enthusiast. Fairly to very interesting for others, depending on the site.

★★ Of some importance and moderately to very interesting for the enthusiast. Slightly to moderately interesting for others. (I recommend reading the text for these sites before deciding upon a visit. You will find some more appealing than others, primarily because of access.)

★ Of interest only to the enthusiast—with one exception that is mentioned in the text. Others may ignore these.

No Stars Of minor importance—only for the avid enthusiast.

LIST OF SITES AND MUSEUMS BY RATINGS

Four Stars ★★★★
Chichén Itzá
Tulum
Uxmal

Three Stars ★★★
Becan
Campeche Museum
Chacmultún
Chicanná
Cobá
Edzna
Hochob
Kabáh
Kohunlich
Labná
Mayapán
Mérida Museum
Sayil
Xpuhil

Two Stars ★★
Acancéh
Aké
Balamku
Balankanche (Cave)
Chichén Itzá Museum
Chuncatzim I
Chunhuhub
Cozumel Museum
Dzibilchaltún
Dzibilchaltún Museum
Dzibilnocac
Ek Balam
El Meco
El Rey
El Tabasqueño
Hecelchakán Museum
Hormiguero

Huntichmul
Ikil
Izamal
Kiuic
Kom
Loltún (Cave)
Muyil
Oxkintok
Playa del Carmen
Río Bec B
Sabacché
Sacbé
San Gervasio
Santa Rosa Xtampak
Uxmal Museum
Xcaret
Xelha
Xkichmook
Xlapak

One Star ★
Almuchil
Balché
Caracol (Cozumel)
Chac II
Chacbolay
Chakalal
Chuncatzim II
Chunhuaymil I
Culucbalom
Dzulá
El Cedral
El Real (Temple 3)
Itzimté
Limones
Manos Rojas
Miramar
Mul-Chic
Nohpat

Payan
Pich Corralché
Puerto Rico
Punta Laguna
Río Bec N
Río Bec I
Sodzil
Tancah
Temple 1
Tohcok
Xcavil de Yaxché
Xcochkax
Xkampon
Xulhá
Yalku
Yamilum

Yaxché-Xlapak
Yaxcopoil Museum

No Stars
Chac I (Gruta)
Cobá-Yaxuná Sacbé
Kancabchén
Ni Ku
Pok-ta-Pok
Río Bec A
Río Bec II
Temple 2
Temple 4

Unrated
Calakmul

PART TWO

• • • •

THE SITES AND MUSEUMS

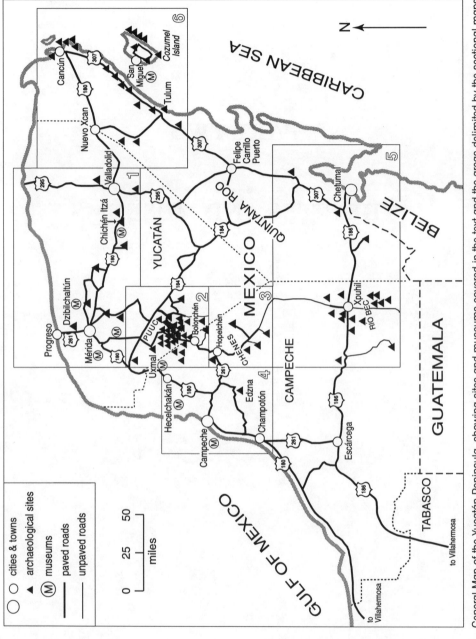

General Map of the Yucatán Peninsula, showing sites and museums covered in the text and the areas delimited by the sectional maps.

SECTION 1

• • • •

NORTHERN YUCATÁN

Bas-relief panel from the east side of the Great Ball Court, Chichén Itzá. Early Postclassic period.

GENERAL INFORMATION
FOR SECTION 1

Point of Reference:
Mérida, Yucatán.
Map: 1

Mileages given to the sites in this section are from the center of Mérida.

The lovely colonial city of Mérida, the largest city on the peninsula, is the capital of the state of Yucatán. It is built on top of the ancient Maya city of Tiho. Since its modern founding in 1542 by Francisco de Montejo the younger, it has retained its place of importance as the commercial, social, and cultural center of the peninsula.

Mérida can be reached by air from some cities in the United States, Mexico City, Cancún, and other parts of Mexico. There are also train and bus connections with central Mexico. If you have the time, you can drive to Mérida from the United States (in five days from Brownsville, Texas, with good stopovers along the way).

As you would expect in a city of over half a million people, there are numerous hotels and restaurants in all price ranges, as well as trailer parks. Hotel rates are the same year-round.

Most visitors fly in, and bus or rent a car to reach the nearby attractions. Car rentals are available at the Mérida airport, south of the city, and at agencies in town. If you want a high-clearance vehicle that will seat five, ask for a Combi—a Volkswagen mini-van.

There are bus connections between Mérida and almost all parts of the Yucatán Peninsula. Exceptions are noted in the text pertaining to the individual sites.

For visitors who intend to explore some of the more remote areas of the peninsula and who need maps that are more detailed than most road maps, a trip to the office of the Instituto Nacional de Estadística, Geografía e Informática (INEGI) in Mérida is recommended.

They have topographic maps of the Yúcatan Peninsula and the rest of Mexico (at various scales). For the peninsula there are maps at scales of 1:1,000,000, 1:250,000, and 1:50,000. The 1:50,000-scale maps are so detailed that they are not really useful for general travel; however, they can be most useful for locating dirt roads that are not shown on less detailed maps.

Master maps at the INEGI office show the areas covered by the more detailed maps, and when you make your selection, someone there will get them for you. The price is reasonable and the office staff is helpful, but it is good to have some idea of what you want beforehand.

The INEGI office is in a building at Paseo de Montejo, no. 442. There is a Xerox sign on the front of the building. As you enter, go straight ahead down a hallway to the end, and turn left. The first door on the left is the entrance. The office is open from 8:00 A.M. to 3:00 P.M. Monday through Friday and does not close for siesta.

If you prefer traveling on conducted tours, try one of the many travel agencies in Mérida, or ask at your hotel for a recommendation. The two oldest agencies are Mayaland Tours (formerly Mérida Travel Service), in the Casa del Balam Hotel, and Yucatán Trails, at Calle 62, no. 482. The most popular tours are to Chichén Itzá and to Uxmal (each daily), but others are available, and special tours can be arranged by car, Combi, or bus.

There is a light-and-sound spectacle at Uxmal, and there are evening tours to the site for the presentation, with a return to Mérida the same night. See "Uxmal" for more details.

Reasonably priced taxis are available in Mérida, and some can be hired to see attractions outside the city. Make price arrangements beforehand.

Mérida has grown steadily and gracefully over the years, and prices in general are reasonable for what you receive in return. Mérida is also known as the "White City" because of its cleanliness, and it is a very relaxed and informal place. Many businesses and shops close for siesta from around 1:00 P.M. until 5:00 P.M., but restaurants remain open.

It is also a good place to shop. The main market is centered on Calle 65 between Calles 56 and 54. This is one block south, and two and three blocks east, of the Main Plaza. Jewelry and handicrafts from all over Yucatán are sold, in addition to the food products found at all municipal markets. Near here is a handicraft market (corner of Calles 65 and 60), and next door is La Poblana, which is probably the largest hammock store in Mérida.

There are all sizes and many colors, and the hammocks are made from a variety of materials. The pure cotton ones are best and, considering the amount of use you will probably give them, will last a lifetime. They are not cheap but are worth the money. Yucatecan hammocks are the best in the world, and if your travel plans indicate you might need one, Mérida is the best place to buy it. *Guayaberas* are also a good buy here. Tony's, on Calle 65 across from the hammock shop, is one of the favorite places to get them. Another shop, Ropa Típica Calderón, is a large place, and has the advantage of being open from 8:00 A.M. to 6:00 P.M., Monday through Saturday, and 8:00 A.M. to 2:00 P.M. on Sunday. It is a bit out of the main part of town at Calle 15, no. 191, in the García Ginéres residential section, northwest of the center. They also sell embroidered blouses and dresses for ladies. A taxi can get you there and wait while you shop.

OTHER STOPOVERS: There are both good and modest hotels in Progreso, and east and west of it, on the north coast of the peninsula. Going east from Mérida on Highway 180, there are hotels in Pisté (just west of Chichén Itzá), at Chichén Itzá (to the east of the site), and Valladolid. Pisté also has a trailer park.

GAS STATIONS: There are several stations in and on the outskirts of Mérida and in Progreso. Along Highway 180 heading east, there are stations at Tahmek, Pisté, and Valladolid. Along the same highway heading south from Mérida, there are stations at Umán and Maxcanú (27.9 miles south of Umán).

GUIDES: A guide is not necessary to reach any of the sites covered in northern Yucatán. For local guides to show you around a particular site, see the coverage of that site.

★ ★ ★

REGIONAL MUSEUM OF ANTHROPOLOGY
(MÉRIDA MUSEUM)

The Mérida Museum is housed in the Cantón Palace on Paseo de Montejo and Calle 43. This elegant building was originally constructed as a residence for General Francisco Cantón Rosado in the early twentieth century. Later, for a time, it became the official residence for the governors of Yucatán.

The entrance to the museum is on Calle 43, and most of the collection is exhibited in several rooms and hallways on the main floor, where there is also a small bookstore selling publications. There are additional exhibits on the second floor.

On the main floor, one room houses the "Piece of the Month"; another, devoted to the geology of the area, has a relief map of the Yucatán Peninsula showing the principal archaeological sites. Early worked stone tools are also displayed.

In other rooms are language charts, displays showing dental and cranial deformations, exhibits of agriculture and methods of

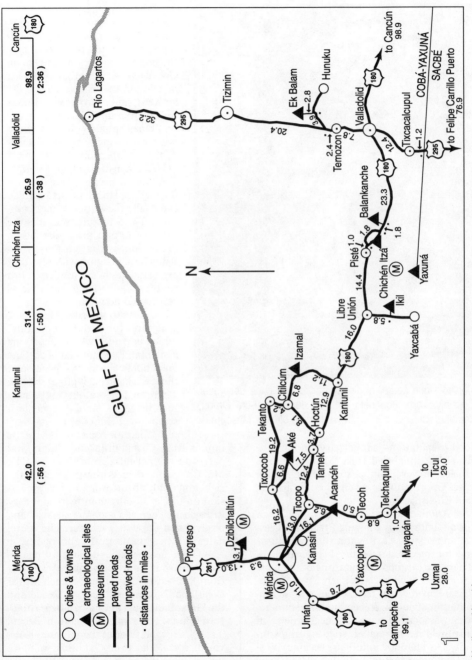

Mérida | 42.0 | Kantunil | 31.4 | Chichén Itzá | 26.9 | Valladolid | 98.9 | Cancún
(:56) | (:50) | (:38) | (2:36)

GULF OF MEXICO

N

cities & towns
archaeological sites
museums
paved roads
unpaved roads
distances in miles •

COBÁ-YAXUNÁ
SACBÉ

Northern Yucatán

There are many large, carved stone monuments from throughout the Yucatán Peninsula, including a paneled stela from Oxkintok, the bottom of a stela from Dzilám González (a site near the north coast of Yucatán that is now mostly destroyed), and a two-headed jaguar throne from the Uxmal region.

One especially unusual piece is labeled as coming from Banqueta-Tunich (a site about 9 miles south of Uxmal) on the lands of Hacienda San Simon. (Some authorities are unconvinced that Banqueta-Tunich is actually the source of the sculpture.) The sculpture, which is the top section of a three-part facade decoration, portrays a grossly inflated human figure with very thin arms. It dates to the ninth or tenth century A.D., though its style is considered non-Classic.

Another unusual piece is a sculpture (or stela) from Tabi, which portrays two men carrying a slain and decapitated deer. One man holds the deer's head, and there is a band of glyphs at the top. There are large cutouts in the stela that bring to mind the modern sculpture of Henry Moore.

Carved stone figure, originally part of a facade decoration, possibly from Banqueta-Tunich (Hacienda San Simon). Terminal Classic period. Now in the Mérida Museum.

food preparation, jade jewelry, and an unusual but unlabeled stela. Most items are labeled, however, and in some of the display cases information is given in both Spanish and English.

Another room is devoted to social evolution, with maps showing Preclassic, Classic, and Postclassic sites and a diagram showing the mechanics of the Maya calendar. There are ceramic exhibits, one of the most interesting of which is an Early Classic cylindrical tripod vessel from Becan with a Teotihuacán-style two-piece hollow statuette found associated with it. The statuette in turn held many smaller, solid figurines inside. The statuette and figurines are typical of Teotihuacán art, while the vessel (the shape of which is also typical of Teotihuacán) portrays Maya deities.

There are copies of some of the murals from Chacmultún and Tulum and part of an original mural from Mul-Chic. The Mul-Chic mural depicts a battle scene on the right and richly attired warriors in a procession on the left (both, admittedly, not easy to discern). There is a poorly preserved band of glyphs in the upper register. The mural dates to the eighth or ninth century A.D.

Other displays include musical instruments, urn burials, a lovely painted capstone from Xnubec, models of the Nohoch Mul at Cobá, the Governor's Palace at Uxmal and the Great Ball Court at Chichén Itzá, Atlantean figures, and a stucco head from Becan.

The second floor of the museum is devoted to material from Oxkintok, some of which was excavated between 1986 and 1991 by the Spanish Archaeological Mission in Hispanic-America.

The museum collection has moved several times over the years, and there has been an increase in the number of items displayed. There have also been improvements in the way the collection is presented. If your last visit was before 1989, I strongly suggest a revisit. Allow 1½ hours to view the collection.

The museum is open from 8:00 A.M. to 8:00 P.M. Tuesday through Saturday and 8:00 A.M. to 2:00 P.M. on Sunday. It is closed on Monday. Photography is permitted, but flash is not.

★ ★

DZIBILCHALTÚN AND DZIBILCHALTÚN MUSEUM

*(tseeb-eel-chahl-*toon; *derivation: Maya for "Where There Is Writing on Flat Stones")*

Location:
   Northern Yucatán.
Map: 1 (p. 27)

The Site

Dzibilchaltún is a very large site, and an extremely important one archaeologically, because of its almost continuous occupation from 800 B.C. to the present. It had its ups and downs and was nearly abandoned for many years, but its stratigraphic sequence is clearly defined.

As you enter the gate to the site, take the trail heading south. The trail passes the small restored temple (Structure 38-sub) and the remains of Structure 38, which once covered it. They are on a platform which supports a few remains of other temple bases. Structure 38-sub dates to the first half of the eighth century, and its simple design is pleasing. There are inset panels in the upper wall zone on all four sides of the building, and it is probably one of the earliest vaulted structures at Dzibilchaltún. In the Terminal Classic period Structure 38 was built on top of Structure 38-sub, and the lower parts can be seen today. At this time the platform supporting the structures was enlarged. A large unrestored mound lies adjacent to the south side of the platform.

A bit farther on, the trail is marked with a sign pointing left to the Temple of the Seven Dolls. There are some architectural remains along the way.

Shortly after the turn, on the left, there is a restored platform and the lower temple walls of Structure 39, one of few at Dzibilchaltún dating to the Early Postclassic period. Stones from Terminal Classic buildings were used in the retaining walls of the platform and in the walls of the structure on top, and in Late Postclassic times a stairway was added and the platform was extended. Next to it on the east is a fair-sized, four-tiered pyramid (Structure 36), with a central stairway facing south toward the Main Plaza. Structure 36 dates to the Late Classic period.

Stela 19 (now in the Dzibilchaltún Museum) was found set into the basal terrace of Structure 36, and a copy has been placed in its original location. Stela 18 was also found set into the terrace, and it as well as the copy of Stela 19 may be seen by descending the modern stairway at the southwest corner of Structure 36.

Part of the Main Plaza, southwest of Structure 36, is occupied by a small, restored open chapel, built by the Spaniards, probably in the 1590s. Some of the stones of the pre-Columbian city were used in its construction.

From there the trail continues east. Along the way it passes a small, low platform—with stairways on all four sides—that supports a plain stela. Over 25 monuments are known from the site; about half are un-

Structure 38-sub and 38, Dzibilchaltún. Late and Terminal Classic periods. Early Spanish chapel on the right.

carved. Farther east is the Temple of the Seven Dolls (Structure 1-sub), the principal restored structure at the site. It is 465 yards from the Main Plaza. There are remains of other structures near this temple. They, along with the platform and stela, are part of the Seven Dolls Group, all of which rests on a large, flat terrace, over 3 feet high.

The Temple of the Seven Dolls is almost square, with a central inner chamber surrounded by a vaulted corridor. There is a doorway on each of the four sides of the temple, and large rectangular windows flank the east and west doorways. The inner chamber had access from the east and west from the outside corridor, and a tower rises above the central part of the roof, over this chamber.

In the upper wall zone of the temple there are inset panels with remains of projecting stone masks above each doorway and on each corner. All were originally covered with stucco to give the final details, and some of this remains on the mask in the center of the south side.

The temple rests on a pyramidal platform with stairways on all four sides. The structure was built during the early part of the Late Classic period. Later in that period it was filled and covered with a much larger construction, the outlines of which can be seen on the north and west sides, where stones on the ground mark its outer limit. Some of the remains of the later structure can be found on the other two sides. It then seems that the later structure fell into disuse and was probably abandoned for 200 years. Then around A.D. 1200–1450 the Maya tunneled into the later construction to the floor of the earlier temple and cut a hole into the rubble below. In this they placed seven crude clay figures, each exhibiting some deformity. These figures, or dolls, give the temple its name. Perhaps they were used in connection with ceremonies for curing diseases, although this is far from certain.

E. Wyllys Andrews IV first saw this structure as a large mound whose superstructure had collapsed, revealing buried chambers. Most of the later construction was removed, exposing the partially intact temple below. Its restoration ensued.

The design of the Temple of the Seven Dolls is unusual for the Maya area because of its truncated tower and unique functional

Temple of the Seven Dolls, west side, Dzibilchaltún. Late Classic period.

windows. It is possible that it was an experimental form of northern Maya architecture.

A dozen Maya *sacbeob* are known at Dzibilchaltún, and although the visitor today will hardly realize it, the approach to the Temple of the Seven Dolls is over one of them (Sacbé 1). It is one of the two major *sacbeob* at the site, both of which extend from the Main Plaza, as do some of the others.

When you return from the Temple of the Seven Dolls and reach the far (west) end of the Main Plaza, take a left turn and go a short distance to the Cenote Xlacah (shlah-*kah*), the largest of several cenotes at Dzibilchaltún. It is 100 feet across at its widest point, at least 140 feet deep, and it goes down at a slant. Numerous artifacts were recovered from its depths. There are shade trees in the area, which is a nice place to relax and have a picnic lunch. Swimming in the cenote is allowed, but a sign informs you that you *must* wear a swimsuit.

From the cenote, return north to the Main Plaza and follow the trail to the left (west). This trail follows Sacbé 2, which goes over 1,000 yards to an unexcavated terrace complex that is similar to the Seven Dolls Group. The *sacbé*, however, is cleared only as far as Structure 57, about 250 yards from the turnoff.

Structure 57 lies north of the *sacbé*, and it was the only structure with a standing vault at Dzibilchaltún when the site was first visited by archaeologists. Since then, it has been consolidated. It probably dates to the first half of the ninth century.

Discovering the exact extent of an ancient city is difficult at best, and this is particularly true of Dzibilchaltún. About 8,400 structures have been mapped in a 7.3-square-mile area, and it is estimated that during its peak period, there was a population of 20,000 people. The agricultural sustaining area for Dzibilchaltún, however, extends far beyond the mapped section.

The area of Dzibilchaltún was apparently first occupied about 800 B.C., by inhabitants with a ceramic tradition related to that in the Petén of Guatemala. Starting around 250 B.C., population increased rapidly and reached a peak around 50 B.C. This was followed by a decline that lasted until about A.D. 600, when Dzibilchaltún again grew rapidly to an enormous size. It probably reached its greatest extent around 830, and about this time a new style of architecture was introduced that continued through the year 1000. This included finely cut veneer facing stones such as those used in the Puuc cities to the south.

During the early part of the following period (A.D. 1000–1200), construction ceased, although small groups of squatters continued to occupy the site. Population dropped to less than 10 percent of its former size. Beginning late in this period and continuing through the next (1200–1540), construction resumed in a modest way, and during this time Dzibilchaltún's inhabitants dug into and reused the Temple of the Seven Dolls (as a shrine). At least one other earlier building was also reused.

Recent History

The existence of Dzibilchaltún was never forgotten, since it was almost continuously occupied up until the Spanish conquest. The open chapel that was erected in the middle of what had been the Main Plaza is one of the earliest colonial structures in Yucatán.

The pre-Columbian structures at Dzibilchaltún were cannibalized for building materials for use in several haciendas, towns, and roads. This went on until the 1950s. The archaeological discovery of the site, however, was by Andrews and George W. Brainerd, who first visited Dzibilchaltún in 1941. They discovered, near the Hacienda Dzibilchaltún, "a large group of hitherto unreported mounds." Brainerd collected pottery sherds, and Andrews explored and recorded the architectural remains. The few weeks they spent there convinced them that they had "stumbled upon the remains of a truly extraordinary city."

World War II interrupted work until 1956, when the Middle American Research Institute (MARI) of Tulane University sponsored excavations. During the next couple of years the National Geographic Society, the National Science Foundation, and the American Philosophical Society helped fund the project, which continued until 1965 under Andrews's direction. Andrews presented a progress report in 1965, published by MARI; a more comprehensive final report, with co-author E. Wyllys Andrews V, was published in 1980.

In 1986 Eduardo Toro Quiñones carried out additional excavations. Fragments of two stelae were discovered, and part of one of the *sacbeob* was consolidated. The work was sponsored by INAH and SEDUE (Secretary of Urban Development and Ecology).

The Mexican government provided funds for some of the restoration at the site.

Connection

Mérida to Dzibilchaltún: 12.4 miles by paved road (:20).

Getting There

From Mérida head north on Highway 261 for 9.3 miles (to just past Kilometer 15), and turn right at the cutoff for Dzibilchaltún (marked with a sign). Go 2.5 miles (part of this road is very narrow), make a right turn, and continue 0.6 mile to the site.

Dzibilchaltún can be reached by private car, taxi, bus, or on conducted tours from Mérida. Cold drinks are available at the site. Since the most interesting structures at Dzibilchaltún face west, the afternoon is the best time for photography. Wear a sun hat, and allow 2 hours to visit the site and museum.

★ ★
Dzibilchaltún Museum

The small but well-arranged museum at Dzibilchaltún is located near the entrance to the site. It displays artifacts from the site as well as photographs taken during excavation. Notable are two fragments of Terminal Classic stelae (Stelae 9 and 19), the seven clay figures discovered in the Temple of the Seven Dolls, and inscribed bones recovered from Cenote Xlacah. Ceramic examples from the earliest through the latest periods at the site are also displayed. The museum is well worth a visit while you are at the site.

Stela 19 from the site, Dzibilchaltún Museum. Terminal Classic period.

★

HACIENDA YAXCOPOIL MUSEUM
(YAXCOPOIL MUSEUM)

Hacienda Yaxcopoil has a small archaeological museum with a collection of artifacts that were found on hacienda lands. Although the items are unlabeled, they come from the greatly ruined nearby site of Yaxcopoil ("Place of the Green Alamo Tree"). Included are carved stone columns and panels depicting standing figures, benches with projecting heads, and other carvings, some of which are well preserved. There is also a display of ceramics.

The museum is in one of the rooms (called the Maya Room) of the main house of the hacienda, and family portraits, furniture imported from Europe, and memorabilia are displayed in other rooms. This is a worthwhile stop when you are driving between Mérida and Uxmal. The hacienda is on the west side of Highway 261, near Kilometer 33; it is 20.7 miles south of Mérida, 9.7 miles south of Umán, and 28.0 miles north of Uxmal. There is a sign on the high-

Carved Stone column from the site, Yaxcopoil Museum. Late Classic period.

way at the entrance to the hacienda and a lovely colonial Moorish double arch that is quite photogenic.

The hacienda, which dates to the seventeenth century, experienced the boom years of sisal cultivation in the late nineteenth and the early twentieth centuries. The hacienda buildings are attractive, and the sisal processing equipment is interesting. All of this is worth a look while you are there.

The hacienda and museum are open Monday through Saturday from 8:00 A.M. until sunset, and on Sunday from 9:00 A.M. to 1:00 P.M. Allow 30 minutes to see the museum and another 30 minutes to tour the rest of the hacienda. Soft drinks are available in one of the rooms of the main house.

★ ★
ACANCÉH

*(ah-kahn-keh; derivation: Maya for "Howl [or Groan] of the Deer";
also the name of an unidentified medicinal plant)*

Location:
    Northern Yucatán.
Map: 1 (p. 27)

The Site

The two structures at Acancéh are both in the town of that name. The first is a pyramid facing an open area—in front of the church and near the Main Plaza—in the center of town, and the other is the Temple of the Stucco Facade, a couple of blocks away.

The pyramid rises in four tiers and has an inset central stairway and apron moldings of the typical Petén Maya type. This Early Classic structure has been compared to the famous Late Preclassic pyramid E-VII-sub at Uaxactún. It is faced with roughly cut stones and must have been plastered originally. Only the front of the structure has been restored. I recommend climbing the pyramid, as there are a couple of pieces of sculpture and carved decorations lying around near the top.

The Temple of the Stucco Facade (Structure 1) is part of a poorly preserved acropolis made up of structures from several periods. There is evidence of a Late Preclassic beginning in this complex, although Structure 1 was built during the Early Classic period. It was then filled with rubble, and another structure was built over

Early Classic pyramid on the Main Plaza, Acancéh.

Detail of the decoration on the Temple of the Stucco Facade, Acancéh. Early Classic period.

it. Ceramic evidence also indicates that Acancéh was occupied from the Late Preclassic to the Late Postclassic period.

The most interesting feature of Structure 1 is the remains of a carved stucco frieze on the upper part of the building. The frieze depicts anthropomorphic bats, birds, and a squirrel. Each figure is surrounded by a terraced border, forming separate panels. Speech scrolls are found with some of the animals, and some glyphlike elements are interspersed between the panels. All the decorations are distinctly non-Maya. Current opinion is that they were done in the style of Teotihuacán, since they especially relate to the mural painting from that site. Few other architectural remains are found in the acropolis.

Recent History

The stucco frieze at Acancéh was discovered in the early years of the twentieth century. It was brilliantly colored when first uncovered, as recorded by Adela Breton, but no real evidence of color remains today.

The site was visited and reported upon by Eduard Seler in 1911, but most of what we know about Acancéh comes from the work done by E. Wyllys Andrews IV in 1941 and 1942 for the Carnegie Institution of Washington.

In 1989 a one-month project of consolidation and restoration was undertaken at the Temple of the Stucco Facade to preserve the stucco frieze. This work was supervised by Beatriz Quintal Suaste, in collaboration with the Restoration Section of the Yucatán Regional Center of INAH.

Connections

1. Mérida to Acancéh (via Kanasin): 16.1 miles by paved road (:35).

2. Mérida to Acancéh (via Ticopo): 19.2 miles by paved road (:46).

Getting There

1. Take Yucatán (state) Highway 18 heading southeast from Mérida to Kanasin and Acancéh.

2. Take Highway 180 heading east from Mérida to the cutoff for Ticopo (13.0 miles). Turn right and go into Ticopo, then right again and proceed to Acancéh.

When you reach Acancéh, you will see the pyramid (behind a locked gate) near the plaza. Ask at the nearby market for the caretaker *(guardián)*, and someone will point out his house across the street. When you find him, he will open the gate for you and take you to the Temple of the Stucco Facade (also behind a locked gate). If he is not at home, try taking a picture of the pyramid, and he will find you.

Acancéh can be reached by private car, bus, or taxi from Mérida. Cold drinks are available in town. Allow 1 hour to visit both structures.

A visit to Acancéh makes an interesting half-day trip out of Mérida when combined with a visit to Mayapán.

★ ★ ★
MAYAPÁN

(mah-yah-pahn; derivation: Maya for "Standard of the Maya")

> **Original Name:**
>   Mayapán.
> **Location:**
>   Northern Yucatán.
> **Map:** 1 (p. 27)

The Site

Although the Late Postclassic site of Mayapán is often described as a sad imitation of Chichén Itzá, said to exhibit poor workmanship and a decadence in all the arts, it nevertheless is an interesting site to visit. Perhaps I enjoyed it more because I was expecting less.

The part the visitor sees today is only the small ceremonial center that stood in the heart of the city, which was a true urban center.

A wall, more than 5 miles long and up to 6 feet high, encircled the city, enclosing an area of 1.6 square miles. Within the confines of the wall some 3,600 structures have been mapped, most of which were residen-

tial. Population estimates for Mayapan's heyday vary from 6,000 to 15,000 people, most authorities settling on a figure around 10,000.

Mayapán is in an infertile region of Yucatán and was supported by tribute from neighboring areas, whose nobles were forced to live as hostages within the city walls, thus ensuring payment from their "home towns."

Most of northern Yucatán was under the control of Mayapán from around A.D. 1250, when it was founded by the tribe of Cocoms, until its looting and destruction around 1440. The destruction is credited to the rebellion of excessively exploited tribes, led by a member of the rival Tutul Xiu family. The city was burned, and the ruling Cocom and all but one of his sons were slain. The survivor was on a trading expedition to Honduras.

Although Mayapán dates to the Late Postclassic period, it incorporated Puuc-style carved and plain stones in some of its structures. These stones are believed to have come from a nearby earlier site, perhaps from Telchaquillo or Santa Cruz, a small site

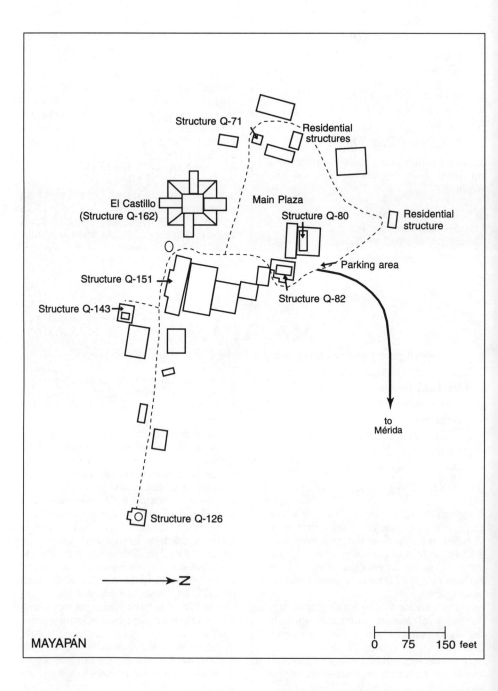

Structure Q-71

Residential structures

El Castillo (Structure Q-162)

Main Plaza

Structure Q-80

Residential structure

Structure Q-151

Parking area

Structure Q-143

Structure Q-82

to Mérida

Structure Q-126

N

MAYAPÁN

0   75   150 feet

El Castillo, northwest corner, Mayapán. Late Postclassic period.

southeast of the main ruins of Mayapán. The Chac masks found on Structure Q-151 at Mayapán were constructed from Classic period Puuc elements in addition to cruder carvings (where a part was missing) produced by Mayapán's artisans, in imitation of the Puuc style. The stone elements forming the masks are practically identical to those found at Kabáh.

You can see Mayapán without a guide, but having the caretaker or his son along will ensure that you do not miss any of the interesting features.

When you arrive at the site, the first building you see on your right is Structure Q-80, a mound with some remains of a vaulted temple on top, entangled with tree roots that seem to be supporting it. A trail leads from there to Structure Q-82, a partly restored temple, a short distance to the southeast. Its pyramidal base rises in two ter-

races, and the lower wall and portions of a column remain, but the most interesting feature is a carved serpent head decorating the top of the stairway on the left.

From here the trail leads southwest and enters the Main Plaza. The plaza itself is of interest for the many pieces of sculpture and carved decorative architectural elements lying around. All are worth a look.

Facing the plaza on the south is the stepped pyramid called El Castillo (Structure Q-162)—the largest at Mayapán. This pyramid, which originally had stairways on all four sides, is obviously a copy of the larger and better-preserved El Castillo at Chichén Itzá. Its north side, facing the plaza, is the best preserved. There are no remains of a temple on top, nor did it ever support a vaulted structure.

The trail leads along the east side of El Castillo and turns to the left, where it im-

Front view of Structure Q-151, Mayapán. Late Postclassic period.

mediately passes Structure Q-151, with its Chac masks. This long, low structure also has remains of numerous columns and small altars and is one of the most interesting at the site. Just behind the mask on the southwest corner is a slab in the exterior wall with an interesting carving of a bird.

The main trail continues east, and soon you come to a cutoff on the right that leads to Structure Q-143, a small ruined pyramid some yards away. It is worth climbing to see the carved serpent heads and columns, the only remains of a small temple that stood on top.

Return to the main trail. By following it east, you pass a number of overgrown mounds. A bit farther, in a clearing at the end of the trail, is Structure Q-126, a circular two-chambered building on a rectangular base. Access is up the partly restored stairway on the south side. This building was one of four observatories reported at Mayapán.

Two other features in this area are a sculptured figure on a base, a few feet to the west of the structure, that you see upon entering the area, and a stela lying at an angle

near the base of the east side of the structure. Both are poorly preserved.

From here you return to the Main Plaza and continue west. The trail leads to Structure Q-71, a small platform with well-made moldings of Puuc stone, a stairway, and a few remnants of the lower portion of a building on top. Structure Q-71 is believed to have been a shrine and is surrounded by many small mounds.

Other structures are found a bit farther north, some of which were clearly residential. One of the features of Mayapán is the large number of rather elaborate residences, their proximity to the main ceremonial precincts, and the relative paucity of religious structures. Authorities explain this by saying that by the time Mayapán was built, religion had lost its predominant place in Maya culture.

Recent History

Since Mayapán was destroyed only a hundred years before the Spanish conquest, memory of it lingered among the native pop-

Detail of the well-preserved Chac mask on the front of Structure Q-151, Mayapán. Late Postclassic period.

ulation. It is mentioned in native documents and was commented on by Bishop Diego de Landa in 1566 from information he gathered.

Its description and location check with the known facts, but some of the data reported in these early sources cannot be substantiated archaeologically. For instance, it is reported that a triple alliance among Uxmal, Chichén Itzá, and Mayapán (the League of Mayapán) existed during the period A.D. 987–1185. Archaeological evidence, however, shows that Uxmal was practically abandoned for the second half of that period and that Mayapán had not yet been founded.

Little note is taken of Mayapán thereafter until John Lloyd Stephens and Frederick Catherwood visited the site. This was followed in 1843 by Stephens's report, which included illustrations by Catherwood. Al-

though the site was mentioned by historians and was known to a few people in the locality, Stephens felt that "ours was the first visit to examine these ruins."

The next visitor of note was Sylvanus G. Morley, almost a hundred years later, but it was only in the 1950s that investigations were begun. The work was sponsored by the Carnegie Institution of Washington, and publications by several prominent archaeologists were issued during the following ten years. These included work by A. Ledyard Smith, Morris Jones, H. E. D. Pollock, Ralph L. Roys, Tatiana Proskouriakoff, Robert E. Smith, Karl Ruppert, and Sir J. Eric S. Thompson.

South side of Structure Q-126, Mayapán. Late Postclassic period.

Connections

1. Mérida to Mayapán (via Kanasin): 28.9 miles by paved road (:55), then 0.2 mile by dirt road (:02).

2. Mérida to Mayapán (via Tixcopo): 32.0 miles by paved road (1:06), then 0.2 mile by dirt road (:02).

Getting There

See "Acancéh" for getting that far. From Acancéh take Yucatán Highway 18 heading south. The highway goes through the town of Tecoh, where there is an interesting huge church and convent, and continues through Telchaquillo. One mile past this last town, (i.e., 12.8 miles south of Acancéh), there is a dirt cutoff that goes 0.2 mile to the right to Mayapán. It passes the caretaker's house on the way to the site.

Mayapán can be reached by private car or taxi from Mérida, and a bus can get you as far as Telchaquillo. There is no food or drink at the site. Allow 1¼ hours for a visit.

AKÉ

(ah-keh; derivation: Aké is an Indian surname)

Location:
  Northern Yucatán.
Map: 1 (p. 27)

The Site

Aké is one of those sites that is a real sleeper. It has interesting remains, is easy to reach, and has been long known, but it attracts few visitors.

When you reach the Hacienda Ruinas de Aké, you can park on the Hacienda Plaza, on the east side of which are remains of two of Aké's ancient structures. Set back from the plaza is Structure 14, a great terraced platform made of huge stones, with the more recent hacienda chapel on the top of the south part of the platform.

Right on the plaza is Structure 15, which rises to a height of about 40 feet. It is a steep terraced pyramid, with a few remains of a summit temple on top. The original pyramidal base was later encased by another, and both construction phases are visible today. On the south side of the structure, the top four courses of stone are part of the summit temple. Just below this is a projecting molding that is part of the original pyramidal base; the remainder is secondary construction with vertical walls and projecting moldings. Both Structures 14 and 15 date to the Early Classic period.

From this area head south, toward the henequen factory and follow the path to Structure 1, the best known at Aké. Structure 1 is a large pyramidal base supporting a platform and remains of 36 stone columns. This monumental structure faces an ancient plaza and is approached on the south side by a stairway over 150 feet wide. The stairway is made of gigantic stone blocks, some over 6 feet long, and some are almost that wide.

The pyramidal base of Structure 1 was encased with another larger construction after it was originally built, but there was probably little difference in time between the two phases, as the use of massive blocks is found in both. The second-phase stonework is found at the lower level of the base, surrounding the structure; what is seen above that is part of the initial construction.

Each column was made of 11 large, roughly squared stones, with smaller stones filling in the gaps, and they were probably thickly coated with lime mortar to give the finished square shape. There are three rows of 12 columns each, and a few still rise to their original height of about 14 feet. It is likely that the structure had a pole-and-thatch roof, as little debris was found atop the platform. Structure 1 dates to the Early Classic period. Although appearing unrefined today, the sheer mass of the structure and its immense facing stones are quite impressive. Aké is a good two-star site.

From the top of Structure 1 you can see other huge mounds on the west side of the plaza and more distant mounds as well. According to Lawrence Roys and Edwin M. Shook, "There are about 25 conspicuous mounds and more than 100 lesser mounds, platforms, and other constructions distributed over an area greater than 2 sq. km. [0.8 square mile]."

Structure 2 lies to the southwest of Structure 1 and is a good vantage point for photographs of the latter. Structure 2 is a terraced pyramid, also with two construction phases, and it originally had stairways on the north and south sides, though little of these remain today. Because of the destruction of the pyramid it was impossible to determine if there was once a stairway on the east (plaza) side.

On the north side of the structure, near the center, an area of the original facing stones of the pyramid is in place. It is made

Structure 1, south side, Aké. Early Classic period.

of stones almost as large as those used on Structure 1, and deeply inset panels formed part of the decoration; these surfaces are believed to have had elaborate stucco decorations originally. The wall at the top of the east end of the north side is a more modern construction, probably built in the late nineteenth century. Against the base of the wall are two small abandoned lime kilns, apparently built around the same time. Modern field walls are also found near the north base of Structure 2. The maximum height of the structure is 59 feet, and a foot trail now gives access to the top.

There are two areas of interest on top of Structure 2. One is a rounded vaulted chamber that was dug into the fill of the pyramid below the top floor of the summit. It is one of the few beehive-type Maya vaults known. The surface of the chamber was plastered several times, and it was most likely a chultun built for water storage, though dry storage or a ceremonial use are possibilities. There are no indications that it was used as a tomb.

Nearby is a small part of a wall, the remains of a building added on top of the pyramid at a later date. Though little remains, the finely cut facing stones, so different from the massive blocks used in the pyramid, are identifiable as Puuc style. Sadly, most of the stones of this building, and parts of the pyramid as well, found their way into the lime kilns. The Structure 2 pyramid was built in the Early Classic period, while the vaulted chamber and the building on top were con-structed in Late Classic or Terminal Classic times.

Immediately to the south of Structure 2 is Structure 6, a huge, long mound with a north-south axis and a centrally located pyramid on top. The structure is greatly ruined, but the central pyramid rises to a height of 59 feet, and a few remains of vertical terrace walls can be seen. Structure 6 is believed to be of Early Classic date.

Due west of the center of Structure 6, in a field planted with henequen and protected by a barbed wire fence, is a standing (and rather eroded) stone, over 10 feet tall. Désiré Charnay believed this to be a *picoté,* or punishment stone, to which an offender was tied before being whipped. Roys and Shook believe the monument is a stela that possibly supported a finished work in lime plaster originally. This is the only known stela at Aké.

In addition to the structures, Aké is also known for its *sacbeob;* the longest is Sacbé 1, which goes almost 20 miles east to Izamal. The remaining seven *sacbeob* at Aké connect the various structures at the site.

Recent History

John Lloyd Stephens and Frederick Catherwood visited Aké in 1842; it was the last ruin they saw on their second trip to Yucatán. Stephens was the first to publish a report on the site, and it included Catherwood's drawing of Structure 1. Charnay reported Aké in 1883 and 1885, and an English translation of the latter appeared in 1887. He too included a depiction of Structure 1, which appeared then much as it does now. Afterward, others visited Aké, including Augustus and Alice Le Plongeon, Sylvanus G. Morley, Marshall Saville, and H. E. D. Pollock, who reported the beehive-shaped vault at the top of Structure 2 in 1936.

The first detailed report of the whole site—called preliminary by its authors Roys and Shook—is the most descriptive. The information was gathered in the early 1950s and published in 1966. Others participating in this project were Tatiana Proskouriakoff, one of whose drawings accompanied the report, and Víctor Segovia, who traced the entire length of Sacbé 1 after its beginning was discovered by Shook. Segovia also located the other *sacheob* within Aké. Although diligently searched for by both Shook and Segovia, the expected *saché* between Aké and Tiho (Mérida) was not found.

Connections

1. Mérida to Aké (via Tixcocob): 22.8 miles by paved road (:53).

2. Mérida to Aké (via Tamek): 25.4 miles by paved road (:38), then 7.5 miles by rock road (:19).

Getting There

In either case leave Mérida as though you were taking Highway 180 east. On the east-ern outskirts of the city, at Kilometer 5, is a Pemex gas station. Here is where you make the choice; the left fork is Highway 80 to Tixpehual and Tixcocob, and straight ahead is Highway 180 to Tamek.

1. From the junction at the Pemex station, take Highway 80 to Tixcocob (13.1 miles), turn right on to an unnumbered road, and go on to Aké. You will pass through the village of Ekmul along the way.

2. From the junction at the Pemex station, take Highway 180 to the cutoff for Aké (22.3 miles). This is 0.5 mile past the cutoff for Tamek. The junction for Aké is marked with a pyramid sign, where you turn left onto a rock road (not shown on most maps). Go 5.7 miles to a cross road, and then turn right for another 1.8 miles to Aké. You will join a paved road shortly before you reach the Hacienda Plaza of Aké, and that is the road to Tixcocob.

If you are going to make a side trip to Aké while driving from Chichén Itzá to Mérida, use the route from Tamek to get to Aké, and the one via Tixcocob (in reverse) to get to Mérida.

Allow 45 minutes for a visit. Cold drinks are available at Aké. You might also want a couple of photos of the old henequen factory on the plaza.

★ ★

IZAMAL

(ee-sah-mahl; derivation: Maya name for the god Itzamná, "Dew of Heaven")

Original Name:
  Izamal.
Location:
  Northern Yucatán.
Map: 1 (p. 27)

The Site

The Pyramid of Kinich-Kakmo in the town of Izamal is one of the largest in Yucatán. As you drive to the town, you can see it rising from the plain. It is also visible from the Main Plaza in Izamal, and so it *should* be easy to

The second, or upper, pyramid of the Kinich-Kakmo, Izamal. The area in front is the flat top of the massive lower pyramid. Early Classic period.

get to. It is not. It is only two blocks north of the church and convent in the center of town, but its base is hidden by modern buildings. Ask directions, and then look for an open gate with some stone steps leading up. The steps ascend right from the street, and from this level, you cannot see the top of the pyramid, so its size is not apparent. When you find the steps, you may still wonder whether you are in the right place. You are. The steps have been restored, and it is an easy—if hot—climb. The pyramid rises in terraces, and part of it is faced with huge stones. Other unrestored areas are grass covered. The base of the pyramid is about 640 feet by 570 feet, and it rises to a height of 56 feet.

It is rather a surprise when you reach the top of the stairs to discover not only that the flat top of the pyramid is so large but also that another pyramid of respectable bulk—and 59 feet high—rises from it.

This partly restored upper pyramid is set over the rear of the first, leaving a large open area in front. This gives the feeling that you are at ground level, which is only dispelled when you turn and look at the town below. Only then does the size of the whole structure become apparent.

The upper pyramid rises in terraces, has rounded corners, and is faced with small boulders. There are remains of a stairway with *alfardas* on the front. You may walk around the base of the upper pyramid, although the path narrows and gets steep at the rear. Although there is no remaining sculpture at Izamal, the massiveness of the Kinich-Kakmo (over 17 million cubic feet) makes a visit worthwhile.

In ancient times Izamal covered an area of about 2 square miles, and the Kinich-Kakmo bordered the north side of a large plaza. On the south side was another pyramid that was partly leveled to form the base of the Franciscan church and convent built in 1553, one of the oldest churches in Mexico. There were other pyramids on the east and west, but they are mostly destroyed. The one on the west originally had large sculptured human heads of stone and stucco, but nothing remains of them today. Other pyramids at Izamal have been totally leveled.

These pyramids date to the Early Classic period, during which time Izamal was the greatest religious center in northern Yucatán. It retained its importance until it was conquered in the Postclassic period by Hunac

Ceel, the founder of Mayapán, and it was occupied at the time of the Spanish conquest. During its heyday Izamal was an important shrine and place of pilgrimage, dedicated to Kinich-Kakmo, a manifestation of Kinich-Ahau, the sun god, and Itzamná. Izamal was also an important trading center for salt found on the nearby coast. It was connected to Aké by a *sacbé.*

Recent History

Izamal is mentioned in the native chronicles and by Bishop Diego de Landa, who said that there was at Izamal "a building of such height and beauty that it astonishes one."

John Lloyd Stephens and Frederick Catherwood visited the site in 1842, near the end of their second trip to Yucatán, and described and drew an illustration of one of the large stucco heads.

Désiré Charnay also visited Izamal, and in 1885 he described and illustrated the site. In 1887 an English translation of the original French text appeared. The stucco head reported by Stephens was destroyed by the time Charnay visited Izamal, but he reproduced the illustration from Stephens's report and included an illustration of his own of another head on the same structure.

Restoration of the Kinich-Kakmo was undertaken by INAH in the 1970s.

Connections

1. Mérida to Izamal: 44.0 miles by paved road (1:03).

2. Chichén Itzá to Izamal: 42.6 miles by paved road (1:07).

Getting There

1. Take Highway 180 heading east from Mérida to Hoctún, turn left on an unnumbered road, and go to Citilcúm. (You will pass through the village of Kimbilá along the way.) In Citilcúm take a right turn and proceed to Izamal.

2. Take Highway 180 heading west from Chichén Itzá to Kantunil. Turn right and continue to Izamal. (You will pass through the village of Sudzal along the way.)

If you are driving between Mérida and Chichén Itzá, a side trip to Izamal will cost you only 13.2 miles (:24), since you can take the two routes described above and eliminate the section of Highway 180 between Hoctún and Kantunil.

There are restaurants in Izamal, some across the street from the Kinich-Kakmo, and the town can be reached by private car, bus, or taxi from Mérida or Chichén Itzá. Allow 40 minutes to visit the Kinich-Kakmo, after you find it.

★ ★
IKIL
*(ee-*keel; *derivation: Maya for "Place of the Wind")*

Location:
    Northern Yucatán.
Map: 1 (p. 27)

The Site

Ikil is worth a visit only if you plan to make the rather difficult climb to the top of the pyramid. The trail is rubble, dirt, and roots, but there are some small trees that provide a handhold.

Although the site of Ikil has not been mapped, it is known that there are some low platform mounds surrounding the pyramid. The mounds, however, do not support standing architecture, and so the pyramid—or, more precisely, the summit temple atop the pyramid—is the feature of most interest.

The pyramid-summit temple known as Structure I is 80 feet high, one of the "largest

The summit temple of Structure I, Ikil. View of the east chamber. Probably early Late Classic period.

architectural monuments of the northern Maya area," according to E. Wyllys Andrews IV and George E. Stuart, who studied the site.

Originally the summit temple rested atop a three-tiered platform. In later times, rooms were added to the outside of each of the three tiers (6 on each side, for a total of 24), and stairways were added on all four sides of the platform. These constructions totally encased the original platform. The stairways are pierced (at least on the two upper levels) by vaulted passageways. The original construction probably dates to the early Late Classic period, and the rooms and stairways were probably added in Terminal Classic times. The stonework in the two construction phases is quite different. None of the stairways affords access to the summit temple today.

As you climb the rocky trail ascending the pyramid, you pass one of the vaulted pas-

sageways beneath the stairway, and later you see another vault that is part of one of the added rooms. As you near the top, you will see the huge rounded corner stones that are part of the summit temple.

The summit temple consists of a rubble core surrounded by a vaulted corridor, although the effect today is of two rooms, the east and west chambers. The extreme weight of the core has caused it to subside, with the result that all but one small section of vault has collapsed, causing the capstone atop this section (in the west chamber) to tilt toward the core at an odd angle.

Each of these chambers has a niche built into the core, and the niches were originally spanned by glyph-carved stone lintels. In the west chamber, a section of the lintel with five glyph blocks and a fraction of a sixth remains in place; in the east chamber only two glyph blocks remain. Originally each lintel contained ten glyph blocks; the portions in place are well preserved.

To the left of the niche in the east chamber is a large stone ring tenoned into the wall of the core. It is assumed that originally there was another ring to the right of the niche. They perhaps functioned as rod holders or tie-rings for curtains, although the remaining ring seems very massive for such a purpose.

The outer walls of the summit temple were constructed of huge stone blocks, some weighing as much as 3,000 pounds, and remains of these can be seen in both east and west chambers. According to Andrews and Stuart, "No such [other] megalithic walls are known from the Maya area," although they note that similar huge stones are used in substructure facings at Aké and Izamal.

Recent History

Ikil seems first to show up in the literature in Sylvanus G. Morley's *Inscriptions of Petén* (1937–1938), where it is listed in the appendixes, and in a later work by the same author, although the site is not described in either publication.

Under the name "Iki," the site is shown on a 1940 map by Tulane University, but the source of information is not listed.

In 1954 an account of the site and sketches of the glyph blocks that were in place was published by Alberto García Maldonado, a Yucatecan artist, in Mérida's newspaper *Diario del Sureste*. García was first brought to Ikil by the Dorantes brothers of a nearby town, and he sent drawings of the glyph blocks to César Lizardi Ramos, a Mexican epigrapher, who identified them as noncalendric glyphs and noted "a number of resemblances to early forms." It was through García that Andrews's attention was brought to the site.

Andrews received permission to search for the missing fragments of the two lintels, and all but two glyph blocks were recovered and recorded in 1956; the two missing ones were assumed to have been pulverized in the collapse of the lintels. The uncovered fragments were reburied for protection, and shortly afterward were dug up by García, who made and published additional drawings.

In 1966 Andrews, Stuart, and Richard Furno returned to Ikil to gather architectural information. Structure I was almost entirely cleared, and enough data were collected to permit a restoration drawing. Although no extensive excavation was carried out, a small sample of ceramics was collected—mostly from the surface—and it gave no evidence to contradict the dates suggested by the architecture or glyphs. This work was sponsored by the National Geographic Society and the Middle American Research Institute of Tulane University, and in 1968 the latter published the information.

Although mask elements, other decorations, and columned doorways were reported by Andrews and Stuart, they are not discernible today when you climb the pyramid.

There is some evidence that the core of the summit temple once supported a roof comb or some sort of superstructure. If indeed it did, this would have added considerably to the height of the structure.

It is thought that perhaps Ikil was an old shrine whose base was added to during the period of dominance by Chichén Itzá.

Connections

1. Chichén Itzá to Ikil: 21.2 miles by paved road (:34), then 300 yards by foot trail (:08).

2. Mérida to Ikil: 63.8 miles by paved road (1:32), then 300 yards by foot trail (:08).

Getting There

From Chichén Itzá head west on Highway 180 to Libre Unión. From Mérida head east on Highway 180 to the same town. In Libre Unión take the unnumbered road heading south (marked for Yaxcabá) to a little past Kilometer 9 (the markers are hard to spot). At this point there is a sign on the left saying San Isidro and a dirt road on the right leading about 300 yards to the small rancho. Ask at the house for someone to show you the way to the pyramid. The residents of the house are familiar with the ruins, but they do not know them by the name of Ikil. When we inquired, we were told that there was no special name for the site.

You will be directed back to the paved road, where you can park on the west side. The foot trail is directly opposite on the east side. The trail soon passes a gate and is easy to follow, but it would be difficult to find the best access route up the pyramid without being shown. For this reason you need to have someone from the rancho along.

Once you begin your climb, you will find a machete helpful to cut back the vegetation for better photographs. Ikil is not a very visited site, and the trail can become overgrown, as is the pyramid and summit temple. Wear boots and have a wide-angle lens for your camera.

Allow 1 hour to walk to the pyramid, climb it, look around at the summit temple, and return to your car. There is no food or drink here, but if you are packing a picnic lunch, there is a nearby cenote that would be a pleasant place to eat. Head north (back toward Libre Unión) for 4.4 miles. At this point there is a rock road to Cenote Xtojil; it goes to the right for 0.6 mile.

You can reach Ikil by private car or taxi from Chichén Itzá or Mérida. A bus can get you as far as Libre Unión, but connections from there are questionable.

★ ★ ★ ★
CHICHÉN ITZÁ AND
CHICHÉN ITZÁ MUSEUM

(chee-chehn eet-sah; derivation:
Maya for "The Mouth of the Well of the Itzás")

Earlier Name:
  Uucil-abnal ("Seven Bushes"),
  according to Michael D. Coe;
  Uuc-hab-nal ("Seven Bushy
  Places"), according to Ralph
  L. Roys.
Original Name:
  Chichén Itzá for the later part
  of its pre-Columbian history.
Location:
  Northern Yucatán.
Map: 1 (p. 27)

The Site

Chichén Itzá is truly a world-class site, one that should be seen by all visitors to Yucatán. It is one of the largest and most studied sites on the Yucatán Peninsula and is better preserved than most others. In addition, many of its structures have been consolidated and restored over the years.

Until 1983, Highway 180 went right through the site, but for ecological reasons this part of the highway was closed, and a bypass was built north of the site. The entrance to Chichén Itzá is by a cutoff from the highway on the west side of the site. The hotels on the east side can be reached by taking the bypass and then heading back toward the site (west) on the old section of Highway 180 that is still open for local traffic.

The ruins of Chichén Itzá can be most easily covered by breaking them into three areas: (1) structures north of the old highway (this is the area you enter from the service building); (2) those immediately south of the old highway, now called the South Group (signs point out the way to this area); and (3) some outlying groups farther south in the bush, misnamed "Old Chichén."

There are two principal styles of public architecture at Chichén Itzá. The first is a local variant of the Puuc style found at sites in west-central Yucatán and northeastern Campeche. The other style, according to Peter J. Schmidt, "is partly derived from the same roots but is vastly enriched by elements

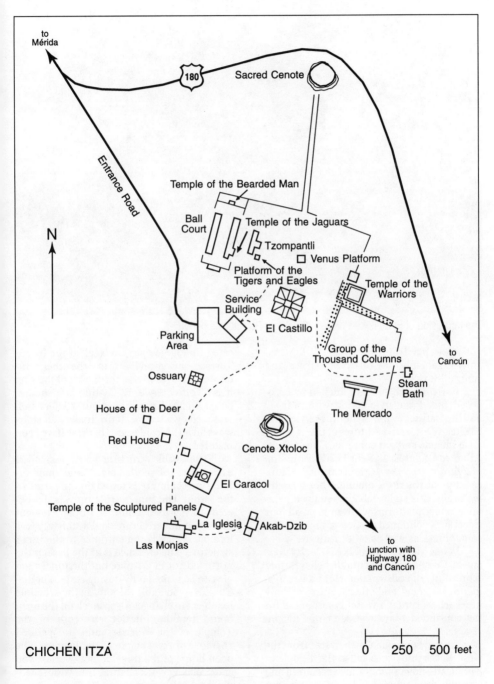

to
Mérida

180 Sacred Cenote

Entrance Road

N

Temple of the Bearded Man

Ball
Court

Temple of the Jaguars

Tzompantli

Venus Platform

Platform of the
Tigers and Eagles

Service
Building

Temple of the
Warriors

Parking
Area

El Castillo

Group of the
Thousand Columns

to
Cancún

Ossuary

Steam
Bath

House of the Deer

The Mercado

Red House

Cenote Xtoloc

El Caracol

Temple of the Sculptured Panels

La Iglesia

Akab-Dzib

Las Monjas

to
junction with
Highway 180
and Cancún

CHICHÉN ITZÁ

0   250   500 feet

The north side of El Castillo, Chichén Itzá. Early Postclassic period.

and concepts from other parts of Meso-america, notably the Gulf Coast, Oaxaca, and central Mexico."

Early investigators of Chichén Itzá proposed that Puuc-style traits were "Maya" and the features found in the other style were "Toltec." Decorative features of the "Toltec" style include serpent columns, Chac Mools, Atlantean figures, serpent heads at the top of *alfardas, tzompontlis,* and carvings of processions of warriors, among others. Architecturally, this style embodies stepped pyramids, dance platforms with stairs on all four sides, large columned porticoes, gallery-patio compounds, as well as other features.

While Mexican influence is clearly present at Chichén Itzá, Schmidt believes that "continuity of construction techniques, residential systems, and other features of daily life, such as ceramic vessel types, argue for the continued Maya character of Chichén Itzá."

As you approach Chichén Itzá from the west, El Castillo—also called the Temple of Kukulcán—towers above the vegetation and is visible from some distance away. It is near the entrance to the site and is centrally lo-

cated in a large open area called the North Terrace, or Central Plaza; like the other principal structures in the north area of the site, it is "Toltec" style. El Castillo is a square-based stepped pyramid about 75 feet tall, crowned by a temple. It originally had stairways on all four sides; two of these have been restored.

The visible structure covers a smaller, earlier one (of similar plan), and some interesting sculpture is found on the inside of the latter. The inner structure was discovered during excavation. A tunnel was cut into the outer structure, and a stairway was located, which is the entrance to the inner structure. The entrance is at the base of the north side of El Castillo, but the inner temple can be visited only during certain hours. Check as you enter the site, as the schedule is subject to change. Also, check on the open hours for the interior structure of the Temple of the Warriors and the painted chamber of the Temple of the Jaguars. The open hours of the three do not overlap; you can probably work all three into your schedule if you plan ahead.

One word about the interior of El Cas-

The Temple of the Warriors, Chichén Itzá. View from the southwest. Early Postclassic period.

tillo: the steep stairway leading up is very narrow, and it is generally hot, steamy, and jammed with people inside. If you are the least bit claustrophobic, you had better pass this up.

If you do go, you will see a Chac Mool and a throne in the shape of a jaguar at the top of the stair. Unfortunately, they are protected by bars, which interfere with photography. If you want some photos anyway, bring a flash unit and a wide-angle lens (for the Chac Mool just behind the bars), and a normal or slightly long lens for the Jaguar Throne some feet behind. The jaguar is painted red and has some jade incrustations depicting the jaguar's spots and jade balls representing the eyes. A turquoise mosaic disc was found on the seat of the throne.

Climbing the exterior of El Castillo is much more pleasant and affords delightful views of the north section of the site. It is a good spot for photos of the Temple of the Warriors, which lies to the east. This latter temple is composed of a pyramidal base rising in three tiers, with a temple on top, approached by a stairway on the west side. There is a large colonnade of stone pillars carved with figures of warriors at the base of the structure on the west side.

At the entrance to the temple there is a Chac Mool and two beautifully carved serpent columns; at the rear are small Atlantean figures supporting an altar. The facade of the temple has sculptures depicting Chac, the Maya rain god. The Temple of the Warriors also had at least two construction phases. There is an earlier inner temple, with pillars sculptured in bas-relief, which retain much of their original color, and murals once adorned the walls of the inner structure. There are also a Chac Mool and the heads of serpent columns inside.

Serpent columns on top of the Temple of the Warriors, Chichén Itzá. Early Postclassic period.

A large courtyard, adjacent to the south of the Temple of the Warriors, is surrounded by numerous ruined buildings known collectively as the Group of the Thousand Columns. The many columns were originally roofed over, forming a colonnade part way around the courtyard.

On the east side of the courtyard is a consolidated building called the Steam Bath, reached by a trail. It has four columns on the west face and remains of simple three-member moldings on the rear of the structure and its eastward projection. The other structure of interest in this area is the Mercado, or Market, on the south side of the courtyard, built on a slightly elevated platform. There is an interesting carved altar in this area and a square patio surrounded by tall columns with simple capitals. The perimeter of the patio was probably roofed with thatch; no stones that could belong to a roof have been found. Other structures in the Group of the Thousand Columns are unrestored, but two ball courts are known.

From here return to the Central Plaza and head north to the Venus Platform. This square platform has a stair on each of its four sides and may have been used as a dance platform. It is decorated with bas-relief sculpture and three-dimensional serpent heads.

Due north of the Venus Platform you come to a trail (built atop an ancient Maya *sacbé*) that continues north 300 yards to the Sacred Cenote. Although the cenote is a natural formation, it may have been altered to achieve its nearly circular shape. It is about 180 feet in diameter, and its sides rise 80 feet above the water level. The Sacred Cenote was apparently not used as a water supply but was reserved for rituals and human sacrifice involving the rain god. The notion that the sacrificed victims were all beautiful young virgins was disproved when human remains of young children and older adults, both male and female, were discovered. The Sacred Cenote is in a depression, and the surrounding dense vegetation cuts off most of the air. On a still day, the heavy atmosphere and buzzing insects can create a hypnotic effect, and one can easily imagine this as a place of human sacrifice. There are remains of a small temple on the edge of the cenote.

When you return to the Central Plaza, head right and visit the Platform of the Tigers and Eagles. This is similar to the Venus Platform, but smaller, and its decorative motifs include jaguars and eagles holding human hearts in their claws, almost identical to some bas-reliefs at Tula in central Mexico.

North of this platform is the Skull Rack, or Tzompantli. The sides are covered with bas-reliefs; some depict skulls in profile, except for the corners, where they are shown full face. Oddly enough, each is different from the other and has its own personality. Other reliefs show warriors in full regalia. Two Chac Mools were excavated from the platform.

Now head west to the Great Ball Court, the largest in Mesoamerica; its walls measure 272 feet long, but the playing area extends some distance beyond. There are interesting bas-relief carvings on the lower walls of the ball court depicting ball game activities and ritual sacrifice. A small temple lies at each end of the ball court, and from in front of the north temple (the Temple of the Bearded Man) a person speaking in a natural voice reportedly can be heard at the other end of the court, about 150 yards away.

The Temple of the Bearded Man gets its name from some bas-relief carvings on the inside of the temple. There are two columns at the entrance to the one-room temple, and these, the interior walls, and the remaining portion of the vault are completely covered with bas-reliefs. In the vault there are some remains of red paint, and this emphasizes the carvings. The larger temple at the south end of the ball court also has remains of columns with carvings, but the walls and vault surfaces are plain.

Even more interesting is the Temple of the Jaguars on top of the south end of the east wall of the ball court, and reached by a steep stair. The roof of the temple is supported by carved serpent columns similar to those at the Temple of the Warriors, and in an inner chamber there are a few fragments of murals that can be seen during the hours when this room is open. Unfortunately, the murals are poorly lighted and hard to make out. A carved wooden lintel spans the doorway to the inner room.

When you return to the plaza level, you can enter a chamber below the Temple of the Jaguars that faces east. It has polychromed bas-reliefs on pillars, walls, and vault in a good state of preservation and a simple three-dimensional sculpture of a jaguar, possibly a throne.

After a visit to this northern section of Chichén Itzá, it is time for a lunch break before you continue to the South Group.

When you reach the South Group, you

A corner of the Skull Rack (Tzompantli), Chichén Itzá. Early Postclassic period.

first come to the Ossuary, or Grave of the High Priest, to the right of the trail. Although mostly ruined, it is similar in design to El Castillo, though built on a smaller scale. There are remains of serpent columns on top, pillars carved with human figures, and the temple walls. Near the base of the Ossuary are some carved-stone panels.

Follow the trail south to the Red House, or Chichán-Chob, to the right of the trail. This small temple is built on a platform with rounded corners and is reached by a stairway on the west side. Simple medial and cornice moldings, a perforated central roof comb, and a flying facade with Chac masks form the exterior decorations. The walls are plain between the upper moldings and below the medial molding, giving a feeling of sober restraint. The Red House (so called because of a red strip painted on a wall) is Puuc style. Its other name, Chichán-Chob, is Maya and

probably means something like "small holes," referring to the latticework in the roof comb. A band of glyphs is found on the vault of the interior of the structure, and it has been dated to A.D. 869.

Northwest of the Red House, and off the main foot trail, is the House of the Deer, named for the depiction of a deer that once existed in one of the rooms. The style of the House of the Deer is similar to that of the Red House.

Follow the main trail south to El Caracol, which lies to the left. This is one of the most imposing structures in the South Group. *Caracol* means "snail" in Spanish and, by extension, "spiral," referring to the stairway found inside the structure. El Caracol is supposed to have served as an observatory, and it is the only round structure found at Chichén Itzá. The upper terrace of El Caracol has some three-dimensional

The Temple of the Bearded Man at the north end of the Great Ball Court, Chichén Itzá. Early Postclassic period.

The Temple of the Jaguar and the Great Ball Court, from the southeast, Chichén Itzá. Early Postclassic period.

Carved pillar in the chamber below the Temple of the Jaguar, Chichén Itzá. A crying rain deity and aquatic animals are depicted. Early Postclassic period.

of Chac masks. A doorway in the east face of the annex forms the open mouth of a monster, a feature associated with the Chenes style, although the rest of the structure is Puuc style. The upper level of Las Monjas has some carved lintels still in place.

Near the annex of Las Monjas is the diminutive La Iglesia, the Church. The lower walls are plain, but the upper facade and roof comb are a riot of Chac masks, many complete with curling snout. These are accompanied by stepped-fret patterns and other interesting designs. Both La Iglesia and Las Monjas are worth some detail photos as well as overall views.

About 100 yards east by foot trail is the Akab-Dzib ("Obscure Writing"), named for some hieroglyphs appearing on a lintel (including a date equivalent to A.D. 870). This structure was built in at least two stages. The central portion was constructed first, and the flanking north and south wings were added later. The Akab-Dzib is undecorated except for simple medial and cornice moldings.

The third section of Chichén Itzá is "Old Chichén," which has both Puuc- and "Toltec"-style remains, as does the rest of the site. The structures are scattered in the bush, but are connected by trails, which begin south of Hacienda Chichén (now a hotel). Visiting "Old Chichén" entails a hot steamy hike into the bush, but some of the structures are worth the effort.

To see the structures you must have a guide. While some of the trails are easy to follow, not all of the branches are marked, and sometimes parts of the trail are overgrown. You can ask for a guide at the ticket office in the service building when you enter the site, or check at the Mayaland Lodge on the east side of the site.

When you visit "Old Chichén," you come first to the Date Group, the most interesting in the area. The name comes from a lintel with an Initial Series date of A.D. 879.

sculpture of human heads. This is a good place for photographs of some of the other buildings.

Due south of El Caracol is the Temple of the Sculptured Panels. The panels are on the north and south exterior walls of the lower portion of the building, and a rocky path leads to the temple on top from the south side. This is a good vantage point for photographs of El Caracol and other structures.

A short distance southwest of the Temple of the Sculptured Panels are two of the most interesting buildings in the area. The largest is Las Monjas, or the Nunnery, with its annex; it is 210 feet long, 105 feet wide, and more than 50 feet high. This building saw several building stages, leading to its present impressive size. There is much interesting detail here, especially in the form

The Red House, or Chichán-Chob, west side, Chichén Itzá. Terminal Classic period.

It is the only Initial Series date known from Chichén Itzá, and the lintel is found spanning the top of two Atlantean figures, which form the doorway of a small temple, only the lower walls of which remain. It has been said that the lintel was previously used in an earlier building. A small Chac Mool is found at the base of the mound that supports the temple.

A bit south is the Puuc-style Temple of the Phalli, and behind this are remains of several structures, Atlantean figures, and carved columns. A short distance northwest is an enclosure with more Atlantean figures and, a bit farther on, a crude sculpture of a serpent. Just west of the Temple of the Phalli is a structure called the Telecotes ("owls"), with remains of carved columns depicting owls and other motifs. The trail to the next area of interest leaves from the Telecotes and heads southwest.

You come next to the Temple of Four Lintels. Little remains of this structure, except for the four carved lintels and the jambstones that support them. The lintels date to A.D. 881 and are carved on some of their edges and on the undersides. The glyphs on the edges of the two lintels that face north are especially well preserved and are very photogenic. Try to do this trip in the morning when they receive the best light.

A short distance southwest is the Temple of the Three Lintels, the only restored structure in "Old Chichén," and a gem. It is a Puuc-style structure, faced with thin veneer masonry associated with the style. Although other structures at Chichén Itzá are also in Puuc style, they generally lack this particular feature. Chac masks decorate the upper facade and are interspersed with engaged columns and a lattice pattern; the lower walls are plain. Two of the lintels, dated A.D. 879,

El Caracol, from the south, Chichén Itzá. The structure shows both Puuc and central Mexican traits. El Castillo rises in the background at left of center.

Las Monjas, or the Nunnery, and its annex, north side, Chichén Itzá. La Iglesia is at far left. Terminal Classic period.

La Iglesia, west side, Chichén Itzá. Terminal Classic period.

are carved on their front edges. The whole has a feeling of quiet dignity.

From the Temple of the Three Lintels, you retrace your steps part of the way before taking a side trail to the left. This brings you to two structures that are kept reasonably well cleared. The one you reach first is mostly a rubble mound but is worth climbing to see the remains of carved rectangular columns on top. A bit southwest is the Castillo of "Old Chichén." It is also mostly rubble, but there are remains of carved facing stones on the west side, a stairway on the north side, and carved columns and jambs on top. There is also a carved serpent head near the base of the Castillo that was probably a part of the original construction. From the top of this structure Las Monjas and El

Castillo of the North Group are visible to the northeast, in the distance.

Ceramic evidence indicates that Chichén Itzá was occupied from the Middle Preclassic period onward. It grew steadily to a position of regional importance, and during the ninth to twelfth centuries it was the political and cultural center of northern Yucatán.

Exactly when Mexican influence first appeared at Chichén Itzá, and how it reached the site, is still being debated and studied, and continuing epigraphic research will doubtless add to our knowledge about the history of the site. At present, some authorities believe that two groups arrived at Chichén Itzá: the Itzás and the "Toltecs." The Itzás are said to have been Putun or Chontal Maya, whose home was along the

The Akab-Dzib, west side, Chichén Itzá. Terminal Classic period.

Gulf Coast of Mexico between Tabasco and Champotón. They were known as sea traders and have been called the "Phoenicians of the New World" by Sir J. Eric S. Thompson. Thompson believed that they had trade connections with the people of central Mexico (through their merchants) and a sea route from Tabasco, around the Yucatán Peninsula, to Honduras.

The Toltecs were the dominant group in central Mexico during the late Terminal Classic and Early Postclassic times. Legend has it that some of this group, led by the famous Ce Acatl Topiltzin Quetzalcóatl, left their capital at Tula and proceeded to Yucatán. It is possible, however, that the "Toltecs" who arrived in Yucatán were a highly Mexicanized group of Chontal Maya who were associated with the Toltecs. Some authorities believe that the Itzás arrived in Yucatán around A.D. 866, led by Kakupacal, and that

the "Toltecs" followed around 987. Other scholars believe that the Itzás arrived after the "Toltecs." Still others believe that there was no "Toltec invasion" and that exotic ideas arrived at Chichén Itzá along with trade goods. Edward Kurjack says, "These new concepts were fused with indigenous art forms to create the mixture observed at Chichén Itzá." He further states that this apparent foreign influence "seems to have been a by-product of native commerce."

According to E. Wyllys Andrews V, "An increasingly accepted argument is that Mexican influence was present in Yucatán considerably before the collapse of the Puuc cities, quite possibly before A.D. 900, and that Puuc and 'Toltec' Chichén Itzá coexisted in northern Yucantán for a century or more." Other authorities also suggest that the two different architectural styles may have been contemporaneous, at least in part.

An Atlantean figure in the Date Group, Chichén Itzá. Early Postclassic period.

After Chichén Itzá went into decline sometime before A.D. 1200, Mayapán became the dominant center in northern Yucatán. Nevertheless, pilgrims still visited Chichén Itzá, as they had for many centuries, and this continued until the Spanish conquest.

Detail of the Temple of Four Lintels, showing the two lintels that face north, Chichén Itzá. Terminal Classic period.

Recent History

In 1528, during the early attempts by the Spaniards to conquer the Yucatán Peninsula, Francisco de Montego the elder established himself at Chichén Itzá for a time, but the hostility of the natives forced him to leave. In 1566 Bishop Diego de Landa described Chichén Itzá as a "very fine site." He gave its location and related the history of the place as given him by local informants. Another Spanish cleric, Diego López de Cogolludo, mentioned the site in 1688. The books of Chilam Balam (native chronicles written in the Maya language, but using the Spanish alphabet) record the history of Chichén Itzá. These early documents plus Landa's work are the principal sources of historical information about the site. Unfortunately, the chronology of the native documents is confused and bathed in legend,

and it is difficult to put the pieces together accurately.

In more modern times, John Lloyd Stephens and Frederick Catherwood explored the site, but Stephens credited the first visit by a "stranger" to a certain John Burke of New York, who was working as an engineer in Valladolid. Stephens also mentions a visit to Chichén Itzá by Baron Friederichsthal in 1840. Stephens said that the baron was the first to bring notice of the site to the public. A much wider audience, however, read Stephens's 1843 publication.

In Stephens's time, the road from Mérida to Valladolid passed through the ruins, much as the modern highway did until a few years ago, and he commented that "the great buildings tower on both sides of the road in full sight of passers-by, and from the fact that the road is much traveled, the ruins of Chichén are perhaps more generally known

The Temple of the Three Lintels, Chichén Itzá. Terminal Classic period.

to the people of the country than any other in Yucatán."

He and Catherwood spent some time at the site and recorded it in text and drawings. Catherwood also produced a map, but for some reason it does not extend far enough north to include the Sacred Cenote, although Cenote Xtoloc (in the South Group), which they used for bathing, is included.

In 1863 Désiré Charnay and E. E. Viollet-le-Duc published a work in Paris, and in 1885 Charnay published another (translated into English in 1887). All these publications include information on Chichén Itzá.

In 1873 Augustus Le Plongeon first visited Yucatán. He and his young wife, Alice, spent seven years there, three months of which they devoted to investigations of Chichén Itzá. He drew plans, copied murals, and took photographs of the site (some in stereo). Although this was clearly a contribution, his fantastic theories were disdained by archaeologists.

Alfred P. Maudslay briefly visited

Chichén Itzá in 1889, and during his stay he surveyed, measured, and photographed the site. He had as his assistant Edward H. Thompson, the American counsul in Yucatán, who later returned to the site after buying Hacienda Chichén Itzá with funds provided by Allison V. Armour, a patron of scientific research. Thompson rebuilt the ruined hacienda and moved his wife and children there from Mérida, intending it to be a profitable enterprise as well as to serve as a home near the ruins. For thirty years he lived at Chichén Itzá and carried out investigations. Some of his reports remain unpublished, although others have found their way into print.

Thompson is best known for dredging the Sacred Cenote, where he recovered artifacts of copper, gold, jade, and clay as well as human bones. Some of these items were given to visiting friends to take back to the Peabody Museum of Harvard University, for whom Thompson was working. The Mexican government learned of this traffic and attached Thompson's hacienda. In 1958 many of these items in the Peabody's collection were returned to Mexico.

Thomspon spent his remaining years a poor man back in the United States, but he had proved his point that the Sacred Cenote was indeed a place of human sacrifice, as legend said.

After Thompson's work, professional archaeologists took over reserach at Chichén Itzá. Sylvanus G. Morley first visited Chichén Itzá in 1907, as a guest of Thompson, and returned to do extensive work for the Carnegie Institution of Washington and the Mexican government. He began his work in 1924 and continued for two decades. In 1926 Sir J. Eric S. Thompson joined the field staff. In 1961 the Sacred Cenote was again dredged. This time a modern air pump was used, and divers explored its depths. About 4,000 artifacts were recovered in four months' work. The project was undertaken by INAH in cooperation with the National Geographic Society and the Exploration and Water Sports Club of Mexico (CEDAM). Additional work at the Sacred Cenote was conducted in the late 1960s, which was reported by Román Piña Chan in 1970.

In 1987 Charles E. Lincoln of Harvard University reported the detailed mapping of a section of "Old Chichén," and in 1991 a project to restore the Group of the Thousand Columns was begun.

Connections

1. Chichén Itzá (hotels) to the parking area for the ruins: 3.0 miles by paved road (:06).

2. Mérida to Chichén Itzá (parking area): 73.9 miles by paved road (1:48).

Getting There

1. From the hotel area on the east side of Chichén Itzá, take old Highway 180 heading east for 0.7 mile (or less—depending on which hotel you are starting from) to the junction with the bypass that goes around the site on the north. Turn left onto the bypass and go 1.8 miles to its other end and the cutoff for the ruins (marked with a sign). Turn left at the cutoff and go 0.5 mile to the parking area.

2. From Mérida head east on Highway 180 to the junction for the cutoff for the ruins (73.4 miles) and continue straight ahead for the remaining 0.5 mile to the parking area.

From the parking area you enter a large, well-designed service building that houses the Chichén Itzá Museum, a restaurant, shops, rest rooms, and a bookstore, in addition to the ticket office. When you leave the far end of the building, there is a trail that goes straight ahead to the Central Plaza and enters it near El Castillo. A marked branch trail heads right (shortly after you leave the service building) and goes to the South Group.

You can reach Chichén Itzá by private car, taxi, bus, or on conducted tours from Mérida. Bilingual guides are available at the site. Wear a sun hat, and if you plan to visit "Old Chichén," wear a long-sleeved shirt and slacks. Allow 2 full days if you want to see the site properly, including "Old Chichén," which takes a tiring 3 hours in itself.

A light-and-sound spectacle is presented in the evening at Chichén Itzá. There is a presentation in Spanish at 7:00 P.M. and another in English at 9:00 P.M. Tickets can be purchased at the site or from some of the larger nearby hotels. For suggestions on photographing the spectacle, see "Uxmal."

★ ★
Chichén Itzá Museum

The nicely arranged Chichén Itzá Museum has displays of various items from the site. Labels are in Spanish, with a synopsis in English and French. Photography is permitted, but flash is not.

There is a rectangular column carved with a figure, with animals in the headdress, that comes from a group to the south of El Caracol. One of the carved panels from the Venus Platform is displayed, and there are other carved columns, both tall and short Atlantean figures, a Chac Mool, and carved serpent heads.

One of the more interesting displays is a ball court ring, carved with a feathered serpent, that was discovered inside the Tzompantli when it was excavated.

Photographs showing the restoration of

Carved panel from the Venus Platform at the site. Chichén Itzá Museum. Early Postclassic period.

El Castillo are exhibited, as are ceramics from the site, and one section gives information on the early investigators of Chichén Itzá.

Outside the museum, in a patio area, there is a large model of the site. You can see the museum collection and the model in half an hour.

★ ★
BALANKANCHE (CAVE)
(bah-lahn-kahn-cheh; derivation:
Maya for "Throne of the Jaguar Priest" or "Hidden Treasure of the Jaguar")

Location:
Northern Yucatán.
Map: 1 (p. 27)

The Site and Recent History

The cave of Balankanche has been known for hundreds of years, but in 1959 José Humberto Gómez, a tourist guide, discovered a sealed section at the end of one of the chambers. He opened it and followed a long passage to a circular cavern. In the center of the cavern was a huge stalagmite resembling a tree trunk with small stalactites forming the "leaves." Around the base of the stalagmite he discovered a treasure trove of pottery, jewelry, and carved artifacts. These items remain in place today and can be seen when you visit the cave. Many of the artifacts date to the "Toltec" period at Chichén Itzá. In a nearby area of the cave is a group of miniature metates with their accompanying manos, and farther on is an underground cenote.

Connections

1. Chichén Itzá to Balankanche: 3.9 miles by paved road (:07).

2. Mérida to Balankanche: 77.3 miles by paved road (1:53).

Getting There

From Chichén Itzá (junction with Highway 180 and the cutoff to the site) or Mérida, take Highway 180 heading east to the cutoff for Balankanche (3.6 miles from Chichén Itzá and 77.0 miles from Mérida). The cutoff is marked with a sign and heads left to the cave.

There are guided tours of the cave in Spanish at 9:00 and 10:00 A.M. and at 12:00, 2:00, and 4:00 P.M. Tours in English start at 11:00 A.M. and at 1:00 and 3:00 P.M.

The caverns are adequately lighted, but the descent at the entrance can be extremely slippery in wet weather, and at these times boots would be best. There are also some low overhangs in spots, through which you must crawl or waddle. Tours last about 20 or 30 minutes.

There is a botanical garden and restaurant at the cave.

COBÁ-YAXUNÁ SACBÉ

*(koh-*bah *yah-shoo-*nah; *derivation: Cobá is Maya for "Ruffled Waters";*
Yaxuná is sometimes given as "Your Green House,"
although some authorities disagree)

Location:
  Northern Yucatán.
Map: 1 (p. 27)

The Site

Many Maya *sacbeob* have been traced, and a good deal has been written about them, but few are discernible today. This is a place to see one.

The Cobá-Yaxuná Sacbé is not terribly impressive visually. You see only a clearing in the trees with weeds on top, but if you stop for a look, you will realize that the *sacbé* is actually a raised roadway made of limestone boulders. See "Cobá" in Section 6, Part 1, for more details.

Highway 295 crosses the *sacbé* at right angles, and the junction is marked with a sign saying Mirador.

Connection

Valladolid to the Cobá-Yaxuná Sacbé: 13.6 miles by paved road (:20).

Getting There

If you are traveling Highway 295 between Valladolid and Felipe Carrillo Puerto, you will cross the *sacbé* 13.6 miles south of Valladolid (and 1.2 miles south of Tixcacalcupul), and you may want to stop for a couple of minutes. Otherwise, it really is not worth the detour from Valladolid and back just to see it.

There is no food or drink at the Mirador, only the sign.

★ ★
EK BALAM
*(ehk bah-*lahm; *derivation: Maya for "Black Tiger")*

Location:
   Northern Yucatán.
Map: 1 (p. 27)

The Site

Ek Balam is a large site with a continuous settlement area covering about 4 square miles. In the center is the site core, surrounded by a double wall. The outer wall is over 4,000 feet in circumference, and it outlines a roughly oval shape that measures over 1,000 feet from east to west (its longest dimension). It encloses an area of about 30 acres. The entrance to the site today is over the West Sacbé, which approaches the wall on that side. When you drive in, you can park near the caretaker's *champa* inside the double wall. In the core area of Ek Balam there are massive structures surrounding a plaza, and though the site is overgrown as a whole, the trails and more interesting features are kept cleared. Unfortunately, most of the architecture is poorly preserved.

As you begin your tour, you first pass the north side of Structure 2, which borders the west side of the plaza. This structure is a huge platform, over 30 feet tall, and some of the facing stone of the platform is in place on the north side. There is a simple molding near the top. A range of rooms on top of the west side of the platform is mostly ruined.

Nearby, on the north side of the plaza, is Structure 1, the largest at Ek Balam. It is over 500 feet long, half as wide, and about 100 feet tall at its highest point. Structure 1 is composed of a 33-foot-high basal platform and the fallen remains of several structures on top. The central structure is the largest and tallest, and brings Structure 1 to its highest point. There is a trail to the top of the platform, and the caretaker will bring along a rope to help you climb. At the top of the platform there is a saucer-shaped depression, dug by looters, and nearby you can see the entrance to a vaulted stairway that goes into the basal platform. From the top of the platform you can see Structure 17 to the south, through the vegetation. The climb to the top of the central structure atop the platform is steeper and longer, and there is not much standing architecture, but reportedly there is a lovely view. We did not climb this part, but we were told that from the top you can see the pyramids at Cobá, over 35 miles away.

After returning to ground level, you walk south to a fair-sized platform with the remains of two identical buildings on top, called Las Gemelas ("The Twins"). The platform and buildings are collectively called Structure 17, and it borders the south side of the plaza. The upper buildings face east and are some of the best-preserved architecture at Ek Balam. The backs and sides of the buildings are standing, and the structures are separated by a passageway. Both structures have a simple, three-member, rectangular medial molding, with a recessed middle section. The temple on the south (right, as you face the back of the structures) has a few stones of its cornice molding in place. In the upper wall zone, between the two moldings, there are projecting tenons that probably supported stucco decorations originally. The fronts of the buildings have fallen, but each structure originally had four rooms. The buildings were once covered with stucco and are believed to have been elite residences. A rocky trail ascends the platform at the rear (west side) of the buildings.

In the plaza, a short distance east of Structure 17, is a stone statue of a headless torso wearing a pectoral. His arms are behind his back, and it appears that the figure depicted is a captive. Close by are a couple of carved stones that were probably part of an architectural decoration. Near this are remains of a couple of carved but broken stelae.

Rear (west) side of the south building of the pair called Las Gemelas ("The Twins") of Structure 17, Ek Balam. Terminal Classic period.

To the east, and occupying the southeast corner of the plaza, is Structure 10, a platform with remains of a small standing temple on top. The temple faces west and has one room and a single doorway spanned by a stone lintel. Much of the facing stone has fallen, but on the south side of the temple (right as you are facing it), part of a three-member molding with a recessed middle part is still in place. Some stones carved with squared spirals are found on the ground nearby. The east and south sides of the platform of Structure 10 have a good deal of their facing stones in place.

From Structure 10 the trail goes to a huge chultun with a large opening at its entrance, and then to a small cleared area where there is a bas-relief stone carving of a profile serpent head with a tenon on the back. Farther on is an eroded circular altar.

You now leave the plaza area and return to where you parked. From there, head west on foot for a short distance to see the remains of one of the walls that encircles the core of the site; nearby, a couple of carved stones are in a cleared area.

Preliminary ceramic studies indicate that Ek Balam was occupied during the Late Preclassic period, although no architectural remains dating to that time have been found so far. Few sherds of Early Classic date have been recovered. The peak period of Ek Balam was the Terminal Classic, when most of the structures were erected and when the site had its greatest occupation. Although this is the same period in which the Puuc cities flourished, there is little evidence of Puuc-style architecture at Ek Balam.

According to William M. Ringle and George J. Bey, the site "appears to have been constructed rapidly by an elite who migrated into the area"; furthermore, "Ek Balam appears to have been occupied for only a few hundred years before abandonment." Ringle and Bey also believe that the walls surrounding the core of the site were symbolic and doubt that they ever served a defensive function.

In addition to the West Sacbé, on which you entered the site, there are others on the north, east, south, and southwest.

Recent History

In 1597 conquistador Juan Gutiérrez Picón prepared the *Relación de Ek Balam* for the king of Spain. Gutiérrez had an encomienda (a grant of land and the labor of the inhabiting Indians) in the region, and he questioned the village elders about the site and the history of the area. His informants told him that the cabecera (principal town of the province) was named Tiquibalon by a great lord called Ek Balam. In the *Relación,* Gutiérrez described the site in some detail and included the history of the area as given him by the Indians. According to Ringle and Bey, however, ceramic studies indicate that "the ethnohistoric Ek Balam was not located in the site center."

In 1886, on his last trip to Yucatán, Désiré Charnay heard rather vague reports about pyramids, vaults, and monuments at Ek Balam. These came from Don Juan Medina, who owned a nearby hacienda, and who offered Charnay assistance with transportation and necessities. Charnay visited and described the site and considered it a great discovery.

Sylvanus G. Morley and Jean Charlot visited Ek Balam in the late 1920s and issued a brief description of the site, which they believed was probably late (Postclassic period). In the early 1980s Ian Graham studied the carved monuments at Ek Balam and produced a preliminary map of the site; in 1984 he gave his information to Ringle and Bey.

Beginning in 1985, several seasons of work were undertaken at Ek Balam, directed by Ringle and Bey, to study the cultural history of the site, its demography, and its political and economic organization. This was sponsored by the National Geographic Society, the Middle American Research Institute of Tulane University, and Davidson College, under the auspices of INAH. Work included mapping of the core area of Ek Balam, its immediate surroundings, and some secondary peripheral sites. Test pits were excavated, ceramic samples were collected and analyzed, and some of the standing architecture was cleared.

Connection

Valladolid (plaza) to Ek Balam: 14.1 miles by paved road (:26), 2.2 miles by rock road (:08), then 0.6 mile by dirt road (:05).

Total from Valladolid to Ek Balam: 16.9 miles (:39).

Getting There

From Valladolid head north on Highway 295 to the cutoff marked for Hunuku. Turn right at the cutoff and go to the village of Santa Rita. Then turn left (the only choice) and go 0.1 mile to the north end of Santa Rita. Then continue 2.1 miles straight ahead on the rock road that goes to the village of Ek Balam. (A right turn at the north end of Santa Rita will take you to the village of Hunuku.) The rock road to the village of Ek Balam is no more than two tire tracks, but the surface is good. This road enters the village on the south side of the plaza. Turn right and then left to go around the plaza, and then take the dirt cutoff on the right to the parking area for the ruins.

When you enter the village of Ek Balam, youngsters will offer to show you the way to the site. Once you reach the site, they or, better yet, the caretaker will show you around. You will see more with someone along. The caretaker of Ek Balam is Anastasio Baas Pomol; he is pleasant, knowledgeable, and helpful.

There is no food or drink at Ek Balam. Allow 1¼ hours for a visit. The site can be reached by private car or taxi from Valladolid. Buses travel along Highway 295 and could drop you off at the first cutoff, but that is as close as you could get to Ek Balam by bus.

If you start from Chichén Itzá, add 26.9 miles by paved road (:38) to the total given above. If starting from Mérida, add 100.3 miles by paved road (2:24) to the total given above. In both cases take Highway 180 heading east to Valladolid and then follow the directions already listed. You can also reach Valladolid by taking Highway 180 heading west from Cancún, 98.9 miles by paved road (2:36).

SECTION 2

• • • •

WEST-CENTRAL YUCATÁN AND NORTHEASTERN CAMPECHE

Mask panels above the center doorway of Structure 1 of Group A, Sacbé. View from the south. Terminal Classic period.

GENERAL INFORMATION
FOR SECTION 2

<table>
<tr><td>

Point of Reference:
Uxmal, Yucatán.
Maps: 2, 2A, 2B, 2B1, 2C, and 2D

</td></tr>
</table>

Mileages given to the sites in this section are from the junction of Highway 261 and the entrance road to the Uxmal ruins.

There is no town at Uxmal, but there are three good hotels near the archaeological zone. The Hacienda Uxmal was the first, and for many years, the only one. It is a charming colonial-style facility; its pool is crystal clear and is surrounded by lush, well-kept gardens. The rooms are spacious, and the floors are cool tile. The rooms have ceiling fans (adequate for most of the year), and many also have air conditioning. Hacienda Uxmal is on the east side of Highway 261, across from the archaeological zone.

Right on the highway (east side) is the restaurant Nicte Ha, open from 1:00 to 8:30 P.M., which is a part of the Hacienda Uxmal operation. It is a convenient place to have lunch or to get a cold drink if you are waiting for a bus back to Mérida. Buses run several times a day each way.

The Archaeological Villa (a hotel operated by Club Med, but open to the general public) is right at the entrance to the ruins and is typical of the Archaeological Villas found at other sites. The rooms are air-conditioned, small, but well designed.

The Mision Uxmal is 1 mile north of the archaeological zone, on the west side of the highway. It is a modern hotel/motel, and all the rooms are air-conditioned.

All the hotels have dining rooms, bars, and swimming pools, and the cost of accommodations for all three is in the same price range.

For the more budget-minded traveler who nevertheless wants to stay near Uxmal, there is the Rancho Uxmal, 2.5 miles north of the archaeological zone, on the west side of the highway. It has 12 rooms, all with ceiling fans. There is also parking for recreational vehicles, electrical hookups, and bathrooms with showers. This is also a good place to eat. Nicely prepared regional specialties, soups, sandwiches, and other fare are available. Their beer is ice cold, and the management is accommodating.

You can, of course, visit the ruins of Uxmal on a day tour from Mérida, but this really does not allow enough time at the site for serious visitors. If you plan to spend more time in the area—and certainly there are many nearby sites to visit—you can drive to Uxmal from Mérida or take a bus. Driving your own vehicle or a rented one is recommended, as this is the only reasonable way to reach some of the isolated sites. Closest car rentals are at the airport in Mérida.

A number of sites in this section lie along the Puuc Highway. There is no regularly scheduled bus service along this highway, but *sometimes* in the high season (July and August, and December through March) buses do run. The service is irregular, but your hotel at Uxmal may have information.

The major sites of Kabáh, Sayil, Xlapak, Labná, and Loltún can be reached on conducted tours from Uxmal. Check at your hotel and make arrangements the day before.

If you drive to Uxmal from Mérida, you will pass through Muna, where there is a small shop selling high-quality reproductions of Maya polychrome pots. This is the establishment of Martín Morales, on Calle 13, a dirt street that intersects the highway at the north entrance to Muna. From the highway go west for one long block. The shop is then the first building on the left. You can easily spot Calle 13, even if you miss the sign. Vendors of huipils hang their wares on lines in this area, and you will see them as you approach along the highway from Mérida. Morales makes, fires, and decorates the pots, and while not cheap, the quality is excellent. There is also an icehouse in Muna on the plaza.

Another interesting place to shop in the area is at Tienda El Chacmool in Santa Elena. The shop is at the south end of the town, on the east side of Highway 261. The shop is actually the home of Miguel Ángel Uc Delgado (son of the caretaker of Sayil) and his attractive young wife. Miguel does excellent wood carvings and stone sculptures of Maya deities and other Maya motifs. His wife sells typical clothing and other interesting items. You will pass right by their shop on your way to Kabáh.

OTHER STOPOVERS: There are modest hotels in Ticul and Tekax on Highway 184; one, the Motel Cerro Inn on the west side of Ticul, has space for a few recreational vehicles.

Food is available at some of the small hotels. Two good spots to eat are Restaurant Los Almendros on the main street in Ticul, serving Maya specialities (they also have a branch in Mérida), and the restaurant of the Hotel Peraza in Tekax, which also serves Maya specialties and other fare as well. Their *poc-chuc* is excellent. This is a marinated and grilled pork steak, served with side orders of grilled, chopped tomatoes, pickled onions, and chili peppers.

GAS STATIONS: The closest station to Uxmal is at Muna, and gas is also available at Ticul, Oxkutzcab, and Tekax. South of Uxmal the nearest station is at Hopelchén, but it is sometimes out of gas.

GUIDES: Miguel Uc Medina, the caretaker of Sayil. He can generally be found at Sayil. If not, someone will be able to tell you when he is expected or where to find him.

Emilio Santos Camal, a resident of Santa Elena. He lives at Calle 27, no. 214, on the corner of Calle 22. His house is only a block or so off the highway. Ask someone if you cannot find it.

Pedro Pacheco Dzul, a resident of Bolonchén. His house is in the center of town, opposite the highway, and near the market and plaza. Ask, and someone will be able to point it out to you. There is no street address.

Bonifacio Canul, the caretaker of Chunhuhub and a resident of Xculoc village. He is generally at Chunhuhub in the morning. Look for him in the village in the afternoon. His house is near the plaza, and someone will be able to point it out. There is no street address.

All of these guides have had experience with archaeologists working in the area, and all are very pleasant, knowledgeable, and trustworthy.

Some of the guides who work at the archaeological zone of Uxmal also know how to reach some of the other sites. They generally do not have a vehicle, but you can arrange for a vehicle and driver through Hacienda Uxmal, and perhaps through the other two large hotels as well. Check with them a day ahead.

★ ★

OXKINTOK

*(ohsh-keen-*tohk*; derivation: Maya for "Three-Day Flint")*

Location:
West-central Yucatán.
Map: 2 (p. 77)

The Site

Oxkintok is a large and important site that was occupied for a long period (from about 300 B.C. to A.D. 1100, according to Ricardo Velázquez Valadéz). It has 11 large temple-pyramids and a number of smaller ones, an internal *sacbé* system, and one *sacbé* that leads to a group of buildings 0.6 mile to the

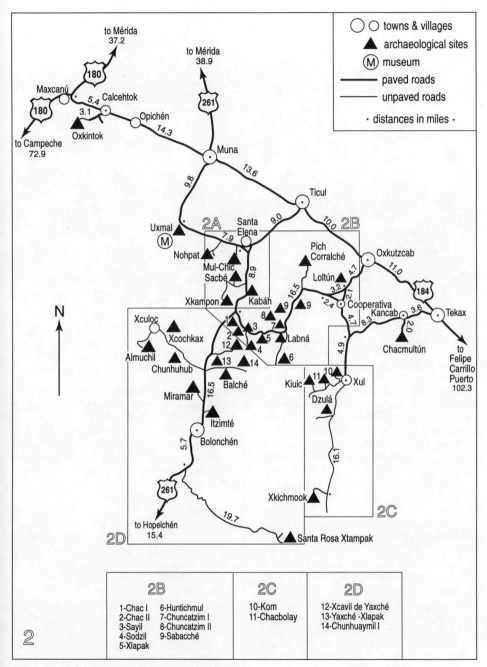

West-central Yucatán and northern Campeche

Map legend:

- ◯ ◯ towns & villages
- ▲ archaeological sites
- Ⓜ museum
- ▬ paved roads
- — unpaved roads
- · distances in miles ·

to Mérida 37.2
to Mérida 38.9
180
261
Maxcanú
180
Calcehtok 5.4
3.1
Opichén
Oxkintok
to Campeche 72.9
14.3
Muna
13.6
9.8
Ticul
Uxmal Ⓜ
2A
Santa Elena
9.0
10.0
2B
7.9
Nohpat
Pich Corralché
Oxkutzcab
11.0
Mul-Chic Sacbé
8.9
Loltún
4.7
184
Xkampon
16.5
Kabáh
3.2
2.1
Cooperativa
Tekax
N
9
9
2.4
Kancab
3.6
2.0
Xculoc
8
7
Chacmultún
8.3
Xcochkax
1
3
Labná
4.9
Almuchil
2
5
to Felipe Carrillo Puerto 102.3
Chunhuhub
12
4
6
13
14
Kiuic
11
10
Xul
Miramar
16.5
Balché
Dzulá
Itzimté
Bolonchén
16.1
5.7
261
Xkichmook
2C
to Hopelchén 15.4
19.7
Santa Rosa Xtampak
2D

2B		2C	2D	
1-Chac I	6-Huntichmul	10-Kom	12-Xcavil de Yaxché	
2-Chac II	7-Chuncatzim I	11-Chacbolay	13-Yaxché -Xlapak	
3-Sayil	8-Chuncatzim II		14-Chunhuaymil I	
4-Sodzil	9-Sabacché			
5-Xlapak				

2

Structure 2B8, with remains of a portal vault, Oxkintok. Late Classic period.

southeast. This may have also continued another 0.6 mile to a pyramidal structure. The earliest known Initial Series date in the Northern Maya area is the equivalent of A.D. 475, on a lintel at Oxkintok. Twenty-one carved stelae, six plain ones, and a number of carved and plain altars have been found at the site. There are also carved lintels—in addition to the one mentioned above—and carved columns.

On the way to the center of the site, the road passes within a couple of hundred feet of Structure 2C1. This structure is on the right side of the road, but sometimes the intervening area is overgrown, which makes the structure hard to spot. Structure 2C1 rests on a platform, and it is a short but steep climb to get to the building. It borders the east side of a courtyard surrounded on the other sides by structures that are now totally fallen. Structure 2C1 has three ranges of rooms and a solid central core. The northeast corner of the building was never completed, but the inner halves of some vaults

on the south and west sides are standing. The stonework employed in the structure is Classic Puuc (A.D. 770–1000).

Continue along the road (heading west). For the moment, pass up the cutoff to the left that goes to the North Plaza, and go beyond it for a short distance to a cutoff on the right that goes to Structure 2B8, a few yards from the road. Only a small part of this Early Puuc–style structure (A.D. 670–770) is standing, but enough is left to show that it had a portal vault. Originally this vault stood in the middle of a single row of four rooms aligned north-south. The room north of the vault and part of the vault itself are standing. A new lintel was placed above the west doorway of the room during consolidation. On the east facade of the room the upper wall zone is in place; it is slightly battered and overhangs the lower wall. There is one tenon in the upper wall zone, and it may have supported some stone or stucco decoration originally. A little farther along the road, on the left, is a broad restored stairway that leads

The Labyrinth, or Satunsat, west side, Oxkintok. Early and Late Classic periods.

to the upper Northwest Plaza of the Dzib Group, which you will see later on your tour of the site.

From here follow the road to its western end, where you will see some remains of more modern ruins—those of an abandoned hacienda. You can turn around here and return to the cutoff for the North Plaza, turn right and drive in part way, and then continue on foot on a clear trail.

Three groups of structures surround the North Plaza, which were given names during the most recent work at the site. They are the Dzib Group, May Group, and Ah Canul Group, and you will come to the Dzib Group first. This group is composed of four plazas, and some of the structures around them have been excavated and consolidated. On the east side of the Northeast Plaza is a rather low spiral structure believed to be a steam bath (DZ-12). If you climb the structure, you can easily see its spiral design. There is a stairway abutting the west side of the structure that descends to the plaza.

On the south side of the plaza is a broad stairway with glyph-carved risers in the center of the lower steps. To the right and on a higher level is a consolidated structure (DZ-15) with an interesting molding, and behind is Structure DZ-8, but they are best reached from the south, later in your tour. At the northwest corner of the plaza is a small consolidated ball court (DZ-10). You now leave the Dzib Group, follow the trail, and take a right branch that goes to the Labyrinth, or Satunsat ("Lost and Lost").

This rather large structure has three levels and has been completely cleared and consolidated. The top level is partly fallen, and the two lower levels are buried within the bulk of the building. Both these levels contain a maze of long, narrow rooms—no wider than the walls that separate them—with interior stairways connecting the two levels. The vaults in the rooms are stepped, and the structure was remodeled in ancient times. Part of the Labyrinth is Early Oxkintok style (A.D. 550–610), and some additions and remodeling were undertaken at the end of the Classic period, hundreds of years later. The only other known example of this type of building is Structure 19 at Yaxchilán, also called the Labyrinth. There are small openings in the interior and exterior walls that

East side of Structure MA-1 (formerly Structure 3B2), Oxkintok. Classic period.

act as ventilators and afford a little light. Access to the interior rooms is from a doorway on the first level, on the west side of the structure. If you plan to take a look, have a flashlight with fresh batteries. If you want a full tour of the inside, it would be best to have a guide (see "Getting There").

During excavation two burials were found in the Labyrinth, one containing four vases, jade earplugs, fragments of a jade mask, and items of shell and stone. One green stone plaque had a glyphic inscription. This burial—believed to be secondary—has been provisionally dated to the Middle Classic period. Indications are that the second burial was several centuries later.

From the west side of the Labyrinth a path leads north and goes uphill to Structures DZ-8 and 15, mentioned before. Structure DZ-8 has a broad stairway on the west that descends to the Northwest Plaza of the Dzib Group. There is a projection on the up-

per part of the stairway, and there are the lower walls of rooms on top. Abutting the structure on the east side, at a slightly lower level, is Structure DZ-15. The roof is gone, but the lower walls of two rooms and the northeast corner of the structure are standing. There is a simple rectangular base, above which is the rounded corner of the wall, and above this a two-member molding, both parts of which are carved. There is a low stairway on the east side, and on the ground in front is a row of carved architectural decorations that were once part of the structure; still others lie about.

When you climb back to the trail, you can see another broad, low stairway to the north, on the east side of the Northwest Plaza, and, on the north side of the plaza, the lower remains of walls of a small structure. Below this is the stairway that leads from the plaza to ground level and the road.

About 40 yards to the southeast of the

Labyrinth is the May Group, a large platform that has a monumental north stairway and that supports several buildings. The dominant feature is the centrally located, tall pyramid with remains of a temple on top (Structure MA-1, formerly 3B2). The structure has been cleared and consolidated and has a stairway on the north side. During excavation, rooms were discovered on two levels on each side of the lower part of the stairway, and this work shows that the structure was built in several phases. Remains of some of these phases can be seen on the east and west sides. The temple atop the pyramid is dated to the Middle Classic period, but the dating of the substructure awaits further study. The structure was probably abandoned before the Late Postclassic period.

During excavation a tunnel was cut into the base of the pyramid through the north stairway, and a rich offering of jade objects was discovered. This ritual deposit included an earplug, a tubular bead, and fragments of a mask. Also included were a shell carving of a crocodile and manta ray spines (now believed by some authorities to have been used in bloodletting rites).

The trail that passes the base of the platform of the May Group continues to the east to the Ah Canul Group, where there are several structures of interest. You first pass Structure CA-5, a range structure with remains of lower walls. Abutting this structure on the east, set back a few feet, is Structure CA-6, another range structure, but one that is larger and better preserved. The westernmost part of the building is intact, including its doorway. Enter the doorway and go to another in the medial wall for a look at the lintel that dates to A.D. 475 (carved on the underside).

Exit this room the way you entered and proceed to the east end of Structure CA-6. There is a transverse room on this end of the

Carved column in the Ah Canul Group, Oxkintok. Late or Terminal Classic period.

building, with part of a stepped vault remaining; a lintel that spans a doorway inside the room is also carved on the underside.

To the east of Structure CA-6 is a plaza, with Structure CA-7 bordering the east side. Structure CA-7 is Puuc style and dates to the Late or Terminal Classic period. It is composed of a double range of rooms with two transverse rooms on each end. On the west side was a portico or gallery originally, with a roof supported in part by four columns carved with figures, two of which remain.

The roof of the portico is gone, while some of the structure behind it is intact and has been consolidated. On the north end part of the front wall of the portico has some remains of decorations; there are plain columns with banded colonnettes as a base and a dentate design that runs vertically between sections of plain stones.

At the south end of Structure CA-7 is the small and greatly ruined Structure CA-8, with a carved column standing in front. From here, cross the plaza to its northwest corner (where you entered) and follow the trail heading north. You next come to Structure CA-4, to the right of the trail. This is a partly consolidated pyramid that rises in tiers and has a western stair. On both sides of the base of the stairway are the remains of small structures.

A short distance to the northwest is Structure CA-3, which has been consolidated. The structure was built in an early style, and it was chosen for study because previously a lintel carved with an Initial Series date, equivalent to A.D. 487, had been found nearby. During excavation a burial was found (believed to be secondary), and grave goods included remains of a jade mosaic mask. The only ceramic vessel in the burial was a Petén type, which dates the burial to between the Early and Middle Classic periods.

Recent History

In 1841 John Lloyd Stephens decided to visit the Cave of Maxcanú, which he had heard was a subterranean construction, with a "marvelous and mystical reputation" in the region. He further said, "The universal belief was, that it contained passages without number and without end." What he was taken to was the Labyrinth of Oxkintok. Until his visit it was believed that this was a natural hill, but his exploration proved that it was a man-made structure, and he described its passages in 1843. He climbed to the top of outside of the structure after visiting its interior and from there saw other mounds, two of which he also climbed, and one of which had remains of standing vaults.

While studying caves in Yucatán in 1895, Henry C. Mercer also explored the Labyrinth. The following year he published plans of the first two levels, a section of the structure, and a description of the building.

Edwin M. Shook explored Oxkintok and published a description and a plan of the site in 1940. George W. Brainerd dug several trenches at Oxkintok to recover ceramic samples in 1940, and his results, published in 1958, show the presence of typical Puuc ceramics of Late Classic (or Terminal Classic) date, as well as some that dated to the Early Classic period. A study of the relationships of the various structures at Oxkintok was published by George F. Andrews in 1975. In 1980 H. E. D. Pollock published details of the standing architecture at the site, and he included additions to Shook's map.

The first extensive excavation at Oxkintok was begun in 1986 by the Spanish Archaeological Mission in Hispanic-America, under the direction of Miguel Rivera Dorado. The mission also help fund the consolidation of some of the structures, carried out by the Salvage Brigade of the Yucatán Regional Center of INAH, under the direction of Velázquez Valadéz. The Spanish Mission's project, which continued through the 1991 season, resulted in a new and more detailed map of the site, a study of the peripheral area around the site core, and the discovery of two carved stelae, as well as the work mentioned above.

Some of the material from the site is now displayed on the second floor of the Mérida Museum.

Connection

Uxmal to Oxkintok: 26.7 miles by paved road (:38), then 0.5 mile by rock road (:02).

Getting There

From Uxmal head north on Highway 261 to Muna and turn left at the sign for Opichén. This paved road is very narrow, but there are wide spots along the way so that oncoming vehicles can pass each other. Go to and through Opichén, and on to Calcehtok. In the center of Calcehtok there is a sign on the left for Oxkintok. If you want a guide for the site who can give you a tour of the Labyrinth, this is where to find him. His name is Roger Cuy, long-time caretaker of Oxkintok, and he lives in the house on the southwest corner of the junction for the road to Oxkintok. Turn left at the junction and go 0.8 mile to another junction on the right. Turn right and proceed to the site, 2.3 miles ahead. The first 1.8 miles of this stretch are paved, the remaining 0.5 mile to the cutoff to the North Plaza is rock.

There is no food or drink at the site; at the least, have cold drinks along and wear a sun hat. Having your own vehicle is the only recommended way to reach the site. Allow 2 hours to see the cleared structures described above. If you have Roger along and want a complete tour of the Labyrinth, add 30 minutes more.

Also of interest in the area are the Grutas ("Caves") of Calcehtok. When you leave Oxkintok and get to the junction for the road to Calcehtok, turn right for 0.9 mile to reach them. Roger can also give you a tour of the caves.

★ ★ ★ ★
UXMAL AND UXMAL MUSEUM
(oosh-mahl; derivation: often given as the Maya "oxmal," meaning "thrice built," sometimes "three times" or "three passed." Ralph L. Roys found these derivations unconvincing. Uxmal is, nevertheless, a very old place name.)

Location:
    West-central Yucatán.
Map: 2 (p. 77)

The Site

Uxmal is a truly beautiful site with an abundance of architecture, though it is more compact than Chichén Itzá. It measures over 0.5 mile from north to south and 700 yards from east to west, with a few buildings scattered outside the main area, mainly lying to the south. A wall surrounds the main part of the site, and some of its east section was traced by John Lloyd Stephens and Frederick Catherwood in 1841. Its location is shown on a site plan published by Stephens in 1843, and it is reported that in recent years the remainder of the wall was traced. Nevertheless, this wall is not apparent to visitors today.

The architecture at Uxmal dates to the Late and Terminal Classic periods and is typical Puuc style (except for a few Mexican motifs and three structures in Chenes style).

The latest recorded date at the site is A.D. 907, and all the stelae at Uxmal date to the end of the Late Classic and Terminal Classic periods. Some authorities believe Ux-mal and other Puuc sites were abandoned around 925–975, while others believe Uxmal was occupied for another hundred years or more. It is known from ceramic evidence that the site was occupied from the Preclassic period.

When visiting Uxmal, some backtracking is necessary to reach the outlying groups. The following sequence is one of several possibilities. Signs in Spanish near the major structures give information about them, with condensed versions in English and French. Other signs point the way to trails that lead to the various groups of buildings.

The first major structure near the entrance to the site is the monumental El Adivino (also called the Temple, Pyramid, or House of the Magician, Soothsayer, or Dwarf). The base is often referred to as oval or eliptical, but since its east and west faces are on a straight line, perhaps it is better described as a rectangle with severely rounded corners.

El Adivino was built during five separate construction periods. The top structure, Temple V, is of course the latest, and it brings the building to its final height of approximately 100 feet. The earliest, Temple I, is beneath the lower portion of the stairway of

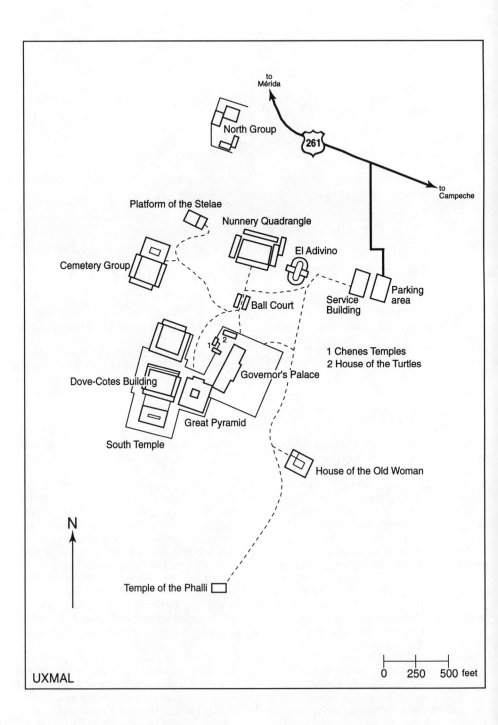

to
Mérida

North Group

261

to
Campeche

Platform of the Stelae

Nunnery Quadrangle

El Adivino

Cemetery Group

Parking
area

Ball Court

Service
Building

1 Chenes Temples
2 House of the Turtles

1 2

Dove-Cotes Building

Governor's Palace

Great Pyramid

South Temple

House of the Old Woman

N

Temple of the Phalli

UXMAL

0   250   500 feet

El Adivino, from the southwest, Uxmal. Terminal Classic period.

the west face, and it was almost totally covered by later construction. Its rooms were filled with rubble beforehand, but portions of two well-preserved Chac masks were visible over the central doorway until fairly recently. Because of the drenching rains spawned by Hurricane Gilbert in 1988, the passageway that led to Temple I had to be blocked off to assure preservation of El Adivino.

Temple II is no longer visible from the outside of the pyramid but may be reached by climbing the east stairway and entering a chamber made during excavation. This temple has only been partly excavated, but its central chamber is supported by columns, and it is topped by a roof comb that is visible in a trench in the floor of Temple V above.

Temple III (no longer visible) was attached to the west side of Temple II. Later, Temple IV was added on in the same direction. Temple IV is visible from the outside of the pyramid on the west side. This temple

has a monster-mouth mask forming its doorway and is referred to as the Chenes temple for that reason. Nevertheless, H. E. D. Pollock considers Temple IV a Puuc copy of a Chenes facade. Certainly the crisp quality of the stonework would seem to substantiate this view. When the crowning Temple V was constructed, it effectively buried the earlier Temples II and III, as well as the rear and part of the sides of Temple IV. Temple I was probably built around A.D. 800, and Temple V about 950–1000. The Magician or Dwarf who gave his name to this structure is a character in Maya folklore.

If you decide to climb El Adivino, you might want to go up one side and down the other. There are interesting Chac masks flanking the west stairway up to the level of Temple IV.

West of El Adivino is another of Uxmal's more impressive structures: the Nunnery Quadrangle, or Casa de las Monjas. This is actually a complex of buildings surrounding a large, roughly rectangular courtyard or

The Nunnery Quadrangle, looking west from El Adivino, Uxmal. Late and Terminal Classic periods.

plaza. The individual buildings are labeled the North Building, the East Building, and so forth, and they rest on platforms that rise above the plaza level. In addition, two smaller structures at plaza level flank a broad stairway that leads to a terrace fronting the North Building. Stela 17 is at the base of the stairway. The plaza-level structure on the west is called the Temple of Venus because of designs on its upper facade, and the smaller structure on the east is Building Y.

A painted capstone was found in Building Y, and the inscription on it includes a probable date of A.D. 907 and the name of Lord Chac, one of Uxmal's rulers. It is believed that several structures at the site were begun or completed during Lord Chac's reign, including the Nunnery Quadrangle, the Ball Court, and possibly the Governor's Palace. This ruler is also named and portrayed on Stela 14 and is possibly mentioned on the Ball Court rings.

The entrance to the Nunnery Quadrangle is through a large corbeled, portal vault in the center of the South Building. There are remains of red handprints in the top of the vault. It is also possible to enter the quadrangle from any of its four corners, as the buildings do not join each other.

There is an inner structure in the North Building, which, along with the South Building, was constructed first, then the East and West buildings. The Temple of Venus and Building Y were added later, and the facade of the North Building was refurbished. All the structures and additions were erected during the late part of the Late Classic and the Terminal Classic periods.

Each of the buildings of the Nunnery Quadrangle has its own individual decorations, which are fantastic in their variety and quantity. This is a great place to take detail photographs with a telephoto lens. Some of the decorations on the West Building show motifs that are considered to be Mexican, such as the feathered serpents. A recent suggestion by Jeff Karl Kowalski is that "'Toltec' traits which appeared during the Terminal Classic may have been introduced by Maya groups such as the Chontal-speaking Itzá, rather than by central Mexicans."

In the late 1980s the South Stairway of the Nunnery Quadrangle was consolidated, as was the north side of the Great Platform

Detail of decoration on the North Building of the Nunnery Quadrangle, showing hut-type niches, Uxmal. Terminal Classic period.

that supports the Governor's Palace and the House of the Turtles.

A path heading south from the Nunnery Quadrangle goes between the two sides of a small ball court. A copy of one of the stone rings, carved with glyphs, is in place on the east side of the western section of the court. The Ball Court is believed to date to around A.D. 905.

The Cemetery Group lies to the west-northwest of the ball court, and there are trails leading to it. This group has several structures surrounding a square plaza, but most are poorly preserved. The most interesting is the central building on the west side, which has been restored. It is a simple, relatively early temple supported by a moderately high pyramidal base. The temple has remains of a roof comb.

In the plaza below are four small platforms decorated with skull-and-crossbones motifs, giving the group its name. These skull racks *(tzompantlis)* are another Mexican trait. Hieroglyphs form the top border on the platforms.

From the Cemetery Group, another trail (sometimes overgrown) goes to the Platform of the Stelae. You should have a guide to reach it. The sixteen stelae originally found scattered around the platform were placed on their sides by Sylvanus G. Morley to facilitate their study. Two of the stelae have been removed, restored, and placed on view in the Uxmal Museum.

The stelae remaining on the platform are mostly broken, eroded, and covered with lichen. Some of the stelae show certain central Mexican traits.

From the Platform of the Stelae you can see the remains of the North Group 200 yards to the northeast. If you wish to see this group, you should have a guide. The North

The Ball Court with the Nunnery Quadrangle in the background, Uxmal. Terminal Classic period.

The partly restored west building of the Cemetery Group, Uxmal. Late Classic period.

Skull-and-crossbones motif decorating the sides of a platform in the plaza of the Cemetery Group, Uxmal. Terminal Classic period.

Group has not been restored, but there are remains of several structures, including one in Chenes style and a portal vault. You can get photos of some of the structures from the Platform of the Stelae and other views from the highway, near the entrance to Hacienda Uxmal.

From here you must retrace your steps almost to the Ball Court, where a path branches south to the Great Pyramid and the Dove-Cotes Building.

The Great Pyramid has had its north stairway and temple restored, and it gleams a brilliant white against the green vegetation. It is an easy climb to the top which is a great vantage point for viewing and photographing the rest of the site. This spot is especially good for telephoto shots of the restored structure on the west side of the Cemetery Group, which rises above the vegetation.

The huge step mask on the interior of the temple is most impressive, as are the Chac masks on the exterior corners. Generally overlooked in the profusion of decorations are some smaller heads that appear to be depictions of the sun god. They are frontal views, framed by what seem to be profile bird heads, and located on the corners just below the snouts of the rain god. Do not miss them.

Adjacent to the west of the Great Pyramid is the Dove-Cotes Building (Casa de las Palomas). It is part of a complex that was originally similar to the Nunnery Quadrangle, but it is not as well preserved. The main feature is the stepped roof comb, which is in excellent condition. Its fancied similarity to dove-cotes gives the building its name.

South of the Dove-Cotes Building is a large unrestored (but cleared) mound called the South Temple. You can get a good view of

The Great Pyramid (left), the Dove-Cotes Building (right), and the remains of the South Temple (right background), from the northwest, Uxmal. Terminal Classic period.

Chac step mask in the temple atop the Great Pyramid, Uxmal. Terminal Classic period.

it from the portal vault entrance of the Dove-Cotes Building, or you can follow the trail from the portal to the South Temple itself.

From the Great Pyramid you can follow the back of the Governor's Palace along its terrace (heading northeast) to the Chenes Temples that lie on the west edge of the terrace. They were mostly covered by the later construction of the terrace but are worth a look. On one there are remains of a Chenes-style monster-mouth mask, and it is possible

that originally the other temple displayed the same motif.

Continue along the terrace to the House of the Turtles. This small but nicely proportioned structure of typical Puuc style has been restored and gets its name from representations of turtles that adorn its cornice molding. That and a continuous row of plain columns in the upper wall zone and simple medial and cornice moldings are the only decorations on the temple. Its sobriety is an interesting contrast to the more elaborate decorations on the other structures at Uxmal.

From the House of the Turtles walk around to the front of the Governor's Palace—one of the real gems of Maya architecture. This exquisite structure lies atop a platform that was built upon a natural elevation. A broad stairway leads to the palace. The structure was built originally as three separate units—a long central building flanked by a smaller building on either end—and the three were joined by two roofed passages with a high vault. At a later date, the passages were blocked up with cross walls, and small rooms with columned porticoes were built on each side. Motifs on the upper facade of the Governor's Palace are corner Chac masks, stepped-fret and latticelike designs, and three-dimensional human figures with elaborate headdresses; together they form a harmonious whole.

Kowalski, who studied the Governor's Palace in great detail, suggests a date of around A.D. 900–915 for its construction, while George F. Andrews dates it to 1000–1050 on the basis of its architectural style. In any case, it is one of the last structures completed at Uxmal; a couple of others were begun but never finished.

Chac masks on the northwest corner of the temple atop the Great Pyramid, Uxmal. Small, humanized faces of the sun god are just below the snouts of the Chac masks. Terminal Classic period.

Two small platforms lie on the terrace in front of the Governor's Palace. One supports a cylindrical column, and the other a sculpture of a bicephalic jaguar that was used as a throne. From this spot (or farther back on the terrace) you can get a good photograph of the Governor's Palace with a wide-angle lens. It is a very long building—322 feet—and the front catches the morning light, which best brings out the detail.

To get to the next area of interest, you have to get off the platform that supports the Governor's Palace; there is a path with steps going down on the north side near the east end of the platform. Follow the trail heading south after you get off the platform and go past its base. Later, take a left branch to the House of the Old Woman. The Old Woman for whom this structure is named is the mother of the Dwarf (already mentioned) in Maya folklore.

There is a two-room, partly standing structure near the base of a large mound. The standing structure is earlier, and it was partly covered and incorporated into the later construction of a pyramidal type. The small lower structure has a roof comb with rectangular slots and some tenons that supported sculpture at one time.

The path that takes you to the House of the Old Woman continues south for about 0.3 mile to the Temple of the Phalli, but you should have a guide to get there. This small,

The Dove-Cotes Building as seen from the Great Pyramid, Uxmal. Note the remains of vaulted rooms. Late or Terminal Classic period.

poorly preserved structure has a sculpture in the form of a phallus that protrudes from the upper part of the building and that served as a drain for water collecting on the roof. It is believed that originally there were more of these drains and that they were nonerotic in nature. It is thought that they were symbolic of fertility of the soil.

From here retrace your steps back to El Adivino and to the exit of the site.

Note: A greatly fallen freestanding arch has been reported at Uxmal and is shown on some site plans. It marked the beginning of a *sacbé* that extended to Kabáh, and it is reported to be very similar to the portal vault at that site. The location of the Uxmal arch, however, is unknown today.

Recent History

Uxmal is one of the few sites on the Yucatán Peninsula whose existence was never lost to human knowledge. It is mentioned in early colonial documents and is shown on a map dating to only fifteen years after the Spanish conquest. According to a genealogical tree, a member of the Xiu family founded Uxmal. Legend relates that Uxmal was one of three centers forming the League of Mayapán (the others were Mayapán and Chichén Itzá). This is not supported by the archaeological evidence, which indicates that Uxmal was virtually abandoned long before the founding of Mayapán. It is possible that Uxmal was reoccupied by the Xiu dynasty many years after its original near-abandonment, which would account for its late date in the native chronicles. Some of the names for the struc-

The House of the Turtles, south side, Uxmal. Late Classic period.

The Governor's Palace, east side, Uxmal. Terminal Classic period.

tures used today were given them by the early Spanish conquerors.

Jean Frédéric Waldeck visited Uxmal for eight days, and he published his information and some fanciful drawings in 1838 in Paris. Waldeck knew of the site from a brief mention of it in an atlas of the two Americas by Alexandre Buchon. Waldeck's volume came to the attention of Stephens, but he and later investigators were unable to find some of the things reported by Waldeck.

Stephens and Catherwood visited Uxmal briefly in 1840, at the end of their first trip to Central America and Yucatán, and returned at the end of the following year for a more thorough investigation. Stephens's measurements and Catherwood's illustrations are much more accurate than the information published by Waldeck.

At the end of the nineteenth century, Uxmal was studied by Augustus Le Plongeon and Edward H. Thompson, and Eduard Seler reported on the site in 1913 and 1917. The first systematic modern exploration of Uxmal was undertaken by Frans Blom in 1929 for Tulane University. A site plan was one of the results of his research.

In 1941 Morley studied the stelae at the site, under the auspices of the Carnegie Institution of Washington.

Since 1938 Mexico's INAH has been in charge of the almost continuous restoration at Uxmal. Directors of the INAH work were José Erosa Peniche, Alberto Ruz Lhuillier, and César Sáenz for the earlier years, and more recently Alfredo Barrera Rubio, Tomás Gallareta Negrón, and others.

Connection

The area of Uxmal is the point of reference for the site. From Mérida (the next nearest point of reference) to Uxmal: 48.7 miles by paved road (1:11).

Getting There

From Mérida take Highway 180-261 heading southwest to Umán. In Umán the two highways diverge. Follow the signs for "Ruinas," which is Highway 261 to Uxmal. The "Ruta Corta" signs indicate Highway 180 to Campeche.

Uxmal can be reached by private car, taxi, bus, or on conducted tours from Mérida, and there is a large parking area near the entrance to the site. A nearby service building houses the Uxmal Museum, a restaurant, artisans shop, book store, rest rooms, and the ticket office—all surrounding a patio.

Note: There is an extra charge to bring a video camera or a tripod into the site.

The major areas of Uxmal are kept cleared, so wear a sun hat, and if you plan to visit some of the outlying groups (those for which you need a guide), wear a long-sleeved shirt. Bring lots of film, and allow a full day to see everything; a day and a half is better.

Bilingual guides are available, and although you can see the major, cleared structures on your own, you should hire a guide to reach the outlying groups as mentioned above.

In the evening a light-and-sound pageant is presented that lasts about 45 minutes. You can buy tickets at your hotel at Uxmal or make arrangements in Mérida for a bus trip that returns after the pageant. You can also buy tickets at the site itself. The schedule includes a 7:00 P.M. presentation in Spanish and a 9:00 P.M. English version, but verify the times. Chairs are provided, and cameras are allowed. Try fast color film (daylight or tungsten), and use the recommended exposure for floodlighted buildings or one stop less exposure. There is not enough light for direct metering with most light meters, and you are too far away from the structures for flash to be useful. Use your fastest normal lens, set on infinity, and open it up all the way. Improvise some sort of support (with your foot propped up on your chair, your knee will serve the purpose, or use another chair if one is available). Be ready to shoot because the lighting changes rapidly. With luck, you may get a few good photos.

Mask of Tlaloc from El Adivino. Late Classic period. Uxmal Museum.

★ ★
Uxmal Museum

The Uxmal Museum is at the entrance to the site in a building complex inagurated in 1985. Photography is permitted, but the use of flash is not.

A site plan of Uxmal, at the entrance to the museum, shows the placement of the major structures and the wall that encircles the main part of the site.

Inside the museum are four carved stone heads representing Tlaloc, the central Mexican rain god, that came from the lower west side (Temple 1) of El Advino.

An interesting set of stone panels, carved with hieroglyphs, comes from El Chimez, a structure that lies to the south of the main part of the site, outside the surrounding wall. Dates recorded in the inscription refer to the ninth and tenth centuries A.D.

There are two restored stelae on display as well as a phallic stone and one of the carved stone turtles from the House of the Turtles. There are also architectural sculptures, ceramic displays, and informative charts. The collection is nicely arranged and labeled.

Outside of the museum, along a wall facing the patio, is a collection of carved stones from the site. Though they are unlabeled, they are worth a look. You can see the museum and the outside display in half an hour.

★
NOHPAT

(noh-paht; derivation: Maya for "large dogfish" or possibly "big lump of clay."
Noh means "large," and Pat is also an Indian surname.)

Location:
West-central Yucatán.
Maps: 2 (p. 77) and 2A (p. 97)

The Site

Nohpat is a very large site, about the size of Kabáh; unfortunately, it is greatly ruined, as it was in 1842 when John Lloyd Stephens first saw it. The site has been looted and stone-robbed for many years, which has contributed to its deterioration.

Undoubtedly, Nohpat was an extremely important place in ancient times. This can be deduced from the abundance of architectural remains and from the fact that it is on a *sacbé* that connects Uxmal and Kabáh.

In visiting the site, you will have to depend on your guide to show you around the more interesting spots. In the area now called Group II, we saw what we took to be two large structures. There may have been more, but the site is so overgrown and fallen that it is difficult to say. We saw remains of some standing vaults, and this may have been part of Structure 4 or 5.

Later we saw the two-story Structure 1, where there were some remains of medial and cornice moldings on the east facade of the upper level. In another area of this structure, one of the rooms has an intact vault and standing jambstones at the doorway, but the lintel is no longer in place, and other parts of the front wall have collapsed. Nearby are the remains of an understair half vault. Structure 1 is Classic Puuc style (A.D. 770–1000).

Getting around Group II at Nohpat is really a bit dangerous. There is loose rubble everywhere, and the ledges around the structures are narrow to nonexistent. It is also a long, rocky way down if you should fall. Exercise extreme caution.

From the upper level of Structure 1 of Group II, you can see the Nohoch Mul ("Great Mound") of Group I in the distance. Group I of Nohpat lies to the northwest of Group II, and the Nohoch Mul, also called Structure 1 of Group I, is the largest construction at the site. This pyramid-temple was described by Stephens as being "150 feet high on the slope, and about 250 feet long at the base."

You can climb the pyramid from the south side, over huge stones that formed a stairway. Other megalithic-style stonework is employed on the terraces around the structure. Only a few stones remain of the summit temple atop the pyramid, but it is probably Early Puuc style (A.D. 670–770), according to Nicholas Dunning. The footing on the way up the Nohoch Mul is fairly good, but the climb is steep.

From the top of the Nohoch Mul, you can see Uxmal to the northwest, Santa Elena to the east, and Kabáh to the southeast.

At the south side of the Nohoch Mul, there are the scattered remains of some carved but eroded stones. We saw one stone that our guide thought may have been carved, but we did not see the others that are reported.

There has been no consolidation or restoration at Nohpat.

Recent History

Stephens reported Nohpat in 1843, and four illustrations of the site, produced by Frederick Catherwood, were included. One is a sketch of the Nohoch Mul, and the others show carved stone monuments. One of the monuments, now called Miscellaneous Stone 4, was found in two parts, a head and a body. Stephens had his helpers put the head back on top of the body, and according to Dunning, they remain that way today.

There were a couple of other early visi-

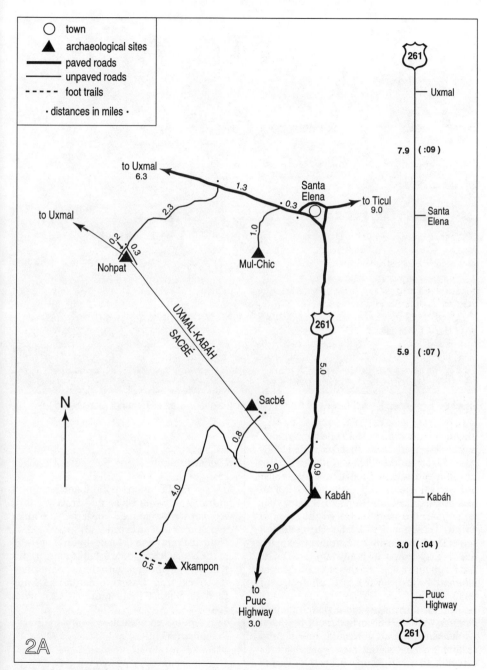

Area near Santa Elena

Structure 1 of Group II, east facade of the second level, Nohpat. Late or Terminal Classic period.

tors to Nohpat, and in 1845 one anonymous writer described a *saché* that connected Nohpat to Uxmal and Kabáh.

The site is mentioned in several publications over the years, and in 1936 H. E. D. Pollock studied the *saché* during his brief visit to Nohpat. His workers traced the *saché* to within 1 kilometer of Uxmal (to the small site of Cetulix, an outlying group of Uxmal), where they lost it in a swampy area. The *saché* runs just west of the Nohoch Mul at Nohpat. Pollock's work was published in 1980.

In 1987 Dunning did a sketch map of Nohpat, and in 1988 members of the Sayil Archaeological Project visited the site, and several changes in the map were made as a result. In 1990 Ramón Carrasco Vargas mapped much of the site in detail.

Connection

Uxmal to Santa Elena: 7.9 miles by paved road (:09).

From the junction of the northernmost entrance to Santa Elena and Highway 261: 1.6 miles by paved road (:03), then 2.6 miles by fair rock and dirt road (:39) to Group II at Nohpat. From there, 0.4 miles by dirt road (:08) to the Nohoch Mul, then 0.1 mile more by dirt road (:04) to the area with the carved stones.

Total from Uxmal to Santa Elena and then to Nohpat (both groups): 12.6 miles (1:03).

Total from Uxmal to Nohpat (direct): 9.4 miles (:57).

Getting There

Guide: Emilio Santos Camal, in Santa Elena. From Uxmal head southeast on Highway 261 to Santa Elena, then return to the cutoff for Nohpat. Turn left and after 2.3 miles take a left branch to reach Group II. After you visit this area, drive back 0.3 mile and take the left fork to the Nohoch Mul. Then go straight ahead to the area with the carved stones. When you are ready to return, you may have to cut back some vegetation to be able to turn your vehicle around.

To reach Nohpat directly from Uxmal, head southeast on Highway 261 for 6.3 miles to the cutoff for Nohpat, turn right, and follow the directions above.

Allow 2 hours to see Group II, 35 min- utes for the Nohoch Mul, and 20 minutes to walk to and see the stones. Wear boots, definitely.

Usually it will take 5 hours from the time you leave Santa Elena until you return. This includes time for a couple of breaks to have cold drinks that you have brought along.

A high-clearance vehicle is recommended to reach Nohpat. If it has been wet, the dirt part of the road will be slippery, and a vehicle with four-wheel drive would make the ride more comfortable, though this is not mandatory.

Buses go to Santa Elena.

★
MUL-CHIC

(mool-cheek; derivation: possibly "Mound Coati" in Maya. Mul means "mound," and Chiic is the name for coati mundi.)

> **Location:**
> West-central Yucatán.
> **Maps:** 2 (p. 77) and 2A (p. 97)

The Site

Mul-Chic is a small site that was discovered in the 1960s. Some excavation and restoration were undertaken, and the site was cleared; unfortunately, it has become overgrown once again. The restored architectural remains face three sides of a small plaza. Some remnants of steps can be seen on the fourth side, but they are unrestored.

The largest and most interesting structure at Mul-Chic is a six-tiered pyramid with a stairway facing the plaza. The pyramid was built on top of an earlier structure—a one-room temple with a vaulted roof and a perforated and decorated roof comb. The roof comb rises from the front of the temple over the single doorway as a flying facade. Some of its stucco decorations may still be seen. The temple was built on the level of the plaza. A simple medial molding forms a border around the building and rises to clear the

doorway; this structure is Early Puuc style (A.D. 670–770).

Originally murals inside the room depicted scenes of warfare, but they have been removed. One wall of the murals can be seen in the Mérida Museum. During restoration of the structure a skylight was installed to illuminate the interior.

Although building over earlier construction was a common practice in the Maya area, here at Mul-Chic it seems a bit unusual in that the earlier structure was a totally different type from the latter.

The remaining architecture on the other two sides of the plaza are, for the most part, the lower walls of small buildings, with some columns in the doorways. One structure has what appears to be a small altar set into the rear wall.

These remains date to a later period than the inner structure with the roof comb.

Recent History

Work at Mul-Chic was undertaken by Mexican archaeologist Román Piña Chan, who reported his findings in Mexico in the early 1960s. George F. Andrews studied the

Principal structure, the tiered pyramid, Mul-Chic. Late or Terminal Classic period. Note part of the roof comb of the inner structure at upper right.

architecture at the site in the 1980s, and reports were published in 1985 and 1986.

Connection

Uxmal to Santa Elena: 7.9 miles by paved road (:09).

From the junction of the northernmost entrance to Santa Elena and Highway 261: 0.3 mile by paved road (:01), then 1.0 mile by rough dirt road (:18).

Total from Uxmal to Santa Elena, and then to Mul-Chic: 9.2 miles (:28).

Total from Uxmal to Mul-Chic (direct): 8.6 miles (:26).

Getting There

In 1982 I wrote that visitors could get to Mul-Chic without a guide. Since then the site has become very overgrown, and you will need a guide to clear it. This accounts for Mul-Chic's rating of one star instead of its original two stars.

Guide: Emilio Santos Camal, in Santa Elena.

From Santa Elena take Highway 261 heading northwest to the cutoff for Mul-Chic, turn left and proceed to the site.

From Uxmal head southeast on Highway 261 to the cutoff for Mul-Chic, turn right and go on to the site.

Note: Emilio may know another way to Mul-Chic, directly from Santa Elena. If he suggests this route, follow his advice.

A wide-angle lens is useful to get shots of the temple with the roof comb while standing on the pyramidal building that encases it.

A high-clearance vehicle is recommended. Allow 30 minutes to visit Mul-Chic once your guide has cleared some of the veg-

Detail of the roof comb of the inner structure, Mul-Chic. Late Classic period.

etation. The clearing will take longer than visiting.

If the road to Mul-Chic is very muddy, you can walk in almost as fast as you can drive. If you walk, wear boots and carry a canteen of water.

Buses go to Santa Elena.

SACBÉ
(sahk-beh)

(SACBÉ-XHAXCHE)

(sahk-beh shash-cheh; derivation: Sacbé is Maya for "white road"; Xhaxche, the name of a nearby savanna)

Location:
West-central Yucatán.
Maps: 2 (p. 77) and 2A (p. 97)

The Site

Sacbé is a real charmer. It has an interesting history, and it is not too difficult to reach. The main feature here is Structure 1 of

Structure 1 of Group A, Sacbé. View of the center and west doorways of the south facade. Terminal Classic period.

Group A, a three-room building that faces south. The east room has fallen, but the center and west rooms are well preserved. The lower walls of the structure are plain, and this contrasts nicely with the highly decorated upper wall zones and medial molding. The decorations above the center room are largely intact; those over the west room have fallen.

There are two stacked, mosaic-style Chac masks above the doorway of the center room, and the lower one has an intact, curled snout. The masks rest upon the rectangular lower course of the medial molding. The middle member of the molding has four rather unusual banded colonnettes—of somewhat spherical shape—on each side of the lower mask. Beyond these, on either side, are geometrical stones that form a stepped-fret design, and beyond that, more of the spherical colonnettes. The top course of the medial molding is rectangular.

Above this molding, on either side of the masks, are plain areas interrupted by a diagonal row of projecting square stones engraved with an X-shaped design. To the left and right of these are large squared spirals, in the background of which are short columns.

Only the lower course of the cornice molding remains, and that is rectangular. Originally it was topped by a continuous row of colonnettes, as depicted by Frederick Catherwood and published by John Lloyd Stephens in 1843. This illustration also shows that there were two stacked Chac masks on the southwest corner of Structure 1, and two above the doorway to the west room. These have fallen, and parts of a couple of snouts are found inside one of the intact rooms. Structure 1 is Classic Puuc Mosaic style (A.D. 830–1000).

Structure 2, about 40 feet to the south-

Detail of stacked mask panels above the center doorway of Structure 1 of Group A, Sacbé. Terminal Classic period.

east, is a partly standing three-room Early Puuc–style building (A.D. 670–770). It also faces south, and the larger center room originally had two columns in the doorway. The one on the west is still in place, and it supports a lintel; the other column is buried in debris. What remains of the back wall of Structure 2 has a simple rectangular medial molding.

Structures 3 and 4 lie to the southwest of Structure 2 and are mostly fallen. There are two chultunes, one near each of these structures.

There has been no consolidation or restoration at Sacbé.

Recent History

Stephens was the first to report Sacbé, and he described the two structures that are now numbered 1 and 2. He commented that another (Structure 3 or 4) was so ruined that "its plan could not be made out." He also re-

ported seeing three ruined buildings on the way to Sacbé.

What Stephens found to be "one of the most interesting monuments of antiquity in Yucatán" was the *sacbé* that he saw near the site. He described it as a "roadway of stone, about eight feet wide and eight or ten inches high." This *sacbé*, of course, is what gives the site its name.

Stephens was told by the natives of the area that the *sacbé* ran from Kabáh to Uxmal, as indeed it does, and he found this to be "the only instance in which we had found among the Indians anything like a tradition." He wanted to trace the route of the *sacbé*, but time and circumstances prevented this.

Teobert Maler visited Sacbé in the late 1800s. He called the site Xhaxche and photographed Structure 1. His photograph was published in 1911 by Henry A. Case and in 1926 by George O. Totten, and Structure 1 appears today almost exactly as shown in the photograph. Maler's text is part of his *Península Yucatán,* volume 1.

In a study of facade masks, Karin Hissink discussed the one on Structure 1 at Sacbé, along with others, in a work published in 1934. Hissink worked from some of Maler's material.

In 1980 H. E. D. Pollock mentioned that Stephens and Maler had visited the site, and he repeated some of Stephens's comments, but he added no new information. He further stated where Maler's photograph had been published.

Sacbé is not included in the 1980 catalog of archaeological sites *Atlas Arqueológico del Estado de Yucatán,* by Silvia Garza Tarazona de González and Edward Kurjack. In the introduction to this work, the authors state that the location of Sacbé had not been identified. Considering the rather vague directions given by Stephens and Maler, which date back a hundred years and more, and the fact that some of the roads they traveled have become overgrown, this is understandable.

On the basis of published illustrations, George F. Andrews classified Structure 1 as Classic Puuc Mosaic style. In summary, of the various authors writing about Sacbé, only Stephens and Maler actually visited the site. It is likely that from Maler's time on, there were no non-Maya visitors until 1987, when Hanns J. Prem, Ursula Dykerhoff, and Nicholas Dunning were taken to Sacbé by Emilio Santos Camal.

Shortly thereafter, Dunning drew a site plan of Group A and reported that Group B, about 500 yards to the north, is made up of three small fallen, vaulted buildings. Perhaps they are the ones seen by Stephens on the way to Structure 1. Dunning calls the site Sacbé-Xhaxche, combining the names used by Stephens and Maler.

In 1990 Ramón Carrasco Vargas of INAH followed and mapped sections of the *sacbé* between Kabáh and Nohpat. He reports that there are settlement remains wherever there is high ground along the way.

Connection

Uxmal to Sacbé: 12.9 miles by paved road (:15), 2.0 miles by fair dirt road (:12), 0.8 mile by overgrown dirt road (:15), then a few hundred feet by foot trail (:05).

Total from Uxmal to Sacbé: 15.7 miles (:47).

Getting There

Guide: Emilio Santos Camal, in Santa Elena. Emilio knows Sacbé by the name Mascarón.

From Uxmal head southeast on Highway 261 to Santa Elena, then south to the cutoff for Sacbé. Turn right onto the dirt road. Along this stretch you will cross the ancient *sacbé,* but unless it is pointed out, you might think it is just another limestone outcrop. Turn right at the overgrown dirt road, which is actually an old wagon road. Along this section you will probably have to stop and cut back vegetation a few times, as this part of the road is seldom used. Once the road is cleared, you should be able to drive out in the time indicated.

Dunning reports that the *sacbé* is very distinct near where it is crossed by the old wagon road. Because of the overgrown conditions of the road, I am afraid I missed it.

Park on the side of the road where your guide indicates, and walk straight ahead for a short distance, then to the left. There is a slight climb to get to Group A. Your guide will lead the way.

Allow 40 minutes to see the two structures once you get there. Wear boots, and have a wide-angle lens for your camera.

A high-clearance vehicle is recommended to reach Sacbé.

Buses go to Santa Elena.

XKAMPON

(shkahm-pohn; derivation: Maya for "Yellow Copal")

Location:
West-central Yucatán.
Maps: 2 (p. 77) and 2A (p. 97)

The Site

There are two structures of interest at Xkampon, both are L-shaped, and both rest on the same platform, where they almost form a quadrangle. Structure 1 is at the southeast corner, and Structure 2 is at the northwest corner. The three corner rooms in each structure are standing or partly standing; the remaining rooms have fallen.

When you reach the site, you come to Structure 1 first. It is a lovely and typical example of Classic Puuc Colonnette style (A.D. 770–830). Most of the facing stone of the lower walls has fallen, but it appears that this area was plain. Above, there is a three-member medial molding with a zigzag-and-triangle decoration in the middle, and rectangular stones above and below. Many of the zigzag, or comb, elements have fallen.

The upper wall zone is a continuous row of split columns, banded in the center. Above this, only the lower course of the cor-

Inside corner of Structure 1, Xkampon. View from the northwest. Late Classic period.

nice molding is in place, and it is rectangular. Whatever base molding exists is buried in debris.

There are three standing doorways in Structure 1, and each is topped by a large stone lintel. Part of the vault of Room 2, the corner room, is intact; it has a row of recessed capstones.

Of Room 3, to the north of Room 2, only the doorway and part of the upper wall zone above it are standing. Room 1, to the west of Room 2, has fared a little better, but even here the area west of the doorway has fallen.

Structure 2 lies about 20 yards to the northwest of Structure 1; it is more ruined and is more buried in rubble than the former. It is also Classic Puuc Colonnette style and has banded, split columns in the upper wall zone. Room 2 of Structure 2 is on the corner. It is relatively small and mostly fallen. Its only entrance is on the inside from Room 1, which abuts it on the south. Room 3, now also greatly fallen in front, is adjacent to the east of Room 2.

One feature of Structure 2, not seen in Structure 1, is the use of *ik-* or T-shaped stones, projecting down from the rectangular molding above the doorway to Room 1, and above the banded columns on the front (south side) of Room 3.

The back vault of Room 1 has collapsed, but in the cross wall, above the lintel of the doorway to Room 2, is a three-member molding with short colonnettes in the middle. Above this is a plain section, and then a simple, two-member rectangular molding near the top of the vault. What little remains of the top of the vault shows recessed capstones.

It is unusual to see this sort of decoration on the inside of a room, but there is a similar case at Chunhuhub, at the north end of the northern longitudnal room of the Main Palace.

There has been no consolidation or restoration at Xkampon.

Recent History

John Lloyd Stephens and Frederick Catherwood visited Xkampon in 1842, and their work was published the following year.

Stephens, believing that what is described above was one structure, said, "Its form was rectangular, its four sides enclosing a hollow square," and further, "Two angles only remain." One of these, now called Structure 2, was illustrated.

A sketch plan of the site by Nicholas Dunning, drawn in 1987, shows that there are actually two structures and that they do not connect on the northeast or southwest corners as presumed by Stephens. Structure 2, already partly fallen in Stephens's time, is now even more ruined.

Teobert Maler photographed Structure 1 in the late 1800s, and his photograph was published by Henry A. Case in 1911 and again by George O. Totten in 1926. Maler's photograph is part of his *Península Yucatán,* volume 1.

In a 1980 publication H. E. D. Pollock mentioned the site briefly as having been visited by Stephens and Maler and described the architecture as "typical Classic Puuc."

Dunning reports that there are several other quadrangles of fallen vaulted buildings at Xkampon. They are spread along a series of outcrops that extend a little over a kilometer (0.62 mile) in length. He also says that Structures 1 and 2 lie toward the eastern end of the site.

Connection

Uxmal to Xkampon: 12.9 miles by paved road (:15), 6.0 miles by fair dirt road (1:00), then about 0.5 mile by foot trail (:20).

Total from Uxmal to Xkampon: 19.4 miles (1:35).

Getting There

Guide: Emilio Santos Camal, in Santa Elena. Try to make arrangements the day before you plan to go, as Emilio will want to find a helper to take along to assist in cutting back the vegetation. There generally is some that must be removed on the last part of the road, the foot trail, and at the site itself. On the way out, once the trail and road are cleared, you can walk and drive in the times indicated. On the way in, it could take up to an hour longer.

From Uxmal head southeast on Highway 261 to Santa Elena, then south to the cutoff for Xkampon. Turn right onto the dirt road and go 6.0 miles. Along the first part of this stretch you will cross the ancient *sacbé* that goes from Kabáh to Nohpat and on to Uxmal, but unless it is pointed out, you might think it is just another limestone outcrop.

A high-clearance vehicle is recommended to reach Xkampon. Have a wide-angle lens for your camera, wear boots, and carry a canteen of water to the site. Wear a sun hat, as the walk is partly through open savanna.

Allow about 1¼ hours to see Xkampon once you reach it. This will allow time for your guide to cut back vegetation so you can photograph the structures.

When you visit Xkampon, you will pass near Sacbé and may want to see that too. The side trip will take about 1½ hours extra. See "Sacbé" for details of that site. If you want to visit both sites, go to Xkampon first and see Sacbé on the way back.

The road to Xkampon goes through irrigated fields, and you will see pipes providing water along the way. The cornfields in this area are truly impressive and are some of the finest we have seen.

Buses go to Santa Elena.

★ ★ ★

KABÁH

(kah-bah; derivation: Questionable. Kabáh may be Maya for "He of the Strong Hand" or "Hand That Nails." Kabahaucán, the name used for the site by Teobert Maler, means "The Royal Snake in the Hand," according to him. Kabáh is, nevertheless, a very old place name.)

Location:
  West-central Yucatán.
Maps: 2 (p. 77) and 2A (p. 97)

The Site

The ruins of Kabáh straddle Highway 261, and most of the cleared structures are on the east side of it. Closest to the road on the east, and one of the most impressive structures at the site, is the well-known Codz-Poop ("Coiled Mat"), named for a supposed resemblance between the curled snouts of the Chac masks (which serve as steps to the inner rooms) and a rolled mat. Today the structure is also known at the Palace of the Masks, or Structure 2C6.

The Codz-Poop is 151 feet long and rests on a platform atop a high terrace, which acts as a court in front. On the west side of the structure there are two rows of standing rooms (five rooms in each row), one behind the other, the rearmost being on a higher level. The end rooms of the structure on the extreme north and south have fallen.

Behind the upper-level rooms on the west side is a solid masonry core, and more vaulted rooms on the north, east, and south surround it. These rooms are also greatly fallen.

It is believed that the core was intended to support a second story that was never built. A roof comb, however, rests on the west side of the core, just behind the upper rooms of the west side. H. E. D. Pollock believes that the roof comb, which was secondary to the early roof, was apparently built in lieu of a second story.

The entire west facade of the Codz-Poop is a mass of Chac masks. This is unusual in Puuc-style architecture, as generally only the upper facades of structures are highly decorated. It does seem a bit overdone when compared to other structures at the site and with palace-type buildings at Uxmal and Sayil.

The Chac masks reportedly number 400, each being constructed of 30 separate pieces. In much of the Puuc area, identical pieces of carved-stone decoration are found,

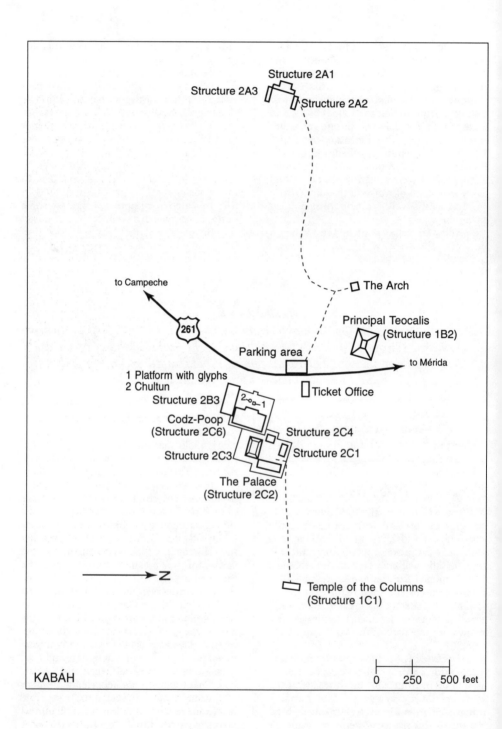

Structure 2A1

Structure 2A3

Structure 2A2

to Campeche

261

The Arch

Principal Teocalis
(Structure 1B2)

Parking area

to Mérida

1 Platform with glyphs
2 Chultun

Ticket Office

Structure 2B3

2—1

Codz-Poop
(Structure 2C6)

Structure 2C4

Structure 2C3

Structure 2C1

The Palace
(Structure 2C2)

Z

Temple of the Columns
(Structure 1C1)

KABÁH

0   250   500 feet

The Codz-Poop, from the southwest, Kabáh. Terminal Classic period.

and a central "factory" has been postulated. One wonders whether the factory didn't overproduce certain designs and sell them at discount to Kabáh's architects.

George F. Andrews feels that the constant repetition of the mask destroys its value as a significant visual form. Tatiana Proskouriakoff says that "the separate motifs merge into a single intricate pattern of shades and deep shadows," and finds the effect disappointing and demonstrating baroque ostentation. Nevertheless, in the warm glow of late afternoon sunlight, the structure is striking. Try to photograph it then.

The roof comb of the Codz-Poop is made of a stepped-fret design, and it was restored in 1991. The rest of the structure and its platform have been partly restored, but many carved stones lie on the ground awaiting incorporation. Two sculptured doorjambs were found in the Codz-Poop. Sir J. Eric S. Thompson dated these jambs to A.D. 879. According to Andrews, the structure is Classic Puuc Mosaic style (830–1000).

In front of the structure is a small platform bearing hieroglyphs on its sides, and nearby is a chultun sunk into the terrace. South of the chultun and bordering the south side of the terrace is Structure 2B3, which rests on a moderately high platform. Though the structure is greatly ruined, the platform is easily climbed, and this is a good place from which to photograph the Codz-Poop.

Behind the Codz-Poop is Structure 2C3; it is more ruined but interesting nevertheless. There are some columned doorways on the lower level, and from the top you get good views of the back of the Codz-Poop and the front of the Palace (Structure 2C2), which lies adjacent to the northeast. This is also a good spot for telephoto shots of some of the ruined structures on the other side of the highway.

The Palace is a multiroomed structure with two columned doorways (out of seven) on the west facade of its upper story. The decoration is much simpler than that on the Codz-Poop, and the Palace also has remains

Detail of Chac masks of the facade of the Codz-Poop, Kabáh. Terminal Classic period.

of a perforated, single-wall roof comb above the medial wall of the second story. A stairway leads to the second story and is pierced at ground level, forming a half vault. The Palace and Structure 2C3 border the east and south sides of a raised plaza respectively. The smaller Structure 2C1 is on the north side of the plaza, and 2C4 is on the west. Consolidation and partial restoration of all these structures were begun in 1991.

A path from the Palace leads about 300 yards to the east to the Temple of the Columns (Structure 1C1). This building is 113 feet long and has five doorways. Its name comes from the engaged columns in between the doorways and banded columns that decorate the upper wall zone. There are also colonnettes as the middle part of the base, medial, and cornice moldings. This temple has been partly restored. Both the Palace and

the Temple of the Columns are Classic Puuc Colonnette style (A.D. 770–830).

There are other structures on the east side of the highway, but they are not cleared and are mostly mounds. The site of Kabáh has major buildings covering about 0.5 square mile, and a settlement area of about 2 square miles.

Now head to the west side of the highway. Kabáh's large Arch is the only restored structure in the west section, but some unrestored remains in two areas are worth a look. As you head along the trail toward the Arch, you pass a large pyramidal mound on the right. This is Structure 1B2, the tallest at Kabáh, called the Principal Teocalis by John Lloyd Stephens, and there are a few remains of a temple on top. The pyramidal base of the structure is unstable, and climbing it is not recommended. From here follow the trail to the Arch.

The Arch spans 14 feet and is very plain when compared to the one at Labná. It also differs in that it has no other structures attached. A *saché* leads from Kabáh's Arch and extends to Uxmal 10 miles away; it passes Sacbé and Nohpat along the way. A similar though fragmentary arch has been reported at the Uxmal end of the *saché,* but its location is unknown today.

When you leave the arch (heading south), look for a trail to the right; it leads about 0.3 mile through the bush to a group of three ruined structures facing a plaza. This whole group is very overgrown, and this area of Kabáh is not often visited. If you climb up the structure where the trail ends, you will find an intact room with a corbeled vault and remains of stucco decoration on a cross wall. This is Structure 2A2. The building and the decoration were reported by Stephens in 1843.

You can climb to the roof of this structure over a steep rocky path for good views of the other two buildings in this group. Structure 2A3 lies on the south side of the

Detail of the Chac mask used as a step to one of the entrances of the Codz-Poop, Kabáh. Terminal Classic period.

plaza and is the building from which Stephens removed sculptured doorjambs, but the structure today is badly fallen. The two-story Structure 2A1 is on the west side of the plaza, and though it too is partly fallen, some remains of vaults and decorative stones can be photographed with a telephoto lens from the top of Structure 2A2. From there, you can also see the Principal Teocalis and structures on the east side of the highway.

There are other ruined buildings on the west side of the highway that I have not seen. Structures 1A5 and 6 are northeast of the group just described and are Early Puuc style (A.D. 670–770). Structures 1A1 and 2 are Classic Puuc Mosaic style, and they are north of Structure 2A2. Structure 1A1 has a Puuc imitation of a Chenes monster-mouth entrance. The masks and other decorative elements are reported to be very similar to those on Temple IV of El Adivino at Uxmal.

Although the architectural remains at Kabáh all date to the Late and Terminal Classic periods, some ceramic sherds found in trenches date to the Late Preclassic period. Apparently Kabáh was at its peak from the eighth through the tenth centuries.

One sculpture found at the site is believed to date to a later period, however, perhaps to the Late Postclassic. This is a three-dimensional male figure with a snake draped over his shoulders. Part of the face of the figure is broken off, but the features that remain appear un-Maya.

The sculpture was found a little south of the Principal Teocalis, along a sacbé that connected to a smaller pyramid to the south. The statue is now installed on the porch of a building near the entrance to Kabáh, next

The Palace, west side, Kabáh. Late Classic period. Photograph taken during restoration.

to another sculpture from the site. It is the three-dimensional figure that is referred to in the derivations of the name Kabáh and Kabahaucán given above.

Recent History

Stephens and Frederick Catherwood visited Kabáh in 1842, on their second trip to Yucatán. They first heard of the site from Father Estanislao Carrillo, the curate of Ticul. Father Carrillo told Stephens that until the opening of the road to Bolonchén (a town farther south), nothing was known of the ruins by the white inhabitants of the area. Stephens speculated that perhaps the Indians knew of them.

Even after the opening of the road, which went right through the ruins, no one but the priest bothered to visit them. Stephens and Catherwood recorded Kabáh in text and illustrations published in 1843, and a rough sketch map of the site was included.

The history of Kabáh in the following years parallels that of Sayil and Labná in that it was studied by Maler, Edward H. Thompson, and Sylvanus G. Morley and was photographed by Henry N. Sweet on an expedi-

tion for Peabody Museum of Harvard University.

Later Alberto Ruz Lhuillier explored the site, and ceramic studies were undertaken by George W. Brainerd and Robert E. Smith. Over the years restoration was undertaken by the Mexican government, and in 1991 a major effort was begun by INAH, under the direction of Ramón Carrasco Vargas.

Connection

Uxmal to Kabáh: 13.8 miles by paved road (:16).

Getting There

From Uxmal take Highway 261 heading southeast and then south to Kabáh. The site is near Kilometer 120, and there is a parking area at Kabáh on the west side of the highway.

Kabáh can be reached easily by private car or on conducted tours from Uxmal. Buses pass the site, but first-class buses will not stop to drop you off. A second-class bus will stop, but ask the driver before you board just to make sure.

Soft drinks and packaged snacks are

Detail of the Temple of the Columns showing banded columns in the upper wall zone, Kabáh. Late Classic period.

The Arch, south side, Kabáh. Late Classic period.

available at the site. Wear a sun hat, and if you plan to see the Temple of the Columns or the three ruined structures on the west side of the highway, wear a long-sleeved shirt.

Allow 1½ hours to see the structures near the highway (both sides), another 30 minutes to get to and see the Temple of the Columns, and an additional 45 minutes for the group of three ruined structures in the west section.

CHAC I
(chahk)
(GRUTA DE CHAC)
(groo-tah deh chahk; derivation: Chac, the name of the Maya rain god, and "Gruta de," is Spanish for "Cave of")

Location:
West-central Yucatán.
Maps: 2 (p. 77) and 2B (p. 115)

The Site

The Gruta de Chac is a deep cave system with a permanent water supply at the bottom. We were told that it was used as such by the local population into the 1950s. Actually it is more interesting to read about the cave than to visit it.

There is not much to see here except the opening to the cave, which was smaller than I expected. The entrance slopes downward, then there is a level area, and you can walk in a short distance. From there it is a vertical drop, and at this small opening you can see the remains of an old, rotted ladder.

John Lloyd Stephens reported the depth of the vertical shaft to be about 200 feet. In *The Hill Caves of Yucatan,* Henry C. Mercer gives the distance as 100 feet, and he counted eight ladders of different lengths in the shaft. From the bottom of the shaft he reported the horizontal passage and final descent to the water level to be 2700 feet—much of it no higher than crawl space.

If you have read Stephens's or Mercer's accounts—and I highly recommend them—and are filled with nostalgia about this infamous cave, you may want to go as far as the opening to the first vertical shaft. Both accounts will convince you that to go beyond the opening would be foolhardy. It would be.

Recent History

Stephens was the first to report the Gruta de Chac in *Incidents of Travel in Yucatán,* published in 1843, and he gives a long description of his harrowing trek to the water level.

Mercer's comments are more concise, but the description of the almost suffocating heat and humidity parallels Stephens's account. In the 1950s Edwin M. Shook visited the cave and collected potsherds, some of which were published by George W. Brainerd in 1958.

In 1962 E. Wyllys Andrews IV was shown an almost complete Maya vessel of unfamiliar design by Jaime Fernández, who had found it in a cave south of Kabáh. Andrews was excited by the story and visited the cave with Fernández and others. He then realized that this was the Gruta de Chac reported by Stephens.

Access was more difficult than in Stephens's and Mercer's time because the ladders had mostly rotted away, and the descent had to be made by ropes.

Andrews was astounded by the amount of pottery in the cave and collected specimens of two main types. One type was

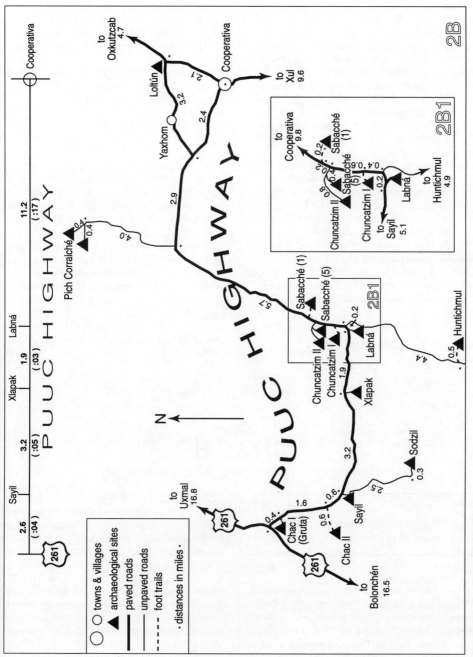

Area along the Puuc Highway

a beautiful black-and-red-on-orange poly-chrome, and the other a slateware with buff slip and black trickle design. The vessels were used to collect and transport water, and many were broken in transit, accounting for the thousands of vessels he found.

In later periods, lighter-weight gourds were used to carry the water, and he found many of these as well.

Andrews was able to reconstruct a number of vessels from the material he collected in the "course of four Sunday visits to the cave." He says, "The deposits still in the cave are inexhaustible." In 1965 the Middle American Research Institute of Tulane University published Andrews's work, which included color illustrations of one reconstructed water jar and polychrome sherds of other jars.

In 1984 members of the Sayil Archaeological Project visited the entrance to the cave and a two-level building complex atop a platform a short distance to the southwest. I have not seen the platform or the structures.

Connection

Uxmal to Sayil: 19.4 miles by paved roads (:24).

From the Sayil junction on the Puuc Highway: 2.2 miles by paved road (:04), about 500 feet walking along the highway (:03), then a few hundred feet by foot trail (:05).

Total from Uxmal to Sayil and then to Gruta de Chac: 21.8 miles (:36).

Total from Uxmal to Gruta de Chac (direct): 17.2 miles (:28).

Getting There

Guide: Miguel Uc Medina, at Sayil.

From Uxmal, take Highway 261 southeast and then south to the Puuc Highway. Turn left and proceed to Sayil. From Sayil, head northwest on the Puuc Highway and park on the right side at Kilometer 30. Return southeast about 500 feet along the highway and take the foot trail (on the right side) to the cave. The distance along the foot trail is short, but the trail may be somewhat overgrown.

Bring a flashlight to see inside the cave entrance and to get as far as the vertical shaft. Allow 20 minutes to take a look.

CHAC II

(chahk; derivation: name of the Maya rain god)

Location:
West-central Yucatán.
Maps: 2 (p. 77) and 2B (p. 115)

The Site

Chac II is a relatively small site with a little standing architecture. The building called Structure 1 by Teobert Maler is a complex one of three stories. There are several partly standing vaults, and the structure was built in two phases. Part of the building is Early Puuc style (A.D. 670–770), and the rest is

Classic Puuc style (770–1000). The facades of the rooms have almost totally fallen, and the structure is overgrown. A columnar altar (or fragmented door column) is found near the west side of the structure.

Maler's Structure 2 (to the southwest of Structure 1) had three rooms and a single doorway (to the central room) on the south side. The central room was mostly intact until 1987, and it had remains of a simple medial molding that rose above the doorway of the facade. Sometime after 1987—and possibly due to the rains of Hurricane Gilbert in 1988—a large part of the central room collapsed, but a small part of the mold-

The central room of Structure 2 (Maler's designation), before it partly collapsed sometime after 1987, Chac II. Late Classic period.

ing remains. This structure is Early Puuc style.

Maler's Structure 3 is southwest of Structure 2. It is a range structure of five rooms, the fronts of which have fallen, but the parts of the vaults that are standing are made of well-cut stones, and the architecture is Classic Puuc Colonnette style (A.D. 770–830).

I have not visited Maler's Structure 4 (reported to be a badly fallen pyramid), but it and Structure 1 are visible from the Palace at Sayil.

There has been no restoration or consolidation at Chac II. Research in the 1980s, by the Sayil Archaeological Project, indicates that Chac II may be connected to Sayil on the south.

In 1990 Miguel Uc Medina showed Michael Smyth (the director of the 1990 Sayil Project) a *saché* that runs in an easterly direction from Chac II for an unknown distance. They lost it where it is buried by the Puuc Highway.

Recent History

During his travels in Yucatán in 1842, John Lloyd Stephens visited the ruins now called Chac II. He described Structure 1 but did not illustrate it in his 1843 publication. He mentions another structure but comments that he "found nothing of particular intrest." From Structure 1 he could see the Casa Grande ("Palace") at Sayil.

Maler visited the site in 1887, and it is included in his *Península Yucatán,* volume 1.

The Early Puuc–style Structure 2 was described by George F. Andrews in 1985.

Connection

Uxmal to Sayil: 19.4 miles by paved roads (:24).

From the Sayil junction on the Puuc Highway: about 0.5 mile by paved road (:02), about 700 feet walking along the highway (:05), then about 0.6 mile by foot trail (:20).

Total from Uxmal to Sayil and then to Chac II: 20.6 miles (:51).

Total from Uxmal to Chac II (direct): 19.6 miles (:48).

Getting There

Guide: Miguel Uc Medina, at Sayil.

From Uxmal, take Highway 261 heading southeast and then south to the Puuc Highway. Turn left and continue to Sayil. From Sayil return along the Puuc Highway, and park on the left (west) at the junction with a small side road. Continue on foot along the highway, then take the foot trail to the left and follow it to the site.

The trail is fairly open as far as Structure 1, but it can be overgrown and generally needs to be cleared to get to the other buildings. A little climbing is involved in getting from one structure to the next.

Have a wide-angle lens for your camera, wear boots, and allow 1¼ hours to see the structures once you get there. Have a canteen of water with you when you walk to the site and visit it.

★ ★ ★

SAYIL

*(sah-*yeel*; derivation: Maya for "Place of the Ants")*

Location:
West-central Yucatán.
Map: 2 (p. 77) and 2B (p. 115)

The Site

Sayil is a large, attractive site with a good deal of standing architecture. It has a settlement area of 1.7 square miles, according to Nicholas Dunning, who further says that the population of Sayil was over 9,000 people during its peak in the Terminal Classic period.

Well-cleared trails at the site lead to the most interesting structures, and one heads east from the parking area and goes to the Palace. On the way it passes a shelter that houses Stelae 3 and 4 from the site. They were moved from their original location on the Stelae Platform (see below) to their present position in 1991, when they were restored. They can now be enjoyed by more visitors, since few made the trek through the high grass to see them. Tatiana Proskouriakoff believed Stela 3 was a Cycle 10 monument (A.D. 830 or later) and that Stela 4 was decadent style (810–889). From the stelae, continue along the trail to the Palace.

The Palace (Structure 2B1) is certainly one of the masterpieces of Maya architecture. It rises in three stories and has 94 rooms (which includes a group of fallen rooms that form a projection at the southwest corner). A wide central stairway divides the structure into two wings, and the second and third stories are set back, so that the roofs of the first and second stories act as terraces for the second and third. You will need a wide-angle lens to get the entire structure in a head-on photo.

The second story has wide doorways supported by two round columns with square capitals, and the upper facade is decorated with Chac masks and depictions of the "diving god" (see "Cobá" and "Tulum," both in Section 6, Part 1, for more on this deity). There are banded facade columns between the doorways and plain columns in the upper wall zone between the masks and depictions of the diving god. The second story is the most interesting of the three and contrasts nicely with the other two, which are simpler. The double-columned doorways give a feeling of lightness to the whole structure, which measures 275 feet wide and 130 feet deep.

Proskouriakoff said of this remarkable building, "This forthright simplicity of arrangement, combined with the casual disregard of minor imperfections of symmetry

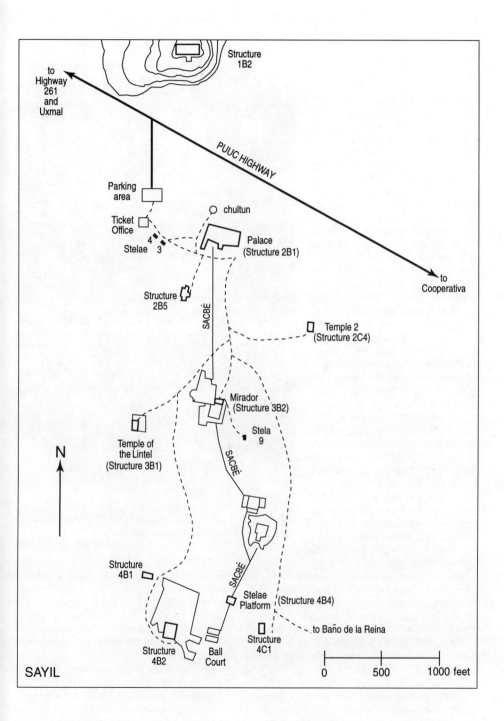

Structure 1B2

to Highway 261 and Uxmal

PUUC HIGHWAY

to Cooperativa

Parking area

Ticket Office

○ chultun

Stelae 4 3

Palace (Structure 2B1)

Structure 2B5

SACBÉ

Temple 2 (Structure 2C4)

Mirador (Structure 3B2)

Stela 9

N

Temple of the Lintel (Structure 3B1)

SACBÉ

Structure 4B1

SACBÉ

Stelae Platform (Structure 4B4)

to Baño de la Reina

Structure 4B2

Ball Court

Structure 4C1

SAYIL

0   500   1000 feet

and a freedom from the oppressively monotonous intricacy of ornament that mars many Puuc structures, makes the Sayil Palace one of the most satisfactory compositions that the Maya ever created." The Palace was not built all at one time. Three of the rooms on the first level (west side and adjacent to the stairway) are Early Puuc style (A.D. 670–770); the first-level rooms on the east side are Classic Puuc Colonnette style (770–830); the second story is Classic Puuc Mosaic style (830–1000). The third story is a local variant style, but it also dates to 830–1000. A catch basin and chultun are found near the northwest corner of the building.

When you leave the Palace, walk past the far east end and follow the trail to the right. This trail goes about 400 yards to the Mirador. Before reaching the Mirador, however, you will find two side trails to other structures. Take these as you come to them. The first side trail heads left and goes to Temple 2 (Structure 2C4) about 200 yards away. Temple 2 is a small structure with three doorways on the west side and two on the east. A simple medial molding runs above the doorways, and the upper facade is plain. The temple is Early Puuc style; though mostly unadorned, it is worth a visit.

From here return to the main trail and turn left. You will soon come to the second side trail, on the right, which goes about 300 yards to the Temple of the Lintel (Structure 3B1). On the way to this temple, the trail branches again, to the left (marked with a sign saying Juego de Pelota, or Ball Court), but pass this up for the moment and continue to the Temple of the Lintel.

The Temple of the Lintel is a small, greatly ruined structure with a fallen front (east) facade but is noteworthy for some carved glyphs that decorate the front of the

Stela 4, Sayil. Terminal Classic period.

lintel (in the doorway on the right as you face the structure). The lintel is on the east side of the medial wall of the bilding, above a doorway that connected two rooms, and is plain on the underside. The faces of the jambs supporting the lintel are also carved with glyphs.

Return now to the trail marked for the Ball Court and turn right for a 7-minute walk. When you reach the end of this trail, you may be surprised that the impressive structure you are looking at is most assuredly

The Palace of Sayil, overall view of the south side, Sayil. Late and Terminal Classic periods.

Detail of the western half of the south side of the Palace of Sayil. Late and Terminal Classic periods.

Temple 2 (Structure 2C4), east side, Sayil. Late Classic period.

not a ball court. Rather, it is a large palace-type building (Structure 4B2), with ranges of rooms on four sides forming a rectangle around a solid core. The east facade has been restored, is in excellent condition, and has seven doorways leading to five rooms; the three center doorways enter the center room, and behind this is another room.

The entire lower facade is decorated with banded columns; those next to the center doorway are larger than the others, and almost all are in perfect condition. The upper wall zone has shorter versions of the same motif in a continuous row. Stacked, frontal Chac masks once adorned the area above the center doorway, but these have fallen. There were also corner masks on each end, and these are also gone. The other ranges of rooms in this structure are poorly preserved. The solid core, in the center of the four ranges, has a platform on top and a few re-

mains of lower walls that formed the four-room second story. Structure 4B2 is Classic Puuc Mosaic style.

Although the low bush in front of the east facade has been cleared, many small trees remain, and even with a wide-angle lens, it is impossible to get a definitive photo of the whole east facade of the building.

What about the sign saying Ball Court? On the site plan of Sayil, Structure 4B2 is about 100 yards west of the Ball Court, so perhaps this general area goes by that name. The Ball Court itself is buried in the bush and not very scenic, according to Dunning.

Return now the way you came. Turn right at the junction with the trail to the Temple of the Lintel and right again at the junction with the trail to the Mirador, and go a short distance to it.

The Mirador (Structure 3B2) is the remains of a temple atop a pyramidal base, and

Structure 4B2, east side, Sayil. Terminal Classic period. (Photograph by author)

The Mirador, view from the north, Sayil. Late Classic period.

when you reach it, you will be facing the back (north side) of the building. The north facade has fallen, but the medial wall and a perforated roof comb with projecting stones are standing. Stucco decorations were supported by these stones when the temple was constructed. The rubble heap to the left (east) of the Mirador is the remains of three fallen rooms, and it shares the pyramidal base of the Mirador. The Mirador is Early Puuc style.

From the Mirador take the trail that leads from the left side of its base. This goes about 140 yards to Stela 9, propped up on a cement base and protected by a thatch shelter. This crudely carved frontal view of a very phallic figure is unlike the other stelae reported from Sayil and is totally un-Maya in feeling. A connection has been suggested with other crude sculpture from Pustunich in west-central Campeche and Telantunich in the southern part of the state of Yucatán. It is thought to be very late and the work of "marginal groups" not sharing in the higher intellectual achievements of Maya civilization.

From here, return to the Palace, go to its west end, and follow a trail to the left for about 100 yards to Structure 2B5. This structure is "unusual in that [the] upper floor rests at half-vault height," according to H. E. D. Pollock. The structure faces east, and the south part of this facade has been restored. The lower wall is plain, while the upper wall zone is decorated with banded colonnettes. Originally there were Chac masks above the two doorways, and perhaps others over the doorways in the north part of the east facade, which is now fallen. Part of the snout of one of the Chac masks is found lying on the ground. The rubble remains of a stairway in the center of the building divides the east facade in two, and only a few stones of the second-story room are standing. Structure 2B5 is Classic Puuc Mosaic style.

Stela 9, Sayil.

You can visit the structures described above on your own, as the trails are well cleared. To reach some other interesting buildings at Sayil, you must have a guide. Ask at the ticket office. These structures are sometimes partly overgrown or are on trails that are overgrown. Their locations and descriptions are given below, but you will have to depend on your guide to get you there.

You can see Structure 1B2 on the top of a steep hill to the north of the parking area and on the other side of the Puuc Highway. You can get a telephoto shot of it from the parking area. This building is a partly fallen Classic Puuc Colonnette–style structure that has been consolidated in part. There is a

Structure 2B5, south part of the east facade, Sayil. Terminal Classic period.

group of three large banded columns in the lower wall, and smaller columns in groups of three, four, and five in the upper wall zone. Anthropomorphic stucco heads were used as decoration within the groups of upper columns, and one eroded example is still in place in the section directly above the columns in the lower wall. I have not visited this structure (having satisfied myself with telephoto shots), but reaching it is reported to be a rather difficult climb.

Structure 4B1 is a small, totally ruined building notable for its carved doorway columns, capitals, and lintels, some of which can still be seen. One column portrays a richly attired figure holding a shield in his left hand and a staff, or lance, in his right hand. For protection, the columns are kept covered with stones (which your guide will have to remove and replace). A capital and lintel lie nearby, and their carved edges are visible in the debris of the structure. Proskouriakoff suggested a late date for the sculpture of Structure 4B1 and calls the style "Late Yuca-

tán, variant," while George F. Andrews believes the structure itself is Early Puuc style. Structure 4B1 is about 150 yards northwest of Structure 4B2.

Structure 4C1 is an Early Puuc–style building that faces east. The north additions to the structure have fallen, but the south room, which once stood as a separate building, has been consolidated. There is no medial molding as such, but the battered upper wall zone overhangs the lower wall, and what remains of the cornice molding is very simple.

About 120 yards to the northwest of Structure 4C1 is the Stelae Platform (Structure 4B4), upon which stood eight of the nine stelae known from Sayil, but all have been removed. Two are at the entrance to Sayil, as mentioned earlier, and the others have been moved to museums in Mexico City and Mérida. Only some plain altars remain on the platform.

The Stelae Platform rests astride a *saché* that leads to other structures, and this is part of a system of *sacheob* that runs roughly

Carved column of Structure 4B1, Sayil. Late or Terminal Classic period.

north-south and bisects the site. It begins near the Palace on the north end and connects to the Mirador Group. Another *saché* leaves that group, and with a few minor changes in direction, wends its way to the Stelae Platform and beyond to the Ball Court, where it ends.

From Structure 4C1 head north to a nearby branch trail that leads to the Baño de la Reina ("Bath of the Queen"), or La Reina Group, about 300 yards away. Only the front of the structure is standing, and it has been consolidated. The lower wall is plain, and the highly decorative upper wall zone is mostly intact. A Chac mask above the single doorway is very similar to the one on the second

story of the Palace, but it lacks the lower curled teeth of the latter. Beyond the mask on either side is a continuous row of colonnettes, each banded at the top, middle, and bottom. The middle part of the three-member medial molding is made of *ik-* or T-shaped stones, and more of these are found in what remains of the cornice molding. The Baño de la Reina would appear to be Classic Puuc Mosaic style; it is altogether delightful.

Recent History

The ruins of Sayil were first reported by John Lloyd Stephens in 1843, and he included en-

Structure 4C1, east face of the south room, Sayil. Late Classic period.

Baño de la Reina, Sayil. Terminal Classic period.

gravings by Frederick Catherwood of the Palace (west side), the Mirador, and Structure 4B2, a plan of the Palace, and a detail of its second level. Stephens saw the figure of the so-called diving god on the facade of the Palace and described it as "the figure of a man supporting himself on his hands, with his legs expanded in a curious rather than delicate attitude" (he later saw the figure at Tulum and made the connection with the one at Sayil).

Teobert Maler published a report on Sayil in 1895, and he mentions the stelae at the site, which were not seen by Stephens. The stelae were relocated by Frans Blom in 1930. In 1946 a beautiful restoration drawing of the Palace, by Proskouriakoff, was published by the Carnegie Institution of Washington, which funded her 1940 trip to the area. Another restoration drawing was published by Andrews in 1975.

In 1980 Pollock reported on the architecture of Sayil in some detail, and he included a site plan drafted for him by Edwin M. Shook. In 1983 the Sayil Archaeological Project began, and it continued into the 1990s, under the direction of Jeremy A. Sabloff and Gair Tourtellot, funded by the National Science Foundation. During this work (among other things) a new and more detailed map was produced, ceramic surface collections were made in various parts of the site, and two residential platforms were intensively excavated.

Ceramic analysis shows that almost all of the collection belongs to the Terminal Classic period, which was the predominant period of occupation and construction at the site. A few sherds were earlier Classic or Preclassic, and some Postclassic ceramics were also found. Michael Smyth was project director in 1990, and major funding that year was through Earthwatch. With the exception of Uxmal, this work at Sayil makes it the most thoroughly studied Puuc site.

Over the years parts of the Palace and other structures were consolidated and restored by the Mexican government, and in the late 1980s the Salvage Brigade of the Yucatán Regional Center of INAH consoli-

dated additional structures at the site. Most notable perhaps was the clearing and consolidation of the west wing of the first level of the Palace. During this work sounding shafts and stratigraphic pits were sunk into the first and second levels of the structure. According to Ramón Carrasco Vargas, the results show that "a two-level structure had existed prior to the erection of the three-level Palace structure."

Connection

Uxmal to Sayil: 19.4 miles by paved road (:24).

Getting There

From Uxmal take Highway 261 heading southeast and then south to the Puuc Highway. Turn left and proceed to the parking area for Sayil (on the right).

Cold drinks and packaged snacks are available at the site, as are rest rooms. If it has been wet, boots would be best, as the trails at Sayil can get muddy. Allow 2½ hours to visit the structures you can reach on your own, and about the same amount of time if you want to see all of those for which you need a guide.

Sayil can be reached on conducted tours from Uxmal as well as in your own vehicle.

★
SODZIL

(sohd-seel; derivation: Maya for "Place of the Bats")

Location:
West-central Yucatán.
Maps: 2 (p. 77) and 2B (p. 115)

The Site

Several structures, in three groups, have been reported at Sodzil, of which we have seen Structures 1 and 2 of the Valley Group.

The main feature of interest at the site are some fragmentary remains of mural paintings in Structure 1 of the Valley Group. Struc-

ture 1 is also called the Conjunto las Pinturas ("Group of the Paintings"). This rather large structure faces east, and there is a single range of eight rooms in the lower section. The four rooms on the south are on a slightly higher level and are larger than the four to the north. According to Nicholas Dunning, the northern rooms employ Early Puuc stonework, which would date them to A.D. 670–770, while the southern rooms could be either Early or Classic Puuc; they date to the Late or Terminal Classic period in any case.

The front facades of all eight rooms have fallen, but the back of the vaults and some

Remains of a mural painting showing a figure with outstretched arm, in Structure 1 of the Valley Group, Sodzil. Late Classic period.

The columned doorway of Structure 2 of the Valley Group, Sodzil. Late Classic period.

cross walls are standing. The murals are found near the center of the structure, in the southernmost of the northern rooms, and they are on the back wall and the adjacent right cross wall.

The largest fragment depicts parts of human figures with outstretched right arms, each holding a sort of stafflike object. Karl Herbert Mayer reported in 1987 that the figures are stylistically similar to the smaller figures in the murals at Chacmultún. When intact, those at Sodzil were about 20 inches tall. Like the figures at Chacmultún, the ones at Sodzil are also in a procession. Several earth colors and Maya blue were used in the murals, and some of the areas of Maya blue are still brilliant. To the right of the main fragment is another, with rectangular designs and a shieldlike object.

Behind the northern rooms, and on a higher level, are the fallen remains of other vaulted rooms of Structure 1.

Across from Structure 1, and facing west, is the smaller, stately, Early Puuc–style Structure 2, which rests on a massive terrace. The facing of the terrace appears to be a huge wall when first observed. On top, Structure 2 has three rooms, one of which is partly intact. Two plain cylindrical columns with square capitals and large cornerstones support three large stone lintels that top the doorways into the room; part of the vault inside the room is intact. A few feet to the south of Structure 2, and still on the terrace, is the opening to a chultun.

Structures 3 through 8 of the Valley Group are all fallen, vaulted buildings, according to Dunning.

There are two hills at the site, each about 130 feet high, and each supports architectural remains. Structure 1 of the East Cerro Group is reported to be a complex building, apparently constructed in several stages, while Structure 1 of the West Cerro Group is much smaller and fallen. Dunning reports that from Structure 1 of the West Cerro Group there is a nice view of Sayil.

Recent History

The location of Sodzil is shown in the *Atlas Arqueológico del Estado de Yucatán* (1980), by Silvia Garza Tarazona de González and Edward Kurjack, where the site is numbered but not named. It is known that archaeologists had visited the site previously, but there were no published reports.

In February 1987, during an archaeological reconnaissance in the area, a group of seven scholars was taken to the site by Marcelino Pech Dzul. The ruins were tentatively named Sodzil, after a nearby *sarteneja* (a natural hollow in the caprock that collects rainwater), and it was soon realized that the site was included in the atlas.

Mayer, who was one of the group, believes that earlier visitors had probably not noticed the paintings. Dunning and George F. Andrews were also part of the group. A month after their first visit, Dunning returned to Sodzil, further explored the site, and mapped it. In the summer of 1987 Rubén Maldonado Cárdenas and Tomás Gallareta Negrón, of the Yucatán Regional Center of INAH, made a plan of Structure 1 of the Valley Group, as did Andrews in 1988. Maldonado Cárdenas also did drawings of the mural fragments, and in August 1987 delivered a report in Campeche at the Second International Meeting of Mayanists.

Connection

Uxmal to Sodzil: 19.4 miles by paved roads (:24), 2.8 miles by dirt road (:35), then about 650 feet by foot trail (:04).
Total from Uxmal to Sodzil: 22.3 miles (1:03).

Getting There

Guide: Miguel Uc Medina, at Sayil. Miguel is definitely the guide of choice in this case. The route to Sodzil goes through Sayil, and as its caretaker, you must have his permission to drive through.

From Uxmal, take Highway 261 heading southeast and then south to the Puuc Highway. Turn left and proceed to Sayil. From the parking area at Sayil, take the dirt road that goes to the Palace (east), and then follow it south. You pass the side trails to other structures of Sayil along the way. After 2.5 miles, take the cutoff to the left for 0.3 mile, and park on the side of the road. Walk to the right to Structures 1 and 2 of the Valley Group. A high-clearance vehicle is recommended.

There may be trees or low-hanging vegetation across the road on the last 0.3 mile. It will take a few minutes to clear the road, but you can drive back to Sayil in the time listed.

Wear boots and allow 45 minutes to see the two structures described above.

Locally, Sodzil is also called "Haltun de Sodzil." *Haltun* is Maya for the Spanish *sarteneja.*

★ ★
XLAPAK
(MALER-XLABPAK)
(shlah-pahk; derivation: Maya for "Old Walls" or "Old Ruined Walls")

Location:
    West-central Yucatán.
Maps: 2 (p. 77) and 2B (p. 115)

The Site

Several structures have been reported at Xlapak, but for the visitor, the building of interest is Structure I, which has been partly

Structure I, north side, Xlapak. Terminal Classic period.

but nicely restored. Structure I has nine rooms, and although two doorways and part of a room have collapsed, the structure is mostly intact.

There are sets of Chac masks in stacks of three on the corners of the upper facade and above the center doorways on the north and south sides. The masks rise above the coping course, which gives them special emphasis. The five existing panels of masks are in good condition and are very photogenic. The snouts of the masks on the corners curve upward, while those in the panels above the doorways have a downward curl.

In the upper wall zone, in between the masks, are stone mosaics with frets and other geometric designs. The base, medial, and cornice moldings have colonnettes in the middle section, and the cornice molding is topped by a coping course.

The lower walls of Structure I are plain except for facade columns at the corners; the columns have rounded bases and capitals. The doorways of the structure are unadorned, but those in the center of the north and south sides are wider than the others.

Although Structure I (to all outward appearances) would seem to have been built all at once, there was actually a sequence in construction. The longitudinal central and south rooms were built first, and at that time there were no doorways on the north wall. The existing north range of rooms was added later, and these rooms do not connect directly with the others.

Near the center of the south side of the structure is a catch basin that drains into a chultun.

A few feet to the southeast of Structure I is a rubble mound that is the remains of Structure II. On the west side, part of a stone mosaic with a fret is still standing. Both Structures I and II are Classic Puuc Mosaic style (A.D. 830–1000).

Recent History

Teobert Maler reported Xlapak under the name of Maler-Xlabpak in 1902, and he included a photograph of Structure I. In 1913 Herbert J. Spinden published a similar photograph of the structure by Henry N. Sweet.

Karin Hissink included Xlapak in her study of masks on buildings in Yucatán in 1934.

In 1980 H. E. D. Pollock published a detailed description of Structures I and II, and the architecture was further analyzed by George F. Andrews in articles published in the 1980s.

Structure I was restored by the Mexican government in the late 1960s, and it is well maintained.

Connection

Uxmal to Xlapak: 22.6 miles by paved roads (:29).

Getting There

From Uxmal, take Highway 261 heading southeast and then south to the Puuc Highway. Turn left and proceed to the parking area for Xlapak (on the right).

Xlapak can be easily reached by private car or on conducted tours from Uxmal.

Cold drinks and packaged snacks are available at the site. Allow 30 minutes to see and photograph Xlapak.

LABNÁ

(lahb-nah; derivation: Maya for "Old Ruined Buildings")

Location:
  West-central Yucatán.
Maps: 2 (p. 77), 2B and 2B1
  (p. 115)

The Site

Labná is a thoroughly delightful site. Its major structures are the Palace and, across a large plaza, the Arch and El Mirador. Another palace-type structure, called the East Building, lies on the east side of the plaza, and there are many unexcavated mounds in the area.

The Palace is a large two-story structure set on a terrace that is over 400 feet long. The first story was a group of separate buildings that were later joined together by the platform built to support the second story. One section of the first story, on a slightly lower level, runs perpendicular to the rest of the building and has a simple molding for decoration. The molding rises above the three central doorways but not the one on the north end. This structure, called the South Wing, is Early Puuc style (A.D. 670–770).

Many interesting and more decorative motifs are found on other parts of the Palace.

Bundles of columns in relief flank some of the doorways, and the ubiquitous masks of Chac are found on the upper facades. Some of the masks are simplified and alternate with stepped-fret designs, and this area of the Palace is Classic Puuc Mosaic style (A.D. 830–1000).

The first story of the Palace has a few jogs in its front, rather than running in a straight line; on one of the outer corners is an interesting sculpture of a serpent head, with an open mouth containing a human head. Below this on the corner of the base molding is a carved head. A few feet away, above the doorway of the west facade, is a Chac mask with a date equivalent to A.D. 862 inscribed on the underside of its elongated proboscis.

The second story of the Palace is made up of separate structures, of which only the easternmost is in fairly good condition. Even here the ends of the building have collapsed, but the center portion retains its two large doorways with two columns each, supporting the lintels. The Palace is a great place for detail photographs because of the multitude of decorations.

An interesting feature at the Palace is a chultun, which is built into the structure.

Overall view of the south side of the Palace, Labná. Late and Terminal Classic periods.

Detail of a Chac mask on the Palace bearing the date A.D. 862, Labná.

The East Building, from the southwest, Labná. Late Classic period.

The circular catch basin that drains into the chultun is located on the terrace that supports the second story, in front of the structure just described. Originally there were 67 rooms in the Palace.

About 100 yards east-southeast of the Palace is the East Building, which is much more sober in its decoration. This L-shaped structure rests on a terrace and has eight rooms; the southernmost room has collapsed, as has part of the end room on the west. The upper wall zone of the facade is decorated with a continuous row of small columns and three-member medial and cornice moldings with colonnettes in the middle part. The lower walls of the structure are plain, and the building is Classic Puuc Colonnette style (A.D. 770–830).

About 200 yards south of the Palace is a group of structures dominated by the pyramid-temple called El Mirador or El Castillo. When John Lloyd Stephens saw this structure in 1842, more of it was standing. According to his description, the temple had three doorways and measured 43 feet in front, although an 8-foot section and one

doorway had already collapsed. As he predicted, another section has since fallen.

The pyramidal base of the structure has not been restored, but its shape is rectangular and is believed to have risen in tiers. Part way up the pyramid are the remains of another room. This room is earlier than the pyramid and was filled in when the pyramid and its stairway were constructed. There are indications that the simple molding adorning this room rose above the doorway.

A rocky path leads to the temple on top of the pyramid and its small restored platform, and from here there are good views of the Palace and the east side of the Arch.

The roof comb of El Mirador is above the front, forming a flying facade. It has rectangular perforations and projecting stones with remains of stucco decoration, including the lower part of a human figure on the southwest corner. El Mirador is Early Puuc style and must have been quite impressive when intact.

The Labná Arch, also called the Portal Vault or Gateway, is one of the gems of this type of structure. It rests on a low platform

West face of the Labná Arch. Terminal Classic period.

(rising in four steps) and forms a passageway between two courtyards, each of which is almost surrounded by structures. Many of these structures have collapsed, but there is some standing architecture north of the Arch.

The west face of the Arch is the most interesting. Above the doorways to its two small rooms is a decorative three-member molding of zigzags and triangles, and above this are depictions of Maya thatch huts with niches in the lower sections. Figures, perhaps seated, are thought to have existed inside the niches originally. Flanking the huts are latticelike patterns and another three-member molding, and the whole is surmounted by the remains of a roof comb. Only a few courses of stone were found and restored, but we know that the roof comb was

Opposite, El Mirador, south side, Labná. Late Classic period.

in three separate sections and was pierced by rectangular openings; it probably had stucco figures as decoration. Tatiana Proskouriakoff believes that there is enough evidence to suggest that the individual sections of the roof comb were stepped, and she shows it as such in her restoration drawing.

On the northwest corner of the upper facade of the Arch is a mosaic Chac mask. The east face of the Arch is simpler in decoration, having stepped frets and geometric designs as its motifs.

A range of rooms extends to the north of the Arch, and some of this is standing. There is one intact doorway. Unusual features here are the use of door jambs imitating banded columns (but carved only on the front) and a lintel that is rounded on its front surface. On either side of the doorway the walls are decorated with a stone mosaic, and some of the individual stones have shallow carving

View of the Arch and remains of structures to the north, Labná. Terminal Classic period. El Mirador is in the background.

as well. The upper wall zone is a continuous row of banded columns, and the three-member medial molding is highly decorative. The Labná Arch and the standing rooms to the north are Classic Puuc Mosaic style.

The other rooms surrounding this courtyard are simply mounds of rubble today.

A *saché* at Labná (about four feet high) runs north-south through the center of the plaza and connects the Palace and the group including El Mirador and the Arch.

Two one-room buildings lie on a hill about 750 yards to the southwest of the Labná Arch; however, there are no trails leading to them. They are called the South Group or Las Gemelas.

Recent History

Stephens first heard of Labná from the brother of a priest from the nearby village of Nohcacab (the modern Santa Elena), but his informant had not personally visited the site. Stephens had the major structures cleared, and they were duly recorded by Frederick Catherwood. An engraving of the front of the Palace was used as the frontispiece for *Incidents of Travel in Yucatán.*

The site, especially the chultunes, was studied by Edward H. Thompson near the turn of the century. Thompson was appointed American consul to Mexico, stationed in Yucatán, and was under instructions to investigate Maya sites in the area. He is better known, however, for dredging the Sacred Cenote at Chichén Itzá. He wrote a book about his work among the Maya in 1932, but his more scholarly reports were published by the Peabody Museum of Harvard University and the Field Columbian Museum of Chicago between 1897 and 1904.

Sylvanus G. Morley visited Labná as well as other sites in the area in his early days in the field. The ceramics of this site and others in Yucatán were reported by George W. Brainerd in 1958. Herbert J. Spinden published photos of the major structures in 1913. These were taken by Henry N. Sweet and Thompson for the Peabody Museum Expeditions.

In 1980 H. E. D. Pollock described and illustrated the structures at Labná in detail, and George F. Andrews analyzed the architecture in several articles published in the 1980s.

Restoration by the Mexican government has been conducted at Labná over the years, and in 1991 a major effort was undertaken by INAH, under the direction of Tomás Gallareta Negrón.

Connection

Uxmal to Labná: 24.5 miles by paved roads (:32).

Getting There

From Uxmal take Highway 261 heading southeast and then south to the Puuc High-way. Turn left and proceed to the parking area for Labná (on the right).

Labná can be reached easily by private car or on a conducted tour from Uxmal.

Cold drinks and packaged snacks are available at the site, and there are rest rooms. Wear a sun hat and allow 2½ to 3 hours for a visit.

Bring lots of film; Labná is a very photogenic site. Its most photogenic feature is the west side of the Arch. Try to see and photograph this in the afternoon.

Note: There is an extra charge to bring a video camera or a tripod into the site.

★ ★
HUNTICHMUL

*(hoon-teech-*mool; *derivation: Maya for "Freestanding Pyramid" or "Ruined Hills")*

Location:
    West-central Yucatán.
Maps: 2 (p. 77) and 2B (p. 115)

The Site

Huntichmul is near Labná and is somewhat larger than the latter. Unfortunately, it is more difficult to reach, has less standing architecture, and has had no restoration and only a little consolidation.

One of the best-preserved and most intresting buildings at Huntichmul is Structure 1 of Group A, called the Half-Column Palace of Four Rooms by Teobert Maler. It has been partly consolidated. The structure faces southwest and rests on a platform built on the slope of a hill. Two of the four original doorways are standing, and a fair amount of the facing stone on the lower front wall is in place. The plain facing stones alternate with columns in groups of three that extend from the base molding to the medial molding. Each column is banded at the bottom, middle, and top. The group of columns on the left, as you face the structure, is intact; some of the others have fallen.

The three-member base molding has a continuous row of colonnettes in the middle, and this design is repeated in the cornice molding. The upper wall zone is a continuous row of split columns, banded in the center, and this rests on a simple, three-member medial molding that offers a nice contrast to the columns in this elegant structure. Structure 1 of Group A is Classic Puuc Colonnette style (A.D. 770–830).

Some distance away, to the southwest in Group E, is a large stone phallus, about six feet long, lying on the ground.

To the west are the remains of Structure 1 of Group C, called the Chief Temple by

Group of three banded columns in the lower wall of Structure 1 of Group A, Huntichmul. Late Classic period.

Maler. This building was constructed in stages on a natural hill that was artificially terraced. It is now almost totally collapsed but is believed to have had rooms on three levels. The most interesting thing about this structure is that the center doorway on the top level carried a monster-mouth facade, typical of Chenes architecture, in an area rather far north of most of the architecture in that style.

Maler published a photograph of this facade in 1895, when more of it was standing. Much had fallen when H. E. D. Pollock visited the structure in the 1930s, and he was unable to determine whether the structure "is built in true Chenes style or whether it is a Puuc copy of a Chenes building."

In the 1980s George F. Andrews reported that the upper level of Structure 1 of Group C used other Chenes construction techniques. This and the existence of some megalithic-style stonework at the site led Nicholas Dunning to suggest that "Huntichmul was one of the first sites established in this area of the Puuc."

A short distance to the north is Structure 2 of Group C, called the Building with the Inscriptions by Maler. This two-story building has fallen, except for the west side of the lower level. Three rooms on this level had doorways on the west facade, and the north doorway is still standing. The center

Structure 2 of Group C, view of the north doorway of the west facade, Huntichmul. Late Classic period. This is a good example of a simple molding breaking above the doorway, a feature typical of Early Puuc–style architecture.

doorway was once topped by a carved stone lintel with an inscription of six glyphs on the face and a standing figure on the underside. Photographs of the lintel, when it was in place, and drawings of both carved faces were published by Pollock in 1980, from material he had gathered in the 1930s.

The center doorway has now collapsed, along with some of the adjacent facade, but according to Dunning the lintel remains in the rubble. Structure 2 of Group C is an Early Puuc building (A.D. 670–770).

These are the only structures I have seen at Huntichmul, but Dunning reports that two others (Structure 3 of Group C and Structure 1 of Group D) are well preserved and are now kept cleared.

Recent History

Maler visited Huntichmul in 1887 and reported the site in 1895. Other data are in *Península Yucatán*, volume 2.

Edward H. Thompson also mentions the site in an 1889 publication. Huntichmul is cited through the years by other authors, and in 1950 Tatiana Proskouriakoff, in her study of Maya sculpture, said that the carved lintel "is difficult to relate to any of the known schools of Yucatán." She could offer no opinion of its date.

In 1970 Pollock described Maler's Chief Temple (Structure 1 of Group C), and in 1980, the other structures at Huntichmul. Andrews published articles in the 1980s that included the architecture at the site, and

Huntichmul was mapped by Dunning in 1987.

Note: There are at least three Maya sites called Huntichmul. The one described above is called "Huntichmul I" by Maler, "Huntichmul, near Labná" by Pollock, and "Huntichmul, Santa Rita" in the *Atlas Arqueológico del Estado de Yucatán.* Locally the site is called Santa Rita after a nearby rancho.

Connection

Uxmal to Huntichmul: 24.7 miles by paved road (:32), 4.4 miles by dirt road (:45), then about 800 yards by foot trail (:30).

Total from Uxmal to Huntichmul: 29.6 miles (1:47).

Getting There

Guide: Miguel Uc Medina, at Sayil, or someone he recommends.

From Uxmal, take Highway 261 head-ing southeast and then south to the Puuc Highway. Turn left and proceed to the cut-off for Huntichmul (0.2 mile past the junction for Labná). Turn right onto the dirt road, and continue for 4.4 miles. Park on the side of the road and walk in an easterly direction to the site. The route of the foot trail as shown on Map 2B is approximate.

The dirt road to Huntichmul is bumpy and is slippery when wet. A high-clearance vehicle is recommended, and four-wheel drive would not be a bad idea. You may lose time on the dirt road removing trees that lie across it. When the road is clear and dry, you can drive it in the time indicated.

Considering the long, hot walk to the site and the time you will spend climbing around it, you should carry a canteen of water with you. Visiting Huntichmul can be exhausting. Allow 2¼ hours to see Huntichmul once you get there. Wear boots and have a wide-angle lens for your camera.

★ ★

CHUNCATZIM I

*(choon-kaht-*seem; *derivation: Maya for "At the Place of the Catzim Tree")*

(XCANELCRUZ)

*(shkah-nehl-*croos*)*

Location:
West-central Yucatán.
Maps: 2 (p. 77), 2B and 2B1 (p. 115)

The Site

Structure 1 is the only well-preserved building here, but it is very worthwhile and easy to reach. It has also been consolidated and partly restored, making it more interesting visually. There are ten rooms on the first story and four on the second.

Structure 1 faces north onto a court, and there are remains of a stairway on the north side that originally led to the second story. The stairway is pierced by a passageway formed of a half vault where it joins the building. There are three doorways on the north side: one beneath the stairway and two others to the east and west of it. Each doorway enters a single room without interior connections.

Beyond these rooms are two others with doorways facing east and west. The side walls of the east and west rooms face north and are set back from the three rooms facing north, giving a certain liveliness to the front facade. The lower wall zone of Structure 1 is plain, and above there is a three-member medial molding. This is topped by a continuous row of split columns, and above this is a cornice molding, with colonnettes in the middle section.

Structure 1, north side, Chuncatzim I. Late Classic period.

The same kind of upper facade decoration continues around the rest of the lower story, though some has fallen. On the rear, three rooms project from the main part of the building, and there are engaged columns with round bases and capitals in place at the two outside corners. A plan of the structure by Teobert Maler and a restoration drawing by H. E. D. Pollock indicate that there were similar columns on the four corners of the main part of the first story as well.

The second story is not only smaller but also simpler in decoration. Most of the facing stones of the upper facade of the second story have fallen, but Pollock shows restorations indicating a two- or three-member medial molding, then a plain section, topped by a three-member cornice molding. No columns or colonnettes are included.

Pollock believed that Structure 1 may have been built in stages, the three north-facing rooms of the first story first, then other parts of the structure. His reasons are that the three rooms facing north are surrounded by unusually heavy interior walls and that the "stairway to the second story overlays upper facade decoration and cornice molding of front range, and is obviously secon-

dary to it." He ends by saying, "All of this must remain conjectural without excavation." In any case, what can be seen of Structure 1 today is Classic Puuc Colonnette style (A.D. 770–830).

On the west side of the court are a few remains of Structure 2. This was either a simple platform, supporting a building of perishable materials, or the lower remains of a building that was never completed. Pollock believed the latter possibility was more likely, since numerous stone spheres, which he determined to be a part of a base molding, were found. A row of five spheres atop a molding of grooved, rectangular stones can be seen in place on the west side of Structure 2, near its south end. Other spheres and pieces of molding lie scattered about.

Recent History

Maler visited Chuncatzim I and drew a plan and section of Structure 1, dated 1886. This was published by Pollock in 1980. Maler called Structure 1 "The Palace-Temple by the Sabacché Road," and the top of the drawing is labeled "Labná." He also wrote, near the top of the drawing, that there were three photographs of the structure—obviously ones he took. He also included a detail drawing of the spherical stones that are part of the base molding of Structure 2.

In 1888 Edward H. Thompson reported upon Chuncatzim I, under the name Chun-Kat-Dzin. Frans Blom wrote about the site in 1935, and he considered it to be an outlier of Labná, a possibility also mentioned by Pollock. Based on his settlement-pattern studies, Nicholas Dunning (1990) concluded that Chuncatzim I (which he calls Xcanelcruz) is indeed a part of greater Labná.

Connection

Uxmal to Chuncatzin I: 25.1 miles by paved road (:33), then about 100 yards by foot trail (:03).

Getting There

Guide: Miguel Uc Medina, at Sayil.

From Uxmal, take Highway 261 heading southeast and then south to the Puuc Highway. Turn left and proceed to the cut-off for Chuncatzim I (0.6 mile past the junction for Labná). You can park on the left side of the highway in front of a fence and walk in from there on a wide trail. Wear boots and allow 20 minutes for a visit.

★
CHUNCATZIM II
(choon-kaht-seem; derivation:
Maya for "At the Place of the Catzim Tree")

Location:
  West-central Yucatán.
Maps: 2 (p. 77), 2B and 2B1 (p. 115)

The Site

The only standing building at Chuncatzim II is Structure 1, but it has a certain undeniable charm. It rests on a slight rise in the ground, faces east, and is multichambered. The vault in the room on the south (left as you face the structure) is intact. That of the room on the right has partly collapsed, as has the rest of the structure.

According to Karl Hebert Mayer, who first reported the structure, it originally had four doorways, only two of which were standing when he visited the site in 1982. Some of the debris burying the lower part of the building at that time has been cleared, exposing the base molding. Some consolidation

and the restoration of one of the doorways have been completed.

The middle part of the base molding has banded colonnettes in groups of three, separated by plain stones. The upper and lower parts of this three-member molding are formed of simple, rectangular slabs. The lower walls of the structure are plain and are faced with well-cut, rectangular stones.

The lower part of the medial molding forms a projection above the doorways and the lower wall between them. The rest of this molding has fallen. Above this are the remains of split, banded columns and the lower part of the cornice molding.

In the debris around Structure 1 Mayer found a curved snout of typical Puuc style and concluded that the upper facade of the building originally had at least one mosaic-style Chac mask. He also found another decorative stone with a "quadrangular frame and a round element in the center," which he interpreted as the rectangular ear plug of

Structure 1, east side, Chuncatzim II. Late or Terminal Classic period.

the postulated mosaic mask. According to Nicholas Dunning, the structure is "Classic [Puuc] Transitional style."

The back of Structure 1 has a simple, geometric, three-member medial molding, running along its length. The wall zone above this molding appears to be plain.

There are rubble remains of other structures nearby, and some decorative elements, primarily parts of banded columns, are lined up neatly. Perhaps eventually they will be reincorporated.

Recent History

In April 1982 Mayer was visiting sites in the vicinity of Rancho Sabacché, guided by Pedro Góngora Interián, a *guardián* of the Zona Puuc. After stopping at Structure 5 of Sabacché, Mayer wanted to visit Chuncatzim, the site reported by H. E. D. Pollock in 1980 and by earlier writers (see "Chuncatzim I"). Góngora Interián told Mayer that there were two sites called Chuncatzim locally, and they visited both. Mayer recog-

nized that the second site they saw was the one reported by Pollock.

He then realized that the other ruin called Chuncatzim by Góngora Interián was an unreported site. In 1984 Mayer published his report on Chuncatzim II. To avoid confusion, Mayer designated the previously known Chuncatzim (Xcanelcruz) as Chuncatzim I, and the previously unreported site as Chuncatzim II. This is the nomenclature used here.

Mayer also commented, however, that his Chuncatzim II might be a part of the nearby dispersed site of Sabacché and that perhaps the structure should be designated Sabacché, Structure 8. He admits that this was difficult to determine. In a 1990 settlement-pattern study, Dunning indicated that Chuncatzim II (under the name of Chuncatzim) is a separate site from Sabacché.

Connection

Uxmal to Chuncatzim II: 25.7 miles by paved road (:34), then about 0.8 mile by good, wide foot trail (:15).

Guide: Miguel Uc Medina, at Sayil.

From Uxmal, take Highway 261 heading southeast and then south to the Puuc Highway. Turn left and proceed to the cutoff for Chuncatzim II (1.2 miles past the junction for Labná). You can park on the left side of the highway, in front of a gate, and walk in from there.

Wear boots and allow 20 minutes for a visit. Try to see Chuncatzim II in the morning, when the front of the structure is best lighted.

★ ★
SABACCHÉ

*(sah-bah-*cheh; *derivation: Maya for "Place of the Ink Tree")*

Location:
West-central Yucatán.
Maps: 2 (p. 77), 2B and 2B1 (p. 115)

The Site

Sabacché is an extremely dispersed site, and remains are found on both sides of the Puuc Highway. Those on the west will be described first.

Structure 5 at Sabacché, also called the Serpent Head Palace, faces east and rests on a platform built on top of a natural rise of limestone bedrock. The structure is one story, and originally there were six rooms in a single row; they are numbered in sequence from 1, at the north end, to 6, at the south end. Rooms 1 and 2 form the North Wing, Rooms 4, 5, and 6, the South Wing; the two are connected by Room 3, an intermediate chamber. The North Wing is on a somewhat lower level than the rest of the structure because of differences in the level of the underlying bedrock.

Structure 5 was constructed in stages, but according to H. E. D. Pollock, we cannot be sure of the exact sequence. Nevertheless,

View of Room 2 of the North Wing, with remains of part of the South wing on the left, Structure 5, Sabacché. Terminal Classic period.

Detail of Room 2 of Structure 5, east side, Sabacché. Terminal Classic period.

he finds it likely that the three rooms of the South Wing were built before the two rooms of the North Wing.

The best-preserved part of Structure 5 is Room 2. The adjacent Room 1 has collapsed, except for the cross wall that connects it with Room 2. The North Wing projects forward from the South Wing by a couple of feet.

Room 2 has an intact doorway and an upper facade that is a riot of decoration. When this entire wing was intact, surely it was one of the architectural gems of the area. On the right, as you face the structure, there is part of a frontal mosaic Chac mask, with a tightly curled snout. To the left of this is a row of columns graduated in length and resting on square stones; they lead to a squared spiral. The background of this area is a checkerboard pattern of projecting and recessed square stones. Beyond this is a part of a corner Chac mask that was restored in 1983,

along with other parts of the facade of Structure 5.

In order to use corner Chac masks, it would have been necessary to place the facade of the North Wing in front of the earlier South Wing, which would account for the projection of the former. Pollock presumed that a mirror image of this design continued to the right, above the fallen Room 1.

The three-member medial molding running across Room 2, and presumably Room 1 originally, is also highly decorated. The middle part is made of flat stones, and some of these are incised with stepped-fret patterns; they alternate with others displaying vertical slashes. Below this is a continuous row of short, banded columns. There are remains of a red handprint on the lintel above the doorway of Room 2.

The base molding, across the front of the north wing of Structure 5, is buried today, but Pollock reports it to be of a typical

Detail of the remains of the frontal Chac mask at the north end of Room 2, Structure 5, Sabacché. Terminal Classic period.

three-member type, with a continuous row of colonnettes in the center. The lower walls of the structure are plain, and the stones are finely cut and dressed. The cornerstone, which provides most of the projection of the North Wing, is slightly rounded.

To the left of the cornerstone is the wall of the small Room 3, the only one without a doorway opening onto the facade. Its only entrance is on the inside, from Room 2. The facing stones of the lower wall of Room 3 were replaced during restoration. There is a large vertical stone in this area that was orig-inally the northeast corner of Room 4 of the South Wing.

Again to the left are vertical jambstones that formed part of the doorway leading to

Room 4. This and the other two rooms of the South Wing have mostly fallen.

The back of Structure 5 is standing in part, though much of its facing stone is gone. The junction of Rooms 2 and 3 is evident here. The rear of Structure 5 is simple in the extreme, compared to the front. On the rear of the North Wing there is a three-member medial molding. The upper and lower parts are mostly plain, and the middle section has groups of colonnettes alternating with plain stones.

The base molding in the rear has colon-nettes in the middle part, in groups of five, separated by plain stones. Structure 5, or at least its North Wing, is Classic Puuc Mosaic style (A.D. 830–1000).

Structure 1, east side, Sabacché. Late Classic period.

The once-lovely Structure 7 at Sabacché, with its latticework flying facade, was illustrated by Frederick Catherwood in John Lloyd Stephens's work and later photographed by Teobert Maler. According to all recent reports, this building has collapsed into a pile of rubble.

On the east side of the highway are Structures 1 through 4, which partially enclose a court (overgrown). Structures 2, 3, and 4 are nothing more than mounds today, but Structure 1 makes this area worth a visit.

This small, one-room building faces east and had a high roof comb on the front as a flying facade. There are large projecting stones on the front wall and smaller ones on the roof comb above. Originally there were more projecting stones on the sides of both as well. These stones once supported stucco decorations, perhaps anthropomorphic, judging by the remains on Structure 4, the Mirador, at Labná.

The single doorway in Structure 1 is in-

tact, and one large stone forms the jamb on the south side. There is also a large lintel spanning the jambs. A simple medial molding crosses the front of the structure and breaks above the doorway. Structure 1 is Early Puuc style (A.D. 670–770).

When Maler photographed Structure 1 in 1887, some of the top of the roof comb had already fallen, but the remaining part spanned the width of the building. Since then, the north end of the structure and the roof comb above it have collapsed. In 1985 George F. Andrews reported that what then remained of the roof comb tilted backward at an angle of more than 12 degrees.

The rains caused by Hurricane Gilbert in October 1988 caused even more of the roof comb and part of the southeast corner of the building to fall. Only part of the lowest section of the roof comb is still in place. Repair work to the walls, corners, and vault was undertaken by Ramón Carrasco Vargas of INAH in 1989, and substantial supports were installed inside the structure to prevent further deterioration.

Recent History

In 1842 Stephens and his artist companion, Catherwood, visited Sabacché. Stephens described four structures in the area, and Catherwood produced drawings of two of them, now numbered Structures 5 and 7. This was published in 1843. Even at that time the now-fallen Structure 7 had a large crack in the front running up from the doorway.

In 1895 Maler reported Sabacché, and he published photographs of Structures 1 and 7. The site is mentioned in other publications but was most thoroughly covered (up until that time) by Pollock in 1980. Later in the 1980s Andrews studied the architecture at the site.

Connection

Uxmal to Sabacché (Structure 5): 25.7 miles by paved roads (:34), then about 0.4 mile by dirt road (:08).

From the Sabacché, Structure 5 junction on the Puuc Highway to the Sabacché, Structure 1 junction: 0.2 mile by paved road (:01), then 0.2 mile by good foot trail (:04).

Total from Uxmal to Sabacché (structures on both sides of the highway): 26.9 miles (:55).

Getting There

Guide: Miguel Uc Medina, at Sayil.

From Uxmal, take Highway 261 heading southeast and then south to the Puuc Highway. Turn left and proceed to the cutoff for Sabacché, Structure 5 (1.2 miles past the junction for Labná). Turn left onto the dirt road, go through a gate, and continue to Structure 5, then return to the highway.

To reach Structure 1, drive north for another 0.2 mile, and park on the right side of the highway. From there, follow the trail to Structure 1. Locally, this structure is sometimes called San Fran, after a nearby rancho.

Try to see both Structures 5 and 1 in the morning, when they are best lighted.

Allow 30 minutes to see Structure 5, and another 20 minutes for Structure 1.

★
PICH CORRALCHÉ

(peech kohr-rahl-cheh; derivation: Maya and Spanish for "Corral Made of Pich Wood")

Location:
West-central Yucatán.
Maps: 2 (p. 77) and 2B (p. 115)

The Site

Pich Corralché is a large site with a settlement area of about 1.4 square miles; it ranks in size near Sayil and Kabáh. Unfortunately, the structures at the site are poorly preserved, which accounts for the one-star rating.

The Main Group at Pich Corralché is made up of numerous quadrangles, and there are pyramids and remains of many vaulted structures as well. Since the architecture is greatly fallen, however, the stelae found in this group will be of more interest to the visitor.

The stelae are broken and lie on their sides, but the carving can be made out, and some parts of it are quite clear. In the same area there is also a short cylindrical stone with the top broken off. What remains of the lower part is carved but eroded.

In 1887 Teobert Maler photographed a building at Pich Corralché (which he called X-corralché) that had a column in a doorway and a medial molding that rose above it. There were also remains of diamond-shaped

Lower part of a stela in the Main Group, Pich Corralché. Late or Terminal Classic period.

decorations on the facade. This structure has not been relocated and may have fallen, but its style was Early Puuc (A.D. 670–770). Nicholas Dunning believes that this structure was probably located in one of the quadrangles of the Main Group. Maler also photographed the stelae in the Main Group, and this was published by H. E. D. Pollock in 1980.

There are two groups of ruins nearby that are considered to be a part of Pich Corralché. The East Group is made up of mounds and a massive rubble platform; the Northeast Group has some remains of Structure 1. This Classic Puuc structure (A.D. 770–1000) is two stories, but like the others at the site, it is mostly fallen.

Recent History

Pich Corralché has been known for some time through Maler's photographs, some of which have been published by others. His text on the site is in *Península Yucatán,* volume 1.

Casts of two of the stelae at Pich Corralché are in the Peabody Museum of Harvard University. According to Herbert J. Spinden, the casts were made by Désiré Charnay.

Several articles that include Pich Corralché were published by George F. Andrews in the early 1980s, and a map of the Main Group was drawn. The map was later updated by Dunning, who also drew sketch plans of the East and Northeast groups.

The site remains inadequately ex-

An interior vault of Structure 1 of the Northeast Group, Pich Corralché. Late or Terminal Classic period.

plored, and there has been no consolidation or restoration of the architecture.

Connection

Uxmal to Pich Corralché: 30.4 miles by paved road (:41), 2.6 miles by fair rock road (:11), 1.4 miles by dirt road (:09). Then 0.4 mile over limestone outcrops (:07) to the Northeast Group.

Return the last 0.4 mile (:07) and continue another 0.4 mile by dirt road (:05) to the Main Group.

Total from Uxmal to Pich Corralché (both groups): 35.6 miles (1:20).

Getting There

Guide: Miguel Uc Medina, at Sayil, or someone he recommends.

From Uxmal, take Highway 261 heading southeast and then south to the Puuc Highway. Turn left and proceed to the cutoff for Pich Corralché. The cutoff is 5.9 miles past the junction for Labná, and just past (east of) an electric substation. Turn left onto the rock road (which later becomes a dirt road), and go 4.0 miles. Then take a right fork for 0.4 mile to reach the Northeast Group. Actually you can walk this last part about as fast as you can drive it, and probably more comfortably. It is all limestone outcrops and loose boulders hidden by weeds.

Allow 20 minutes to see the remains of Structure 1 of the Northeast Group. Then return to the dirt road and continue for 0.4 mile to reach the Main Group. Allow 30 minutes to see the stelae and the few remains of fallen, vaulted buildings.

A high-clearance vehicle is recommended. Wear boots and have a wide-angle lens for your camera.

★ ★

LOLTÚN (CAVE)

(lohl-toon; derivation: Maya for "The Rock of Flowers")

Location:
West-central Yucatán.
Maps: 2 (p. 77) and 2B (p. 115)

The Site

For the enthusiast the primary reason for a visit to Loltún is to see the well-preserved bas-relief sculptured figure on the outside rock wall, near the Nahkab entrance to the cave. This bigger-than-life-sized figure of a man in profile with an elaborate costume is believed to date to the Late Preclassic period (or possibly the late part of the Middle Preclassic). It is one of the earliest known sculptures in Yucatán, indeed in all the Maya Lowlands.

The figure is holding a lance in his right hand and may represent a warrior, though some authorities believe that the relief is related to Maya deities. A vertical row of glyphs is carved above and to the left of the figure; these are the earliest reported from Yucatán. The numeral 3 accompanies the top glyph, but no date has been deciphered; the relief is dated by its style. A drawing of the relief in the INAH guide for Loltún lists the sculpture as Preclassic Maya and says that in a study, Anthony P. Andrews compared the relief to the Late Preclassic Stela 11 from Kaminaljuyú, in the Guatemala highlands. The guide further states that the Loltún relief is between 2,200 and 2,500 years old.

When you tour the cave, you are shown through several caverns, some of which are gigantic. In several spots there are remnants of paintings, including both positive and neg-

ative painted hands, a motif seen in many parts of the Yucatán Peninsula.

The Loltún Head, discovered in the cave in 1960 by Jack Grant and Bill Dailey, was for several years in the Mérida Museum. It has been returned to the cave, where you can see it when you take a tour. The head is about two feet tall and is rather crudely carved. When displayed at the Mérida Museum, it was labeled as in Olmec style or showing Olmec influence, a view that some authorities reject.

In a large chamber that you visit near the end of the tour are several carvings on boulders and wall surfaces. Although they have been recorded and were reported many years ago, they have not been dated, nor have the paintings. The carvings include spirals, crude faces, and geometric designs.

The chamber in which these carvings appear has an opening to the surface, so there is some light. You need fast film for available-light shots; a flash is also useful here and to shoot the paintings, where there is no natural light.

A nearby chamber with another opening to the surface has a ladder and steps carved into the rock, and this is your exit to the surface. From there you walk aboveground back to where you parked.

Excavations at Loltún show that the cave was used from very early times. Some lithic artifacts associated with animal remains were found in a preceramic level that dates to around 2200 B.C., and the earliest ceramics date to the Middle Preclassic period, around 700–650 B.C. Ceramics from succeeding periods were also discovered, and analysis by Fernando Robles Castellanos and

Preclassic bas-relief carving at the entrance to Loltún Cave.

Glyph-carved jamb from the Main Group at Yaxhom, on display at Loltún Cave. Late or Terminal Classic period.

Eduardo Toro Quiñones indicates that a climax was reached during the Late Classic period. Little material from the Postclassic and colonial periods has been found.

There are four monuments displayed at Loltún near the ticket office, and all are worth a look while you are there. One is a six-foot-tall stone phallus from Nohoch Cep (one of the groups at Yaxhom); two others are glyph-carved jambs from the Main Group

at Yaxhom. Both jambs have an Introducing Glyph at the top, but the double columns of glyphs below (where an Initial Series date would normally be found) have no numerical coefficients, and according to Nicholas Dunning, "only a few calendrical signs are identifiable."

Another carved stone comes from Group B at Yaxhom; it is circular and has a single large glyph. All the groups at Yaxhom from which these monuments come are 2 to 2½ miles from Loltún.

Recent History

Loltún Cave was first studied by Edward H. Thompson, who reported his findings in 1897 while working for Peabody Museum of Harvard University. He worked at Loltún on two occassions. The first expedition was during the 1888–1889 season, and the second was two years later. He explored the cave and discovered several carvings on the walls and boulders of one of the chambers. He also excavated in that area and found fragments of pottery and stone implements at various depths. Photographs of these items and of the sculptured figure on the outside wall appear in his publication.

A few years later Henry C. Mercer explored the cave, undertook some excavation, and published photographs of the carvings inside the cave. Oddly enough, he made no mention of the Preclassic figure at the entrance.

Drawings of the sculptured figure were published by Tatiana Proskouriakoff (1950) and Miguel Covarrubias (1957).

The most recent work at the cave was sponsored by the Southeast Regional Center of INAH and the Yucatán State Government.

Connections

1. Uxmal to Loltún (via Santa Elena, Ticul, and Oxkutzcab): 31.6 miles by paved road (:57).
2. Uxmal to Loltún (via the Puuc Highway): 36.5 miles by paved road (:59).

Getting There

Both routes from Uxmal to Loltún are good; use the one that best fits with your travel plans. If you take the first route, leave Uxmal heading southeast on Highway 261 to Santa Elena, then go northeast on an unnumbered road to Ticul, then southeast on Highway 184 to Oxkutzcab. When you reach Oxkutzcab, go two blocks past the Main Plaza to a sign indicating the way to Loltún. Turn right and continue to the cave. The entrance is marked and is on the right side of the road.

If you use the second route, take Highway 261 southeast and then south to the Puuc Highway. Turn left and go 16.5 miles to the junction with a road (on the left) that goes to the village of Yaxhom. Take this road and go 3.2 miles to the junction with the road to Oxkutzcab, and then turn left. When you join this road, you will be just about at the entrance to Loltún (on the left). You can also go to the end of the Puuc Highway at Cooperativa and turn left to reach Loltún, but this is 1.3 miles (:02) longer than taking the cutoff to Yaxhom.

There is a parking area at Loltún and a restaurant. Tours of the cave (some in English) are conducted on Tuesday through Sunday. They start at 9:30 A.M. and thereafter at 1½-hour intervals; the last tour begins at 3:30 P.M.

As you approach the entrance to the cave, the bas-relief figure is on the rock wall to the left of the main entrance, a bit above eye level. Once you reach it, you can see and photograph it in a few minutes. Avoid the use of flash; it washes out the figure and emphasizes the discoloration in the rock. This is especially true if the sculpture is wet, as it sometimes is. When it is wet, good photos are extremely difficult to get. Try fast film and available light. There are some trees you can lean against for support. The sculpture never gets direct sunlight, but there is likely to be more ambient light in the morning, especially in the rainy season, so if you plan to see Loltún and other sites the same day, go to Loltún first.

If you want to see the bas-relief sculpture at the entrance to the cave but do not wish to tour the cave itself, ask at the ticket office. They will probably allow you to see the sculpture without taking a full tour of the cave.

Bring your own flashlight for extra light in the cave and for reading your camera dials when setting up for flash shots in dark areas.

Allow 1½ hours to visit the cave and walk back to your car, and a few minutes more to see the monuments near the ticket office.

You can reach Loltún on conducted tours from Uxmal or by taxi from Oxkutzcab, as well as in your own vehicle.

★ ★ ★
CHACMULTÚN

*(chahk-mool-*toon; *derivation: Maya for "Mounds Made of Red Stone")*

> **Location:**
> West-central Yucatán.
> **Map:** 2 (p. 77)

The Site

Chacmultún is a real sleeper. There is a good deal of standing architecture that has been restored, some interesting decorations, and remains of polychrome frescoes. The site has been known for a long time, is easy to reach, and is kept cleared, yet it attracts few visitors.

While it may not be quite equal to the more popular Sayil and Labná, it is certainly in the same class, especially since its restoration.

There are three groups of structures at Chacmultún, all of which you should see. As you enter the site, the road passes the first group, a complex of buildings on the right. This group is called Chacmultún, the same

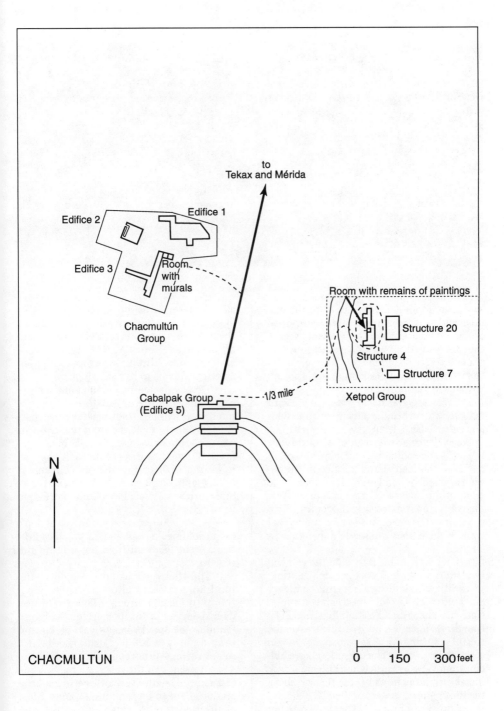

to
Tekax and Mérida

Edifice 2

Edifice 1

Edifice 3

Room
with
murals

Chacmultún
Group

Room with remains of paintings

Structure 20

Structure 4

Structure 7

Cabalpak Group
(Edifice 5)

1/3 mile

Xetpol Group

N

CHACMULTÚN

0   150   300 feet

Edifice 5, north side, lower level, Cabalpak Group, Chacmultún. Late Classic period.

as the site as a whole. Pass it by for the moment and continue about 250 yards to the end of the road. Facing you is the second group, called Cabalpak (meaning something like "Lower Terrace") or Edifice 5. This is a multistoried structure, although that fact is not apparent at a glance.

Its lower story has twelve rooms, with many of the corbeled vaults intact, and with a facade that has been nicely restored. The upper wall zone is formed of a continuous row of banded columns, and there are colonnettes in the medial and cornice moldings, each of which is composed of five parts. The front of the lower-level rooms is divided by a partly restored stairway in the center. Climb the stair to the top of this lower section, and walk to the left side to see the opening to a chultun.

Then walk to the right side and you will see a trail going uphill. As you climb this trail, you will see architectural remains on higher and higher levels. Only then can you appreciate that the structure is multistoried. The first three stories are built on terraces on the side of a natural hill; the fourth story is on top of the hill itself. The upper levels are hidden from view by trees when you are standing at ground level or on the terrace above the lower story.

The remains on the other levels are not as well preserved as the first but are worth a look. There are four ranges of rooms above the first, for a total of five in all. Two ranges are on one level, however, so Edifice 5 is generally considered to be four-storied, although some consider it to have five stories.

There are some intact vaults and in-place stone lintels in the upper stories. Another interesting feature is the crudely carved foot-shaped stones projecting from the vaults in one of the upper rooms. The soles of the feet face out, and the toes point up. They appear to be too high to function as convenient hooks, and one wonders about their use. Structure 5 is Classic Puuc Colonnette style (A.D. 770–830).

When you return to ground level, look for a trail heading east (left as you face Edifice 5) that takes off from the front of the structure.

The trail leads about 0.3 mile to the third group at Chacmultún, called the Xetpol ("Broken Head") Group. (This group was named for an anthropomorphic sculpture found in the area.) The last part of the trail is up a hill over 100 feet high, making it a rather tiring, but not too difficult, climb.

At the top of the hill is a long building (Structure 4) with five doorways in a central section, flanked by projecting rooms. Most of the structure is remarkably intact, and

Structure 4, west facade of the central section, Xetpol Group, Chacmultún. Late Classic period.

part of it has been restored. In the far left room of the central section of the structure, there is an altar or bench, with niches below. This room has no doorway to the outside and can be entered only through the adjacent room on the south, through the far left doorway of the central section. Even more interesting are fragmentary remains of wall paintings found in the center room, on the rear wall on either side of a doorway that leads to an upper chamber. Little remains except black line-work, but the sure flow of the lines indicates the hand of a master artist.

The west facade of Structure 4 is extremely plain. The base molding is a single course of rectangular stones, and the three-member medial and cornice moldings are very simple. George F. Andrews considers this structure to be an intermediate type of Classic Puuc architecture.

You can get to a higher level with more architectural remains by going around either end of Structure 4. A stairway on the south side has been restored. The upper building (once considered an upper level of Structure 4, but now designated Structure 20) is set back from Structure 4, and the terrace in front of Structure 20 forms the roof over Structure 4. From this terrace you can see the two other groups at Chacmultún below in the distance.

The two-storied Structure 20 has been partly restored and has a number of vaulted rooms on its lower level. There are some stone lintels in place in the first story and a partly restored stairway on the north side

Structure 20, west side, Xetpol Group, Chacmultún. Late Classic period.

Structure 7, south side, Xetpol Group, Chacmultún. Late Classic period.

Edifice 1, southwest corner, Chacmultún Group, Chacmultún. Terminal Classic period.

(left as you face the structure). The second story was greatly fallen when the site was first reported, but it is known that the rooms of this story rested on a platform, and this has been restored. The decoration on the building is very simple. The original construction of structure 20 is Early Puuc style (A.D. 670–770), but the building was added to later.

As you face Structure 20, look for a trail that leads to the right for a short distance to a small two-room building (Structure 7). It is simple in design with a single regtangular course of stone for a medial molding, but it is worth a few minutes to visit. Structure 7 is Early Puuc style.

Now return to ground level and your car for a cold drink and a rest. You will need both.

After this break, drive back to the Chacmultún Group, which you saw when you entered the site. Across the road from this group are a couple of small mounds that form the Central Group, but there is no standing architecture there.

The Chacmultún Group has the most extensive architectural remains at the site, consisting mainly of three major buildings:

Edifice 3 on a lower level, and Edifices 1 and 2 on a higher terrace.

Edifice 3 is composed of about 20 rooms, and remains of mural paintings can still be seen in one of them. They are located on the back wall of the second room on your right as you approach the building. The opening to this chamber faces south. The murals are in poor condition, but figures in a processional, wearing ritual regalia, can still be discerned. There is a padlocked door to this room, but the caretaker will open it for you. There are many intact vaults in Edifice 3, and the remaining medial molding has a design carved on its middle member.

Climb now to the upper level of the group. Edifice 1 is a large building with a central stairway on the south, banded columns decorating the upper wall zone, and three-member medial and cornice moldings, the middle parts of which are carved. There are projecting stone phalli in the middle of the cornice molding; these are best observed on the west end of the building. The west part of the south facade of the structure has been restored, and the large center doorway (of three) is supported by two cylindrical

Detail of the west facade with hut-type niche above the doorway, Edifice 1, Chacmultún Group, Chacmultún. Terminal Classic period.

columns with rectangular capitals. There are two hut-type niches in the upper wall zone of this area, and another on the west end of the building. For this and other reasons, Edifice 1 (as well as Edifice 5) reminds you most of Labná.

The remaining rooms of Edifice 1 are unusually wide, and one of them has six projecting foot-shaped stones like those mentioned earlier in the upper level of Edifice 5. The east side of Edifice 1 (right as you face the structure) is mostly collapsed. On the west end of the building are the remains of a stairway, supported by a vault, that once led to the roof of the structure. It is of more modest dimensions than the south stairway, and both were built after the construction of the rooms. Although there were several stages of construction in Edifice 1, the exact sequence has not been determined. It is believed that second-story rooms were planned but never built. On the northwest corner of

the building there is an extension formed of three rooms. These are mostly fallen, but jambstones and lintels that were part of the entrance to one of the rooms are standing, and there are remains of lower walls and a three-member medial molding like the one on the main part of the structure. Edifice 1 is Classic Puuc Mosaic style (A.D. 830–1000), and it must have been a truly outstanding piece of architecture in its heyday.

The other structure on this upper level, Edifice 2, is a most unusual one. Its east face has a recessed central stairway flanked by remains of vaulted rooms—one on each side. This is backed by a large core of a solid mass of rubble. It is theorized that this solid core was meant to support an upper story that was never built. The core and stairway of the structure were built first and are Early Puuc style; the vaulted rooms flanking the stairway are Classic Puuc Colonnette style and were added later.

Edifice 2, northeast corner, Chacmultún Group, Chacmultún. Late Classic period.

The north and south sides of Edifice 2 have no openings in the exterior walls, but there is a small opening in the west wall several feet above ground level, but no stairway leading to it has been discovered. The opening enters a narrow chamber that makes a 90-degree turn to the right, goes up a few steps, and continues straight ahead almost to the south end of the building. The purpose of this crudely vaulted chamber has not been determined; it seems to go nowhere in particular. Sunk into the terrace between Edifices 1 and 2 is a chultun with a catch basin on the surface.

Although the structures at Chacmultún were erected during the Late and Terminal Classic periods, the general area was inhabited earlier. Late Preclassic ceramics were found in a cave 2.5 miles from the site. There are Late Postclassic ceramics at the site itself, indicating that it was occupied, at least to some extent, long after the latest buildings were erected.

Recent History

Teobert Maler described Chacmultún in works published in 1895 and 1902, and he gave the structures such fanciful names as "The Chamber of Justice" for Edifice 2. Edward H. Thompson, working for the Peabody Museum of Harvard University, explored and mapped the site in 1899 and did a watercolor copy of the murals. This is fortunate, for when he returned two years later, they had been greatly defaced. He reported his findings in 1904.

Mexican scholars who studied Chacmultún in the early and mid-twentieth century were Federico Mariscal, José Erosa Peniche, and Enrique Juan Palacios. In 1980 H. E. D. Pollock described and illustrated the major structures at Chacmultún, and Andrews analyzed the architecture in articles published a few years later.

In the early 1980s major restoration at the site was undertaken by the Mexican government, and nearby groups were explored and recorded, some of which were dwellings.

Some of this work was reported by Antonio Benavides Castillo in 1985.

Connections

1. Uxmal to Chacmultún (via Santa Elena, Ticul, Oxkutzcab, and Tekax): 43.5 miles by paved roads (1:19).

2. Uxmal to Chacmultún (via the Puuc Highway): 50.7 miles by paved roads (1:18).

Getting There

Both routes to Chacmultún are good; use the one that best fits with your travel plans. If you take the first route, leave Uxmal heading southeast on Highway 261 to Santa Elena, then go northeast on an unnumbered road to Ticul, then southeast on Highway 184 to Tekax. As you enter Tekax, you will see a pyramid sign for Chacmultún. Turn right at the sign and go a long block to a cemetery. Then turn left—the only choice—and go another block to a junction with a road that has a sign for Kancab. Turn right at the

junction and take the road west through the village of Canek and on to Kancab. In Kancab take the cutoff to the left for Chacmultún (marked with a sign).

If you use the second route, take Highway 261 from Uxmal heading southeast and then south to the Puuc Highway; turn left and continue to Cooperativa. Turn right at the end of the road (left goes to Loltún and Oxkutzcab), and go to the junction for Chacmultún (marked with a sign). Turn left and go to Kancab. This part of the road is narrow. In Kancab turn right at the sign for Chacmultún and proceed to the site.

The road from Kancab to Chacmultún is now paved, but there are lots of dips and curves along the way. Drive slowly.

Chacmultún can easily be reached by private car, but buses go only as far as Tekax. From there you could probably get a taxi to the site. There is no food or drink at Chacmultún. Wear boots and allow 3 hours to see the three groups at the site. On the way back to Uxmal treat yourself to a lunch of *poc-chuc* at the Hotel Peraza in Tekax.

KOM

(kohm; derivation: Maya for "depression" or "ravine")

Location:
West-central Yucatán.
Maps: 2 (p. 77) and 2C (p. 165)

The Site

Kom is a dispersed site with three main groups—A, B, and C—and two other groups of somewhat lesser importance. All three main groups are very worthwhile, and the site as a whole, according to George F. Andrews, shows "considerable variety in building form and architectural style, including both early and late [Puuc] styles."

When you drive to the site you reach Group C first. Park on the dirt road, and fol-

low a foot trail for a short distance to the right to Structure 1, the only standing building in Group C. Originally this structure had six rooms in a double range of three rooms, back to back. Those on the south have totally collapsed, and of those facing north, only the center room is fairly well preserved.

The north facade of Structure 1 originally had five doorways, one in each end room and three entering the center room. Only the central doorway of the center room remains intact, though jambstones of the other doorways, nearest the one in the center, are still in place. Many of the facing stones of the north wall have fallen, but those that remain would indicate that the lower part of the wall was plain. The upper section (but still below the molding) has a recessed,

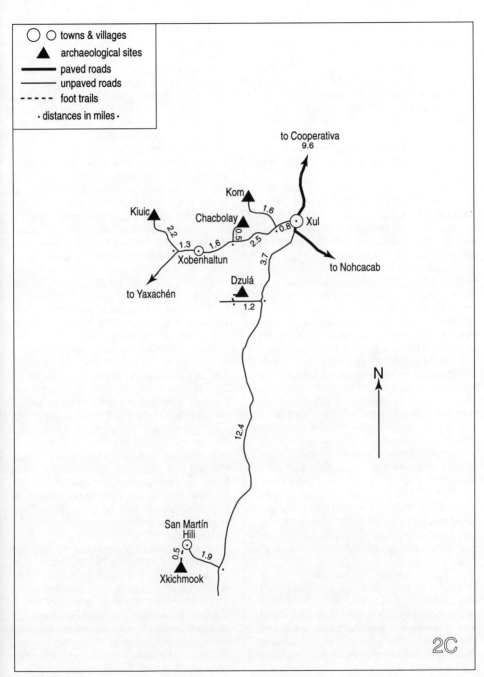

Area near Xul

geometric design in the form of a horizontal cross, with a projecting stone in the center. This feature is best observed on the extreme left (east). A reconstruction drawing by Andrews shows two more crosslike designs on the facade of the central room.

The interior of the central room is partly intact, and the vault is complete in the middle of the room. It is gracefully curved and is topped by a line of recessed capstones. Structure 1 of Group C is Early Puuc style (A.D. 670–770).

Return to your vehicle and follow the road north for 0.3 mile. This brings you to the base of a low hill that is topped by Group A, the largest architectural assemblage at Kom. A trail leads up the hill and passes between Structures 4 and 6.

These two structures are at right angles to each other, and each is a single range of rooms. Both lie along the edge of the flattened top of the hill. The doorways of both face downhill, and both bildings are fallen or partly fallen, though remnants of vaults can be seen.

At the top of the hill you come first to Structure 2, which borders a plaza on the south. (Structure 1 is on the west side of the plaza, and the few remains of Structure 5 are found on the north side.) Structure 2 has four rooms in a line facing north, two of which have been consolidated and partly restored. Though the facing stones of the lower walls of the north facade are gone, two doorways are intact, with their jambstones and lintels.

Remains of a simple medial molding are found above each doorway and in one place in the wall between them. The molding seems to overhang the doorways more than is usual and appears today to be almost a sort of canopy.

To the southeast of Structure 2, away from the plaza, is Structure 3, a building with seven rooms in two rows, back to back. It is partly fallen, but the exterior east end wall and some of the interior cross walls are standing. The exterior east wall is decorated with a typical three-member medial molding with columns above it.

From here, head northwest, passing the side of Structure 2, and continue across the plaza to Structure 1, the largest at Kom. This 13-room building appears to have been built in different stages. Its east facade has mostly fallen, and decorative fragments lie in heaps on the ground in front. One large section has columns and a three-member molding, of which the middle part is colonnettes. The south wall and some of the interior doorways of Structure 1 are intact, and some of the rooms have been consolidated.

Part of Structure 1 is two stories, and the rest is one story. One single range of three rooms, extending to the east, is mostly rubble. The rear (west face) of the structure has many decorative elements in place in the upper section (of the same type that lie on the ground in front of the building). Below the decorations the facades of the rooms have fallen, but the inner parts of the vaults are standing, as are a couple of cross walls and an interior doorway. When intact, Structure 1 must have been a truly impressive piece of architecture. It appears to be Classic Puuc Colonnette style (A.D. 770–830).

When you leave Group A, follow the road as it curves to the right, to the base of a hill supporting Group B. The largest building in this group is Structure 1, with six rooms. The three on the west were constructed first and are Early Puuc style, and at that time the structure was L-shaped. The central room on the west has three doorways, and there are remains of a simple rectangular molding that rises above them. Between the molding and the lintels over the doorways are some diamond-shaped stones for decoration. The south room of this part of the structure projects from the rest of the west facade and has one doorway on the south side.

During Classic Puuc times three rooms were added on the east side. The center room on the east, which projects from the others, is mostly fallen, but most of the north and south rooms are standing. A cornice molding with a continuous row of colonnettes is still in place in a few spots, and more of this decoration can be seen in the large clumps of the fallen facade of the center room. The structure has been partly restored.

A few feet to the north of Structure 1 is Structure 2, which faces south. Of the original three rooms, only the one on the west is

Structure 1 of Group B, view of part of the west side, Kom. Late Classic period.

in good condition; the others are greatly fallen. In the lower wall there are three large banded columns on the southwest corner, two of which are complete. The upper wall zone displays a continuous row of colonnettes, banded in the center, and it is separated from the plain lower wall by a simple three-member medial molding. Shorter colonnettes adorn part of the cornice molding.

A short distance to the northeast is Structure 3 of Group B, with one of its two original rooms still standing. It is also decorated with banded colonnettes in the upper wall zone and smaller plain colonnettes in the middle of the three-member medial and cornice moldings. Structures 2 and 3 of Group B appear to be Classic Puuc Colonnette style.

Recent History

In 1928 José Reygadas Vértiz described several sites in a Mexican publication, including Groups A and B at Kom. In 1936 H. E. D. Pollock visited Kom, and in 1980 he published a brief report (and a synopsis of Reygadas's information).

The site is included in the 1980 *Atlas Arqueológico del Estado de Yucatán* by Silvia Garza Tarazona de González and Edward Kurjack.

Andrews studied the architecture at Kom and published his findings in several articles in the 1980s. In late 1987 the Salvage Brigade of the Yucatán Regional Center of INAH, under the direction of Ricardo Velázquez Valadéz, carried out consolidation in Groups A and B at Kom. The site was mapped by Uwe Gebauer in 1988.

Connection

Uxmal to Kom (via the Puuc Highway): 45.3 miles by paved road (1:09), 0.8 mile by rock road (:04), then 1.6 miles by dirt road (:15) to Group C at Kom.

Total from Uxmal to Kom (Group C): 47.7 miles (1:28).

Getting There

Guide: Miguel Uc Medina, at Sayil, or ask around in Xul.

Structure 2 of Group B, south facade, west room, Kom. Late Classic period.

From Uxmal, take Highway 261 heading southeast and then south to the Puuc Highway. Turn left and go to Cooperativa, then right and continue to Xul. In Xul turn right at the sign for Kom, pick up the rock road, and go to the dirt cutoff for Kom. Turn right and proceed to Group C. There are some limestone outcrops along the dirt road, but they can be crossed in a standard vehicle if you take it slowly.

Bring a wide-angle lens for your camera, and wear boots. Allow 2 hours to see the three major groups at Kom, including travel time between them.

Buses go as far as Xul.

★
CHACBOLAY
(CHACBOLAI)
(chahk-boh-lahee; derivation: Maya for "jaguar")

Location:
West-central Yucatán.
Maps: 2 (p. 77) and 2C (p. 165)

The Site

The Castillo at Chacbolay is the only well-preserved structure at the site, but to the southeast the fallen remains of two vaulted buildings have been reported. Chacbolay is better than the average one-star site, even with its single standing building.

The Castillo has eight rooms around a central, solid core, and a stairway on the west side. Beneath the stairway there is a doorway entering the central room of the west facade, and two other doorways enter rooms on either side. In the upper wall zone, above the north and south doorways (in the rooms on the west side), are niches that perhaps originally housed some decoration. Today the niches are empty except for the remains of red paint.

The niches are bordered by sections of plain stone, and there are groups of three

The Castillo, from the southwest, Chacbolay. Late Classic period.

banded columns at the north and south corners of the upper wall zone on the west side. Below these, in the otherwise plain lower wall zone, are tall, single, banded columns. There are also upper wall zone niches on the north and south sides of the structure near the west end, and probably there were more originally, but parts of the other facades have fallen.

The building has the usual base molding, but one variation in the medial and cornice moldings is the inclusion of spherical stones in groups of three near the corners. The rest of the two upper moldings is made up of the more common colonnettes, as is the base molding.

Two vaulted passages pierce the stairway; the one nearest the bilding is mostly intact, while only a small part of the other vault is standing (at the base of the stairway). Only the upper part of the stairway remains, but originally it descended to the base of the natural hill that supports the structure.

The Castillo at Chacbolay was not built all at once, and authorities differ about which parts were built first. There seems to be agreement, however, that the west rooms were a later addition. The best place to see two different construction phases is on the north side of the building, a few feet to the east of the doorway. At this junction there are large vertical stones on the left (east), next to smaller square stones on the right.

Teobert Maler speculated that the core of the building might contain rooms that were later filled in, but H. E. D. Pollock found no evidence for this. Pollock believed that a second story was planned but never constructed, a situation also found in Edifice 2 at Chacmultún.

Recent History

Maler visited Chacbolay in 1888 and first reported it in 1902. More information is contained in *Península Yucatán,* volume 1.

The site is later mentioned in works published in Mexico and the United States. Pollock described the Castillo in detail in 1980. On the basis of the architecture, George F. Andrews classifies the Castillo of Chacbolay, at least its west rooms, as Classic Puuc Colonnette style (A.D. 770–830).

No extensive excavation has been undertaken at the site, but it was mapped by Uwe Gebauer in 1988.

Connection

Uxmal to Chacbolay: 45.3 miles by paved roads (1:09), 3.3 miles by rock road (:14), then 0.5 mile by poor dirt and limestone road (:05).

Total from Uxmal to Chacbolay: 49.1 miles (1:28).

Getting There

Guide: If this is the only site you will be visiting in the area, you can ask for a guide at the village of Xobenhaltun, 1.6 miles past the cutoff for Chacbolay as you drive west from Xul, or ask in Xul. If you plan to see other sites on Map 2C on the same trip, check with Miguel Uc Medina, at Sayil.

From Uxmal, take Highway 261 heading southeast and then south to the Puuc Highway. Turn left and go to Cooperativa, then right and continue to Xul. In Xul turn right at the sign for Kom and pick up the rock road. Go to the dirt cutoff for Chacbolay, turn right, and continue to the site.

Wear boots and allow 30 minutes to see the Castillo. A wide-angle lens is a must here, and even with that you will not be able to get a shot of the entire west facade of the structure.

Buses go as far as Xul.

★ ★
KIUIC
(kee-week; derivation: Maya for "plaza," "market," or "market place")

Original Name:
  Possibly Kiuic.
Location:
  West-central Yucatán.
Maps: 2 (p. 77) and 2C (p. 165)

The Site

Kiuic is a fascinating site with several well-preserved structures. Some consolidation and restoration have been undertaken, and if access were easier, it clearly would be a three-star site.

There are three numbered groups at Kiuic, and the sequence in which you visit them will depend on which branches of the dirt access road are open at the time. Here, the groups will be described in numerical order. Depend on your guide to get you around.

There are four standing, or partly standing, structures in Group 1 that are of inter-est. Structure 3 has been restored and is a fine example of Classic Puuc Colonnette–style architecture (A.D. 770–830). It is one story, with four rooms facing north. In the upper wall zone, decorations include split columns in groups of three, separated by plain sections. There are restrained base, medial, and cornice moldings decorated with colonnettes.

Nearby, to the southeast, is Structure 4 of Group 1, which faces east. Though badly fallen, one of its original five doorways remains intact. The upper zone of the facade overhangs the lower wall without the usual medial molding. This uper zone rises at the doorway, and the effect is similar to the broken medial molding seen in other Early Puuc–style structures (A.D. 670–770). A carved capstone was found inside the room with the standing doorway, but it has been looted and was replaced with a plain stone. At the back of Structure 4, on a higher level, is an almost completely fallen double range

Structure 3 of Group 1, north side, Kiuic. Late Classic period.

Structure 4 of Group 1, east side, Kiuic. Late Classic period.

of rooms. These may be a part of Structure 4 or may be a separate structure.

Adjacent to the south of Structure 4 is Structure 5, originally with six rooms. Only part of it is standing now, but what remains of the east facade is exquisite. John Lloyd Stephens, who saw this structure in 1842, described it as "remarkable for its simplicity ... and, for its grandeur of proportions." He removed a painted capstone from the interior of the room by digging down through the roof.

The walls of the facade are decorated with banded columns, alternating with diamond-shaped designs, and Frederick Catherwood, who accompanied Stephens, produced an engraving showing wall segments on either side of a doorway. In the early 1930s the northern part of the facade collapsed, perhaps in part because of the removal of the capstone. This structure is Classic Puuc Colonnette style.

The most monumental building at Kiuic

is Structure 6 of Group 1, also called the Nohochpak, about 200 feet to the southeast of Structure 5. At ground level Structure 6 has a range of 12 rooms facing north, in a single line, divided by a central stairway (now rubble) that leads to the roof of the structure. Set back from the top of the stairway is another range of rooms that is mostly fallen. The lower-level rooms on the west side of the stairway are well preserved and have been consolidated, and the upper facade is decorated with a continuous row of split columns. Colonnettes also decorate the middle member of the medial and cornice moldings. Structure 6 is Classic Puuc Colonnette style.

Group 2 lies to the northeast of Group 1, and Structure 1 is the best preserved of this group, with three existing rooms that face west, two of which are intact. The entrance to each room was originally supported by two columns, forming three doorways, though the facade of the southernmost room

Structure 5 of Group 1, remains of the east facade, Kiuic. Late Classic period.

has collapsed. The columns in the center room are plain, while those in the north room (and originally the south room as well) were constructed in three parts.

Each of the three-part columns has a center section in the form of molding, though the columns in the north room had a different design from those on the south. The batter of the upper facade of the building, its simple cornice molding, and the subtle variety of its columns give the structure a certain charm and elegance. Behind these rooms are the rubble remains of three others that faced east, and they were back-to-back with those described. Structure 1 of Group 2 has been consolidated and is Early Puuc style.

A short distance to the northeast are the remains of Structure 2, a fair-sized pyra-midal mound with a range of three vaulted rooms at ground level on the west side. Though the mound is mostly rubble, there are remains of geometric decorations in the upper facade of the rooms. The decorations include a stepped-fret design and split columns, and above this a three-member cornice molding.

H. E. D. Pollock reported that the pyramid appears to have been built against the back of these rooms and that the rooms were supposedly filled at that time. He further reported that "the pyramid presumably supported a temple building now completely fallen." This is the only temple-pyramid at the site. Mapping of Kiuic by Uwe Gebauer indicates that a stairway ascended the pyramid on the east side.

Structure 6 of Group 1, the Nohochpak, view of the west half of the north side, Kiuic. Late Classic period.

Group 3 is east of Group 2, and the best-preserved building is Structure 2. Its center room, of three that face west on the first level, has two columns with capitals in the doorway and remains of triangular and diamond-shaped decorations above the massive stone lintels. The lower wall is plain, and much of the facing stone of the upper walls has fallen, as has the north room. A simple doorway to the south room is intact, and the structure has been partly restored. There is a badly fallen room above and behind the central room of the first level, and indications are that a stairway on the east side led to it. Structure 2 of Group 3 is Early Puuc style.

Structure 1 of this group lies a few feet to the west and is mostly collapsed, but a partly standing vault can be seen.

Recent History

In 1843 Stephens was the first to report the site of Kiuic, and his work included two illustrations by Catherwood, Structures 5 and 6 of Group 1. Teobert Maler visited Kiuic in 1888, and his text and illustrations are in *Península Yucatán,* volume 1.

Kiuic is included in many publications through the years, but those works are mainly descriptive. No extensive excavation has been undertaken at the site, but some of the structures were consolidated in the 1980s. Pollock covered the architecture of Kiuic in some detail in 1980, and George F. Andrews analyzed several of the structures in articles published in the mid-1980s. The site plan drawn by Gebauer in 1988 indicates

Structure 1 of Group 2, view of the west facade, Kiuic. Late Classic period.

Structure 2 of Group 3, view of the west facade, Kiuic. Late Classic period.

the presence of a number of buildings at Kiuic not described above.

Connection

Uxmal to Kiuic: 45.3 miles by paved road (1:09), 6.2 miles by rock road (:29), then 2.2 miles by poor dirt road, with bumpy limestone outcrops (:30—but see below).

Total from Uxmal to Kiuic: 53.7 miles (2:08).

Getting There

Guide: Miguel Uc Medina, at Sayil.

From Uxmal, take Highway 261 heading southeast and then south to the Puuc Highway. Turn left and go to Cooperativa, then right and continue to Xul. In Xul turn right at the sign for Kom, pick up the rock road, and go to the dirt cutoff for Kiuic. Turn right and continue to the site.

You must have a high-clearance vehicle to reach Kiuic, and while four-wheel drive may not be absolutely necessary, it would be a help in getting over the limestone outcrops.

There is a gate at the entrance to the dirt road. If no one has recently driven this road, there may be some trees lying across it, in which case it will take you longer than the 30 minutes indicated above.

Allow 1 hour and 45 minutes to visit the three groups described above. Though there is a lot to see at Kiuic, it is fairly easy to get around, and little climbing is involved. Wear boots and bring a wide-angle lens for your camera.

Buses go as far as Xul.

★
DZULÁ
(TZULÁ)

(tsoo-lah; derivation: Maya for "Well [Waterhole] of the Foreigner")

Location:
    West-central Yucatán.
Maps: 2 (p. 77) and 2C (p. 165)

The Site

Dzulá is known mainly for its remains of mural paintings. Structure 1 though, which houses them, is in itself quite impressive.

This two-story building rests atop a hill, and originally there was a stairway on the southwest side. A plan of the structure drawn by Uwe Gebauer shows that there are 17 rooms in the upper story, arranged in a square, with openings on all four sides. There are possibly as many as 25 rooms below, concealed in the first story, according to Nicholas Dunning. Structure 1 is a truly massive building, though much of it has fallen.

To reach the upper level and the murals, you make a not-too-difficult climb over rubble fallen from the structure. On the way you will see the remains of large vaulted rooms.

The outside wall of the room with the major fragments of the murals has collapsed, but the murals are protected by a thatch shelter.

The best-preserved section of the paintings is on the inner vault, just above the spring line, in the corner of the room. There is a line of five figures, though only the legs of three and the legs and torsos of two more are in place. They are easier to discern, however, than the figures in Edifice 3 at Chacmultún.

The abutting end wall also has remains of paintings, and there are a few fragments at the top of the vault nearby, all depicting figures. The figures form three rows and are separated by painted borders on which they stand. Some sort of ritual procession may be indicated, perhaps an offering of tribute or the installation of a Maya lord.

Elsewhere in this room, and elsewhere in the structure, areas of plaster remain attached to the underlying wall. A few small areas retain some paint, but the designs are difficult to make out. Some of the larger areas of plaster appear to have been unpainted.

Other structures are reported at Dzulá, to the northeast, east, and west of the hill topped by Structure 1, but these are greatly fallen. The site as a whole is medium size and dates to the Late Classic Period, and Structure 1, probably to around A.D. 770–830.

Recent History

In 1842 John Lloyd Stephens visited Dzulá and saw the paintings described above, but he gave no name for the site. He commented that the murals were "by far the most interesting paintings we have seen in the country." Unfortunately, he did not visit Chacmultún, where the murals with the figures were then in good condition.

Edward H. Thompson published a short report on Dzulá in 1904 and illustrated it with a photograph of the inner corner of the room with the paintings and a drawing of some of the figures in the two upper rows. A native of the area told Thompson that he and his friends called the ruins "Tzula," and this is the name Thompson used in his report.

Some of Thompson's work was republished in Mexico in the 1920s and 1940s, and Dzulá was mapped by Gebauer in 1988, completing the work of George F. Andrews.

There has been no in-depth excavation, and no restoration or even consolidation, except that the edges of the painted plaster fragments have been cemented to the walls to prevent further deterioration.

Connection

Uxmal to Dzulá: 45.3 miles by paved road (1:09), 3.7 miles by fair rock road (:20), 1.2 miles of somewhat worse rock and dirt road (:12), then a short distance by foot trail (:05).

Total from Uxmal to Dzulá: 50.3 miles (1:46).

Getting There

Guide: Miguel Uc Medina, at Sayil, or ask around in Xul.

From Uxmal, take Highway 261 heading southeast and then south to the Puuc Highway. Turn left and go to Cooperativa, then right and continue to Xul. In Xul go straight ahead at the sign for Dzulá. Shortly south of Xul the paved road veers to the left (to Nocacab), and a rock road goes straight ahead. Follow the rock road south, then turn right onto another rock road. Go 1.2 miles, park on the side of the road, and walk to the site from there.

A wide-angle lens and fast film are recommended for photographing the paintings in natural light. Otherwise, bring a flash unit. Allow 30 minutes to see Structure 1 and the paintings, and wear boots for the climb to the room that houses them.

Buses go as far as Xul.

★ ★

XKICHMOOK

*(shkeech-mook; derivation: Maya for "The Buried Beauty,"
according to Edward H. Thompson)*

Location:
West-central Yucatán.
Maps: 2 (p. 77) and 2C (p. 165)

The Site

Xkichmook is actually a very good two-star site. A number of structures are reported, and four of them are of interest to the visitor.

Mask panel in the upper facade of the south wing of the Palace, Xkichmook. Late Classic period.

As you climb to the site from the north, you first come to the rear of the Palace (Structure 1), an L-shaped structure and the largest at Xkichmook. You can actually see the structure as you begin to climb to the site. The main facade of the Palace faces south. In the center of this facade is a stairway (now in ruin) from a plaza to a two-room temple on top; the rest of the structure is one story. On either side of the fallen stairway are remains of decorations.

Rooms project from each side of the stairway, and on the west a range of five rooms extends to the south. The corners of the rooms of the upper story are decorated with stacked, projecting Chac masks reminiscent of those on Structure XX at Chicanná. To get a good view of the masks, climb the rubble stairway and head left (west). The masks on the northwest corner are well preserved, and there are also masks in the upper wall zone of the building.

Four of the rooms that extend to the south also face the plaza (east); the fifth room (on the northwest corner) has a doorway facing west. The upper facades of these first four rooms are highly decorated with remains of mask panels and columns. In this row the two rooms in the center project in front of those on each end. The mask panels on the two center rooms were larger (occu-

pying the entire upper facade) and somewhat different from those on the end rooms (where the masks are confined to the space between the medial and cornice moldings). The mask on the room farthest right (north) as you face this row is the best preserved.

To the southeast of the Palace (and once considered a part of it) are two well-preserved rooms that face west onto the same plaza. This is Structure 12, and it originally had nine rooms, though much of it has fallen. The upper wall zone of the standing rooms is decorated with large rosettes that have a rectangular, lower extension. This is a unique feature, although small rosettes are sometimes found in the cornice molding on some other structures. There is a two-member cornice molding, as well as a three-member medial molding with an unusually high upper part. The lower walls of Structure 12 are mostly plain, but there is a vertical recess (one of three originally) that divides the two rooms. The base molding is in three parts, with groups of three colonnettes in the middle section.

You now leave the plaza area the way you came in and take a trail to the right. A short distance away is the partly ruined Structure 4. This building had eight rooms surrounding a solid central core, and part of the north facade (west side) is fairly well preserved. The upper wall zone is decorated with groups of three columns separated by plain areas, and in the area above the standing doorway are triangular decorations in a panel that is divided by a horizontal course. The medial and cornice moldings have groups of three colonnettes as part of the decoration.

From Structure 4 the trail continues to Structure 6, a two-room building that is fairly well preserved. It faces west, and there is a stack of three frontal Chac masks in the lower wall between the doorways. Three similar masks decorate the upper wall zone, which also has plain columns. Most of the fine detail of the masks is executed in stucco. The medial and cornice moldings include a mat-symbol motif that is seldom seen.

The two standing rooms of Structure 12, Xkichmook. Late Classic period.

In a detailed study of the structures at Xkichmook, George F. Andrews concluded that Structures 4, 6, and 12 are in a transitional style that he calls Chenes-Puuc, and earlier investigators had also noticed some Chenes traits at the site. Andrews believes that Structure 1 is "almost purely Chenes in conception and execution," while H. E. D. Pollock saw the style of this structure as "something of a blend of Puuc and Chenes traditions, but basically Puuc." Andrews's work on Xkichmook was published in 1984 and 1985. He believes the structures at Xkichmook date to the Late Classic period, while other authorities prefer a Terminal Classic date.

Recent History

Xkichmook was discovered in 1886 by Thompson, who first reported it—under the name Kich Moo—in an 1888 publication of the American Antiquarian Society.

Thompson returned to the site in 1891 and conducted research over a period of several years. His detailed report on Xkichmook was published by the Field Columbian Museum of Chicago in 1898, for whom he was working, with the sponsorship of Allison V. Armour.

Some authorities disagree with Thompson about the derivation of the name of the site and offer other possibilities. Locally the site is sometimes called Kichmo, but Xkich-

Upper facade of Structure 4, north side, Xkichmook. Late Classic period.

mook is the generally accepted name today in the literature.

Teobert Maler visited Xkichmook in 1889, and three of his excellent photographs of the site were used in *Arquitectura Prehispánica*, by Ignacio Marquina (1951). Maler's other data are in *Península Yucatán*, volume 1.

In 1979 some clearing of the structures was undertaken, and lithic studies were carried out in the late 1980s.

Connection

Uxmal to Xkichmook: 45.3 miles by paved roads (1:09), 16.1 miles by rock road (:53), 1.9 miles by fair to poor dirt road (:12), then about 0.5 mile by foot trail (:10).

Total from Uxmal to Xkichmook: 63.8 miles (2:24).

Getting There

Guide: Miguel Uc Medina, at Sayil, or ask around in Xul.

From Uxmal, take Highway 261 heading southeast and then south to the Puuc Highway. Turn left and go to Cooperativa, then right and continue to Xul. In Xul, go straight ahead at the sign for Dzulá. Shortly south of Xul the paved road veers to the left (to Nocacab), and a rock road goes straight ahead. Follow the rock road south to the cutoff for San Martín Hili, and turn right onto the dirt road to reach the Ejido of Xkichmook (in San Martín Hili).

Once you reach the ejido, whoever you have brought along as a guide should ask permission to visit the site. Since the trail to the site is through ejido fields, someone from the ejido will accompany you.

Driving your own vehicle is the only reasonable way to reach Xkichmook, since regular bus service goes only as far as Xul.

Wear boots, have a wide-angle lens for your camera, and allow 1 hour to visit the site.

★
XCAVIL DE YAXCHÉ

(shkah-weel deh yahsh-cheh; Xcavil is Maya for "second sowing" [land that is sown with seed]; Yaxché means "ceiba" and is also the name of a nearby hacienda or rancho. Note: Xcavil is the spelling used in the literature; however, the pronunciation shown is that used locally.)

Location:
West-central Yucatán.
Maps: 2 (p. 77) and 2D (p. 182)

The Site

Several groups of structures are reported at the dispersed site of Xcavil de Yaxché, some with well-preserved architecture. The only one I have seen, however, is Structure 1 of the Central Group, called the Temple-Palace by Teobert Maler.

This large structure must have been a splendid building when intact; even in partial ruin it is impressive. It faces west, and the first story is composed of a double range of eight very wide rooms that run north-south. Three other smaller rooms form an extension to the rear, and there are several intact doorways on this lower level. The upper wall zone of this level includes highly decorative banded columns, squared spirals, and a simple two-member medial molding.

The west facade is divided in the center by a stairway that ascends to a smaller second-story structure of five rooms. The stairway is mostly rubble, but parts of the upper structure are standing, and its west facade is the best preserved. There is a medial molding with a continuous row of colonnettes in the middle part, and in the upper wall zone some plain columns and remains of a stepped-fret design.

When Maler photographed the Temple-Palace, there was a mask panel above the doorway of the center room, in the rear extension on the first level. The mask has since fallen, although the doorway is still intact. On the north side of the rear extension is an extremely narrow doorway—barely should width. The doorway is very low, though this is due in part to rubble on the floor.

The Temple-Palace is Classic Puuc Mosaic style (A.D. 830–1000), as are some other structures at Xcavil de Yaxché, while other buildings at the site are Early Puuc style (670–770).

Recent History

Xcavil de Yaxché was first reported by Maler in 1902, and he included a photograph of the mask panel mentioned above. In 1934 Karin Hissink, in a study of mask panels in Yucatán, presented a drawing of the same mask done from Maler's photograph. Maler's plan and elevation of the Temple-Palace were reproduced by H. E. D. Pollock in 1980.

The site was mapped by Nicholas Dunning in 1987, and George F. Andrews studied the architecture and presented his results in 1988. There has been no extensive excavation or consolidation of the structures.

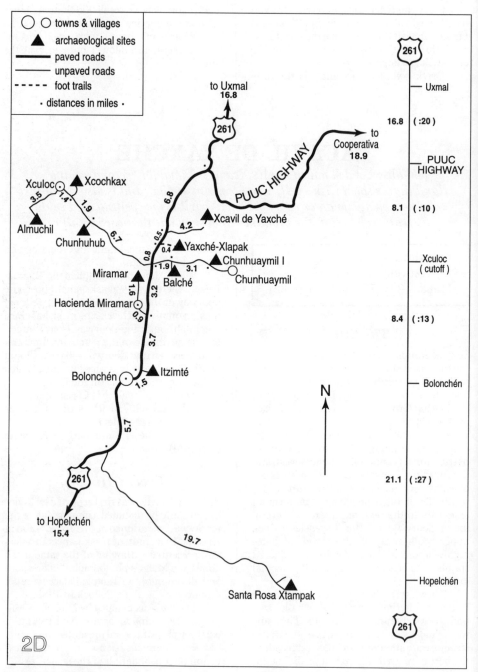

Legend:
- ○ ○ towns & villages
- ▲ archaeological sites
- —— paved roads
- — unpaved roads
- - - - foot trails
- · distances in miles ·

to Uxmal
16.8

261

to Cooperativa
18.9

PUUC HIGHWAY

Xculoc
Xcochkax
3.5
1.4
1.9
6.8
Almuchil
Chunhuhub
6.7
0.5
4.2
Xcavil de Yaxché
0.8
0.4
Yaxché-Xlapak
1.9
3.1
Chunhuaymil I
Miramar
3.2
Balché
Chunhuaymil
1.6
Hacienda Miramar
0.9
3.7
Bolonchén
1.5
Itzimté
5.7
261
to Hopelchén
15.4
19.7
Santa Rosa Xtampak

N

Mile markers (Highway 261):
- Uxmal
- 16.8 (:20)
- PUUC HIGHWAY
- 8.1 (:10)
- Xculoc (cutoff)
- 8.4 (:13)
- Bolonchén
- 21.1 (:27)
- Hopelchén

261

261

2D

Area near Bolonchén

Structure 1 of the Central Group (the Temple-Palace), from the southwest, Xcavil de Yaxché. Terminal Classic period.

Connection

Uxmal to Bolonchén: 33.3 miles by paved road (:43).

From the plaza in Bolonchén: 9.7 miles by paved road (:15), 3.7 miles by poor dirt road (:55), then 0.5 mile by foot trail (:10).

Total from Uxmal to Bolonchén and then to Xcavil de Yaxché: 47.2 miles (2:03).

Total from Uxmal to Xcavil de Yaxché (direct): 27.8 miles (1:33).

Getting There

Guide: Pedro Pacheco Dzul, in Bolonchén.

From Uxmal, take Highway 261 heading southeast and then south to Bolonchén.

From Bolonchén return north on Highway 261 to the cutoff for Xcavil de Yaxché (unmarked), and turn right onto the dirt road. This road has lots of bumpy limestone outcrops. If it is wet, you will probably need a vehicle with four-wheel drive; when dry, you can drive it in a high-clearance vehicle. After you park near the site, follow the foot trail to the north to reach it. Allow 1 hour to visit the Temple-Palace.

Note: If the dirt road looks so bad that you decide to walk in from the highway, wear boots and carry a canteen of water.

Buses go to Bolonchén.

★
YAXCHÉ-XLAPAK

*(yahsh-cheh shlah-pahk; derivation: Yaxché is Maya for
"ceiba" and also the name of a nearby hacienda or rancho;
Xlapak is Maya for "Old Walls" or "Old Ruined Walls")*

Location:
   West-central Yucatán.
Maps: 2 (p. 77) and 2D (p. 182)

The Site

Mapping of Yaxché-Xlapak in 1987 by Nicholas Dunning shows that the site covers an area of over 1.5 square miles, larger by far than previously thought and roughly equivalent in size to Sayil. Several groups are reported at the site, with structures, platforms, plain conical altars, and six stelae, some of which are carved. The stelae and the platform on which they lie were discovered by Dunning during his work at the site. The architecture at the site ranges from Proto-Puuc to Early Puuc to Classic Puuc Colonnette style, covering a time span from about A.D. 610 to 830.

Dunning notes that unlike other large sites, there are no particularly large structures at Yaxché-Xlapak; "Rather, there are numerous medium-large structures and hundreds of smaller vaulted buildings spread across a large area." The only structure I have seen at Yaxché-Xlapak is Structure 1 of the East Cerro Group (called Structure III or the Castillo by Teobert Maler). It is one of the largest and best-preserved buildings at the site.

This structure is Classic Puuc Colonnette style (A.D. 770–830). It rests atop a hill and faces west, with a range of six rooms running north-south. The doorways to the four center rooms are intact, and remains of a stairway are found in the center of the west facade. The base of the stairway is pierced by a passageway formed of a half vault, and the stairway itself leads to the flat roof of the structure. A low platform is reported on the roof, but no rooms.

The lower west wall of the structure is plain, and the upper wall zone has a continuous row of banded columns. Colonnettes are used, also in a continuous row, as part of the medial and cornice moldings. This range of rooms was built first, according to Antonio Benavides Castillo and Abel Morales López. Later, nine rooms were added to the east side in three more construction stages, and five of the rooms form an eastern projection.

The most interesting of these is the room with a doorway on the north, supported by two intact round columns with square capitals. This is the largest room in the structure, the only one with a columned entrance, and it has a pointed vault without capstones, which is rarely found in Puuc architecture, although other examples are reported from Sayil and Itzimté. The exterior north facade of this room has groups of three plain columns in the upper wall zone, separated by flat stones, and continuous rows of colonnettes in both the medial and cornice moldings.

Recent History

Maler visited Yaxché-Xlapak in 1887 and reported the site under this name because Yaxché was the name of a nearby hacienda that is still in operation today. His report was published in 1902 and included a photograph of the west facade of the Castillo. The structure seems to have suffered little since that time. He described, but did not illustrate, four other structures at the site, three of which have not been relocated.

The site was briefly mentioned by Alberto Ruz Lhuillier in 1943, and in 1979 Benavides Castillo and Morales López published a detailed description of the Castillo, including photographs, a plan, and brief notes on other structures at the site. The architecture was studied by George F. Andrews in 1985; later, Dunning explored Yaxché-Xlapak, discovered the stelae, and mapped the site.

Structure 1 of the East Cerro Group (the Castillo), from the northwest, Yaxché-Xlapak. Late Classic period.

Connection

Uxmal to Bolonchén: 33.3 miles by paved road (;43).

From the plaza in Bolonchén: 9.2 miles by paved road (:14), then 0.4 mile by foot trail (:30).

Total from Uxmal to Bolonchén and then to Yaxché-Xlapak: 42.9 miles (1:27).

Total from Uxmal to Yaxché-Xlapak (direct): 24.5 miles (:59).

Getting There

Guide: Pedro Pacheco Dzul, in Bolonchén.

From Uxmal, take Highway 261 heading southeast and then south to Bolonchén.

From Bolonchén return north on Highway 261 to the stopping place along the highway (east side). There is no real shoulder to the road in this area, but there is a limestone outcrop on which you can park. If you are driving a high-clearance vehicle, you can pull off the road a bit farther and park under the shade of a tree. You walk to the site from there, and the last part is very uphill.

Wear boots and a sun hat, carry a canteen of water, and have a wide-angle lens for your camera. Allow 35 minutes to see the Castillo.

Buses go to Bolonchén.

★
BALCHÉ

(bahl-cheh; derivation: Maya name for a tree used in making a native alchoholic drink, and the name of the drink as well)

Location:
West-central Yucatán.
Maps: 2 (p. 77) and 2D (p. 182)

The Site

Balché is a dispersed site with several standing, or partly standing, structures reported. Unfortunately, they are all on the tops or sides of hills, so a good deal of climbing is involved in visiting the site. If you do not mind climbing, rate Balché two stars.

I could not begin to give a written, detailed "tour" of this site, so the following is simply a description of the structures we saw. Depend on your guide to get you around.

From where you park your vehicle you can see a structure atop a tall hill. We were told that there was no trail to it and did not attempt to reach it. From there you walk for some distance and climb about 150 to 200 feet to reach Structure 6. Actually, you climb, descend a bit, and climb again. From the top of the first climb, Structure 6 is clearly visible.

On the lower level, Structure 6 has a row of three rooms in a line. The end rooms are smaller than the central room, and each end room has a single narrow doorway; the central room has three doorways that are wider, and all five doorways are intact. The lower walls of the building are plain, and the upper wall zone overhangs the lower. There is no projecting medial molding as such, but the overhang would seem to serve the same aesthetic purpose. The decoration of the upper wall zone is completely geometric. There is a lower rectangular section, above which are alternating recessed and projecting square stones; above this is another continuous rectangular course.

In this upper course, projecting stones above each doorway are shown in a recon-struction drawing by George F. Andrews. The one above the second doorway from the right, as you face the structure, is still in place. Perhaps the stones supported some decoration that is now fallen. At yet a higher level is a section of vertical, recessed and projecting stones.

Behind these three rooms, and on a higher level, are three more. The central room has three doorways, and the two projecting end rooms each have a doorway on the side. A simple, rectangular medial molding—or perhaps the lower course of an overhanging upper wall zone—is the only decoration remaining.

At one time this upper level was thought to be a separate structure, but now it is known to be the second story of a two- story building. Structure 6 is Early Puuc style (A.D. 670–770).

Near Structure 6 is another building, of which only a small part is standing. Part of the vault of one room is intact, and there are two cylindrical columns with square capitals at the doorway. A simple, rectangular medial molding projects above the lintels. I am not sure of the number of this structure, but it appears to be Early Puuc style.

On the way back to your vehicle you pass the base of a hill that supports Structure 4, and you can see it from ground level. Structure 4 is part way up the hill, and a section of the building is well preserved, though other parts have fallen.

The lower walls of Structure 4 are plain, and some of the facing stone is gone. There is one intact doorway and, above the lintel that spans it, a three-member medial molding. The middle part of the molding is a continuous row of colonnettes. What remains of the upper wall zone is plain, and a single rectangular course of stones is all that is left of the cornice molding. Structure 4 is Classic Puuc Colonnette style (A.D. 770–830).

Recent History

In 1887 Teobert Maler visited a site that he called Xbalché, where he saw several small buildings. His information on the site is part of *Península Yucatán,* volume 1. It is believed that these structures are part of Balché, but they have not been relocated, and Maler apparently did not see the ones described above. These were first reported in 1978, and Balché is not included in the *Atlas Arqueológico del Estado de Yucatán.* For a while after its rediscovery, Balché was thought to be a part of nearby Yaxché-Xlapak. Recent authors, however, primarily Andrews and Nicholas Dunning, consider it to be a separate site. Andrews, the principal investigator of Balché, reported on the architecture in articles published in 1985 and 1986, and Dunning's settlement-pattern study appeared in 1990.

There has been no consolidation or restoration at the site.

Connection

Uxmal to Bolonchén: 33.3 miles by paved road (:43).

From the plaza in Bolonchén: 8.4 miles by paved road (:13), 1.9 miles by fair dirt road (:09), 0.1 mile by a spur dirt road (:01), then about 0.9 mile by foot trail (:20).

Total from Uxmal to Bolonchén, and then to Balché: 44.6 miles (1:26).

Total from Uxmal to Balché (direct): 27.8 miles (1:00).

Getting There

Guide: Pedro Pacheco Dzul, in Bolonchén.

From Uxmal, take Highway 261 heading southeast and then south to Bolonchén.

From Bolonchén return north on Highway 261 to the cutoff for Balché, on the right. This is the same cutoff that goes to Chunhuaymil I. (This is exactly opposite a cutoff on the left that goes to the village of Xculoc.)

Turn right onto the cutoff and right again at the spur road, then park. You walk to the site from there.

Allow 1¼ hours from the time you leave on foot until you return to your vehicle. This will give you the time to walk and climb to the structures, and see them.

Wear boots, and carry a canteen of water for the climb to Structure 6.

Buses go to Bolonchén.

★
CHUNHUAYMIL I

*(choon-wahee-*meel; *derivation: Maya for "Place of the Trunk of the Uayam [Guava] Tree")*

Location:
  West-central Yucatán.
Maps: 2 (p. 77) and 2D (p. 182)

The Site

Chunhuaymil I is a small site, and of its five numbered buildings, only Structure 1 is partly standing. The site is also overgrown, so the one-star rating is a bit generous.

Structure 1 is made up of five rooms— three in a row facing south onto a court, and two abutting the rear, forming an L-shaped section. Each room has a single entrance, and there are no interior connections.

Of the rooms facing south, only the doorway to the central room is intact. There are remains of a simple, rectangular medial molding above the lintel and running along the front wall. In one section, a second rectangular course lies above the first and projects from it. The east and west rooms each had two columns in the doorways originally. The west room is now a pile of rubble, and the front of the east room has fallen. Nicholas Dunning reports that the columns of this room are carved in high relief but poorly preserved, and one is said to be in situ. The other is on the ground in front of the structure. I am afraid I missed the columns.

Dunning also reports that Structure 1 is Early Puuc style (A.D. 670–770) and appears to have been built in two or three stages. He says further that the central capstone of the central room facing south has been removed. He believes that it was probably painted.

Structures 2 and 3 are on the east and west sides of the same court faced by Structure 1. Structure 2 shows Classic Puuc (A.D. 770–1000) stonework in its lower walls, and door columns are found in the rubble of Structure 3.

Across the dirt road from these structures are two mounds, the remains of Structures 4 and 5 that have been mostly destroyed by stone removal.

Recent History

The location of Chunhuaymil I is shown on one of the maps in the *Atlas Arqueológico del Estado de Yucatán.* The site is numbered but is not named in the accompanying text.

Dunning described the site and did a sketch map of it, which was part of his doctoral dissertation (1990). This is the major reference for the site.

Connection

Uxmal to Bolonchén: 33.3 miles by paved road (:43).

From the plaza in Bolonchén: 8.4 miles by paved road (:13), then 5.0 miles by dirt road (:30).

Total from Uxmal to Bolonchén, and then to Chunhuaymil I: 46.7 miles (1:26).

Total from Uxmal to Chunhuaymil I (direct): 29.9 miles (1:00).

Getting There

Guide: Pedro Pacheco Dzul, in Bolonchén.

From Uxmal, take Highway 261 heading southeast and then south to Bolonchén.

From Bolonchén return north on Highway 261 to the cutoff on the right. (This is exactly opposite a cutoff on the left that goes to the village of Xculoc.)

Turn right onto the dirt road, and proceed to Chunhuaymil I. The road is narrow and rather bumpy and actually goes through the site on the way to the village of Chunhuaymil. Although Structure 1 is only about 100 feet to the left of the road, it is almost impossible to see because of the intervening vegetation. Your guide will have to open the trail or cut a new one to reach the structure, which will take a few minutes.

Wear boots, have a wide-angle lens for your camera, and allow 10 minutes to see Chunhuaymil I once you reach it.

There is a cleared area on the south side of the road, between the mounds of Structures 4 and 5, where you can turn your vehicle around.

Buses go to Bolonchén.

★ ★
CHUNHUHUB
(*choon-hoo-*hoob; *derivation: Maya for "Place of the Huhub Tree"*)

Location:
   Northeastern Campeche.
   Maps: 2 (p. 77) and 2D (p. 182)

The Site

Chunhuhub is a very good two-star site and is highly recommended to the serious enthusiast. The two principal structures of the

The Main Palace, west facade, Chunhuhub. Terminal Classic period.

Main Group are easy to reach; they are the Main Palace to the north and the Adjacent Palace to the south. They lie at the rear of a large terrace and are separated by a pile of rubble believed to be the remains of a stairway that led a raised court. Both buildings face west, so the afternoon is the best time for photography. There is a pile of rubble to the west of the structures that offers a good vantage point for photographing the palaces. Even from this distance you will need a wide-angle lens to get both palaces in an overall view.

The Main Palace is about 115 feet long and has six rooms. There are four in a north-south line, each with a doorway facing the terrace, one transverse room on the extreme north end, and one inner room behind the central room. (From the outside, the entrance to the central room is the second doorway from the left as you face the structure.) The structure has been restored, and during this work new lintels were installed to replace those that had fallen in the two middle doorways of the north-south line of rooms. The lower walls on either side of the doorway to the central room are decorated with stepped-fret elements and rows of colonnettes above and below. Beyond this, on each side, are three facade columns. The rest of the lower walls of the Main Palace are plain.

The three-member base molding has a top and a bottom rectangular section, and the middle part has stepped frets alternating with groups of three colonnettes. The medial and cornice moldings are unusual in the number of parts included. There are six in the medial molding and five in the cornice molding; both have rectangular courses and short colonnettes. On the north part of the upper facade, the moldings and upper wall decorations have fallen, except for the lowest course of the medial molding. In the center and south part of the facade, a good deal of decoration is in place.

Above the central room the medial molding was reduced to four parts so that it rose above the doorway, and it projects from the walls more than the adjacent molding. This can best be observed to the south of the doorway to the central room.

Between the moldings in the upper facade are frets, plain and banded split columns, and, originally, anthropomorphic figures carved almost in full round. The figures are no longer in place.

The doorway from the central room to the inner room is more than 6.5 feet wide

solidated. It is about 85 feet long and has three rooms, each with a doorway. The center doorway is wider than the others, and the lower walls of the structure are plain. There is an interesting section of base molding in place between the north and center doorways. It is made up of stepped frets, alternating with groups of three colonnettes, and above there is a running design formed of loops.

Both the medial and cornice moldings are made of five members, and both include rectangular sections and colonnettes, some in groups of three, and others in a continuous row. The upper facade is decorated with stepped frets, banded columns, and panels with projecting tenons. According to H. E. D. Pollock, there were weathered remains of a human figure on the tenon of the panel over the central doorway when he visited the site. He says, "Judging from the tenons still in place, there once were eight such figures." The architecture of both the Main and Adjacent Palaces is Classic Puuc Mosaic style (A.D. 830–1000).

Behind the Main and Adjacent palaces is a raised court that you can reach by climbing the rubble between the two palaces. There are a few remains of fallen architecture, including a partly intact vault, and mounds of rubble that are the fallen remains of other structures. To the southwest of the Adjacent Palace is a large rubble mound with a couple of columns on top.

There are four other groups of structures at Chunhuhub that we have not seen. One is the Temple Group, a large greatly ruined pyramid with fallen structures on the top, and three outlying hilltop groups. These last were called the First, Second, and Third Castillos by Teobert Maler, and locally the Third Castillo was called Xpostan in his time. It is now called Xpostanil.

Reportedly, the Temple Group lies a short distance to the west of the Main Group. The three castillos are from 0.6 mile to 1.2

Three-member molding in the north longitudinal room, at the entrance to the north transverse room, the Main Palace, Chunhuhub. Terminal Classic period.

and is intact with its massive lintel and full-width jambstones. A short flight of three or four steps leads from the outer room to the inner room.

The only access to the north transverse room is from the northernmost, longitudinal room. Above the doorway that enters the transverse room is a three-member rectangular molding. (This is the inside of the north wall of the north longitudinal room.) It is unusual to see this kind of molding on the interior of a room, but there is a similar example in Structure 2 at Xkampon.

At the south end of the Main Palace, set back from the front of the building, is an understair half vault, indicating a stairway to the top of the structure on the south side.

The Adjacent Palace is about 25 feet south of the Main Palace, and it has been con-

The Adjacent Palace (center right) and the Main Palace (left), view from the southwest, Chunhuhub. Terminal Classic period.

miles to the north and northwest of the Main Group. If you wish to see these, your guide will be able to get you there. The most interesting would seem to be the Third Castillo, but getting to any of them would require a good deal of climbing.

Recent History

In 1843 John Lloyd Stephens was the first to report Chunhuhub. Three illustrations by his artist companion, Frederick Catherwood, were included. These depicted the Main Palace, a detail of the doorway to the central room of this structure, and the Adjacent Palace. Stephens found the doorway to the central room of the Main Palace to be "the largest and most imposing we had seen in the country." He mentions other structures in the area, and they may be the ones called the Castillos and the Temple Group by Maler.

Pollock's description of the architecture was published in 1980, the same year that Edward Kurjack cleared some of the structures at Chunhuhub as part of the work to produce an atlas of the archaeological sites in Campeche.

In 1989 the site was mapped and the structures recorded in detail. This work was conducted by the French Center of Mexican and Central American Studies, and the French National Center of Scientific Research, Unit 312, under the direction of Pierre Becquelin. This was part of the fourth and final season of field work in the Xculoc area. In the earlier seasons other nearby sites were studied. All of the work was undertaken with the collaboration of the Campeche Regional Center of INAH.

Connection

Uxmal to Chunhuhub: 24.9 miles by paved road (:30), 6.7 miles by rock road (:30), then 300 yards by dirt road (:03).

Total from Uxmal to Chunhuhub: 31.8 miles (1:03).

Getting There

From Uxmal head southeast and then south on Highway 261 to the cutoff for Chunhuhub (also the cutoff for Rancho Yaxché and Xculoc village). It is sometimes marked with a sign for Xculoc, and sometimes with a handmade sign for Yaxché that is not easy to spot. A good landmark is a small abandoned building just before the cutoff, a few feet to the right of the highway.

Turn right on the rock road, go to the dirt cutoff, and turn left. The dirt road is no more than a wide path through cornfields, and from this junction you cannot see the ruins, as they are hidden by trees. If you cannot spot the dirt road, continue along the rock road for about 0.5 mile, stop and turn around. Look to the right, and you will be able to see the structure. This will help you find the dirt road to them when you drive back.

Drive the dirt road slowly, and watch out for one high limestone outcrop near the end. Stop before the outcrop and walk in the rest of the way if you do not have a high-clearance vehicle.

If you would prefer to have a guide with you, go first to Bolonchén and find Pedro Pacheco Dzul. This is 8.4 miles (:13) along Highway 261, past the rock cutoff for

Chunhuhub, so you will have to add 16.8 miles by paved road (:26) to the total given above.

If you are going to Chunhuhub in the afternoon, there is another option. Stay on the rock road and go on to Xculoc village. This is 3.3 miles (:13) past the dirt cutoff for the site. Ask for Bonifacio Canul, the caretaker of Chunhuhub. If he is there, he will be happy to take you to the site. If he is not, one of the other villagers will probably be able to get you there. If you choose this option, add 6.6 miles by rock road (:26) to the total given above. Bonifacio is generally at Chunhuhub in the morning.

Wear boots and a sun hat, and allow 1 hour to see the two palaces. There is no food or drink at the site.

Buses go to Bolonchén but do not run along the rock road to Chunhuhub. The closest you could get by bus would be the junction of the rock road and Highway 261.

★
XCOCHKAX

(shkohch-kahsh; derivation: Maya for "wild ix-koch," wild castor bean)

Location:
   Northeastern Campeche.
Maps: 2 (p. 77) and 2D (p. 182)

The Site

The Main Group at Xcochkax has structures on five levels, on the sides and top of a hill. This small site also includes other outlying buildings to the north, northwest, and east. Depend on your guide to get you around.

Much of the architecture at Xcochkax is greatly fallen, but some details can still be seen. On the lowest level of the Main Group are fragmentary remains of a lower wall with three short columns. This building is Classic Puuc Colonnette style (A.D. 770–830). Higher up the hill is a partly ruined, L-shaped structure. There are glyph-carved panels lying

around that once formed a decoration surrounding one of the doorways. At one time a glyph-carved lintel was in place over one of the doorways as well. This structure is Early Puuc style (670–770).

On top of the hill are some badly fallen buildings, but of more interest here are some carved figures that were once jambstones or columns of one or more of the buildings. There are other carved and decorated stones, including a lintel, and a panel of five carved glyphs.

Recent History

In 1980 H. E. D. Pollock reported on the architecture at Xcochkax from data he had collected many years before. Tatiana Proskouriakoff mentions one of the carved columns in her 1950 study of Classic Maya sculpture and lists it as "Late Yucatán, variant?" She considered the high-relief column to be of a non-Classic type.

In 1986, during the first field season of the Xculoc (Campeche, Mexico) Project, the mapping of Xcochkax was started, and the architecture was studied in detail. A number of previously unreported buildings were discovered, and the site proved to be somewhat larger than originally thought. Ceramic studies were also undertaken, and of the identified fragments, 99 percent dated to the Terminal Classic period, and only 1 percent to an earlier period.

This work was undertaken by Unit 312 of the French National Center of Scientific Research and the French Center of Mexican and Central American Studies, under the direction of Pierre Becquelin and Dominique Michelet, and with the collaboration of the Campeche Regional Center of INAH. Work began in 1986, and preliminary reports were issued in 1987 and 1988.

Connection

Uxmal to Bolonchén: 33.3 miles by paved road (:43).

From the plaza in Bolonchén:

Glyph-carved panel from the Main Group, Xcochkax. Late or Terminal Classic period.

8.4 miles by paved road (:13), 8.6 miles by rock road (:39), 0.2 mile by dirt road (:02), then about 0.5 mile by foot trail (:15).

Total from Uxmal to Bolonchén, and then to Xcochkax: 51.0 miles (1:52).

Total from Uxmal to Xcochkax (direct): 34.2 miles (1:26).

Getting There

Guides: Pedro Pacheco Dzul, in Bolonchén, or Bonifacio Canul, at Chunhuhub or in Xculoc village (see below).

From Uxmal take Highway 261 heading southeast and then south to Bolonchén.

From Bolonchén return north on High-

way 261 to the cutoff for Xculoc village (see "Chunhuhub" for landmarks). Turn left onto the rock road and continue to the dirt cutoff for Xcochkax (on the right). Drive in the short distance and park, then continue to the site on foot.

If you go to Xculoc village to get Bonifacio as a guide, add 2.8 miles of rock road (:08) to the *direct* total from Uxmal. Wear boots and allow 50 minutes to see Xcochkax once you arrive.

Buses go to Bolonchén but do not travel the rock road to Xcochkax.

★
ALMUCHIL
*(ahl-moo-*chel; *derivation: Maya for "Place of the Young Toads")*

> **Location:**
> Northeastern Campeche.
> **Maps:** 2 (p. 77) and 2D (p. 182)

The Site

Almuchil is a small site, and the best-preserved building is Structure 3, also called the Ball Palace. This is the only structure at Almuchil that we have visited. Five other structures at the site are partly or greatly fallen, and they are reported to be 200 to 250 yards to the northwest and southwest of Structure 3. There are also some outlying hilltop buildings.

Structure 3 was originally two stories, but the upper rooms have totally collapsed. The structure has four rooms on the first story, and three of these, in a north-south line, are intact. The structure faces west, and behind it to the east is a platform that once supported the second story. Teobert Maler believed that there was once a stairway on the east side.

The lower walls of Structure 3 are plain, and some of the facing stones have fallen. Those that remain are finely cut, faced, and fitted. The interior masonry is cruder. There are plain but well-cut lintels above the doorways, as well as full-width jambstones. The medial and cornice moldings are each made of three rectangular parts.

The upper wall zone is made up of simple but varied and unusual decorations. Above the north doorway (left as you face the structure) there are three spheres, or balls of stone, arranged vertically, followed by six split columns. The use of stone spheres is rare in Puuc architecture, but other examples are found at the Castillo of Chacbolay and on Structure 2 at Chuncatzim I. The arrangement of spheres and columns is repeated three more times across the front of Structure 3 and ends above the center doorway. Beyond this some of the upper wall zone has fallen, but on the south part of the facade, continuing to the end of the south room, there is a different motif.

In this area there are groups of three split columns, separated by plain areas that are bordered with dentate elements arranged vertically. Maler believed the plain areas may once have been decorated with sculpture, but there do not seem to be remains of tenons in these areas.

On the inside of the south room (right as you face the structure) are the remains of a column of small, painted glyphs. They are on the north (left) cross wall near the top.

Structure 3 at Almuchil is Classic Puuc Colonnette style (A.D. 770–830).

Recent History

Maler visited Almuchil in 1887 and published some of his findings in 1902. More information is contained in *Península Yucatán,* volume 2.

The site is mentioned in works published in Mexico in the 1940s and 1950s, and H. E. D. Pollock described six structures at Almuchil in 1980. In an analysis of Puuc architecture, George F. Andrews lists Structure 2 as Early Puuc style (A.D. 670–770), and Structures 1, 4, and 6, in addition to Structure 3, as Classic Puuc Colonnette style. There has been no restoration at Almuchil.

Connection

Uxmal to Almuchil: 24.9 miles by paved road (:30), 10.0 miles by rock road (:43), 3.5 miles by rough rock road (:40).

Total from Uxmal to Almuchil: 38.4 miles (1:53).

Getting There

Guide: Bonifacio Canul, at Chunhuhub or in Xculoc Village.

Structure 3 (the Ball Palace), west facade, Almuchil. Late Classic period.

From Uxmal take Highway 261 heading southeast and then south to the cutoff for Xculoc village. See "Chunhuhub" for landmarks. Turn right and go to Xculoc village.

From the plaza at Xculoc village take the rock road heading left. This is a wretchedly bumpy road that goes over groups of limestone outcrops and hills. You will need a high-clearance vehicle, and four-wheel drive would be useful. The road *must* be driven slowly, or you will certainly damage your vehicle. As you near the site, there are large stones hidden by weeds; be especially careful in this area. Having your own vehicle is the only recommended way to reach Almuchil.

Since some clearing may have to be done, allow 45 minutes to see and photograph Structure 3—more time if you plan to try to see some of the other structures. Try to see Structure 3 in the afternoon when the light hits the main facade. Have a wide-angle lens for your camera, and wear boots.

★
MIRAMAR

(mee-rah-mahr; derivation: Spanish for "Look at the Sea."
Miramar is the name of a nearby hacienda)

Location:

Northeastern Campeche.

Maps: 2 (p. 77) and 2D (p. 182)

The Site

Miramar is a small to medium size site with two structures that can be visited. It also has some unique features, one of which is the

Corner Chac mask, Miramar. Terminal Classic period.

ward, and above them and in between the eyebrows of the mask is a stone that is incised with a curved chevronlike design. There are many carved stones lying around in front of the structure, and these were originally parts of the masks.

A short walk in a northerly direction will get you to the next structure. This one is greatly ruined, though an interior doorway with an intact lintel can be seen.

Recent History

We were told that Miramar was known to people in the area for some time but that it was reported to the authorities in Campeche only in 1979, by Pedro Pacheco Dzul. Andrews visited the site in 1984 and mentions it briefly in an article published in 1985. The site is also mentioned in articles by Andrews, Paul Gendrop, and others in 1987, but no specific architectural style or date is given for the buildings.

decoration on the main structure. This makes Miramar a decidedly good one-star site—I was really tempted to give it two stars.

The main structure faces north and originally had two sets of stacked Chac masks, one set each on the northeast and northwest corners. One set has been moved to the Campeche Museum. These masks projected in front of the facade of the east and west wings of the structure; according to George F. Andrews, the projection is about five feet. He further says, "The two sets of masks are separated by a long passageway at right angles to the main facade which does not appear to have been vaulted. This is also a unique architectural feature."

The corner masks are constructed in the usual mosaic style, but they are different from any I have seen. You first notice the teeth, which seem clenched and almost humanlike. The snouts of the masks curl down-

Connection

Uxmal to Bolonchén: 33.3 miles by paved road (:43).

From the plaza in Bolonchén: 5.2 miles by paved road (:08), then 2.5 miles by fair dirt road (:20).

Total from Uxmal to Bolonchén, and then to Miramar: 41.0 miles (1:11).

Total from Uxmal to Miramar (direct): 30.6 miles (:55).

Getting There

Guide: Pedro Pacheco Dzul, in Bolonchén. Locally Miramar is also sometimes called Dios Chac.

From Uxmal take Highway 261 heading southeast and then south to Bolonchén. From Bolonchén return north on Highway 261 to the cutoff for Hacienda Miramar, which is on the left. Drive in on the dirt road to the hacienda. Your guide should ask permission there for you to visit the site, as it is on hacienda lands.

From the hacienda, turn right onto another dirt road and continue to the parking area. From there it is a few minutes on foot, with a short climb, to the main structure.

The route of the dirt road from the hacienda to the site (and the location of the site itself) as shown on Map 2D, is approximate.

Wear boots, have a wide-angle lens for your camera, and allow 40 minutes to see the two structures at Miramar.

Buses go to Bolonchén.

ITZIMTÉ

(eet-seem-teh; derivation: Maya name for a plant used to flavor posole, a beverage of ground maize and water)

Location:
Northeastern Campeche.
Maps: 2 (p. 77) and 2D (p. 182)

The Site

Itzimté is a fairly large site, but unfortunately most of its structures are greatly ruined. This is partly due to removal of the cut-stone facing (by people living in the area), which has been going on for over a century. Nevertheless, there are three spots that are worth a look.

You first climb to Structure 1, a large building that bounds the south side of a raised plaza. This structure originally rose in three levels and had stairways on both the north and south sides. It is noteworthy for a well-preserved room with an intact vault under the north stairway. Northeast of Structure 1 is Structure 4, only one wall of which is standing. Just below the spring line of the vault are remnants of a painted band of hieroglyphs.

From here you climb back down to the road and proceed east, where another uphill trail will get you to Structure 63. This structure, which faces west, is the largest at the site and the tallest, with a maximum height of 71 feet. The front of the structure is formed of artificial terraces, while the back is part of a natural hill. A stairway (in ruin) leads up the west side to a platform that supports a row of ten rooms (mostly collapsed),

and above this is a pyramidal base that supports the remains of the topmost structure.

Many other structures have been mapped at Itzimté, and as you wander around, you will see the remains of some of them looming above the surrounding fields.

There is a dispirited air about the site because of its near destruction, and it would take a very fertile imagination to picture it in its prime.

Recent History

In 1842 when John Lloyd Stephens visited Itzimté, he was the first person to record the site; his brief description was published in 1843. At the time of his visit many cut stones had already been removed from the structures, and even though the site had been cleared so that he could study it, he commented, "It was melancholy that when so much had been done for us, there was so little for us to do." He published no illustrations of the site.

Teobert Maler visited Itzimté in 1887, and in 1902 he reported his findings, which included one photograph. Unfortunately, the structure that he showed, with a well-preserved Chac mask above the doorway, has since collapsed. This structure was Classic Puuc Mosaic style (A.D. 830–1000), and at least one Early Puuc–style structure (670–770) has been reported at Itzimté.

Although mention of the site was made in some later publications, it was only in 1973 that the existence of inscribed stelae and a lintel was ascertained. These were recorded by Eric von Euw that year and beautifully presented in a 1977 publication. Some of the stelae have been restored and are in the Stelae Gallery in Campeche City.

Von Euw calls the site Itzimté-Bolonchén to distinguish it from a site in Guatemala called Itsimté, which also has inscribed monuments. The latter is generally spelled with an "s," however, and is sometimes called Itsimté-Sacluk.

Although there has been no extensive excavation at the site, H. E. D. Pollock considers Itzimté "essentially a Puuc city." There has been no consolidation of the structures.

Connection

Uxmal to Bolonchén: 33.3 miles by paved road (:43).

From the plaza in Bolonchén: 1.5 miles by paved road (:02), 0.2 mile by dirt road (:02), then a few hundnred feet by foot trail (:03).

Total from Uxmal to Bolonchén and then to Itzimté: 35.0 miles (:50).

Total from Uxmal to Itzimté (direct): 32.0 miles (:46).

Getting There

Guide: Pedro Pacheco Dzul, in Bolonchén.

From Uxmal take Highway 261 heading southeast and then south to Bolonchén. From Bolonchén return north on Highway 261 to the cutoff for Itzimté (unmarked), and turn right onto the dirt road. Drive in the short distance, park, and continue on foot to Structure 1.

Wear boots, and have fast film and a wide-angle lens for your camera. Allow 1½ hours to see Itzimté.

Buses go to Bolonchén, and cold drinks are available there.

★ ★
SANTA ROSA XTAMPAK

(sahn-tah roh-sah shtahm-pahk; derivation: Santa Rosa is Spanish for "Saint Rose," the name of a nearby hacienda; Xtampak is Maya for "In Front of the Wall" or "Wall in Sight")

Location:
  Northeastern Campeche.
  Maps: 2 (p. 77) and 2D (p. 182)

The Site

Santa Rosa Xtampak is a very good two-star site, and although it is on the northern edge of the Chenes region, it is considered by many to be its capital city. It is a large site with a core area that is "nearly as large as the entire group of major structures at Uxmal," according to George F. Andrews. There is a fair amount of standing architecture at Santa Rosa Xtampak, but unhappily, a great deal has fallen.

Sixty-seven chultunes for water storage were carved into the limestone bedrock at the site, and these were recorded by Evan I. DeBloois. Based on their maximum capacity, it has been calculated that they could have supported a population of 12,000. Andrews believes that a figure of 8,000 to 10,000 "seems fairly reasonable at the height of the Classic period." Another indication of the importance of Santa Rosa Xtampak is that more hieroglyphic inscriptionos have been recorded at the site than at any other in the Chenes region.

The trails at the site are kept cleared, and getting around is not too difficult. Unfortunately for the photographer, many trees and other vegetation remain, and this obscures some of the structures—and often you cannot back off far enough from a building to get a definitive photo. A wide-angle lens

Standing room on the north part of the rear (west side) of the first level of the Palace, Santa Rosa Xtampak. Late Classic period.

and fast film will improve your chances a little.

As you walk to the site, the foot trail passes a fallen building and, nearby, a piece of architectural sculpture in the form of a human torso, said to have come from the building. A short distance later the trail enters the site core at the rear (west side) of the Palace, the largest and finest Chenes structure known. The Palace is 146 feet long and 79 feet wide at ground level, and about 50 feet tall. It rises in three stories and contains 41 rooms, some of which have fallen.

On the west side you can see the remains of multiple rooms, some with partly collapsed vaults. On the first story, the end rooms on the left (north) are the best pre-served, with a standing exterior wall. There are tenons in the upper wall zone, just above the medial molding, that no doubt once supported sculptural decorations.

There are two interior stairways in the west side that can be reached only from adjacent exterior rooms. The more northerly stairway is completely intact, and you can climb it to the second and third stories. The southern stairway is a mirror image but is not as well preserved. These stairways offer the only currently visible access to the second story, according to Andrews. The stairways change direction ten times on the way up to the third story.

The west side of the third story of the Palace is well preserved, with doorways leading to the interior stairways. The remainder of the west side of this story is a solid wall that has five recessed panels as decoration. Recessed panels are also reported from some structures in the Río Bec region.

On the south side of the Palace most of the outside parts of the vaults of a long central room have collapsed, but part of the southwest corner of the structure is intact, and next to it is a standing doorjamb with a three-member upper molding as decoration. The interior back wall of the long central room has two doorways to interior rooms. The wall between the doorways was once decorated with a panel carved with figures, but this, as well as a corresponding panel in the north part of the Palace, was looted at least by 1969. A carved geometric design remains in place above the area where the panel with the figures was once installed. To the left of the left (west) doorway is a plain split column in the wall. It is one of three that originally formed a panel, and the center column was carved. The carved column was also looted before 1969.

The most interesting feature of the east side (front) of the Palace is two walls, or pylons, that form the entry to a small court on the third story. They are at the top of the now-fallen monumental stairway and are decorated with stone and stucco. The motif is the typical monster-mouth doorway used in Chenes architecture, and the design is similar to that on the Building with the Serpent Mouth Facade at the site. The decorations are fairly well preserved and can be best photographed with a telephoto lens.

In 1977 David F. Potter said, commenting on the monster-mouth facade design, "This motif, when complete, typically extends to include the upper wall zone above the doorway," meaning that originally the two walls would have been joined at the top, forming a complete doorway. He believes this to be the case, and this also seems to be indicated on Teobert Maler's elevation drawing of the Palace. Restoration drawings by Paul Gendrop and Alejandro Villalobos also show it as such.

The first-story rooms adjacent to the stairway are partly collapsed, but doorways to interior rooms are still standing, with their wooden lintels intact. On the wall that forms the north side of the stairway are remains of a few facing stones, and enough is left to show that this area was banded. On the second level of the east side there were structures with a single room on the north and south corners; they are detached from the other rooms on that level. Some remains of the structure on the south are still standing.

The best-preserved parts of the north side of the Palace are the first-story rooms on the northwest corner and the center rooms on the second story.

In 1843 John Lloyd Stephens described the Palace as "the grandest structure that now rears its ruined head in the forests of Yucatán." More than a hundred years later, Andrews had this to say, "In virtually every respect, the three story palace is a unique building and it has no counterpart anywhere in the Chenes region." From the details of construction he further states that the Palace "appears to have been conceived at the outset as a three story structure," unlike many other multilevel Maya buildings. It is true, however, that some secondary construction was found, but most authorities agree with Andrews on this point.

About 50 yards northeast of the Palace is the Building with the Serpent Mouth Facade, which faces south. The room that supports this facade projects in front of those on either side and is mostly intact. Only small parts of the adjacent rooms are standing, and the rest of the structure has collapsed. A good deal of the facade decoration has fallen, but enough remains for it to be easily identified—even today—as a typical Chenes monster-mouth doorway. Behind this room are rubble remains believed to have been a stairway to the roof of the structure.

A few feet to the southeast are the remains of two structures with standing back walls only a yard apart. The building on the west is composed of three rooms running north-south and originally had a doorway to each room on the west side. This side of the building is now fallen, but the back of the vaults and parts of the cross walls are standing. Maler called this structure the Red House, but very little of the red paint he observed remains.

The south wall, or pylon, of the third level of the Palace, east side, Santa Rosa Xtampak. Late Classic period.

Building with the Serpent Mouth Facade, south side, Santa Rosa Xtampak. Late Classic period.

The adjacent building is L-shaped and also has three rooms. The back wall and one cross wall are all that remain.

About 40 yards to the east is the Cuartel, an assemblage of structures surrounding a courtyard. The North, West, and South Ranges are connected at the corners, and the three form a U. The East Range is a separate structure, and access to the courtyard is at the northeast and southeast corners. (At one time the name Cuartel applied only to the North Range of this complex, but now it generally includes the entire group.)

As you approach the Cuartel, you come first to the outside of the West Range, with part of its wall intact. You then head north and turn right and follow the back of the North Range, the best preserved of the build-ings in this group. Both the West and North ranges have large stairways—now mostly fallen—in the center, which go from the outside to the top and continue to the inside of the courtyard. It has not been determined whether the rubble at the top of the stair-ways indicates the existence of rooms or whether it was only a platform. There are no doorways on the outside of the West or North ranges; all the rooms faced inward toward the courtyard.

The back of the North Range is deco-rated with a three-member base molding that has groups of three colonnettes in the mid-dle member, separated by plain sections. Above the colonnettes in the base molding (in the lower wall of the structure) are two long inset columns. Remains of the medial

East wing of the North Range of the Cuartel, south facade, Santa Rosa Xtampak. Late Classic period.

molding, upper wall zone, and cornice molding are still in place.

You now enter the courtyard of the Cuartel at the northeast corner. The inside of the North Range is well preserved and has some intact decorations. There are three rooms in a line on each side of the stairway of the North Range, and while part of each end room has fallen, the rest is intact. The center room of each wing is set back from the adjacent rooms, and this three-part facade is typical of Chenes architecture. Not so typical is the broken medial molding that rises above the center doorway of the East Wing. It is unusual to find this style of molding in this area, as it is almost exclusively found in the Puuc region in some of the early architecture. The instance at Santa Rosa Xtampak is believed to postdate the Early Puuc–style examples (A.D. 670–770). So, while Chenes-style architecture predominates at Santa Rosa Xtampak, influences from the Puuc and Río Bec regions are also evident.

On each side of the center doorways, on each wing of the North Range, are panels of three stacked masks in frontal view, a motif seldom found on Chenes-style buildings but used on a number of Río Bec–style structures. The masks on the left (west side) of the doorway of the East Wing are the best preserved.

Other facade decorations include corner columns in the lower walls at the junction of the rooms and inset split columns as well. There are also groups of colonnettes in the medial and cornice moldings. Projecting stones above the medial molding and in the cornice molding probably once supported sculptural decorations.

You leave the Cuartel at the southeast corner of the courtyard and head south to the Southeast Quadrangle, about 150 yards away. You pass rubble mounds of fallen architecture along the way.

The Southeast Quadrangle is made up of four ranges of rooms surrounding a courtyard that you enter at the northwest corner. The West Range is a row of single rooms, and the north and south ends of it are well preserved. In the center of this range is an opening to the outside that is believed to be a portal vault. The South Range is mostly collapsed, but it had a double row of rooms. From the amount of rubble, it is believed that there may have been a second story over at least some of the rooms of the lower story.

At the south end of the East Range of the Southeast Quadrangle is a narrow vaulted passageway that leads to the outside of the courtyard. In the north part of the East Range there is a faintly painted capstone and a fragment of painted stucco just above the spring line of the vault.

The North Range of the Southeast Quadrangle is poorly preserved, but it is a double row of rooms, and there is a pyramidal mound of rubble at the center that may be the remains of a stairway and a second-story structure. In the center of the courtyard of the Southeast Quadrangle is a small platform and, nearby, a plain cylindrical stone column that once may have stood upon it.

As you wind your way back to the Palace, about 270 yards to the northwest, you pass the base of the Central Pyramid—at 50 feet high it is the tallest of four pyramids at Santa Rosa Xtampak. The Central Pyramid is actually "a series of three overlapping pyramids with flat summits, the central one being the highest," according to Richard B. Stamps. The Central Pyramid is today a rubble mound, but its size can still be appreciated.

Eight stelae were found at Santa Rosa Xtampak, and they were all located on the east side of the South Plaza, which is immediately south of the Central Pyramid. All of them had been removed by 1969.

Recent History

In 1843 Stephens was the first to report Santa Rosa Xtampak, and his text was accompanied by engravings of the rear of the Palace and the two carved panels he found on the first level. The engravings were produced by Frederick Catherwood, and a plan of the first floor of the Palace was also included. Stephens mentioned the "vestiges of six buildings," but only the Palace is illustrated. From his description, however, it is evident that one of the other buildings he saw was the Cuartel.

Maler visited Santa Rosa Xtampak in 1891 and reported the site in 1902. His work included the Palace and some of the other structures. More information is found in *Península Yucatán,* volume 2.

In 1936 H. E. D. Pollock investigated the site for the Carnegie Institution of Washington (CIW), along with Henry B. Roberts, who was conducting a ceramic survey. It was they who discovered the eight stelae, seven of which were analyzed by Tatiana Proskouriakoff in 1950. Pollock's report, published in 1970, covers both the architecture and brief notes on the stelae. He also published a photograph of the one stela not included in Proskouriakoff's work and a site plan drawn earlier by George W. Brainerd, Lawrence Roys, and Karl Ruppert, who, in 1949, also conducted studies for CIW.

Brainerd's final ceramic study was not published before his untimely death, but in an article in 1958 he mentioned the presence of Middle and Late Preclassic wares as well as Late Classic specimens.

In 1945 Alberto Ruz Lhuiller reported on several Chenes sites, including Santa Rosa Xtampak.

Ray T. Matheny of the Brigham Young University–New World Archaeological Foundation (BYU-NWAF) visited Santa Rosa Xtampak as part of the foundation's Campeche Project. This led to a more thorough study of the site in 1969 by Stamps and DeBloois. Stamps recorded the architecture in detail during the ten weeks he spent at the site, and this formed the basis for his master of arts thesis for BYU in 1970. A brief ceramic analysis was included, and some of the collection was gathered by DeBloois in and around the chultunes at the site.

The limited ceramic sampling indicates that Santa Rosa Xtampak was extensively occupied during the Late Preclassic period and again in the Late Classic. It seems to have been unoccupied during the Early Classic, and there is no evidence that it remained occupied into the Postclassic period. Two possible Middle Preclassic sherds were found, but Stamps believed that more excavation was needed to show whether the site was truly occupied at that time as Brainerd suggested.

DeBloois also surveyed the west end of

the site and discovered additional structures. He also found a *sacbé* that led from the northwest corner of the Palace to a group of buildings to the west.

By the time Stamps and DeBloois reached Santa Rosa Xtampak, all of the stelae (except for a few small fragments), the carved panels and columns of the Palace, and most of the painted capstones had been looted.

In 1987 Andrews reported on Santa Rosa Xtampak, and his article included a detailed analysis of much of the standing architecture at the site. He also made corrections to the plans of some of the buildings previously reported. He dates the structures to A.D. 650–850, which agrees well with the probable dates of the stelae (751–889). Stamps suggests a slightly longer time span for the architecture (600–900).

In a 1989 article Karl Herbert Mayer described a carved but eroded altar at Santa Rosa Xtampak, which he believes is a "stela" that was briefly reported earlier by Stamps and DeBloois. This altar bears the longest hieroglyphic inscription not only at Santa Rosa Xtampak but also in the entire Chenes region. Mayer further reports that one of the stelae removed from the site is in the National Museum of Anthropology and History in Mexico City, while two others are in private collections.

Restoration of the most critical sections of the Palace began in November 1991, and additional work was undertaken there and at other structures in 1992. Another project was the mapping of 3.5 square miles of the site by the Center of Historic and Social Investigations of the Free University of the Southeast (Campeche), in collaboration with INAH, with funds provided by the Foundation for Latin American Anthropological Research. Rogerio Cohouh Muõz was in charge of the topographical work, and Abel Morales Llópez drew in the architectural and cultural features.

Connection

Uxmal to Santa Rosa Xtampak: 39.0 miles by paved road (:51), 19.7 miles by fair rock road (1:15), then a couple of hundred yards by foot trail (:10).

Total from Uxmal to Santa Rosa Xtampak: 58.7 miles (2:16).

Getting There

From Uxmal head southeast and then south on Highway 261 to Bolonchén, and continue south to the cutoff for Santa Rosa Xtampak. The cutoff—near but before Kilometer 79— is marked with a pyramid sign that indicates it is 32 kilometers to the site (although which site is not stated). Turn left at the cutoff, onto the rock road, and go 18.8 miles to the caretaker's house (on the right). You should stop and tell the caretake that you are going to the site, even if you have a local guide with you (see below). The caretake will either come with you or bicycle over and meet you there; you will definitely need someone to show you around the site.

There is a fork in the road 0.3 mile after you leave his house. Take the right branch and go another 0.6 mile to the dead end which is the parking area. This is at the base of the low hill on which Santa Rosa Xtampak is situated. The climb to the site is steepest at the beginning and gentler afterward, but not too difficult in any case.

There are two caretakers for Santa Rosa Xtampak who generally alternate duties. The one we met was Miguel Arcángel González Pacheco, who was very pleasant, enthusiastic, and helpful, and who introduced himself as Mike. The other is Fidel Contún, who no doubt would be equally agreeable. You will be asked by whichever one you meet to sign a small registration book that they carry; as you can imagine, you will not see a lot of entries.

While it is possible to drive to Santa Rosa Xtampak without a local guide, you might feel more comfortable having someone along. In that case contact Pedro Pacheco Dzul, in Bolonchén, and if possible make arrangements ahead of time.

Having your own vehicle is the only recommended way to reach the site. There is no food or drink available. Carry a canteen of water when you climb to the site, and allow 3 hours for a visit.

COLOR PLATES

Stacked, corner masks on Structure I, Xlapak. Terminal Classic period.

Unless otherwise noted, color photographs by the author.

Temple of the Seven Dolls, west side, Dzibilchaltún. Early part of the Late Classic period.

El Castillo, from the northwest, Chichén Itzá. Early Postclassic period.

The Governor's Palace, from the northeast, Uxmal. Terminal Classic period.

Structure 1 of Group A, south facade, Sacbé. Terminal Classic period.

Codz-Poop, west facade, Kabáh. Terminal Classic period.

Structure 5, east facade, Sabacché. Terminal Classic period.

The Palace, west part of the south façade, Sayil. Late and Terminal Classic periods.

West face of the Labná Arch, Labná, Terminal Classic period

Edifice 1, west part of the south facade, Chacmultún Group, Chacmultún. Terminal Classic period.

Structure 5 of Group 1, detail of the east facade, Kiuic. Late Classic period.

West facade of the Main Palace, Chunhuhub. Terminal Classic period.

The center room of the south facade, Principal Palace (Structure 2), Hochob. Late Classic period.

The Temple of Five Stories, west side, Edzna. Late Classic period.

Jaguar panel on the structure with the bas-relief stucco facade, Balamku. Classic period.

The west facade of Structure III, Calakmul. Classic period.

Central part of the west facade, Structure II, Chicanná. Late Classic period.

Structure I, from the southeast, Becan. Late Classic period.

Structure I of Group B, east side, Río Bec. Late Classic period.

Frontal mask panel on Structure I of Group I, Xpuhil. Late Classic period.

Structure II, south facade, Hormiguero. Late Classic period.

Mask on the Pyramid of the Masks (Structure I), Kohunlich. This mask is on the lowest level, south of the stairway. Early Classic period. Photograph by Jerry Kelly.

Temple of the Frescoes (Structure 16), from the northwest, Tulum. Late Postclassic period.

Nonah (Structure 32-a), San Gervasio. Late Postclassic period.

SECTION 3

• • • •

EAST-CENTRAL CAMPECHE

The north facade of the second-story temple, Structure 1, El Tabasqueño. Late Classic period.

GENERAL INFORMATION FOR SECTION 3

Point of Reference:
Hopelchén, Campeche.
Maps: 3 and 3A

Mileages given to the sites in this section are from the Main Plaza in Hopelchén (and the junction for the road to Dzibalchén).

The only hotel in this area is the modest Los Arcos, in Hopelchén, which is sometimes filled. If you want to stay there and are coming through Hopelchén early in the day, it would be prudent to get a room (and pay for it), go on to the ruins, and return later. There are a couple of small restaurants in Hopelchén and an icehouse on the plaza.

If you would prefer better accommodations when you visit the ruins in this area, it would be best to plan an overnight stop at Uxmal (1:08 to the north) or Campeche, (1:23 to the west). These are the only nearby stopovers. See Section 2 for the Uxmal area and Section 4 for the Campeche area, and their related maps.

You can reach Hopelchén by bus and can get another to Dzibalchén, but the best way to visit sites in the area is in your own vehicle. The closest car rentals are in Campeche.

From the outskirts of Dzibalchén there is a road that goes 86.0 miles to Xpuhil. Though passable for standard vehicles, it is a rather long (about 4 hours) and somewhat bumpy ride, and as you would expect, there are no accommodations, food, drink, or gas along this route. The first 12.4 miles of this road (out of Dzibalchén) are paved, as are the last 6.1 miles (on the Xpuhil end); the 67.5 miles in the middle are rock.

GAS STATIONS: There is a gas station in Hopelchén, but it is sometimes out of gas. The nearest station to Hopelchén is in Campeche City.

GUIDES: Hortensio Camal Ku, the caretaker of Hochob. He lives in the village of Chencoh, and residents can point out his house. Since you have to pass through Chencoh on your way to Hochob, look for him in Chencoh first. If he is not in there, you can probably find out if he is at Hochob; if so, look for him there.

Another guide is José Williams, a resident of Dzibalchén. His house is right on the highway, on the east end of Dzibalchén, just before the cutoff for Kancabchén and Xpuhil. When you drive from the Dzibalchén Plaza to the cutoff, his house is on the right, and there is a sign (in English) indicating that he can get you to sites in the area. Although we have never gone on a trip with José, we have met him, and he seemed affable and well informed.

If you do not have your own vehicle, he can get you to Hochob by bicycle (5.6 miles by the old dirt road) or can arrange to rent a truck to get you there, to Dziblinocac, or to El Tabasqueño. Discuss the price of a trip and the cost of vehicle rental beforehand.

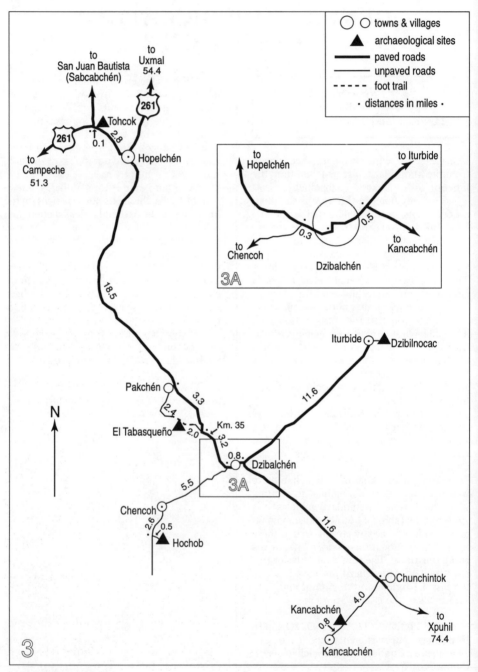

towns & villages
▲ **archaeological sites**
paved roads
unpaved roads
foot trail
· distances in miles ·

to
San Juan Bautista
(Sabcabchén)

to
Uxmal
54.4

261

▲ Tohcok

261
0.1
2.8

to
Campeche
51.3

○ Hopelchén

to
Hopelchén

to Iturbide

0.3

to
Chencoh

0.5

to
Kancabchén

Dzibalchén

3A

18.5

Iturbide ○ ▲ Dzibilnocac

Pakchén ○

3.3

11.6

2.4

El Tabasqueño ▲

2.0

Km. 35

3.2

N

0.8

○ Dzibalchén

3A

5.5

11.6

Chencoh ○

2.6

0.5

▲ Hochob

○ Chunchintok

4.0

Kancabchén ▲

0.8

to
Xpuhil
74.4

Kancabchén

3

East-central Campeche

★
TOHCOK
(TOHKOK)

(toh-kohk; derivation: "toh" is Maya for "motmot";
"kok" is Maya for "nightingale")

Location:
East-central Campeche.
Map: 3 (p. 210)

The Site

Part of one of the structures at Tohcok has been cleared, and it is just a few feet off Highway 261 (north side), from which it is easily visible. The cleared part of the building has remains of several vaulted rooms, and

Columned and vaulted structure alongside the highway, from the southeast, Tohcok. Late Classic period.

there is a doorway with two round columns with rectangular capitals on the east side.

The lower rooms on the west side were filled after the original construction, and an upper level was added, though little of that remains today. Beyond the cleared portion, more rooms extend to the north and then turn to the east.

Sometimes another structure is visible nearby, but sometimes it is overgrown. It is 0.2 mile east of the cleared structure, also on the north side of the highway, but farther from it. From the road it appeared to be on top of a small hill or pyramidal platform. Because of its proximity to the cleared structure, it seems reasonable to assume that it is a part of the same site.

Recent History

Tohcok is shown on a 1940 map compiled by Tulane University. H. E. D. Pollock noted that the site is incorrectly placed north of Hopelchén, rather than west, on this map. In a 1951 work published by the Carnegie Institution of Washington, Edwin M. Shook and Tatiana Proskouriakoff described Tohcok as having architecture that is "of neither the distinctive Chenes nor Puuc style; it appears rather to be a blend of the two." In 1985 George F. Andrews described

the structure mentioned by Shook and Proskouriakoff and also found both Chenes and Puuc traits. Tohcok is in a border area; it is near the Chenes region (to the south), the Puuc region (to the north), and the Edzna region (to the west). Andrews found ten other sites in this border region with a blend of architectural styles, to which he gave the name Chenes-Puuc. The structure of Tohcok dates to the Late Classic period.

Connection

Hopelchén to Tohcok: 2.8 miles by paved road (:05).

Getting There

Head west from Hopelchén on Highway 261 to Tohcok. You will pass the second structure described above (although it may not be visible) before you reach the cleared structure on the highway. The highway structure is also 0.1 mile before (east of) a side road heading north to the village of San Juan Bautista (Sabcabchén).

You can get to Tohcok by taxi from Hopelchén if you are without a vehicle. Allow 15 minutes to see and photograph the cleared structure.

★ ★

EL TABASQUEÑO

(ehl tah-bahs-keh-nyoh; derivation: Spanish for "the Tabascan" [see text])

| Location: |
| East-central Campeche. |
| **Map:** 3 (p. 210) |

The Site

El Tabasqueño (sometimes simply Tabasqueño) is named for a man from Tabasco who at one time owned a ranch of the same name near the archaeological site. The site name is sometimes shortened to Tabas.

The site is reported to be fairly large, but visitors today see only two structures in the main part of the site; the remains of the rest are reported to be collapsed. The most important area is a plaza with structures surrounding it, although the visitor is not really aware of this. The plaza is reported to be about 260 feet (north to south) and 165 feet (east to west); Structure 1, which faces north, borders the plaza on the south.

Structure 1, also called the Temple-Palace, is an impressive, if partly fallen, two-story building. Its most outstanding fea-

Structure 1 (the Temple-Palace) second story, north facade, El Tabasqueño. Late Classic period.

ture—which is really spectacular—is an almost totally intact Chenes-style monster-mouth mask surrounding the doorway on the north facade of the second-story temple. The mask is executed in finely cut stone with the delicate details worked out in stucco, some of which remains. H. E. D. Pollock notes that the stone cutting in the mask "is of high order and shows mastery of the art." Paul Gendrop dates the temple to around A.D. 710.

On the corners, flanking the Chenes mask, are stacks of Chac masks. Of the original eight on each corner, six remain on the northeast corner and seven on the northwest, and they are almost totally intact, including the downturned snouts. The north facade of Structure 1 has been compared—

with good reason, because of a distinct similarity—to the north facade of Structure V at Hormiguero in the Río Bec region, although on the latter, the snouts of the Chac masks are mostly gone.

The room entered by the monster-mouth mask is narrow, and the capstones that once formed the top of the vault are mostly gone. The back wall of this room is actually the medial wall of the two-room temple, although the adjacent south room has collapsed, except for its back vault, which abuts the medial wall. There are no interior doorways connecting the two rooms. There are remains of a perforated roof comb above the medial wall, and this is best observed from the back (south side) of the structure. The lintel in the second story temple is wood,

Structure 2, the tower, El Tabasqueño. Late Classic period.

while those in the first story are stone. A stairway on the north, now fallen, connected the second story temple to the plaza.

On the first level, rooms extend to the west (and originally they extended to the east as well), and parts of the west rooms are standing. On the west wing of the north facade (first level) there is a three-member medial molding, and part of this is well preserved, with remains of modeled stucco in the middle member. The motif is reported to be an anthropomorphic figure that is extended and undulating. There are remains

of red paint in this area and on the stucco of the wall below.

There are projecting tenons just above the medial molding, as well as in other parts of the building, indicating that there was once a rich display of architectural sculpture—probably of stucco—on Structure 1.

About 170 feet to the southwest of Structure 1 is Structure 2, very plain by comparison with the former, but decidedly most unusual. Structure 2 is a solid masonry tower, square in cross section, measuring about 5 feet wide and deep at the base. It is currently 15 feet tall, but some of the top has fallen, and its exact original height is unknown.

There is a simple, single-course projecting molding 3 feet from the top, with smaller projecting stones on the north and east sides. These may have once supported stucco sculptures, as projecting stones are presumed to have done on Structure 1 and many other buildings.

George F. Andrews reported that the cut-stone facing of the tower is "indistinguishable from the facing stones used in the outer walls of Structure 1." He also says that the tower stands on a low platform in front of a collapsed building, and "I believe that the platform which supports the tower was incorporated into a stairway leading to the building behind."

Freestanding, solid towers such as Structure 2 at El Tabasqueño are extremely rare in lowland Maya architecture. Only three others are known in the Chenes region: Structure 1 at Chanchén and Structures 1 and 2 at Nocuchich, sites that are 13 and 19 miles north of El Tabasqueño respectively.

Structure 1 at Nocuchich had a colossal head on the north side, but this tower has fallen. It was originally cross-shaped in cross section, but a later addition on the south side made it rectangular with a protrusion on the north. The cross section of Structure 2 at Nocuchich is nearly square, and Structure 1 at Chanchén is rectangular. These last two towers are taller than the one at El Tabasqueño and have larger bases, and both have vertical slots in the upper section, similar to slots found on the roof comb of Structure 1 at El Tabasqueño and many other sites. Andrews, who studied the towers, believes that the one at El Tabasqueño also may have had slots in its now-fallen upper section.

He compared the four known towers in the Chenes region and believes that they "can best be described as symbolic representations of conventional temple buildings with high roof combs." He professes to have no answer for why this symbolic device was chosen.

Andrews also commented on the cylindrical tower at Puerto Rico in the Río Bec region and states that it "differs considerably from the towers in the Chenes region." See "Puerto Rico" in Section 5 for details of that tower.

Recent History

In 1895 Teobert Maler was the first to report El Tabasqueño, and more information is included in his *Península Yucatán,* volume 1. His photograph of the Chenes monstermouth doorway of Structure 1 shows that it has suffered little since he took the picture in 1887. Only a few stones immediately above the doorway have fallen since then.

Pollock visited El Tabasqueño in 1936 and published his findings on this and other Chenes sites in 1970. He reported details of the architecture of Structure 1, but neither he nor Maler mentioned the tower.

In 1956 Ricardo de Robina published a plan of the main part of the site and another of Structure 1, but the tower was not included. Apparently the first publication of the tower was by Paul Gendrop in 1983, and Andrews's analysis of the tower followed in 1989.

There has been no excavation or restoration of the architecture at El Tabasqueño, but the doorway of the second-story temple of Structure 1 has been consolidated.

Connections

1. Hopelchén to El Tabasqueño (via Pakchén): 18.5 miles by paved road (:29), 1.5 miles by rock road (:04), 0.9 mile by dirt road (:17), then a couple of hundred yards by foot trail (:16).

Total from Hopelchén to El Tabasqueño (Connection 1): 20.9 miles (1:06).

2. Hopelchén to El Tabasqueño (via the entrance near Kilometer 35): 21.8 miles by paved road (:34), 0.9 mile by dirt road (:09), then about 1.1 miles by foot trail (:25).

Total from Hopelchén to El Tabasqueño (Connection 2): 23.8 miles (1:08).

Getting There

Guides: Hortensio Camal Ku, in Chencoh, or José Williams, in Dzibalchén.

If you have a guide with you when you

leave Hopelchén, then either connection will get you to El Tabasqueño in about the same time. Use whichever route your guide recommends. If you get Hortensio or José to take you, the route via the entrance near Kilometer 35 will be shorter. In either case you will have to add driving time to the totals given above to pick them up. To go to Chencoh and get Hortensio and return to the Kilometer 35 cutoff for El Tabasqueño, add 1:06. (See "Hochob" for details on reaching Chencoh and for options if you do not have your own vehicle.) To go to José's house in Dzibalchén and return to the Kilometer 35 cutoff, add :22.

1. When you reach Pakchén (from Hopelchén), turn right into the village on the rock road, and left onto the dirt road. After 0.2 mile take a sharp left and go another 0.7 mile. From there you walk to the site.

2. When you are approaching from Dzibalchén, go to the Kilometer 35 marker and a few hundred feet beyond, and look for two dirt trails on the left; they join a few feet later in the woods. Turn left and go 0.6 mile; turn left again, proceed for another 0.3 mile, and park. (In wet weather you may have to walk in part of this last 0.3 mile.) From here you walk, gently uphill, to the site over a clear trail. On the way out, walking downhill, you can make it a little faster than the time indicated.

A high-clearance vehicle is recommended to reach El Tabasqueño if you take the route through Pakchén; a standard vehicle will suffice for the other route.

Allow 1 hour and 10 minutes to see El Tabasqueño once you get there. Wear boots, carry a canteen of water to the site, and have a wide-angle lens for photos of the front of Structure 1 if you want to get an overall view including the remains of the first level. Have cold drinks in your vehicle. The nearest restaurants are in Hopelchén.

★ ★ ★

HOCHOB

*(hoh-*chohb*; derivation: Maya for "Place Where Ears of Maize Are Stored")*

Location:
    East-central Campeche.
Map: 3 (p. 210)

The Site

Hochob has been cleared and consolidated and is spectacular. It is one of the best preserved and most studied of all the Chenes sites. Though it is relatively small, the distinctive architectural remains make a visit very worthwhile.

Several structures are arranged around a plaza, and together they occupy most of a low natural plateau that dominates the surrounding plain. Of prime interest is the Principal Palace (Structure 2), which bounds the plaza on the north. This building is composed of a central section and two lateral wings, each containing one vaulted room, with the central section recessed from the adjacent wings. Much of the west wing has collapsed, as has the eastern part of the east wing, but the central section is mostly intact.

The entire facade of this section (south, or main face) is decorated with an incredibly intricate monster-mouth mask, typical of Chenes sites. The design was constructed of stone and stucco, and there are a few remnants of red paint in the eyes of the serpent. A perforated roof comb rises above the front of the structure and originally supported stucco figures. Only the lower part of the roof comb remains today.

The lower wall of the main facade of the east wing is plain, while the upper portion is decorated with a monster-mouth motif, similar to that on the central portion. On the southwest corner of the upper section of the east wing, there are stacked Chac masks.

Structure 2 (the Principal Palace), center section, south facade, Hochob. Late Classic period.

Wooden lintels originally spanned the tops of the doorways of all three rooms, but they fell many years ago. A new lintel was placed above the doorway of the central room during consolidation.

For many years the sequence of construction of Structure 2 was debated. In 1956 Ricardo de Robina suggested that the three rooms were built separately (perhaps the central room first) and later joined together by walls and fill. H. E. D. Pollock felt that the lateral wings were built first; although there were definitely phases in the construction, he believed that the structure was conceived as a unified whole. During clearing and consolidation of the structure, Ramón Carrasco Vargas found evidence that the end rooms were constructed first, and then the center one.

Bounding the plaza on the east is Structure 1, similar to Structure 2, but not as well preserved. There are three rooms in a line facing west, and the front wall of the central room has remains of a monster-mouth facade. This room projects in front of the end rooms, and at the junctions there are stacked, corner Chac masks. The lower walls of the end rooms are plain. Here too there

Structure 1, center section, west facade, Hochob. Late Classic period.

was a sequence of construction, as the monster-mouth doorway decoration was added to the simpler facade of the center room after the initial construction.

On the south side of the plaza are remains of a range of rooms running east-west, and at each end there are pyramidal bases with structures on top. Structure 5 (the pyramid and temple on the east end) is better preserved than its western counterpart (Structure 6), and it consists of a two-room temple, almost square in plan, with doorways facing north and south. There are indentations, or false doorways, in the east and west walls, and no interior connection between the two rooms. Projecting tenons are found above the medial molding and in the cornice molding, and they probably supported some sculptural decoration originally. There is a perforated roof comb above the medial wall, and a fair amount of it is intact.

A good part of the pyramidal base of Structure 5 is rubble, but several of the lower steps on the north side are in place and indicate an extremely steep, but functional, stairway.

Details of construction indicate that the lower range of rooms was built first and that the pyramidal bases and their temples, on the ends, were added later. Beyond Structure 6 (to the west) are the rubble remains of Structure 7, and bordering the plaza on the west is a mound called Structure 8.

The structures at Hochob are Late Classic. Ceramics found at the site date from the Late Preclassic period to postconquest times.

Recent History

The first scientific report on Hochob was published in 1895 by Teobert Maler, although he had discovered the site some eight years earlier. He explored Hochob and produced photographs, a site plan, and elevations of Structures 2 and 5. Other works were published by Eduard Seler in 1916 and by Karin Hissink in 1934. The site is also covered in a 1945 report by Alberto Ruz Lhuillier, and in 1956 a more thorough investigation of the site was published by Robina. In 1970 Pollock's report on Hochob and other Chenes sites appeared, although he had visited the area in 1936, when he was working for the Carnegie Institution of Washington.

Structure 5, north side, Hochob. Late Classic period.

Up to this point, all of the work at Hochob had been exploratory and descriptive. In 1982 and 1983 Hochob was cleared, studied, and consolidated by Carrasco Vargas, and his work has made the site a great deal more interesting for visitors.

In a 1985 article Carrasco Vargas and Sylviane Boucher state that they believe the corner masks on buildings at Hochob and elsewhere, commonly called Chac masks, are actually representations of Itzamná.

Connection

Hopelchén to Hochob: 25.0 miles by paved road (:41), 5.5 miles by poor rock road (:27), then 3.1 miles by rough dirt road (:25).

Total from Hopelchén to Hochob: 33.6 miles (1:33).

Getting There

Head southeast from Hopelchén to the cutoff for the village of Chencoh. The cutoff is near the Kilometer 40 marker and shortly after the entrance sign for Dzibalchén; there is a cemetery on the left and a soccer field on the right. (There is not always a sign indicating that the rock road on the right goes to Chencoh, but there may be a sign indicating a junction on the right.) Turn right and proceed to Chencoh. In Chencoh take a left at the plaza, and then another left to get on the road to Hochob. If you cannot find this road, anyone around will be able to direct you. Follow the dirt road, take a left at the fork 2.5 miles out of Chencoh (the only one you will encounter), and proceed to the site. You can park at the base of the plateau and make the easy climb to the site from there.

Having your own vehicle is the best way to reach Hochob, but there are other options. You may be able to find a guide with a vehicle through one of the travel agencies in Campeche City. If you start from there, add 54.2 miles by paved road (1:23) to the total given above. Another option is to take a bus to Dzibalchén and contact José Williams, who can arrange for transportation. José would also be the one to have along if you would prefer to have a guide with you when you go to Hochob in your own vehicle.

Allow 1 hour to visit Hochob. Have a wide-angle lens for your camera, and at least have cold drinks along. There is no food or drink at Hochob or nearby.

★ ★

DZIBILNOCAC

(tseeb-eel-noh-ahk; derivation: Maya for "Painted Vault." The spelling and derivation given above are those used in the literature; however, the pronunciation is that used in the area, where the second-to-last c is not pronounced. When the name is spelled the way it is pronounced locally (Dzibilnohac), the meaning changes to "Large Turtle That Writes" or "Large Turtle with Writing on It.")

Location:
East-central Campeche.
Map: 3 (p. 210)

The Site

Although Dzibilnocac is a large site, there is really only one structure of interest for the visitor, but that one—or a least a part of it—is superb. Dzibilnocac is also the easiest to reach of all the Chenes sites.

The Temple-Palace (Structure A1) rests on a platform roughly 250 feet long and 98 feet wide. The structure consists of a double range of vaulted rooms at ground level, eight of which have an east-west axis, and two that run north-south. In the center and on each end of the lower rooms are pyramidal bases with temples on top that form towers. Each of the temples had two rooms. The central

Structure A1 (the Temple-Palace), eastern temple and adjacent room, north side, Dzibilnocac. Late Classic period.

temple was a bit larger than the other two, but most of it has collapsed. The western temple is in a ruinous state, but the eastern temple is well preserved, has been cleared, and is nicely consolidated. The lower range of rooms of Structure A1 was built first, and the towers and temples added later.

All four facades of the eastern temple bear relief sculpture of the monster-mouth type made from stone and stucco. The east and west facades have false doorways, while the north and south faces supported the real doorways that gave access to the back-to-back rooms. The real doorways collapsed some time ago, but the one on the north side has been restored. There are remains of the lower section of a roof comb above the medial wall of the temple, and stacked Chac masks on three of the four corners. Those on the southwest corner have fallen.

The eastern temple is approached by

steep but functional stairways on the north, east, and south sides, with some of the lower steps in place. The corners are rounded on the pyramidal base that supports the temple. Two of the lower rooms next to the eastern temple have been cleared and consolidated, and benches are found in the south room.

On the north exterior face of the lower part of the structure is an indentation in the front wall, and rounded corners are found there as well. A three-member base molding runs along the building, and in the middle part are groups of three colonnettes, separated by plain stones.

Beneath the mound that is the remains of the central temple are the two rooms of the lower range that run north-south, and you can reach the eastern room through an eastern doorway by an easy trail from the back (south side) of the building. There are some remnants of paint in the eastern room, and in one area there is the upper part of a figure in profile with an elaborate headdress (difficult to discern). Originally there were painted capstones, one each in the eastern and western rooms under the central temple, but both have been removed. Fortunately they were well documented by scholars before their disappearance.

During clearing and consolidation, another capstone—fragmented, but with most of its parts recovered—was found in the north room of the eastern temple. This capstone is now in the Mérida Museum. Another capstone, of which only three small fragments remain, was found in the lower range of rooms.

Other remains at Dzibilnocac include seven major pyramids (overgrown) and numerous minor ones, as well as structures of collapsed architecture. The proximity of the town of Iturbide has contributed to the extensive damage done to the site.

Recent History

In 1842 John Lloyd Stephens and Frederick Catherwood visited Dzibilnocac, and Catherwood did a drawing of Structure A1 that shows the remains of the three towers but no details of the relief sculpture. They explored the other ruined mounds, and Stephens commented that "beyond [Structure A1] were towering mounds and vestiges, indicating the existence of a greater city than any we had yet encountered."

Teobert Maler visited the site in 1887, and his photograph and notes were used by Eduard Seler—who also visited Dzibilnocac—in a 1916 publication. More of Maler's information is contained in *Península Yucatán*, volume 3. Other reports on Dzibilnocac were published by Karin Hissink (1934), Alberto Ruz Lhuillier (1945), and Ricardo de Robina (1956).

In 1949 Karl Ruppert and George W. Brainerd, sponsored by the Carnegie Institution of Washington, visited the site. Brainerd collected ceramic samples, but Brainerd died, and the ceramic analysis was not completed, although a map of the site was produced.

The New World Archaeological Foundation sponsored work at Dzibilnocac from 1968 through 1970. The site was remapped and proved to be larger than originally thought. Many test pits were dug to study the ceramics, and six eroded stelae were discovered. These finds were reported by Fred Nelson, Jr., in 1973.

This work shows that Dzibilnocac was first occupied late in the Middle Preclassic period and that the population grew in the Late Preclassic. At the end of the Late Preclassic, the population declined drastically, and there is scant evidence for occupancy during the Early Classic. Again in the Late Classic, there is evidence for a large population. The structures visible at the site today date to this period, although in some cases these cover Late Preclassic construction. The site was abandoned around A.D. 950.

In 1982 Ramón Carrasco Vargas, working for the Southeast Regional Center of INAH, cleared and consolidated the east part of Structure A1. During this work he discovered the two previously unreported capstones.

Connection

Hopelchén to Dzibilnocac: 37.4 miles by paved road (1:01), then a couple of blocks by rock road (:03).

Getting There

From Hopelchén take the road that goes southeast to Dzibalchén. Turn left at the Dzibalchén Plaza, then right at the end of the plaza, and follow the road as it bears to the left to exit the town. Continue to the town of Iturbide, where you will enter its plaza at the southwest corner. Go to the end of the plaza and turn right; this street then continues as the road to Dzibilnocac, and you can drive right to Structure A1. Allow 45 minutes to see the structure.

Cold drinks are available in Iturbide, and when you return to the plaza, take a look at the structure on the east side. The pyramidal base is pre-Columbian, although the stair and guardhouse on top are modern additions. Part of Iturbide overlies the ancient site.

East face of the eastern temple of Structure A1 (the Temple-Palace), Dzibilnocac. Late Classic period.

KANCABCHÉN

*(kahn-kahb-*chehn; *derivation: Maya for "Spring [Well] of the Yellow Earth")*

<table>
<tr><td>

Location:
   East-central Campeche.
Map: 3 (p. 210)

</td></tr>
</table>

The Site

Kancabchén is a small site with one partly standing building (Structure 1). Its vault is mostly intact, but the remains of the building and a few mounds that lie to the west have been greatly stone-robbed. Structure 1 faces south and has one room, and the north, south, and west walls are standing. Most of the east wall has fallen, and this opening provides access to the room.

There are offsets in the spring line on the long (north and south) walls, but none on the end walls. One feature of interest in this structure is the unusually thick front (south) wall, which measures seven feet at the single doorway. The doorway is spanned by three large stone lintels, one behind the other; two are intact, while the outermost is broken and partly hanging, though still in place.

Almost all of the exterior facing stone has been removed, but near the doorway are remains of a medial molding or, according to George F. Andrews, possibly a sloping upper wall zone.

Recent History

Teobert Maler visited Kancabchén in 1894, and in 1895 was the first to report the site. Although it is known that he took a photograph of Structure 1, he did not include it with his text. Additional information on the site is part of his *Península Yucatán,* volume 3.

Andrews visited the site in 1986 and reported his findings the following year. He comments that his notes are at odds with Maler's description. Maler believed that the room described above was an inner or rear room. Andrews believes this was probably the only room, and today there is no obvious evidence of a front room. Andrews further comments that because of lack of facade detail, "it is difficult to assess the architectural style of Structure 1." He found that the style of the interior stonework (and the fact that it was held together with clay rather than limestone mortar) "differs sharply from typ-

Doorway with three lintels in the south wall of Structure 1, Kancabchén. View from inside the room. Late or Terminal Classic period.

ical Chenes construction technology." He was unable to say whether the construction was early or late.

Connection

Hopelchén to Kancabchén: 37.4 miles by paved road (:57), then 4.0 miles by dirt road (:18).

Getting There

From Hopelchén take the road that goes southeast to Dzibalchén. Turn left at the Dzibalchén Plaza, then right at the end of the plaza, and follow the road as it bears to the left to exit the town. Continue for a short distance to the junction with the road that goes to Chunchintok (marked with a sign). Turn right at the junction and go 11.6 miles to the dirt cutoff for Kancabchén.

Turn right and proceed to the site (on the right side of the road and just a few feet from it). Structure 1 is 0.8 mile (:05) before the village of Kancabchén.

Bring your own food and drink, and a wide-angle lens to photograph the doorway from the inside of the room. Allow 10 minutes to visit Structure 1.

SECTION 4

• • • •

NORTHERN AND
WEST-CENTRAL CAMPECHE

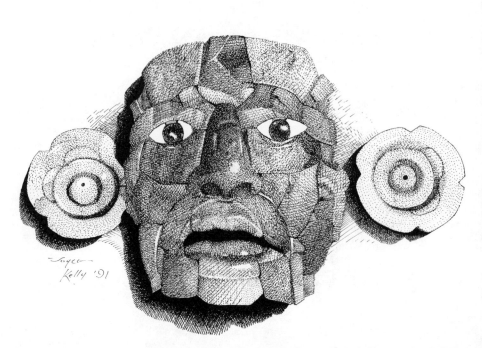

Jade mosaic mask found in Structure VII, Calakmul. Late Classic period. Now in the Campeche Museum.

GENERAL INFORMATION
FOR SECTION 4

> **Point of Reference:**
> Campeche, Campeche.
> **Map** 4

Mileages given to Edzna are from the Main Plaza in Campeche City.

Campeche City is the largest town on the west coast of the Yucatán Peninsula. Like Mérida, it is a charming colonial city, and it has the advantage of a location right on the Gulf of Mexico.

There are three good large hotels. The Baluartes and the Ramada Inn are next door to each other, and both are on the *malecón*—near the Main Plaza. The newer Hotel Debliz is 2.0 miles northeast, at Avenida Las Palmas, no. 55. This avenue parallels the *malecón,* one block inland. Somewhat more modest than the others is the Hotel Alhambra, also on the *malecón,* 1.3 miles southwest of the Baluartes. There are several smaller places around town, and also a trailer park.

There are many restaurants in Campeche. An old-time favorite is the Miramar, visible from the two large hotels on the *malecón.* It is frequented by business people as well as travelers, does a brisk lunchtime business, and provides fast service. It is also open for dinner, when the pace is a bit more leisurely. Try its steamed Moro crabs.

Campeche City can be reached by train from central Mexico or Mérida, or by bus from anywhere on the peninsula or central Mexico. You can drive to Campeche City from the United States (four days from Brownsville, Texas, with good stopovers along the way). Car rentals are available in town and at the large hotels. Campeche has an airport, and flights connect with some other cities in Mexico, but road connections are probably easier.

There are travel agents in Campeche, and some can arrange visits to Edzna or even Hochob.

In Lerma, south of Campeche along the coast, there is a good icehouse.

OTHER STOPOVERS: Sihoplaya, 25 miles south of Campeche on Highway 180, has a rather good hotel, and farther south there are a couple of modest hotels in Champotón.

Champotón is a good place to stop for a shrimp cocktail. There is a small restaurant (El Paso del Viajero) across the highway from the gas station and north of the bridge. Another restaurant, El Manglar, is just south of the bridge.

GAS STATIONS: There are a few gas stations in and on the outskirts of Campeche City, and going north on Highway 180, at Tenabo and Calkiní (50.3 miles from Campeche City). Heading south on Highway 180, there are stations at Seybaplaya (20.8 miles from Campeche City) and Champotón. South of Champotón there is a station on Highway 261 at Escárcega.

GUIDES: A guide is not needed to reach Edzna, the only site covered in this section, but if you are using Campeche as a stopover and point of departure for El Tabasqueño, see "General Information for Section 3" for a guide.

★ ★ ★
REGIONAL MUSEUM OF ARCHAEOLOGY (CAMPECHE MUSEUM, CAMPECHE CITY)

The collection of the Campeche Museum has had a number of homes over the years and is now housed in the Casa del Teniente del Rey, a historic building in the center of Campeche City. The museum was inaugurated at its present location in September 1985.

At the entrance to the museum is a large, Late Classic stone sculpture from the region of Chunchintok. Other displays are in rooms surrounding a patio and along the corridor walls facing the patio. One room is devoted to early Maya history, and another has Stela 9 from Calakmul, polychrome pots, and figurines. There is a model of Becan with its encircling ditch and earthwork.

There are stelae, carved panels and columns, and other stone sculpture from various parts of the state of Campeche, including Edzna (Stelae 8, 9, and 15), Chunhuhub, Xculoc, Xcalumkin, and Xcocha. One especialy interesting display is the unusual corner Chac masks from Miramar, which have been restored (see "Miramar" in Section 2 for a description).

The real gems of the collection are the jade mosaic masks and jade jewelery from Calakmul, discovered in the 1980s. These are truly

Carved column (provenience unknown) depicting five individuals, the most shown on any of the known carved columns. Probably Late Classic period. Campeche Museum.

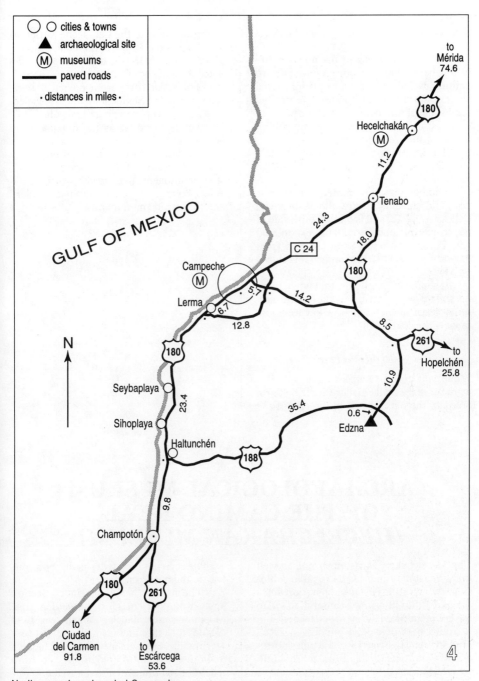

GULF OF MEXICO

to
Mérida
74.6

180

Hecelchakán
M

11.2

Tenabo

24.3

18.0

C 24

180

Campeche
M

5.7

14.2

Lerma

6.7

8.5

12.8

261

to
Hopelchén
25.8

N

180

10.9

Seybaplaya

23.4

35.4

0.6

Sihoplaya

Edzna

Haltunchén

188

9.8

Champotón

180

261

to
Ciudad
del Carmen
91.8

to
Escárcega
53.6

4

Northern and west-central Campeche

spectacular. There are two large masks and three smaller ones, and all have been restored.

Most of the items in the museum are well labeled, but the provenience of two painted capstones and an exquisite carved column are unknown. In an open area behind some of the rooms are stelae and other carved stones that are unlabeled but still interesting and worth seeing.

The second floor of the museum houses colonial period material and is also worth a visit.

Photography is permitted, but flash is not. The museum is on Calle 59 between Calles 14 and 16, and is on the south side of the street. It is open from 8:00 A.M. to 8:00 P.M. Tuesday through Saturday, and from 8:00 A.M. to 1:00 P.M. on Sunday. It is closed on Monday.

It should be mentioned that when there is a shift of personnel during the day, the museum closes for ten minutes. Allow 1½ hours to view the collection.

Added Extra

While you are in Campeche you will also want to see the Stelae Gallery at the Baluarte Soledad, the old fort just to the east of the Main Plaza in town. The Baluarte Soledad (once the home of the Campeche Museum) now houses the offices of the Campeche Regional Center of INAH, and one room is devoted to the Stelae Gallery.

The stelae come from Edzna, Itzimté, Xcalumkin, and Xculoc, and they are labeled. The gallery is open during the regular office hours of the Regional Center, and there is no charge.

Outside the fort and facing the plaza are some interesting (but unlabeled) carved stone monuments that are also worth a look. Allow 20 minutes to see the Stelae Gallery and the outside monuments.

★ ★
ARCHAEOLOGICAL MUSEUM OF THE CAMINO REAL (HECELCHAKÁN MUSEUM)

The Hecelchakán Museum is not as well known as some others on the Yucatán Peninsula, though it has been in operation since the mid-1960s. It is in the center of town, to the left of the Main Plaza (as you face it), and occupies part of a long building. (Hecelchakán is on Highway 180, 35.5 miles northeast of Campeche City and 74.6 miles southwest of Mérida.)

In the plaza at Hecelchakán is a tall, rectangular stone column (unlabeled) carved with hieroglyphs. You will pass by it on your way to the museum.

The museum has both an indoor section and an outdoor corridor and garden area. Most items are unlabeled, but the wealth of carved stone monuments makes a visit very worthwhile. Some displays are well lighted, and others are not. Photography is permitted, but flash units are not allowed.

Inside the museum are a couple of carved and beautifully preserved glyphic columns, one of which came from Xcalum-kin. A display case holds a nice collection of figurines from Isla Jaina, and large transparencies show aerial views of the island and its pyramids. There are also a large model of a pre-Columbian Maya village and chronological charts.

Along the corridor outside are more carved columns, one with a frontal figure, and another (from Xcalumkin) that is totally glyphic.

Carved panels and more carved columns, some with capitals carved with hieroglyphs, are displayed in the garden abutting the corridor.

Allow 45 minutes to view the collection.

Carved column from Xcalumkin. Late Classic period. Hecelchakán Museum.

EDZNA
(ETZNA)
(ehds-nah; derivation: Maya for "House of the Grimace [or Visage]")

Location:
West-central Campeche.
Map: 4 (p. 231)

The Site

Edzna is a splendid site with a good deal of standing architecture, some of which has been consolidated and restored over the years. Lamentably, it still attracts relatively few visitors, though it is easy to reach if you are driving.

The monumental zone at Edzna covers an area of 2.3 square miles; the site was occupied from around 400 B.C. to A.D. 1500. Thirty-two stelae have been reported at Edzna, and fragments of two of them are Cycle 8 monuments (pre–A.D. 435), according to Antonio Benavides Castillo, who dated the fragments stylistically. The lastest stela from Edzna is dated A.D. 810, and the study of these monuments indicates that they record information relating to five apparent rulers of the site.

All of Edzna's structures described below have been partly or completely consolidated or restored, though this is only a small part (albeit the most important part) of the site. Great hydraulic works are also found at Edzna, but the visitor is unaware of these. Twelve canals and a number of reservoirs have been recorded. One canal heads for over 8 miles in a southerly direction from near the southeast part of the Great Acropolis.

As you enter the site, you come first to the Platform of the Cuchillos ("Knives"), named because of a rich offering of obsidian blades found there. The platform is over 250 feet long and 90 feet wide and is oriented roughly east-west. This was a residential unit of 20 rooms, 12 of which were vaulted. None of the vaults is intact, but there are two

columns in the entrance to the easternmost center room. Stairways of varying widths give access to the rooms from each side of the platform, and the broadest stairway is on the south side, facing the Great Plaza.

The west end of the platform borders the east side of a smaller plaza surrounded by structures on the other three sides. This is called the Annex of the Cuchillos, and there is an altar in the center of the plaza. On the southeast corner of the plaza is an intact portal vault that once was the access from the plaza to a *saché* that leads to the Great Acropolis. The vault was later covered by another large structure with a stairway facing the plaza and a room in the upper part.

Other rooms around the plaza have columned entrances and lower walls in place. This area also shows different periods of construction.

To the south of the Annex of the Cuchillos is the Nohoch Na ("Great House"), a high platform over 370 feet long, oriented north-south. Excavation of the structure shows that its entire length is faced with a grand stairway that leads to two long rows of double rooms, separated by a narrow opening. Only the lower walls of the rooms are standing, and they were originally roofed with perishable materials. The structure faces west, across the Great Plaza and toward the Great Acropolis, and there is evidence that the Nohoch Na covers an earlier building.

The South Temple is a few yards southeast of the Nohoch Na and borders the south side of the Great Plaza. Its pyramidal base rises in five tiers and has an inset stairway on the south side (facing away from the Great Plaza), and there are remains of the lower walls of a temple on top. The South Temple is Petén style, and next to it is the Ball Court.

The Ball Court also borders the south side of the Great Plaza and abuts the east side of the South Temple. The two walls of the

The South Temple, the rear (north) side, Edzna. Classic period.

Ball Court are sloped, and there are remains of the lower walls of a room on top of each side. The butt of a ball court ring is in place in the middle of the west side of the court.

Jutting eastward from the east side of the Ball Court is a small Early Classic Petén–style construction, of which the low platform and lower walls remain. To the south of the Ball Court is Structure 418, a platform with the lower remains of a room on top, unimpressive visually but interesting because it was originally a Petén-style construction to which Puuc-style cut stones were added during the Postclassic period.

A short distance to the southeast is the Temple of the Masks (Structure 414), and here there is more to see. This Early Classic structure rises in tiers, has remains of a stairway on the north, and on either side of it displays elaborate mask panels. There is one mask on each side on the lower level and fragments of another on the east side (left as you face the structure) on the level above, which formed part of a second pair. The masks are made of stucco, are well preserved, and have remains of paint. It appears that a humanized form of the sun god is depicted. Though smaller, they are similar to the lower four masks at Kohunlich, which are also of Early Classic date. The masks at Edzna are pro-

tected by thatch shelters, but there is enough light for photography.

A few yards to the northeast of the Temple of the Masks is the stairway that ascends the Small Acropolis on its west side. The Small Acropolis is a square platform over 240 feet on each side, and there are four structures on top arranged around a patio. At the foot of the stairway is a group of fragmented stelae, mostly lying on their sides, but with some clear carving that you can easily photograph.

At the top of the stairway is the Temple of the Stelae (Structure 419-2), and it too has a western stairway that gives the impression of being an extention of the stairway that ascends the Small Acropolis. On the lower level of the Temple of the Stelae, to the north of the stairway (left as you face the structure), are a few remains of a stucco mask, and another mask once adorned the other side. On top of the temple are the remains of the lower walls of a room that was possibly roofed with perishable materials originally.

Also atop the Small Acropolis, behind the Temple of the Stelae, is the Temple of the Stairway with Reliefs (Structure 419-3), resting on the east side of the acropolis. This Petén-style structure has a broad stairway on the west, and some of the stones that form it

Stucco mask on the Temple of the Masks (Structure 414), Edzna. This mask is on the lower level of the temple's north side, on the east side of the stairway. Early Classic Period.

are carved in low relief with various designs. The remains of a temple on top were constructed with stones from other buildings, and fragments of stelae were also incorporated. On the north and south sides of the Small Acropolis are two more structures with stairways and the lower parts of temple walls.

Immediately to the north of the Small Acropolis is the Great Acropolis, the largest and most impressive architectural assemblage at Edzna. The Great Acropolis is a platform constructed over 20 feet high and measuring over 500 feet on each side. A broad stairway on the west side provides access to the top of the platform and its several structures. The buildings are arranged around a plaza, and there is an altar in the center.

When you climb the stairway to the Great Acropolis, you come face to face with the most interesting structure at Edzna, the beautiful Temple of Five Stories or Templo Mayor, with a height of 100 feet to the top of its roof comb, and 126 feet above general ground level. This is the tallest structure at the site, and it dates to the Late Classic period. It covers an earlier Petén-style pyramid-temple. On the front of the structure the first four stories are composed of rooms

flanking a central stairway, the left side of which has been restored, and the fifth story is the temple with a roof comb.

The stairway is pierced by vaulted passages on the first two levels, allowing foot traffic to pass beneath the stairway from one side of the building to the other. At the foot of the structure a broad stair of four steps leads to the first level rooms. Glyphs are carved on the risers of the steps, some of which are well preserved. On the first and fourth stories the doorways are supported by columns, and those on the fourth story also had capitals.

The whole feeling of the structure is one of restraint. Simple moldings form the most prominent feature, although projecting tenons indicate that stucco figures once adorned the facade. This is especially true of the perforated roof comb, which was both literally and figuratively the crowning glory of the structure. Since the temple faces west, the afternoon is the best time to photograph it. From the top of the temple you have a gorgeous view of the other restored structures around the plaza and beyond. From this vantage point you can appreciate what a magnificent city Edzna must have been in its heyday.

Abutting the southwest corner of the

The Temple of Five Stories, from the southwest, Edzna. Late Classic period.

Temple of Five Stories (and called its "Annex") is a small structure with a western stair and the lower walls of a room on top. It dates to the time of the Petén-style structure beneath the Temple of Five Stories. West of the annex is the House of the Moon ("Casa de la Luna"), which rests on the south side of the Great Acropolis and faces north onto the plaza. It rises in seven tiers, has a broad inset stairway, and boasts a long temple on top that originally was roofed with perishable materials. The temple is composed of three rooms, a large one in the center, flanked by much smaller rooms on each end. There are three pillars at the entrance to the center room, and the base of the structure covers an earlier construction.

On the southwest corner of the Great Acropolis is the Southwest Temple, the base of which rises in two sloped tiers. It has an eastern stair and the remains of the lower

walls of a temple on top. Adjacent to the north are two long low buildings with columns and lower walls. The space between the two is the access to the stairway of the Great Acropolis. The room just to the north of this space was originally one of the two rooms of the building, but later it was closed in and converted to a steam bath ("temazcal").

To the north of this structure is the Northwest Temple—a counterpart of the Southwest Temple—with a base that rises in five tiers, an eastern stairway, and remains of the lower walls of a temple on top. From the top of this structure you can look down, on the north side, into the Puuc Patio and the structures that border it. The North Platform (Structure 343-3) is on the north, and the lower walls of several rooms are standing atop a low platform. On the west is the Puuc Platform (Structure 343-2), the base of which has colonnettes as part of the

House of the Moon, north side, Edzna. The thatched roof (no longer in place) is believed to be like the original roof. Late Classic period.

decoration; on top of the platform are the remains of lower walls.

When you are ready to leave the Great Acropolis and are standing at the top of its stairway, you can see the broad *sacbé* that goes from it to the north end of the Nohoch Na and the Annex of the Cuchillos, one of three *sacbeob* known at Edzna.

Before you leave Edzna, stop for a look at some carved stelae lying on their backs under a thatch shelter next to the ticket office. There is enough light for photography.

Recent History

The name Etzna was given the site by scholar Nazario Quintana Bello in 1927, although the site's existence had been known for many years to people living in the area. Mexican historian Héctor Pérez Martínez later changed the name to Edzna because

there is no word "etz" in the Maya language. Although both spellings are found, Edzna is now preferred.

In 1928 Federico Mariscal published some drawings and plans of Edzna; Sylvanus G. Morley and Enrique Juan Palacios later deciphered some of the dates on the stelae.

The first extensive exploration of the site was undertaken by Alberto Ruz Lhuillier and Raúl Pavón Abreu in 1943. They determined the extent of the principal ceremonial center and the characteristics of the Temple of Five Stories, and the information was published by Ruz Lhuillier in 1945. Pavón Abreu conducted further work in 1958 and 1962, and the Temple of Five Stories was partly restored. In 1968 a survey of the main area and some peripheral areas was made by the University of Oregon, and it was reported by George F. Andrews in 1969.

In 1970 additional excavation and restoration was undertaken by Pavón Abreu and Román Piña Chan for INAH, and in 1983 the New World Archaeological Foundation reported on the hydraulic systems and ceramics at Edzna, in works authored by Ray T. Matheny, Donald W. Forsyth, and others.

From 1986 through 1989 major excavations were undertaken at Edzna, and several structures were consolidated and restored. Archaeologists involved in this work were Pavón Abreu and Luis Millet Camara of the Campeche Regional Center of INAH, and it was reported by Benavides Castillo in 1989 and 1990.

Guatemalan refugees formed part of the work force, and funds were provided by agencies of the United Nations and Mexico devoted to helping refugees. A truly international community was involved and included Spain and Norway.

In 1991 additional excavation on the north side of the Main Acropolis and consolidation of the Temple of Five Stories were undertaken.

Connections

1. Campeche to Edzna: 39.9 miles by paved road (1:03).

2. Uxmal to Edzna: 91.7 miles by paved road (2:06).

Getting There

From Campeche head east on Highway 180 to the cutoff for Edzna (28.4 miles). The cutoff is on the right and well marked. Turn right (onto Highway 188) and continue to the site. There are two branch roads—one on each side—about 0.6 mile *before* the entrance to Edzna. The one on the right is actually the continuation of Highway 188. The entrance to Edzna is straight ahead on a spur road.

From Uxmal head south and then west on Highway 261 to the cutoff for Edzna and turn left. Then follow the directions above.

Soft drinks and packaged snacks are available at the site, and there are rest rooms at the ticket office. Wear a sun hat and allow 3 hours for a visit. Edzna is best reached in your own vehicle or by private tour from Campeche.

SECTION 5

• • • •

SOUTHEASTERN CAMPECHE AND SOUTHERN QUINTANA ROO

Grotesque mask panel from Balamku; west panel on the south side of the structure with the stucco facade. Classic Period.

GENERAL INFORMATION
FOR SECTION 5

Point of Reference:
Xpuhil, Campeche.
Maps: 5, 5A, and 5A1

Mileages given to the sites in this section are from the crossroads at Xpuhil.

Although ruins abound in this area, accommodations, unfortunately, do not. This is actually still a frontier that had poor road connections to the rest of the peninsula until 1972, when Highway 186 was paved. The area lacks the colonial charm of Mérida and Campeche and the burgeoning tourist development of Cancún. Nevertheless, it is an area of extreme importance for the visitor interested in the archaeology of the region.

There are no hotels as such in Xpuhil, although there are a few modest cabañas (pole-sided and thatch-roofed) with hammocks available at the Mirador Maya Restaurant. There is also parking space for vehicles if you are prepared to sleep in your car. Bathrooms and showers are available. You can spot the Mirador Maya Restaurant by its large thatch roof. It is a half-mile west of the crossroads at Xpuhil, on the south side of the highway, on a rise of ground. If you plan to spend a night or more in the area, this is probably your best bet.

The crossroads at Xpuhil are roads that intersect the highway, in what has become the center of town. The road heading north goes to Zoh Laguna, and on to Dzibalchén. See "General Informaiton for Section 3" for details. You will take the first part of this road to get to Culucbalom and Puerto Rico. The rock road heading south from Xpuhil is the first part of the route to Hormiguero and the Río Bec sites.

There are several restaurants near Xpuhil crossroads. The Tulum, on the south side of the highway is probably the best. There are also a couple of grocery stores and a bus station near the junction. Xpuhil is the major bus stop between Escárcega and Chetumal.

If sleeping in a hammock or in your vehicle does not appeal to you, the alternative is to get an early start from Escárcega or Chetumal and visit some of the five more-accessible sites along the highway (Balamku, Chicanná, Becan, Xpuhil, and Kohunlich) in one day, driving between the two cities or working out of one of them and returning. To visit all five sites and drive between Escárcega and Chetumal would take more than 12 hours (if you spend the recommended time at each site).

This is one area where having your own vehicle is extremely important. Closest car rentals are in Chetumal at the Hotel del Prado.

OTHER STOPOVERS: The nearest good hotels are in Chetumal: the four best there are the Hotel del Prado, the Continental Caribe, and the Caribe Princess (all centrally located) and the Principe, a little north of the others. There are a few more-modest places in town as well. On the western outskirts of Chetumal (before you reach the center of town when driving in from Xpuhil) is the Paradise Motel, fair at best. The large hotels all have restaurants, and there are several others around the city.

There are modest hotels in Escárcega; the best is probably the Hotel Escárcega. The town also has a number of small restaurants.

Bacalar has a fair hotel with a restaurant, and a trailer park with a restaurant and clean bathrooms. Both are on the loop that passes Bacalar Lagoon. When you are heading north on Highway 307 and leave the highway to take the loop, you come to the trailer park almost immediately. The hotel is farther along the loop.

GAS STATIONS: Xpuhil has a gas station at the crossroads, and there is another at Ucum, 58.0 miles to the east (shortly before the junction with Highway 307). There is also gas at Escárcega and Chetumal, but none between Escárcega and Xpuhil.

GUIDE: Juan de la Cruz Briceño, caretaker of Becan. Look for him at Becan. If he is not there, someone will be able to tell you where he is or when he is expected. Juan is the guide of choice for all the archaeologists who work in the area. He knows the jungle like the back of his hand, is a pleasant and reassuring companion to have along, and is highly recommended.

★ ★

BALAMKU

*(bah-lahm-*koo; *derivation: Maya for "Jaguar Temple")*

(CHUNHABIL)

*(choon-hah-*beel*)*

Location:
Southeastern Campeche.
Map: 5 (p. 245)

The Site

Balamku—at least a part of it—is truly spectacular! It comes close to being a three-star site. The main feature of interest is a magnificent and well-preserved bas-relief stucco facade, with remains of red, black, and yellow paint. In the center of the best-preserved portion of the facade is a panel with a stylized jaguar in profile, seated on a border made of a zigzag design, interspersed with circular elements. The figure wears a belt with a bow below it, bracelets, a collar, and a pectoral. The head of the jaguar seems to be skeletal, and it wears a circular earplug with a lower tau element and a curved, three-part component above. This figure is what gives the site its name.

On each side of the jaguar are two large horizontal panels with grotesque frontal masks, each with two serpents extending from the mouth. The heads of the serpents are rather naturalistically portrayed on the west panel (left as you face the facade) and can only be described as vicious looking. The masks are similar but not identical, and above each are representations of animals, said to be tapirs. However, the animal on the right appears to me more like a monkey, while the other looks somewhat like a

pot-bellied rabbit, although the feet seem froglike.

There are vertical sections above each animal, and each is decorated with a seated human figure facing front with legs crossed and with arms and hands on the chest. The head is gone from the figure on the left, while the other is better preserved. Above the head of the figure on the right is a face that forms the headdress, and the head of the figure itself wears earplugs. Below the chin are the eyes and part of the nose of another face, and yet another is found on the figure's abdomen.

To the right of the east grotesque mask is another seated jaguar, whose accoutrements are the same as those on the one described above. The extreme left part of the facade is not as well preserved, but it appears that there might have been yet another seated jaguar and another frontal mask.

The style of the bas-relief is distinctly unusual; it seems unrelated to the Río Bec style found at nearby sites to the east or to the Chenes style to the north. When further study is conducted, it will be interesting to see how it is classified.

This elaborate facade occupies the west end of a building reported to be 130 feet long and 49 feet high. The structure borders the north side of a plaza and faces south onto it. The stucco facade was covered with rubble that was part of a later construction, and this protected the bas-relief. The uncovered section of the facade is about 30 to 40 feet long, stretching from the west end of the building toward the center, and you can clearly see

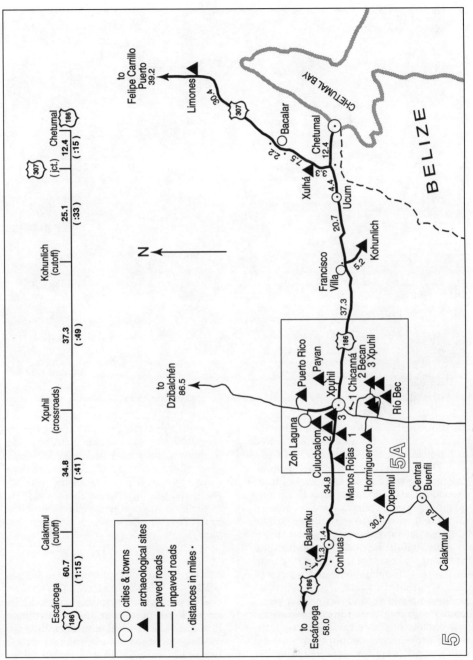

Southeastern Campeche and southern Quintana Roo

Part of the south side of the structure with the bas-relief stucco facade, Balamku. Classic period.

that the bas-relief continues toward the center, though the remainder is still covered with rubble.

When viewed from the plaza, this building has a top profile that is formed of three humps, perhaps indicating that three individual upper structures shared a common platform, or that there were three separate buildings that have slumped together. There are some indications that a stairway once existed in the center of the building (east of the bas-relief facade), but it and the rest of the structure are rubble, as are the structures on the east and south sides of the plaza. There is a pyramidal mound on the west side, with remains on the east side of a wide stairway of gentle slope. Behind (north of) the building with the bas-relief facade is another large rubble mound, but I do not know how far the site extends, since it is just beginning to be studied.

You will want to have a wide-angle lens for overall views of the stucco facade, and a telephoto lens would be useful for detail shots of the upper section. There have been many changes at Balamku in the past two years, and perhaps there will be more. If so, by the time you get there, you may find it to be a three-star site.

Recent History

Balamku was officially discovered in November 1990 by Florentino García Cruz, an archaeologist for the Campeche Regional Center of INAH, and four INAH guardians. Previously, looters had been discovered uncovering the stucco facade, and local people (who call the site Chunhabil) reported these illicit activities to INAH.

Sometime after its official discovery guardians were assigned to the site, and a protective metal roof was installed over the bas-relief facade. The stucco facade was repaired and consolidated by a team of restoration experts headed by Julio Chan. The plaza was completely cleared of low bush, but some small trees were left. The rubble core between the two seated human figures was consolidated.

A short note in the March 1991 issue of *Mexicon* reported the discovery of the site, the result of newspaper reports the journal had received. In this note, the date of the structure with the bas-relief facade is given as around A.D. 500–700, although some authorities believe it may be a little earlier. A May article in the same journal described the stucco facade in more detail, and four photographs of it were included. This article also states that the ceramics collected from a surface survey date from around 300 B.C. to A.D. 600.

Connection

Xpuhil to Balamku: 37.5 miles by paved road (:45), then 1.7 miles by rough dirt road (:20).

Getting There

Head west from Xpuhil on Highway 186 to the cutoff for Balamku (at Kilometer 93.3).

The cutoff is 1.3 miles past (west of) the center of the village of Conhuas. A better check is that the cutoff is 1.0 mile west of the Kilometer 95 marker and the west entrance sign for Conhuas.

If you are approaching from Escárcega and do not spot the dirt road, go on to the Kilometer 95 marker, turn around and go back 1.0 mile. The cutoff is on the north side of the highway, and the dirt road winds around a bit on the way to the site. The first part is bumpy limestone outcrops, but afterward it is a little smoother.

After driving in 1.7 miles, you will see (to the right) what looks like a branch road that goes up a rise (blocked by large stones). This rise is actually part of the structure that borders the south side of the plaza. Park at the branch and walk over the rise to reach the plaza. (The road you came in on actually continues straight ahead and then makes a U-turn and enters the plaza, but this part is steep and bumpy, so it is easier to walk in the last few feet.)

Allow 45 minutes for a visit, and have your own food and drink along—there are none at the site or nearby.

We were told that the road to Balamku would likely be improved in the future, but until it is, a high-clearance vehicle is recommended.

Unrated
CALAKMUL

(kah-lahk-mool; derivation: Maya for "Place [City] of Two Adjacent Mounds [Pyramids]")

> **Location:**
>   Southeastern Campeche.
> **Map:** 5 (p. 245)

The Site

Calakmul is impossible to rate fairly using the criteria applied to the other sites covered in this work. It is truly a special case. Calakmul is enormous and immensely important, with over one hundred reported stelae, re-

cording numerous dynastic texts. William J. Folan, current director of the Calakmul Project, says, "It is one incredible place to do problem oriented research." In the early 1980s the site was mapped, and excavations began later. Significant work was undertaken to clear and consolidate some of the structures. During this work, two magnificent jade mosaic masks were discovered and restored.

On the minus side (for the visitor), there is not a great deal of standing architecture, and most of the stelae are fairly

mask of the 25- to 30-year-old male who was interred—a seventh-century nobleman of Calakmul—and there were also jade plaques, beads, ear flares, and a ring. This burial was discovered in 1985, and the mask and some of the jewelery are now displayed at the Campeche Museum.

Structure VII faces south on to the Central Plaza, and a row of plain stelae is found in front of its base. On the east side of the plaza are more stelae, mostly lying on their sides, but with some carving still discernible. Structure IV, behind these stelae, is overgrown with vegetation.

Bordering the Central Plaza on the south is the small, ruined Structure V, with two fairly well-preserved stelae on the north (plaza) side. Stela 29 (on the right as you face the pair) portrays Ruler 2 of Calakmul, and his wife is depicted on Stela 28 on the left. This royal couple face each other, and both stelae date to A.D. 623. Each figure stands on top of a bound captive, and they too face each other.

Stela 29, depicting Ruler 2, Calakmul. Early part of the Late Classic period.

The sides of the stelae are totally covered with glyphs, some of which record their dates, and there are panels of glyphs on the front of each stelae as well. The stelae are over nine feet tall, and the backs are uncarved.

According to Joyce Marcus, who studied the hieroglyphic inscriptions at Calakmul, "This marital pair from A.D. 623 is the first of at least five royal couples depicted on Calakmul stelae." Along the south base of Structure V are more stelae, most of which are standing and all of which are greatly eroded.

To the south of Structure V is Structure II, the largest at Calakmul. This is a pyramidal base with an assemblage of buildings on top. It rises 175 feet from a base that is nearly 500 feet square and is very similar in dimensions to El Tigre pyramid at El Mirador in Guatemala, 23 miles to the south-southwest. Structure II and the nearby Structure

eroded. The real minus, however, is access to the site, which can range from difficult to impossible. Folan says that in the rainy season it can take two to four days to reach Calakmul. When conditions are ideal—meaning when the road is bone dry and cleared of vegetation—you can drive from the highway to the site in 4 or 5 hours. In any case, reaching Calakmul requires an expedition that should not be undertaken lightly. For those who may wish to try, the site is included here.

As you enter Calakmul, you come first to Stela 1, still standing, and carved on all four sides, but very eroded. To the west is Structure VII, a fair-sized but ruined pyramidal mound with remains of a temple on top. Below the floor of this temple a vaulted burial crypt was found, and it contained approximately 2,000 pieces of jade. Some of these were part of a jade mosaic portrait

I are the two "mounds," or "pyramids," that give Calakmul its name. At the north base of Structure II are some standing but eroded stelae; one is encapsulated by the roots of a tree.

From here it is about 130 yards east to Structure III, the best preserved at the site and by far the most photogenic. Structure III is small when compared to the massive pyramids of Structures I and II, but is still a fair size and contains the remains of 12 rooms resting on a platform about 15 feet high. The platform rises in tiers, and there is a broad stairway on the west side that is the approach to Structure III. Many of the rooms have intact vaults, some of which are stepped, and a good deal of plaster remains on the walls. Ancient graffiti are scratched into the plaster. A more modern inscription was left by Cyrus L. Lundell when he visited Calakmul in 1931; he recorded his name and the date of his visit, and it was he who named the site. A few wooden lintels remain in place in Structure III, and the second jade mosaic mask found at Calakmul was discovered beneath the floor in one of the rooms. This mask, discovered in the late 1980s, portrays an Early Classic ruler who was buried there about A.D. 500. This mask is also in the Campeche Museum.

About 200 yards south-southeast is Structure I, the second largest at Calakmul. This is also a tall pyramid about the height of Structure II but rising from a smaller base. There is also a structure on top. The one standing stelae at the west base of Structure I has had its front and top cut off, and there are glyphs on the sides.

Although there are many other large structures in the central area of Calakmul, they are mostly overgrown, so those described above are the main features of interest for the visitor, except for a sculptured

Stela 28, depicting the wife of Ruler 2, Calakmul. Early part of the Late Classic period.

rock outcrop that I have not seen. It lies about 360 yards to the west of Structure VII and represents seven bound, nude captives; it is reported to be very eroded.

The "downtown" area of Calakmul, which has most of the monumental architecture and stelae, covers an area of 0.7 square mile. The site nucleus, which is surrounded by a system of canals, is 8.5 square

Structure III, west side, Calakmul. Classic period.

miles, and the whole site occupies 27 square miles. This is the size of (or larger than) Tikal, making it one of the largest sites in Mesoamerica. Over 6,500 structures have been mapped at Calakmul, and the population is estimated to have been 60,000 during Late Classic times.

Calakmul went through several developmental stages, spanning the Middle Preclassic through the Terminal Classic periods, with much evidence of a Post-Classic occupation. The stelae at the site date from A.D. 514 to 830.

In addition to being an important individual site, Calakmul during the Late Classic period was also a regional center, dominant over some smaller surrounding sites such as Oxpemul, La Muñeca, Naachtún, and Uxul.

Recent History

Lundell, a botanist working for a chicle firm, was led to Calakmul by chicleros in December 1931. Apparently there were at least a couple of earlier visitors who scratched

their names into the plaster of Structure III, but Lundell was the first to report the site and is credited with its discovery. He found 62 stelae, drew a map of the site, took photographs, and gave the information to James C. Brydon, who worked for the same chicle company. Brydon showed the material to John C. Merriam, then president of the Carnegie Institution of Washington (CIW), when they were both passengers on a boat bound for New Orleans. Merriam forwarded the report to Sylvanus G. Morley, who was then working at Chichén Itzá. Morely, whose major interest was deciphering dates on inscribed monuments, was greatly excited by the news and had Lundell come to Chichén Itzá. Lundell arrived on March 5, 1932, and less than a month later Morley left on the hastily arranged First Campeche Expedition, sponsored by the CIW, to investigate Calakmul. Morley discovered 41 stelae that Lundell had not seen, bringing the total to 103, more by far than reported from any other Maya site. Of the total, 79 were carved. John S. Bolles was a member of the expedition, and he prepared a map of Calakmul.

In 1933 the Second Campeche Expedition returned to Calakmul, with John H. Denison, Jr., as epigrapher. Other expeditions were undertaken in 1934 and 1938, and other sites were investigated, but these expeditions did not return to Calakmul. The information gathered during these four expeditions was published by the CIW in 1943 under the title *Archaeological Reconnaissance in Campeche, Quintana Roo, and Peten.* The authors of this classic work were Karl Ruppert, who studied the architecture, and Denison, who reported on the carved monuments. Their volume, covering twenty-nine sites, is still one of the best sources of information for the area.

After 1933 Calakmul was virtually abandoned for almost fifty years, except for possible visits by chicleros, howler monkeys, and looters, and rare visits by archaeologists and others. In 1982 Folan, as field director and subproject director, undertook work at the site. This was sponsored by the Center of Historic and Social Investigations of the Free University of the Southeast in Campeche, with Román Piña Chan as project director. Later, Folan became project director.

Work continued during the 1980s, which included detailed mapping of the 11.6-square-mile central part of the site. In this work Folan was assisted by Jacinto May Hau. Excavation of the buildings atop Structures I and II, consolidation of the upper part of Structure VII, and clearing and consolidation of Structure III were also undertaken. Some tombs and several stelae and carved boulders were discovered during this work.

Folan long promoted the idea of a national park at Calakmul. In May 1989, the president of Mexico, Carlos Salinas de Gortari, created the Calakmul Biosphere Reserve, which encompasses 1.8 million acres.

Connection

Xpuhil to Calakmul: 34.8 miles by paved road (:41), 13.9 miles by fair rock road (:25), then 24.3 miles by dirt road (variable time, see below).

Total from Xpuhil to Calakmul: 73.0 miles.

Getting There

Guide: Juan de la Cruz Briceño, at Becan.

Note: Visitors are allowed at Calakmul *only* when Folan and his staff are working there, but not at other times without a current written permission from INAH. Juan will know if work is underway at the site and if you may visit it.

From Xpuhil head west on Highway 186 to the cutoff for Calakmul. This is near Kilometer 97 and is a short distance east of (before) the community of Conhuas. Turn left on to the rock road and continue for 13.9 miles. Up to this point you should have no difficulties. When the rock road ends and you start on the dirt road, it is impossible to say what conditions you will encounter. Sometimes in wet weather, long stretches of the dirt road will be under water. At the very least, the road will be slippery and have deep mud; getting stuck will be more than a distinct possibility. For a graphic depiction of what the road can look like, see the photograph on page 460 of the October 1989 issue of *National Geographic.*

If you are still determined to try to reach Calakmul, you must have a high-clearance vehicle with four-wheel drive and a winch, your own food and drink for a couple of days, and a hammock or camping equipment, unless you plan to sleep in your vehicle. At the very least have a machete and ax with you to clear vegetation from the road; a chain saw, in addition, is advisable. Make sure your gas tank is filled before you start, or carry extra gas. You get very poor gas mileage on bad roads.

You should also be able to make minor repairs to your vehicle, because if your have a problem, you are a long way from help. Before you start on the dirt road remove your windshield wiper blades and pull any side-view mirrors in toward the windows. Both wiper blades and mirrors are easy targets for hanging lianas, and both can be ripped off even at speeds of five miles per hour. Be prepared to have branches, twigs, and insects fly into your vehicle, unless it is air-conditioned and you can keep the windows rolled up—which is ideal, of course. Also expect to hear a lot of screeching and thumping as vegetation hits the sides and top of your vehicle. With luck you may not get a broken windshield, but you may lose some trim.

Have a wide-angle lens for your camera and fast film. Wear boots and allow 2 hours to visit the part of the site described above. If you want to climb to the top of Structures VII, II, and I, double or triple that amount of time.

Note: When you leave Calakmul and are heading back to the highway, you pass a cutoff, on the right, that goes about 5 miles to Oxpemul. The cutoff is 13.7 miles past (north of) Central Buenfil. Shortly after the cutoff there are a couple of spots where you get a view of Oxpemul. It appears to be two small hills on top of a larger one, and they are distinct on the eastern horizon. Juan will point them out to you, and it is worth a telephoto shot if you are not pressed for time. It is better to do this on the way out; on the way in, concentrate your efforts on reaching Calakmul.

★

MANOS ROJAS

*(mah-*nohs* roh-*hahs*; derivation: Spanish for "Red Hands" [see text])*

Location:
Southeastern Campeche.
Maps: 5 (p. 245) and 5A (p. 253)

The Site

The name Manos Rojas was given this site because of red-painted handprints found in one of the structures. Manos Rojas is reported to be a scattered site, with several structures and a stone-lined *aguada*, but it is the structure of Group C that is of interest to the visitor. This structure is the northernmost at the known site and is closest to the highway. It is a large building with more than one level and is much destroyed or buried, but there are some remains of corner masks in a vertical row, made of stone and stucco. They are similar to those on Structure XX at Chicanná. To the left of the corner masks (as you face them) are a few remains of relief carving depicting profile masks. Some carved stones that were once a part of the building are found on the ground nearby.

There are two narrow vaulted corridors running at right angles to each other, which begin on each side of the corner masks. The vault on the left is made of well-cut stone and is particularly well preserved. The one on the right is cruder, and both corridors have an offset at the spring line of the vault. Some remains of larger vaults—originally a part of rooms—may be seen on another corner of the structure.

Recent History

Manos Rojas was discovered in 1971 by Jack Eaton during a reconnaissance conducted for the Middle American Research Institute of Tulane University.

Although Manos Rojas has been recorded and the existing architecture studied by David F. Potter and the masks by Paul Gendrop, no excavation or restoration has been undertaken, so little can be said about the site except that the architectural remains date to the Late Classic period and the corner masks are typical of others found in the region.

Connection

Xpuhil to Manos Rojas: 13.6 miles by paved road (:17), then about 200 yards by foot trail (:05).

Getting There

Guide: Juan de la Cruz Briceño, at Becan.

From Xpuhil head west on Highway

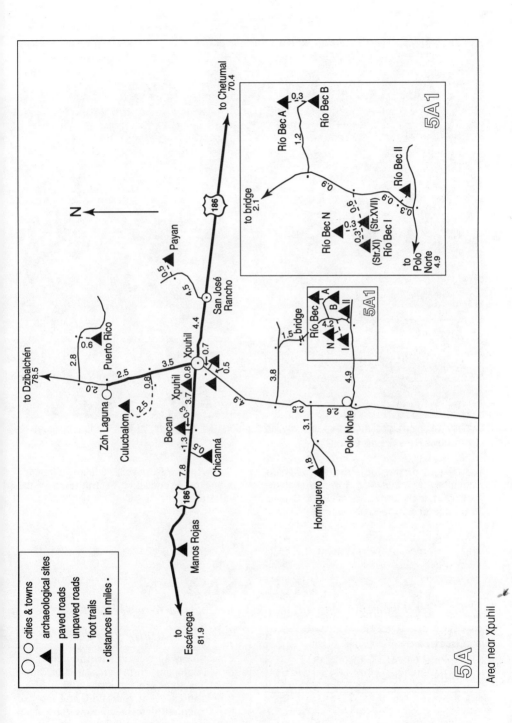

N

to Chetumal
70.4

186

Payan
0.5

San José
Rancho
4.5

4.4

Puerto Rico
0.6
2.8

Xpuhil
0.7

to Dzibalchén
78.5

2.0
2.5
Zoh Laguna

Culucbalom
2.5
0.8
3.5

0.8
3.7
0.3
Xpuhil
0.5

Becan
1.3

Chicanná
0.5

7.8

186

Manos Rojas

to
Escárcega
81.9

4.9

3.8
1.5
bridge

Río Bec
A
B
II
4.2
N
I

5A1

2.5
3.1

2.6
4.9
Polo Norte

Hormiguero
1.8

5A

Area near Xpuhil

5A1 (inset)

Río Bec A
0.3
Río Bec B
1.2

to bridge
2.1
0.9

Río Bec N
(Str.XI)
0.3
0.3
(Str.XVII)
Río Bec I
0.9
0.9

Río Bec II
0.3

to
Polo
Norte
4.9

5A1

Legend

○ ◯ cities & towns
▲ archaeological sites
▬ paved roads
— unpaved roads
· · · foot trails
· distances in miles ·

Remains of corner masks (center) and vaulted corridors (left and right) of the Structure of Group C, Manos Rojas. Late Classic period.

186 and park on the side of the road between Kilometers 131 and 132. From there you walk south to the Structure of Group C, over a trail that may have to be cleared.

Wear boots, have a wide-angle lens for your camera, and allow 30 minutes to see the building.

★ ★ ★
CHICANNÁ

*(chee-kah-*nah; *derivation: Maya for "Serpent-mouth House")*

Location:
    Southeastern Campeche.
Maps: 5 (p. 245) and 5A (p. 253)

The Site

Chicanná is an elegant site and one of the most photogenic in the area. It is medium-sized, but some of its monumental architecture is in excellent condition, and most of the structures described below have been consolidated and restored.

Structure II, Group A, west side, Chicanná. Late Classic period.

When you enter the site, you come first to Group A, with buildings surrounding a plaza, the only well-defined plaza group at the site. Structure II borders the plaza on the east, and it alone would make a visit to Chicanná worthwhile. Its highly ornamental main facade features a typical Chenes-style monster-mouth (or open serpent-mouth) doorway, flanked by profile masks. These are quite similar to the decorations on Structure 2 at Hochob in the Chenes region, 65 miles to the north. It is Structure II at Chicanná that gives the site its name.

This structure is one story with eight rooms; the front row with three, and the rear with five. There are also a few remains of a roof comb above the medial wall. Most of the wall surfaces and the roof comb were originally painted red, as shown by traces of remaining paint. Flanking the decorative facade of the center room are two relatively plain lateral wings, and there is a broad, low stairway on the west (plaza) side. Some of the stucco remains on the interior walls, where interesting graffiti are also found. One is assumed to portray the facing Structure I with its towers, stairways, and simulated temples.

Remains of some red, painted glyphs are found on the exterior of Structure II, immediately to the right of the Chenes monster mask and just below the medial molding, at the top of the plain lower wall of the south room. These glyphs were revealed when a layer of stucco that covered them fell from the surface in 1986. Structure II dates to A.D. 750–770. (All the dates given here for the structures at Chicanná are those presented by David F. Potter, based on the ceramic sequence established by Joseph W. Ball.) For really dramatic results, try to photograph Structure II in the afternoon when the Chenes monster mask is catching the sunlight. It is spectacular.

Structure I, on the west side of the plaza, is a typical Río Bec twin-towered building with a range of rooms connecting the towers. The towers have the usual rounded corners and banded tiers, and there are remains of steep nonfunctional stairways. The towers once supported ornamental simulated temples. There are two rows of three rooms each between the towers, and three doorways face the plaza. There are also two small transverse rooms behind each tower. The vaults of some of the rooms are intact.

Flanking the three exterior doorways are vertical inset panels with carved decorations. Only the lower part remains of the panels next to the center doorway, but the others are better preserved and show profile masks. Structure I rests on a low platform with a broad stairway on the east (plaza)

Central part of the west facade, Structure II, Group A, Chicanná. Late Classic period.

side. On the south side of the structure, part of the facade is standing, and it too has an inset panel. Access to the transverse rooms behind the tower is from this side, and the inner room is intact. A similar entrance is found on the north side of the structure. The back wall of Structure I is solid, the lower wall zone is plain, and there are remains of simple three-member base and medial moldings. Structure I was built slightly earlier than Structure II.

On the north side of the plaza are the remains of Structure III, which has plain, inset facade columns and two doorways with a circular carved stone in front of each. There are other entrances to the structure from the east and north. To the west (left as you face the structure) is another building that is mostly rubble, and both structures have broad stairways on the south, facing the plaza. Structure III was an elite residence built during the Terminal Classic period.

Three other groups at Chicanná can be reached from the Main Plaza. Structure VI, the principal building of Group B, lies about 130 yards southeast of the Main Plaza and is notable for some intact relief sculpture of profile masks and a perforated roof comb, much of which remains. The perforations were partly lined with marine shells. Slabs projecting from this roof comb presumably once supported stucco figures. Structure VI rests on a platform and faces south. It has two rooms, one behind the other, though part of the front room has collapsed. Later, additional rooms were constructed on the east and west sides of the building. Structure VI dates to the same time as Structure I.

About 130 yards southwest of the Main Plaza is Group C, with Structures X and XI. Structure X, with three rooms facing onto a broad terrace, is greatly ruined, but it originally had a panel with a profile mask. Structure XI has 11 or 12 rooms on one level and

Structure I, Group A, east face, Chicanná. Late Classic period.

Structure III, Group A, south side, Chicanná. Terminal Classic period.

was intensively excavated. It shows a developmental type of vaulting, which, along with the associated ceramics, indicates the structure is of relatively early date (A.D. 550–650). Stone lintels are in place in some of the interior rooms. Structure XI-sub, under the visible building, is the earliest structural unit examined at the site; it dates to 400–550.

Farthest from the Main Plaza, about 370 yards northwest, is Group D, with the well-preserved and exuberant Structure XX. This building is composed of two stories and is

Structure VI, Group B, south side, Chicanná. Late Classic period.

one of the latest major constructions recorded at Chicanná. It dates to A.D. 770–830 and it was constructed in two phases; the lower rooms were built first, then the upper rooms and an annex on the first level were added. The first-level rooms are arranged in a rectangle around a central core that supports the upper rooms, and the annex projects to the west.

The front (south) facade of Structure XX is outstanding. The doorway ot the center room on the lower level is surrounded by a monster-mouth doorway, a good deal of which remains. Above this, on the second level, is a doorway with the same motif, also partly intact, and this is flanked by stacked, corner Chac masks that are well preserved. Above the upper rooms are remains of a perforated roof comb. Access to the upper level is by a stairway at the back of the lower central room on the south side of the structure. The stairway ascends for several steps, then divides in two at a landing, and other stairs continue upward, 90 degrees to the right and left. Structure XX rests on a low platform approached by a stair that is divided

in the center by a rectangular construction that has the remains of the lower curled teeth of the lower-level monster-mouth mask.

As you walk around Structure XX, you will see remains of vertical inset panels of profile masks on the facades of both the upper- and lower-level rooms. The lower rooms also have benches decorated with small heads made of stucco, inside a rectangular motif.

There is evidence for a short occupation at Chicanná during the Late Preclassic period, but it was not extensive, and there are no structural remains that date to that period. During the early part of the Early Classic period there is a surprising gap in the ceramic sequence, with no evidence that the site was occupied from about A.D. 250 to 400.

Structural activities began between A.D. 400 and 550, though these constructions are not visible today. The following period, 550–750, was a time of major construction; much of the standing architecture seen today dates to that period. In the next period, 750–830, more architectural activity took place—notably the construction of Structures II and XX. during the last period (830–

Structure XX, Group D, south facade, Chicanná. Late Classic period.

1050) Structure III was built. The site continued to be occupied until around 1100, and there is evidence for ritual activity during this late period, demonstrated by the presence of censers.

Recent History

Chicanná was discovered in 1966 by Jack Eaton during exploration of the area before the formal start of the extensive project jointly sponsored by the National Geographic Society and the Middle American Research Institute of Tulane University. Though Eaton discovered other sites, this find is perhaps the most noteworthy.

It is surprising that Chicanná was not discovered earlier during the Carnegie Institution of Washington's extensive reconnaissance of the area in the 1930s, especially considering its proximity to Becan. This says something about the density of the vegetation in the area.

In 1970 Eaton excavated, consolidated, and partly restored Structure II, and Structure XX was discovered. In the mid–1980s additional excavation and consolidation were undertaken by Román Piña Chan and Ricardo Bueno Cano. The latter was also coordinator of another project that began in October 1991.

Connection

Xpuhil to Chicanná: 5.8 miles by paved road (:09), then 0.5 mile by rock road (:02).

Getting There

Head west from Xpuhil on Highway 186 to the cutoff for Chicanná (marked with a sign), turn left, and proceed to the site. There is no food or drink at the site. Allow 2 hours for a visit.

Buses stop at Xpuhil crossroads.

★ ★ ★
BECAN
(beh-kahn; derivation: Maya for "Ditch Filled with Water")

Location:
Southeastern Campeche.
Maps: 5 (p. 245) and 5A (p. 253)

The Site

Becan is built on a limestone outcrop that is as much as 30 feet higher than the surrounding countryside and is visible from the top of Structure I of Group I at Xpuhil about 4 miles away. The site is famous for its "moat," which gives the site its name. The moat is actually an earthwork made of a ditch and embankment that never held water. The earthwork fortification surrounds the site and conforms well to the edge of the limestone outcrop on which Becan was built.

The ditch is roughly kidney-shaped, with a perimeter of 1.2 miles, and it encloses the 46 acres of the site. It is one of the most massive fortifications known in the Maya area, as well as one of the earliest. A comparison with other Maya fortifications shows the one at Becan to be by far the largest when seen in profile. The ditch is crossed by seven causeways, one of which is the entrance to the site today.

As you enter the site, you come first to Structure I, which borders the south side of the Southeast Plaza. This structure has two massive towers (on the northeast and northwest corners) and two double ranges of rooms running along the complete length of the building on the south side. The rooms are on two levels, and the doorways open to the south, onto a large terrace. The towers, which are about 50 feet high, rise in tiers and have rounded corners, but there is no evi-

Structure I, south side, Becan. Late Classic period.

Structure II, east side, Becan. Late Classic period.

dence for temples on top. The towers are joined by a solid mass, with no openings on the north (plaza) side of the structure, and they had steep nonfunctional stairways on all four sides.

Flanking the central doorway of the lower-level rooms are remains of profile mask panels; presumably there were more stacked above these originally, but only the lower walls of the room are intact. On either side of the doorway on the east side of the lower-level rooms are a pair of recessed panels with a cross motif, near the southeast corner of the building. Next to this, on the right, is another doorway that leads to a narrow interior stairway that is the access to the upper-level rooms. Structure I dates to around A.D. 750; it has been cleared, excavated, and consolidated.

On the terrace to the south of Structure I (east side) is Structure I-a, of which the basal platform remains. It is believed to have been an elite residence, constructed in the Early Postclassic (or Terminal Classic) period. A short distance to the southwest you can see part of the south retaining wall of the terrace, and nearby on the south, Structure I-b. Only a low platform with a western stair remains, and it may once have been topped by a building of perishable materials.

Proceed now to the Southeast Plaza, either by a trail from the upper level on the east side of Structure I or by an exterior stairway on its west side that goes up to plaza level.

Structure II borders the Southeast Plaza on the west. It is composed of a lower range of rooms on the east side, which backs up to a tall pyramidal mound with the remains of a temple on top. This part of Structure II has been cleared and consolidated. On the west side there is also a range of rooms and the

Structure III (left), Structure III-a (center), and the northeast corner of Structure I (upper right), Becan. Structure III was built in the Late Classic period but was enlarged during the Terminal Classic or Early Postclassic period. Structure III-a is believed to be of late date.

main stairway to the top of the structure. The lower walls of the rooms on the east side are standing, and the east facade is decorated with panels of checkerboard designs bordered by stepped elements and with other panels with cross motifs. During excavation two empty tombs were found in one of the lower level rooms.

Structure III, on the east side of the plaza, has three rooms on a lower level and remains of others higher up. There is a broad stairway from the plaza between the central and south rooms on the lower level and a narrower inset stairway between the central and north rooms. Some stucco medallions decorate the edge of the benches in one of the rooms. Structure III was apparently built around A.D. 600–730 but was modified in the Terminal Classic or Early Postclassic period.

In the Southeast Plaza, just in front of the broad stairway of Structure III, is Structure III-a, a low circular construction with a western stair that is thought to be a late-date altar.

Perhaps the most impressive building on the Southeast Plaza is Structure IV, which borders the plaza on the north. This was one of the first and most extensively excavated

structures at Becan. It is also one of the most complex. Structure IV is formed of a pyramidal base, with a broad stairway on the south leading to an upper courtyard surrounded by rooms on three sides.

On the back (north side) of the lower level of the structure are terraces on four levels with additional rooms. There are also Río Bec–style nonfunctional stairways on the east and west sides of the building, as well as interior stairways, one of which exits through the base of the west nonfunctional stairway on its north side. There is a multitude of decorations on Structure IV, and the building totally encases the earlier Structure IV-sub.

On the east side (right as you face the structure) of the front wall that forms the entrance to the upper courtyard of Structure IV are remains of relief carving. The decoration is believed to have once surrounded the doorway. There are also similar remains on the west facade of the structure at the top of the nonfunctional stairway, and both may have represented Chenes-style monster-mouth motifs. There are seven rooms around the upper courtyard, and three have doorways facing it. On either side of these door-

Structure IV, from the southeast, Becan. Late Classic period.

ways are inset panels with cross motifs, bordered on the bottom with stepped elements.

On the north side of Structure IV is a cascade of rooms that form the four levels of the terraces. Access is from the west to Level 2, and you enter from two steps that are supported by decorative stones. On Level 2 there are profile mask panels flanking some of the doorways, and the steps to these rooms are formed of frontal masks. On the first level there are remains of an inset panel with a cross motif. According to E. Wyllys Andrews V, Structure IV-sub dates at the latest to A.D. 150–250 and may have been earlier (100 B.C.–A.D. 150), while Structure IV dates to A.D. 770–830.

To the north of the terraces of Structure IV is Structure V-A, a six-room building that faces east on to a courtyard. There is a double range of three rooms, and the east facade has remains of checkerboard panels, bordered by stepped elements, on either side of the central doorway.

To the northwest of Structure V-A is the greatly ruined Structure VI, which has not

been excavated. This is a large platform with mounds on top. One feature of interest here is a vaulted tunnel, aligned east-west, that runs along the south side of the structure; the western entrance to the tunnel can be seen next to the south side of the platform of Structure VI. On its eastern end, the tunnel connects to the courtyard faced by Structure V-A.

Adjacent to the north of Structure VI is Structure VIII, a massive building with a pyramidal base, remains of rooms and two large round pillars on top, and towers near the northwest and southwest corners of the upper level. Structure VIII dates to around A.D. 600–730. It had a broad stairway on the front (west) that faced the Central Plaza and the stairway may have risen in two sections, according to David F. Potter. One exploratory excavation was made at Structure VIII on the north end of the lower stairway some years ago. Consolidation of Structure VIII was begun in 1992. The top of Structure VIII is a good vantage point for photographs of Structure X across the Central Plaza to the west.

Intact mask panel and step mask on Level 2 of the north side of Structure IV, Becan. Late Classic period.

Inside the pyramidal base of Structure VIII is a series of vaulted rooms connected by narrow passageways. The rooms are undecorated and relatively small, especially compared to the height—over 25 feet in one area. The purpose of the rooms is unknown. The entrance to these rooms is on the south side of the pyramidal base of the structure, near its east end. If you decide to visit these interior rooms, have a flashlight and extra batteries—it is pitch black inside—and a flash unit for your camera. It would also be best to have someone along who knows the layout of the rooms. Ask Juan de la Cruz Briceño, the caretaker of Becan, when you enter the site.

To the northwest of Structure VIII is Structure IX, bordering the Central Plaza on the north. At 100 feet high, this is the tallest structure at Becan, and we were told there are plans to consolidate it. It probably had a southern stairway (facing the Central Plaza) and a temple on top.

Structure X on the west side of the Central Plaza is better preserved and has been partly excavated and consolidated. This structure has rooms on two levels and a stairway on the east (rising in two tiers with a landing in between) facing the plaza. One of the risers of the lower stairway is incised with an *ahau* sign. (This sign is a stylized face that signifies "lord." *Ahau* is also a day in the Maya month.) At the level of the landing there is a small, rectangular opening into the upper stairway.

The first-level rooms formed lateral wings on the north and south sides of the stairway. The upper level originally had two rows of three rooms each, but most of the end rooms have fallen, except for parts of a couple of doorjambs. The center rooms are better preserved, and the most notable feature of Structure X is the sculptured remains of a Chenes-style monster-mouth doorway on the east facade of the center doorway. The vault above the doorway has fallen, and along with it the upper part of the design, but a fair amount is in place on either side. There are remnants of red, yellow, and blue-green paint on the thin layer of stucco that covers the stone reliefs.

The doorway in the medial wall between the center rooms is intact and is still spanned by its original, well-preserved wooden lintels. Above the medial wall of the structure is the lower part of a perforated roof comb. Structure X dates to around A.D. 600–730 and covers an earlier building.

Structure X, east side, Becan. Late Classic period.

To the west of Structure X is the West Plaza, surrounded by long, low platforms on the north and south sides and by a group of greatly fallen buildings, collectively called Structure XIII, on the west. Structure XI, a ball court, is on the east side of the West Plaza and abuts the southwest base of Structure X. Outside this plaza, to the north and near the north edge of the ditch, is the ruined Structure XII, on the south side of which is the one standing stela (Stela 1) known from Becan; unhappily, it is uncarved. The three other stelae reported were originally carved but are badly eroded and broken.

Ceramic and lithic evidence indicates that Becan was occupied from the late part of the Middle Preclassic period (550 B.C.), possibly by colonists from the Petén in Guatemala. During the Late Preclassic (after about 50 B.C.) the first architectural activity began, notably, but not only, Structure IV-sub; the monumental earthworks were built around A.D. 150–250. There was an apparent decline in population from around 250 to 450, and little architecture from this part of the Early Classic period is known at Becan. From 450 to 600 population increased, and there is evidence of Teotihuacán influence in the ceramics. One outstanding example is in the Mérida Museum; see that section for details.

Between A.D. 600 and 730 the ditch began to be used as a refuse dump. Río Bec–style architecture flourished during this period, and this style continued into the next period (730 to 830). From that time to 950 there is evidence of a possible invasion by people from the northwestern part of the Yucatán Peninsula, and some of the existing structures at Becan were adapted and modified "following new spatial requirements," according to Ricardo Bueno Cano. Between 950 and 1050 there are signs of cultural decline, and major architectural activity stopped. From around 1200 to 1450 the only evidence of occupation are some Mayapán-type censers. From then until the early twentieth century, the area was virtually unoccupied.

Recent History

From 1932 through 1938 the Carnegie Institution of Washington sponsored explorations in the Río Bec region and adjacent areas. The results of these efforts were published by Karl Ruppert and John H. Denison, Jr., in 1943. During their reconnaissance, they discovered many sites, including Becan in 1934.

E. Wyllys Andrews IV was project director of work carried out in the Río Bec region (including Becan) from 1969 through 1971, sponsored jointly by the National Geographic Society and the Middle American Research Institute (MARI) of Tulane University. Under his directorship, a great deal of new information was gathered. Extensive ceramic analysis was undertaken by Joseph W. Ball (who returned in 1973 for additional research), the lithic assemblages were studied by Irwin Rovner, the fortifications by David Webster, the architecture by Potter, and the cultural ecology by Ingolf Vogeler. In addition, Jack Eaton, of the field staff of MARI, undertook extensive reconnaissance, discovering numerous sites and relocating sites previously reported.

The prehistoric settlement of the Becan area was studied by Prentice Thomas, Jr., for a joint University of Tennessee–National Geographic Society expedition in 1972 and 1973. The area studied extended from Xpuhil to beyond Chicanná, or over 6 miles from east to west, by 0.6 mile to 1.5 miles from north to south. The preliminary report published by MARI in 1974 was compiled by Richard E. W. Adams, who was also director of the work at Becan during the 1970 season.

Additional work on the lithic artifacts was undertaken by James B. Stoltman in 1973, and there was further study of the Preclassic architecture in the same year by E. Wyllys Andrews V. MARI published these more extensive reports from 1976 through 1981.

From the mid–1970s through the mid–1980s, the Southeast Regional Center of INAH and the state government of Campeche carried out explorations and consolidation of some of Becan's major structures. This work was directed by Román Piña Chan and Bueno Cano. In October 1991 the latter became coordinator of a new project of consolidation.

Connection

Xpuhil to Becan: 4.5 miles by paved road (:07), then 0.3 mile by fair rock road (:03).

Getting There

Head west from Xpuhil on Highway 186 to the cutoff for Becan (marked with a sign). Turn right onto the rock road, and continue to the site. There is no food or drink at Becan. Allow 2 hours for a visit.

Buses stop at Xpuhil crossroads.

★ ★ ★
XPUHIL

(shpoo-heel; derivation: Maya for "Place of the Cattails"; named after a nearby aguada)

Location:
Southeastern Campeche.
Maps: 5 (p. 245) and 5A (p. 253)

The Site

The lovely Structure I of Group I at Xpuhil is a rather typical example of Río Bec–style architecture, with towers joined by a lower range of rooms. One unusual feature here, however, is the incorporation of three towers, rather than the two generally encountered.

The structure has been cleared and consolidated, and it rests atop a platform with rounded corners. The structure faces east, and there are three doorways on that side to the lower-level rooms. Flanking the doorways are vertical inset mask panels; those next to the center doorway portray frontal masks, while the panels adjacent to the other doorways have profile masks. The center room is recessed from the others, and at the junctions the lower walls are rounded, giving the feeling of corner facade columns. Much of the upper walls of the rooms has fallen. There are three rooms behind the front row, each with a single entrance from the room in front. There is a step up, from the front to rear rooms, and one step is decorated with *ik-* or T-shaped motifs.

Behind the towers on each end of the structure are two rooms, entered from the

Structure I of Group I, the back (west) side, Xpuhil. Late Classic period.

Detail of the mask panel and simulated temple on the upper part of the west tower, west side, Structure I of Group I, Xpuhil. Late Classic period.

north and south sides of the building. Inset panels also decorate these areas, though only parts of the decoration remain.

The central tower is the best preserved, especially its west side, with its rounded corners, banded tiers, and some steps remaining of its ornamental stairway. Its simulated temple and parts of the monster-mouth decoration that surrounded the false doorway are in place. (The simulated temple and those that originally topped the other two towers may or may not have had roof combs.)

Even better preserved is a frontal maks panel just below the temple of the west tower. You will want a telephoto lens to get shots of the temple and mask. Originally there were three masks along this stairway (and it is believed that there were also three on the east side on each of the north and south towers);

according to David F. Potter, the masks are "obviously feline." This is an interesting point; most of the mask decorations in the Río Bec region are reptilian in nature.

The north and south towers have some of their lower steps in place, and according to Tatiana Proskouriakoff, who did a restoration drawing of the structure, the stairs incline only 20 degrees from the vertical. For this reason, the risers had to be given an outward batter to provide the indication of steps. There is an interior stairway in the south tower. Paul Gendrop dates Structure I of Group I to around A.D. 760.

About 60 yards to the east of Structure I is Structure II, which has been cleared and consolidated. Structure II rests on a platform with a broad stairway on the east side (flanked by *alfardas*) and rooms on the north, west, and south. Only the lower walls of the rooms remain. According to Ricardo Bueno Cano, Structure II was an elite residence constructed during the Postclassic period. He also notes that the *alfardas* flanking the stairway are an uncommon characteristic in Río Bec–style architecture.

Recent History

Group I of Xpuhil was discovered by Karl Ruppert and John H. Denison, Jr., in the 1930s, while they were working for the Carnegie Institution of Washington. They reported this find as well as others in 1943, and Proskouriakoff's drawing of Structure I accompanied their volume.

This drawing plus photos and a model of Structure I at Río Bec B were the main sources of information on Río Bec–style architecture until the work in the area sponsored by the National Geographic Society and Tulane University in the late 1960s and 1970s. During this work Jack Eaton discovered Groups II, III, and IV at Xpuhil, and Structure I was cleared. Some additional clearing and minor restoration were undertaken in 1977.

In the mid-1980s further work was conducted by Bueno Cano, and Structure II was consolidated. In October of 1991 a new project began at Xpuhil, coordinated by Bueno Cano.

Note: Two other structures that may be a part of Xpuhil lie along the rock road that heads south from Xpuhil crossroads. The first is 0.7 mile (:02) south of the crossroads and a few hundred feet to the left of the road, from which it is visible. It is on the land of a lumberyard, and you can ask permission there to visit the structure. A fair amount of the walls of the structure are standing.

The second structure is 0.5 mile (:02) south of the first, along the rock road, and is immediately to the right. In fact, when the road was constructed, it actually cut through part of the building. This appears to have been a rather large structure that possibly had a tower, and we were told that it once had a mask that is now completely gone.

Pitifully few facing stones remain on the structure. In one area there are about two dozen that formed part of a simple, rectangular three-member molding, with the center part recessed, and in another area a few stones are stacked vertically, apparently part of an exterior wall.

Connection

Xpuhil (crossroads) to Xpuhil (ruins): 0.8 mile by paved road (:01), then a couple of hundred yards on foot (:03).

Getting There

From Xpuhil crossroads head west on Highway 186 to the parking area for the site (on the right). Structure I is on the north side of the highway, from which it is easily visible, and you walk there from the parking area. There is no food or drink at the site. Allow 45 minutes for a visit.

Buses stop at Xpuhil corssroads.

★
CULUCBALOM

(koo-look-bah-lohm; derivation: the intended meaning is "Men Seated at a Conference" in Maya [see text])

Location:
    Southeastern Campeche.
Maps: 5 (p. 245) and 5A (p. 253)

The Site

Culucbalom is principally composed of a plaza with five structures arranged around it, although another structure and a low mound are also reported. The site is totally

Inset panel to the right (north) of the central doorway, east side, Structure V, Culucbalom. Late Classic period.

overgrown, and although we were told the plaza was 50 meters wide, we could not see across it because of the vegetation. Today only two of the plaza structures are of interest to the visitor.

Structure I, the larger and better preserved of the two, bounds the plaza on the north and faces south. It is reportedly composed of six rooms, although only the two center rooms are easily discernible today, since much has collapsed. The center rooms, one behind the other, are on a high platform; the east and west rooms are on a lower level. The center rooms are reached by a rocky foot trail up the south side. On each side of the central doorway are two inset panels with applied carved columns, and each column bears the depiction of two seated figures, one above the other.

According to Karl Ruppert and John H. Denison, Jr., "The native workmen gave the name Culucbalom to the site because they said that the name meant 'men seated at a conference.'" Only three of the original columns remain, and they are rather eroded. A fourth, reported to be the best preserved of the lot, has been removed from its place and is believed to have been looted. Above and

below the columns are short sections of a three-part molding, which give the effect of capitals. There is a perforated roof comb on Structure I, with a few remains of projecting figures. Graffiti, both ancient and modern, are found on the interior plaster walls of the center rooms.

To the southwest of Structure I is Structure V, set atop a low platform. Three rooms are reported, but only the center one is easily visible today, and much of its vault has collapsed. The most interesting feature is a pair of inset carved panels flanking the central doorway. They depict stylized profile masks similar to those on the north side of Structure IV at Becan.

Adjacent to the south of Structure V is a rubble mound that is the remains of Structure VI.

In a chart published in 1987, Paul Gendrop dates Structure I to around A.D. 640, and Structure V to about 740.

Recent History

Culucbalom was discovered in the 1930s during extensive exploration by the Carnegie Institution of Washington (CIW). This site and many others were reported on by Ruppert and Denison in a 1943 CIW publication. The site is also mentioned by Alberto Ruz Lhuillier in 1945.

In a 1987 study, Gendrop attempted a new stylistic evolution of profile mask panels in the Río Bec style, and the panels on Structure V at Culucbalom were included.

Connection

Xpuhil to Culucbalom: 3.5 miles by paved road (:04), 0.8 mile by poor dirt road (:10), then about 2.5 miles by foot trail (1:00—but see below).

Total from Xpuhil to Culucbalom: 6.8 miles (1:14).

Getting There

Guide: Juan de la Cruz Briceño, at Becan.

From Xpuhil head north on the road that goes toward Zoh Laguna. Turn left onto an unmarked dirt car trail, and proceed to the caretaker's house. Drive this part *very* slowly because the road goes over limestone outcrops that are hidden by vegetation.

From the caretaker's house proceed on foot to the site. This sounds relatively easy, but it is not. Sometimes years go by without a single visitor going to Culucbalom, so the trail is often completely overgrown in parts, and not too well defined in other parts.

The first section is generally in fairly decent shape, but it soon gets worse, and then much worse. Perhaps it would be more accurate to say that in some areas there *is* no trail and that a new one has to be cut. Most of the way you are traveling through dense second-growth vegetation. There is no way to describe this to someone who has not experienced it. Suffice to say that it requires constant machete work.

It took us 2 hours and 20 minutes on foot to reach the site, including time for Juan to relocate the trail. Of course, if a trail has been recently cut, you could make it much faster. On the return trip it took us only 1 hour at a fast pace. The vegetation can completely obliterate the trail in a matter of a few months. This is unquestionably the worst foot trail I have ever traveled.

Wear boots and a long-sleeved shirt because there are many thornbushes and some wasps. It is also a dandy place to pick up *garrapatas* ("ticks"). Bring a canteen of water, fast film, and a wide-angle lens for your camera. You do not need a sun hat, but having your own machete along to help clear the trail is a good idea. Allow 1 hour to visit the site once you reach it.

★
PUERTO RICO

*(poo-*ehr*-toh* ree-*koh; derivation: Spanish for "Rich Port")*

Location:
   Southeastern Campeche.
Maps: 5 (p. 245) and 5A (p. 253)

The Site

The main feature of interest at Puerto Rico is an almost solid, large cylindrical tower that once had a stepped, pointed top. The tower rests on a conical platform that is now mostly destroyed, although the tower itself is well preserved. It reaches an impressive height of about 20 feet and is about 10 feet in diameter, but it bears no decoration.

The facing stones on the tower are meticulously cut and carefully laid and are intact for the most part. The tower is pierced by a few small shafts or ducts, but there are no rooms on the inside. The original function of the tower remains uncertain, although it has been speculated that the shafts were used in some way for astronomical determinations. This, however, has not yet been demonstrated. Without excavation it is

Solid cylindrical tower, Puerto Rico. Late or Terminal Classic period.

impossible to tell if the tower contained a tomb, which would indicate a funerary function. In any case, the Puerto Rico tower is unique, not only in the Maya area, but also in all of Mesoamerica. The details of construction of the tower date it to the Late Classic or Terminal Classic period.

About 160 feet east of the tower is a plaza surrounded by remains of ancient structures, but these are simply mounds today. There are openings into the plaza in the center of the mounds on the north and west sides, and reportedly on the other two sides as well.

Recent History

Puerto Rico was discovered by Jack Eaton and Loring M. Hewen in 1967, and the tower was reported upon by E. Wyllys Andrews IV in 1968, in a work published in Mexico.

In 1980 archaeoastronomer Anthony F.

Aveni wrote about the Puerto Rico tower and noted that "the shafts were evidently constructed with great care for they are perfectly straight and dead level with the horizon." His measurements of the direction of the shafts confirmed Andrews's report, but Aveni could find no important astronomical significance to them. He suggested other possibilities for the construction of the shafts but ends by admitting that "the exact function of the circular tower at Puerto Rico must remain a total mystery to us, at least for the present."

In 1989 George F. Andrews analyzed four freestanding towers in the Chenes region; in a comparison, he says that the Puerto Rico tower "shows no real affinities with the Chenes towers and the only similarity between them is that all can generally be described as having tower-like forms." (See "El Tabasqueño" in Section 3 for more on the Chenes towers.)

There has been no significant excavation at Puerto Rico.

Connection

Xpuhil to Puerto Rico: 6.0 miles by paved road (:07), 2.0 miles by good rock road (:05), 2.8 miles by poor rock road (:11), then 0.6 mile by dirt (grass) road (:05).

Total from Xpuhil to Puerto Rico: 11.4 miles (:28).

Getting There

Guide: Juan de la Cruz Briceño, at Becan.

Head north from Xpuhil on the paved road that later becomes a rock road, to the cutoff for Puerto Rico. Turn right on another rock road and go to the next cutoff. Turn right onto the dirt (grass) road and continue to the site. If the dirt (grass) road is blocked by trees lying across it, you can walk to Puerto Rico in just a few minutes more than it will take you to drive this last part.

Wear boots and allow 30 minutes to see the tower and visit the plaza.

A NOTE ON THE RÍO BEC SITES

> **Maps:** 5 (p. 245), 5A and 5A1 (p. 253)

There are a number of groups called Río Bec scattered in this immediate area. They are numbered I to VIII, lettered A through E, and G, H, J, K, L, M, and N. The group originally reported as F was later designated number I, and to avoid confusion, there is no letter I in the series. Some of these groups have several structures, while others are a single building, and some of them are separated by a fair distance.

According to H. E. D. Pollock, "There is no reason to believe that these groups form a single site, but further explorations might disclose a continuous pattern of remains over much of the area." Since Pollock wrote this in 1965 several new groups have been discovered; his statement, however, still seems to hold true today.

Of the many groups so far reported, Group B is by far the most interesting to visit. Five of the groups are covered here: Groups I, II, A, B, and N, and they will be considered separately, except for the capsule information at the beginning that relates to all the groups, which is covered under Río Bec B. The "Recent History" for Río Bec B also includes the pertinent information on Groups A, I, II.

While it is possible to visit all five groups in one day from Xpuhil if conditions are *ideal*—meaning that the dirt roads are bone dry and you do not have to spend time removing trees that have fallen across them—it would still be a long and tiring trip of 7 to 8 hours, bumping along bad roads and walking along foot trails.

I recommend going to Río Bec B first for best photographs of the front of Structure I. Reaching Río Bec B will give you a fair idea of what the dirt roads in the area are like at that particular time. You can then decide whether you want to visit the other groups. Since these are less photogenic and often overgrown, the time of day that you reach them is less important.

After Río Bec B, the two most interesting are Group I, Structure XVII, and Group N, Structure I.

Guide: Juan de la Cruz Briceño, at Becan. Juan will point out the cutoffs to the various groups, which would be easy to miss even with the maps included here. None of the junctions is marked.

★ ★

RÍO BEC B

*(ree-oh behk; derivation: Río is Spanish for "river,"
and Bec is Maya for "evergreen oak" [see text]).*

Location:
   Southeastern Campeche.
Maps: 5 (p. 245), 5A and 5A1
   (p. 253)

The Site

Structure I at Río Bec B is magnificent; it is one of the best-preserved buildings in the region and has been consolidated. It was one of the first buildings discovered in the area and has the romance of having been "lost" for over sixty years before it was relocated

(see below). If access were easier, Río Bec B would be a three-star site.

Structure I has six rooms on one level, two in the center (one behind the other) and two smaller ones on each end. Some of the corbeled vaults supporting the roof over the rooms have collapsed, but essentially the feeling of the whole is preserved. When you look at it, you know exactly how the Maya architect who designed it wanted it to look.

There is a central doorway on the front (east) side and a doorway on each of the north and south sides. Flanking the central doorway in the lower wall zone are inset panels with a checkerboard design, framed by a

Structure I of Group B, east side, Río Bec. Late Classic period.

---

274   •   *THE SITES AND MUSEUMS*

Detail of the south part of the roof comb (east side), Structure I of Group B, Río Bec. Note remains of the mask panel at lower right. Late Classic period.

stepped pattern. The three-member base molding has colonnettes in groups of three in the middle part, bordered by plain stones on either side.

There are 55-foot-high towers on each end of the front facade, with typical rounded corners, banded tiers, and nonfunctional stairs leading to simulated temples on top. The temples are decorated with monster-mouth masks on the east and west sides and with inset panels bearing a cross motif (repeated four times vertically) on the north and south sides. The stairways of the towers incline only about 8 degrees from the vertical and have the same outward batter seen at Xpuhil.

The doorways of the structure, including those in the simulated temples, were topped by wooden lintels. Some of these were still in place when the building was rediscovered, but they were replaced with new lintels to protect the structure when it was consolidated.

Above the medial wall of the central part of the structure and in between the towers is a two-part perforated roof comb. The lower portion is decorated with stylized masks of stone; above this were three-dimensional human figures made of stucco. The figures

are almost totally gone, but the masks are mostly intact.

There are also remains of checkerboard panels flanking the doorways on the north and south sides of the building and colonnettes in the base molding. The rear of the structure is plain except for simple moldings, and the base molding has plain colonnettes in groups of three.

There are some interesting graffiti on the plaster walls on the interior of the rooms. They are not difficult to photograph, but you will need relatively fast film. Most of the graffiti are of a type commonly found at other Maya sites, and include depictions of temples, processions, and typical (if rather crude) Maya-style profiles. All are worth a photograph. The most unusual graffito, however, is a naturalistic, two-foot-high nude female torso that is quite contemporary in feeling. It was dubbed the "Botticelli Nude" by Hugh Johnston, who discovered it and apparently believed it to be quite old. Some authorities, however, feel that it was probably incised in the last century. In any case, it is completely un-Maya in feeling.

While it is undisputed that Structure I at Río Bec B was constructued during the Late Classic period, its exact date within this period is still debated. In 1987 Paul Gendrop proposed a date of A.D. 630 for the first phase of construction and 680 for the second phase. Other authorities believe the structure was built somewhat later (700–850).

A few yards to the north of Structure I is another greatly fallen and overgrown building. According to Juan de la Cruz Briceño, this structure has two rows of two rooms each, the same north-south alignment as Structure I, but no towers. Considering what we saw of it, this sounds reasonable.

Recent History

Structure I at Río Bec B has—to me at least—one of the most interesting histories of all the sites in this guide. In 1906–1907 French archaeologist Maurice de Périgny explored the Río Bec region and was the first to record the existence of pre-Hispanic buildings in the area. One of the structures he found had square towers with rounded corners and was unlike other known Maya buildings in the Petén or Yucatán. He named it Río Beque, after a small stream (or dry watercourse) in the area, of which there are precious few.

In 1912 Raymond E. Merwin and Clarence L. Hay, under the auspices of the Peabody Museum of Harvard University, visited the area and relocated the structure discovered by Périgny. In addition they discovered others. One of these was near Périgny's building, was similar to it in design, but was much better preserved. To distinguish the two, Périgny's structure was called Río Bec A, and the one found by Merwin and Hay Río Bec B. They also discovered Groups C through F.

Merwin and Hay spent some time at Río Bec B and cleared Structure I of its mantle of vegetation. Hay then took some excellent photographs of the temple; one classic shot has been widely reproduced.

Merwin's work formed part of his doctoral dissertation but was never published. Not until 1935 did Hay publish an article in *Natural History Magazine* about the structure; this was occasioned by the completion of a model of the temple, produced by Shoichi Ichikawa for the American Museum of Natural History. The model was produced from Hay's photographs and Merwin's field notes and at the time was considered "the finest reproduction of a Maya temple ever constructed."

In the 1930s several expeditions to the area were sponsored by the Carnegie Institution of Washington, and these were reported by Karl Ruppert and John H. Denison, Jr., in 1943. During these expeditions only Merwin's Group F was relocated, and since additional structures were discovered in this group, it was relabeled Group I. Other new groups (II through V) were also discovered, but Structure I at Río Bec B was not to be found. You could look at photographs and a model of this large temple, but no one really knew where it was. It seemed almost inconceivable that, once found, it could be lost again. That, however, is exactly what happened.

In 1971 Jack Eaton of the field staff of the Middle American Research Institute of Tulane University (working under the sponsorship of the National Geographic Society) methodically cut a grid system through much of the area. Using Merwin's information and reports of local residents who claimed to have seen it a few years earlier, he fruitlessly attempted to relocate Structure I at Río Bec B; he did, however, find three new groups (VI, VII, and VIII).

Also in 1971 Hugh and Suzanne Johnston, a documentary film team from Princeton engaged by WNET/13 to do a film on "Mystery of the Maya" for television viewing, visited the area and were shown around by Eaton. The Johnstons returned to the area in 1972 and 1973. On their third trip they were accompanied by Gillet Griffin, pre-Columbian art historian at Princeton University, and Andrea Seuffert, an artist with the Mexico City Museum.

In between trips the Johnstons had studied Merwin's field notes, and they drew their own map from his data. The field notes and dissertation were contradictory. The dissertation located Structure I at Río Bec B and other structures in a north-south direction from a given point. The field notes, which turned out to be correct, pointed east-west.

With this preliminary work, the aid of

workmen in the area, and Juan de la Cruz Briceño as their chief guide, they rediscovered Río Bec B in May 1973. This was a truly exciting find for the world of archaeology. It became known that the elusive Structure I at Río Bec B lay but a stone's throw from one of the trails previously cut by Eaton. The discovery was reported in June 1973, and Río Bec B rejoined other sites in the annals of Maya archaeology.

Structure I was cleared once again and filmed by the Johnstons. It was presented on television as part of "Mystery of the Maya" in April 1974.

In the late 1970s and 1980s Structure I was further cleared and consolidated, and its architecture and decoration were studied by Gendrop and George F. Andrews.

In 1984 the South Frontier Archaeological Project was undertaken, and in 1986 the results were reported by Ramón Carrasco Vargas, Sylvian Boucher, and Agustín Peña, all of the Yucatán Regional Center of INAH. Most of the previously reported groups at Río Bec were relocated, and several new groups were reported. Additional work at Río Bec began in October of 1991, coordinated by Richardo Bueno Cano.

Connection

Xpuhil to Río Bec B: 6.1 miles by good rock road (:15), then 8.6 miles by variable dirt road (1:06).

Getting There

Guide: Juan de la Cruz Briceño, at Becan.

Take the rock road that heads south from Xpuhil for 6.1 miles, turn left onto a dirt road, and go 3.8 miles. Take the right branch at this junction and go 1.5 miles to a small bridge (actually nothing more than a few planks, but it is usable). Continue another 2.1 miles to the cutoff for Río Bec B. Turn left at the cutoff and go 1.2 miles to the site.

A high-clearance vehicle is needed to reach Río Bec B (and the other Río Bec sites covered here as well), and four-wheel drive will be necessary if the dirt roads are wet. Have a wide-angle lens for overall shots of the front of Structure I, and allow 1 hour to visit the site.

Note: When you take the rock road heading south from Xpuhil, you will pass two ruined structures alongside it. See "Xpuhil" for more details.

RÍO BEC A

The Site

Structure I at Río Bec A is not as well preserved as its counterpart of Group B, but it also had towers with rounded corners. Eight rooms are reported, but much of the structure has fallen, although part of the back wall is standing. The base molding of the structure is like that of Structure I of Group B, with plain columns separated by flat stones in the middle part; remains of this can be seen on the back wall.

Connection

See "Río Bec B." Río Bec B to Río Bec A: about 600 yards by foot trail (:15—see below).

Getting There

From Río Bec B you can walk to Río Bec A, which lies to the north. If the trail is clear, you can walk there in the time indicated; if it is overgrown, it will take somewhat longer.

Allow 15 minutes to see Río Bec A. Have a wide-angle lens for your camera.

★
RÍO BEC I

The Site

Río Bec I is a rather large group with 17 numbered structures aligned roughly east-west. Most of the structures have fallen, but two are of interest to the visitor today. On the east edge of the site is Structure XVII (formerly Merwin's Group F), which has been consolidated. The structure rests on a platform that also supported two other buildings that have collapsed. A short climb from the south to the top of the platform brings you to Structure XVII. Of the six original rooms of the structure, the two in the middle (one behind the other) are partly intact, although the vaults have fallen. The structure faces

west and is most notable for the remains of a monster-mouth doorway on the west facade that is fairly well preserved. This building has been dated to around A.D. 800 by Paul Gendrop.

About 470 yards to the west is Structure XI of Group I, which can be reached by foot trail. This is a rather large twin-towered structure with eight rooms that have mostly fallen. The structure faces east, and the twin towers are standing, with remains of typical rounded corners and banded tiers made of well-cut stones. The facing stones of the nonfunctional stairways have fallen, and there are no remains of the simulated temples that probably once topped the towers. The rear

Detail of the center of the west facade, Structure XVII of Group I, Río Bec. Late Classic period.

(west side) of the structure is plain and without doorways.

When Structure XI was first reported, there were remains of beautifully executed, well-preserved stone and stucco relief sculpture on the east facade, between the central doorway and the north tower, depicting a monster-mouth motif. Unhappily this sculpture has totally fallen. Gendrop dates Structure XI to around A.D. 780. The structure is overgrown and will require some clearing to photograph the towers.

Connection

Xpuhil to Río Bec I (Structure XVII): 6.1 miles by good rock road (:15), 8.3 miles by variable dirt road (:56), then 0.6 miles by foot trail (:19).

Total from Xpuhil to Río Bec I (Structure XVII): 15.0 miles (1:30).

Getting There

See "Río Bec B" for getting as far as the last cutoff for that site. When you reach the cutoff for Río Bec B, instead of turning left, continue straight ahead for another 0.9 mile. Park on the side of the road and walk to the right to Structure XVII. At one time you could drive this last part, but it has become too overgrown for vehicles. From Structure XVII to Structure XI is 0.3 mile, a 14-minute walk.

Allow 15 minutes to visit each of the structures, plus some extra time to clear Structure XI. Carry a canteen of water, and have a wide-angle lens for your camera.

★
RÍO BEC N

The Site

Structure I at Río Bec N is remarkably like its counterpart at Río Bec B, though the former is not as well preserved. Although mounds are reported in the area, Structure I is the only numbered building at Río Bec N. This structure faces north and is slightly smaller than Structure I at Río Bec B, but the floor plans of the two are almost identical. At Río Bec N the two towers are standing, with some of the rounded corners and banded tiers intact. The facing stones that formed the steps have fallen, but a good deal of the simulated temples atop the towers is intact.

Another similarity with Structure I at Río Bec B is the use of inset checkerboard panels flanking the central doorway on the main facade and the use of inset cross motifs on the sides of the simulated temples.

Minor differences include the number of squares in the checkerboard pattern—11 across on the panels on the front of Structure I at Río Bec B, and 9 on Structure I at Río Bec N—and four cross motifs on the simu-

lated temples at B and three at N. The great similarity of the two buildings led George F. Andrews to conclude that Structure I at Río Bec N "appears to have been modeled after Río Bec B (or vice versa)."

It is not known whether there were checkerboard panels flanking the doorways on the sides of Structure I at Río Bec N (as there are at B), since much of this part of the structure has fallen. According to Hasso Hohmann, "There is no evidence of the existence of a roof comb [at Río Bec N] as in Río Bec B." Structure I at Río Bec N has not been cleared, much less excavated; no doubt if it were, some of the questions about its architectural details would be clarified.

Recent History

In 1974 Andrea Seuffert published an article about the rediscovery of Río Bec B in the bulletin of INAH. In the article, another twin-towered structure—with checkerboard panels having nine squares across—was mentioned, and it is believed that this was Structure I at Río Bec N. In 1974 Andrews

Structure I of Group N, north side, Río Bec. Late Classic period. This photograph was taken with a wide-angle lens pointed upward, which causes distortion. Although the towers appear to be tilted, they are actually vertical.

visited and photographed the building, and in 1985 Hohmann did the same. Later that year, Hohmann published a brief description and sketch of the structure, and in 1987 another report with drawings and photographs, including one taken by Andrews in 1974. Hohmann was taken to Río Bec N by Juan de la Cruz Briceño, who told Hohmann that he had discovered the structure by chance around 1970.

In 1986 Ramón Carrasco Vargas, Sylviane Boucher, and Agustín Peña published a article on regional settlement patterns in the Río Bec area, and Structure I at Río Bec N was included; it was illustrated with photographs and a plan.

In 1989 Andrews published a study of checkerboard panels and cross motifs, including those at Río Bec N.

Connection

See "Río Bec I." Río Bec I (Structure XVII) to Río Bec N: 0.3 mile by foot trail (:12).

Getting There

See "Río Bec I." From Structure XVII at Río Bec I, head north on the trail to Río Bec N.

Allow 15 minutes to see the structure at Río Bec N. (Juan thinks of this structure as "Templo Juan," and I suggest you use this name when you ask him to take you there.)

Carry a canteen of water, and have a wide-angle lens for your camera.

RÍO BEC II

The Site

Río Bec II is composed of several greatly fallen structures surrounding a plaza. This assemblage of buildings is similar to Group E at Uaxactún, in the Petén of Guatemala, which was used for solar observations. Over a dozen groups of this type have been reported, although those are not as rigidly oriented as the one at Uaxactún. This led Karl Ruppert to conclude that while the other groups may have copied Group E at Uaxactún, they were nonfunctional copies of the working-model solar observatory at that site.

You enter Río Bec II from the west, through remains of a ball court (Structure IV). Abutting the south side of the court is Structure III, a rather tall pyramidal construction that borders the plaza on the west. Structure I, on the east side of the plaza, is simply rubble, but in front of it are the remains of two carved stela and a plain one, in a north-south row.

The lower part of Stela 3 is on the right as you face the row; it is standing but very eroded. The legs of a figure can be discerned on the front—if you look very carefully—and there are remains of glyphs on the sides of the monument. Stela 2, in the center, is plain. On the left is Stela 1, with remains of glyphs on its two sides but no discernible carving on the front; the top of the stela is gone.

Connection

See "Río Bec I." From the cutoff for the foot trail to Río Bec I to Río Bec II: 0.9 mile by variable dirt road (:11), then about 100 feet by foot trail (:02).

Getting There

See "Río Bec B" and "Río Bec I." From the junction with the foot trail to Río Bec I, continue along the dirt road for 0.9 mile and park

on the side. From there you walk left to Río Bec II. Allow 5 minutes to see and photograph the remains of the stelae and have a look at the overgrown mounds.

If you get as far south as Río Bec II, you may want to consider another route back to Xpuhil, but only if you have found the roads to be completely dry so far. From the parking place at Río Bec II, continue 0.3 mile south along the dirt road (:04), and turn right onto another dirt road. After going 4.9 miles (:34), you will connect with the good rock road that goes to Xpuhil. This junction is at the village of Polo Norte. Turn right onto the rock road and go 11.2 miles to Xpuhil (:27).

This was the original route to Río Bec and was used before the bridge, mentioned earlier, was installed. There are low spots along the route from Río Bec II to Polo Norte that will be muddy or covered with water if there has been rain recently, and the road is very narrow, since it is no longer used much. If it is dry and you decide to take it, it will be 1.1 miles shorter and will save about 17 minutes in getting back to Xpuhil. If it has been wet, it would be better and safer to return the way you came, via the bridge.

★ ★
HORMIGUERO

(ohr-mee-geh-roh; derivation: Spanish for "anthill" [see text])

Location:
    Southeastern Campeche.
Maps: 5 (p. 245) and 5A (p. 253)

The Site

Hormiguero is one of the major sites in the Río Bec region, and it is stupendous; if access were easier, it would clearly be a three-star site. Structure II at Hormiguero is one of the largest and best-preserved buildings in the area. When I first saw this structure in 1978, it could only be seen rather piecemeal because of the surrounding vegetation. Even with some clearing, it was impossible to get an overall photograph of the building. Over the years Structure II was cleared, and in 1984 it was excavated and

consolidated, so now the visitor can fully appreciate it.

When Hormiguero was first reported, it was said to be composed of three groups, with an informal layout and an extent of 900 feet from north to south and 650 feet from east to west. Since then, the East group was discovered lying 700 feet to the east of Structure II.

Structure II is over 150 feet long from east to west; it faces south and rests on a platform. During excavation 3 rooms on a lower level of the south side were discovered, bringing the total number of rooms to 11. The center room on the main level is surrounded by an incredible Chenes monster-mouth mask, made of stone and covered with stucco, with much of the stucco detail intact. The original wooden lintels above the doorway are still in place. This part of the facade recalls

Structure II, south side, Hormiguero. Late Classic period.

Detail of the Chenes mask on Structure II, south side, Hormiguero. Late Classic period.

Structure II at Chicanná and Structure 2 at Hochob, but the mask at Hormiguero is larger and the effect is bolder.

On either side of this central mask are tall Río Bec–style towers with typical rounded corners, banded tiers, and steep false stairways. The towers project in front of the central facade, and each is pierced at its base by a vaulted passage. A few of the steps are in place near the top of the east tower (on the right, as you face the structure), and there are four masonry blocks on top of each tower.

Beyond the towers are sections of facade with vertical rows of inset mask panels in frontal view. Flanking the panels are applied columns made of small stones, which originally formed the jambs of doorways for the two end rooms, but these rooms have mostly collapsed. The lower-level rooms on each end also have remains of inset mask panels and columns forming the jambs of doorways.

From the central room (main level) there is a step up to a rear room, and there are three doorways connecting the two. The central doorway is very wide, while the others are narrow, and the one on the east has an intact stepped vault.

At the rear (north side) of Structure II are remains of a projecting stairway, and above, on the main level of the building, the lower part of large constructed columns. One of the two doorways on this side of the building is mostly standing. Each doorway entered a single room—without other connections—behind the towers. You can climb the west tower from the rear (north side) over rubble. When you reach the height of the top of the main-level rooms, you will see a short, steep stair with *alfardas*, leading to the four masonry blocks that are the remains of the temple on top.

From this vantage point you can look

Inset panel with frontal masks, south facade, west side, Structure II, Hormiguero. Late Classic period.

down into the central rooms of the main level. According to Ricardo Bueno Cano, these rooms were sacked and destroyed when Hormiguero was vandalized. Paul Gendrop dates Structure II to around A.D. 700.

Structure V is about 190 feet to the north of Structure II, and it has also been partly cleared and consolidated. Structure V consists of a rather tall pyramidal base with a one-room temple on top that faces north and, to the west of the temple, a solid tower. When the structure was first reported, it was speculated that perhaps there was a tower on the east side originally as well, and though this has not yet been demonstrated, there is a good deal of debris on that side.

The north facade of the temple displays a typical Chenes monster-mouth motif surrounding the single doorway, and there are stacked, corner Chac masks on the northeast and northwest. These are similar to the masks on Structure XX at Chicanná, Structure A1 at Dzibilnocac, and Structure 1 at El Tabasqueño; like these, the relief sculpture is made of stone, covered with stucco, and well preserved. The wooden lintel above the doorway is still in place, although the east and west walls of the temple have fallen. The rear (south) wall is partly standing and is curiously plain compared to the highly ornamented north facade. The south facade has only simple rectangular moldings as decora-

Structure V, upper temple (left) and tower (right), north side, Hormiguero. Late Classic period.

tion, but the upper wall zone may have had some stucco decoration originally.

There is an opening into the pyramidal base of Structure V on its north side. Within it you can see a doorway with a stone lintel and parts of a wall. These are part of the earlier Structure V-Sub.

Some of the facing stones on the tower are in place, and they show that it had rounded corners and banded tiers of typical Río Bec style. There is no evidence, however, that the tower ever had a nonfunctional stairway or a simulated temple on top, features that are characteristic of these towers. Structure V dates to around A.D. 790, according to Gendrop.

Structure VI is a short distance to the northwest of Structure V, and on your way there you pass another, almost totally fallen building, with remnants of masks in stone and stucco at present ground level. On the right are two corner masks, stacked one

above the other, and on the left the remains of what appears to be part of a Chenes monster-mouth motif.

Structure VI is greatly fallen and unrestored and is reported to be a four-room building facing south, with towers on the southeast and southwest corners. Apparently there were no false stairways or simulated temples on top of the towers. An unusual feature is the use of buttresses on the outer sides of the towers. The buttress on the west side of the west tower is partly standing and exhibits banded tiers. This structure dates to about A.D. 810, according to Gendrop. Near Structure VI is the opening to a large chultun.

Return now to Structure II and head to the East Group. I have not seen this group, but Structure E-1 is reported to be the most important building there. It has Río Bec–style towers and well-preserved panels of profile masks on each side of a doorway on the west side of the structure. Another building in this group is a habitational unit; there are chultunes and an *aguada* nearby.

Bueno Cano reports that Hormiguero was possibly occupied beginning around the Protoclassic period (A.D. 50–250) and that this is the only site known so far in the area that has pre–Río Bec structures (550–600). These are found below Structures II and V and are called II-Sub and V-Sub. Hormiguero was at its peak during the Late Classic period and apparently was abandoned before Postclassic times.

Recent History

In 1933, during one of the Carnegie Institution of Washington's extensive reconnaissance missions in Campeche, the existence of some well-preserved ruins was reported to the members of the expedition by the workman's cook. The site was then visited by members of the expedition in April of the same year.

The name Hormiguero was in local use at that time for an *aguada* near the ruins and was applied to the ruins as well. This probably refers to the many anthills found in the area.

The exploration of Hormiguero was reported, along with the results of other expeditions in the area, by Karl Ruppert and John H. Denison, Jr., in 1943. The site was partly cleared and photographed, and a site plan was drawn. The architecture at Hormiguero is covered in a 1977 publication by David F. Potter for the Middle American Research Institute of Tulane University.

In 1984 the Campeche Regional Center of INAH conducted work at Hormiguero under the field direction of Bueno Cano and the general direction of Román Piña Chan. Major efforts were concentrated on Structures II and V. Structure II was cleared, excavated, and consolidated, and the lower-level rooms on the south side and the large columns on the north side of the structure were discovered. In 1984 and 1985 the East Group was investigated, and a brief report on this group was published in 1987. In Oc-

tober 1991 a new project began, with Bueno Cano as coordinator.

Connection

Xpuhil to Hormiguero: 8.6 miles by good rock road (:21), then 4.9 miles by dirt road (:41).

Note: Hormiguero is actually about 15 kilometers (9.3 miles) east of where it is shown on most maps.

Getting There

Guide: Juan de la Cruz Briceño, at Becan.

Take the rock road that heads south from Xpuhil and go 8.6 miles. Turn right onto the dirt road and go 3.1 miles. Then take a right branch for 0.5 mile, and then a left turn, and proceed 1.3 miles to the site.

You need a high-clearance vehicle to reach the site, and four-wheel drive if it has been wet. Wear boots, have a wide-angle lens for your camera, and allow 2½ hours for a visit.

Note: There is a problem concerning the best time of day to visit Hormiguero. Structure II gets the best light in the afternoon, while Structure V is best lighted in the morning. In the rainy season it is better to make the trip in the morning, since rain is less likely. If you reach the site early, you might try taking a brief look at Structure II, going on to the others, and returning to Structure II later when the light will be better. Even an hour or so can make a difference.

Note: When you take the rock road heading south from Xpuhil, you will pass two ruined structures alongside it. See "Xpuhil" for details.

PAYAN

(pah-yahn; derivation: Maya for "first" [see text])

Location:
Southeastern Campeche.
Maps: 5 (p. 245) and 5A (p. 253)

The Site

The explored portion of Payan reportedly includes several widely scattered mounds and a high pyramid faced with large stone blocks. There is some evidence of the former existence of a building atop the pyramid.

A number of other structures are found to the southeast, but only Structure I is in fair condition, and this is the feature of interest for visitors today. On the way to Structure I, however, you pass some mounds and the remains of another small building.

Structure I has 16 rooms on one level, and it is reported that there are suggestions of 6 others at a lower level. Much of the structure has fallen, but the front (west) facade has some bas-relief sculpture that is well preserved. This facade is broken by three doorways, and it is possible that originally there were two other smaller doorways in projections at either end. The relief sculpture on

Structure I, west side, showing relief sculpture surrounding the central doorway, Payan. Late Classic period.

each side of the central doorway (in the lower wall zone) depicts stylized serpent profile masks in inset panels. The motif is repeated three times vertically, although the lowest sections are mostly covered with debris. The two panels are mirror images of each other, and the masks face away from the doorway. They are similar to the relief sculpture found on Level 2 on the north side of Structure IV at Becan, but more detail is preserved at Payan, especially in the south panel (the one on the right, as you face the structure).

On an inclined upper wall zone above the panels is more relief sculpture of a different type. The part over the central doorway has fallen, but from what remains above the panels (and the amount of debris in the central doorway), it is believed that the upper-zone sculpture continued above the doorway. In a restoration drawing, Paul Gendrop shows the now-missing portion as the upper part of a monster mask, and he considers this facade at Payan to be one of the most representative examples of a partial zoomorphic doorway. His drawing was done following an unrestored version of the remaining sculpture by George E. Stuart of the National Geographic Society. In a chart prepared by Gendrop, Structure I at Payan is dated to around A.D. 650. Remains of wooden lintels (reportedly zapote) are found in the doorways.

The other feature of interest at this structure is some graffiti on the plastered walls of one of the interior rooms. Enter the north doorway of the front of the structure (the one to the left as you face it). You will have to duck to get through because the doorway is partly filled with rubble. Proceed straight through the remains of two rooms and into the third, then turn left and enter a small chamber. As you enter, look to the wall on your right. Most of the graffiti are found on this wall and include a rather fat jaguar, a geometric design that looks like a stylized profile serpent head, geometric human heads, what appears to be a canoe, and large platted motif. On the opposite wall, at the level of the debris, are remains of small circular designs.

Recent History

Payan was explored by the Fourth Campeche Expedition, sponsored by the Carnegie Institution of Washington (CIW) in February 1938. The site was named Payan ("first"), as it was the first site visited on this expedition.

This site and many others were reported upon in a 1943 CIW publication by Karl Ruppert and John H. Denison, Jr.

Payan is included in David F. Potter's comparative study of the architecture in the central Yucatán Peninsula, published by the Middle American Research Institute of Tulane University in 1977.

In the 1980s Gendrop published several articles on mask panels in the Río Bec, Chenes, and Puuc regions, and the Payan example is included.

There has been no extensive excavation at the stie.

Connection

Xpuhil to Payan: 4.4 miles by paved road (:06), 4.5 miles by rock road (:27), then 0.5 mile by foot trail (:10).

Total from Xpuhil to Payan: 9.4 miles (:43).

Getting There

Guide: Juan de la Cruz Briceño, at Becan.

Head east from Xpuhil on Highway 186 to San José Rancho and stop on the north side of the road at the entrance to the ranch. Juan will ask permission there for you to drive through their property to reach the site. There are a couple of gates along the way. To the left of the road you will pass a ruined structure in a milpa. Afterward park and take the foot trail to the right to reach Structure I.

Wear boots and have a wide-angle lens to photograph the front of Structure I, and fast film or a flash unit to photograph the graffiti on the inside. Since Structure I faces west, the afternoon is the best time to photograph the sculpture on its facade. Allow 45 minutes to see and photograph the building.

★ ★ ★
KOHUNLICH

(koh-hoon-leech; derivation: possibly a corruption of
"Cohune Ridge," since the cohune is a species of palm)

Location:
  Southern Quintana Roo.
Map: 5 (p. 245)

The Site

Kohunlich is a large site with some sizable structures that have been partly cleared and consolidated. As you walk along the road that enters the site, you come first to the Acropolis Plaza and its surrounding buildings on the left. The main structure in this group is the Acropolis (Structure VII), bordering the east side of the Acropolis Plaza and the north side of the Great Plaza. (The numbers of the structures given here are those used by George F. Andrews.) The Acropolis is a large rectangular platform approached by a stairway on the west. There is also an extension on the southwest corner and remains of rooms on top of both; the Acropolis was built in two or three construction phases.

The original platform and four of the rooms on top "show classic Río Bec style architectural details," according to Andrews. In the rooms, these details include rounded doorjambs, three-member base moldings, and, on the exterior of the rooms, large inset corner columns made of smaller stones. Between the two rooms at the top of the stairway is a restricted-entry passage to the upper courtyard. These rooms were a later addition, as was the southwestern extension and its rooms on a lower level. The platform itself was added to on the east and south sides, and the later construction covered two Río Bec–style towers, one on each of these sides. The towers were set into the original platform and have steep nonfunctional stairways; the towers were revealed during excavation.

Bounding the Acropolis Plaza on the north is Structure VIII; it is greatly ruined and only partly excavated. Structure IX, on the west side of the plaza, is simply a rubble mound.

The Great (or Ceremonial) Plaza is a few yards to the southeast. In addition to Structure VII on the north side, there are three large buildings on the other sides: Structure IV on the east, Structure V on the south, and Structure VI on the west.

Structure IV has been partly excavated, and there are remains of rooms atop a platform with a western stair. Three of the lower rooms have been cleared, and it is possible that there were second-level rooms, but this part is now mostly rubble. There is a simple, one-course rectangular molding above the doorway to the best-preserved room, but the facing of the upper wall zone has fallen, so the architectural details of this area are unknown. About centered on the stairway are three stelae, each on a different level, but they are so badly eroded that it is impossible to tell if they were once carved.

Structure V is a long platform of irregular shape with remains of the lower walls of buildings on top; it was built in at least three construction phases. There is a monumental stairway on the north (plaza) side and a smaller stairway on the south that leads to another plaza, surrounded by unexcavated buildings. One of the structures on top of the platform has remains of large constructed columns, some of which formed doorjambs. These are similar to those on Structure II at Hormiguero.

Structure VI is also of irregular shape and is made up of several platforms and a broad stairway on the east that ascends a large mound to a two-room temple on top. Only the lower walls of the temple are standing, but they have rounded doorjambs and, on the exterior corners, constructed columns. The temple also has a three-member base molding with groups of colonnettes in

Structure IV, from the northwest, Kohunlich. Late Classic period.

the middle part. All these features are typical of Río Bec–style architecture.

A short distance northeast of the Great Plaza is a large paved, sunken plaza, with a platform projecting into it on the east and a stairway on the south side of the projection. Bordering the south side of this plaza is a low circular construction. There are no remains of buildings surrounding the plaza.

About 300 feet to the east is the Pyramid of the Masks (Structure I), the real gem of the site. It rests atop a small hill, and the structure itself is about 50 feet high. Structure I was built in two construction stages, the first during the Early Classic period. The original building (Structure I-sub) is a stepped pyramid rising in four tiers, with a five-room temple on top and a broad stairway on the west. The pyramidal base has rounded corners and overhanging apron moldings and is similar to some structures in the Petén of Guatemala and in Belize.

The most interesting part of the struc-ture is, of course, the beautifully executed and well-preserved masks. They belong to the first construction stage and are found on each side of the stairway of Structure I-sub. The four lower masks are very humanized depictions of the sun god, with elaborate decorations on either side. The two upper masks are smaller and show the same deity in a more stylized form. The masks are made of carved stucco over a stone base. Remnants of paint are visible on some of the masks, and each is a bit different from the others. Certainly these masks rank as some of the finest and most sensitive Maya sculptures ever produced. The masks are protected by thatch shelters, so for best photographic results, have fast film and a wide-angle lens.

At a later date the pyramidal base was encased in another structure, thanks to which the masks are so well preserved. Much of this later construction has fallen or been removed, and little of it remains today, though a few remnants can be seen at the base of the

Structure I-sub (the Pyramid of the Masks), northeast corner, Kohunlich. Early Classic period.

pyramid on the southeast corner and the north side.

Only the lower walls of the temple on top of the pyramid are standing, but enough is left to show that the rooms were once vaulted. It is not known if the later structure that encased the pyramidal base of Structure I-sub also covered the temple on top.

About 400 feet to the southwest is the Ball Court (Structure II). The court is I-shaped and has sloping lower walls topped by vertical sections. Its size is impressive.

Recent History

According to Fernando Cortés de Brasdefer, Raymond E. Merwin, in 1913, was the first to report the site of Kohunlich, although it was then called Clarksville, and a site of this name is shown on the 1940 Tulane Map. Clarksville also appears in the 1959 atlas of Quintana Roo by Florencia Muller, with her reference being the Tulane Map, and the characteristics of the site are listed simply as *montículos* ("mounds"). This would seem to imply that all Merwin saw were mounds, and not the mask panels.

In 1967 looters reportedly discovered the site, removed some of the outer covering of Structure I, and revealed the masks. Ignacio Ek, of the nearby village of Francisco Villa, came across this work and reported it to authorities, who then took steps to protect the masks and the site, which was known locally by the name Kohunlich at that time.

Shortly thereafter, Víctor Segovia, an archaeologist with INAH, excavated the upper level of Structure I-sub, which was reported in 1969. Work at the site continued under Segovia's direction from then until 1981, and other structures were cleared and consolidated.

A preliminary ceramic report in 1981 by Diana Z. De Dávila indicates that there were two major occupation and construction periods at Kohunlich, one in the Early

Mask on the lower level of the south side of the stairway, Structure I-sub (the Pyramid of the Masks), Kohunlich. Early Classic period.

Classic (A.D. 450–600) and another in the Terminal Classic (800–1050).

In 1987 Andrews published an analysis of the excavated architecture at Kohunlich, noting the various Río Bec–style details on Structures V, VI, and VII (first phase). He discussed three chronological possibilities for the existence of these traits but preferred the one that would have the Río Bec–style architecture appearing at Kohunlich during the Xcocom ceramic phase (A.D. 800–1050), postdating this style in the Río Bec region. He noted that the Río Bec–style buildings at Kohunlich incorporated rather crude stonework, compared to the Late Classic examples in the Río Bec region, and felt this was "indicative of the kind of 'decadence' one would expect to find at a provincial site far from the Río Bec heartland."

Connections

1. Xpuhil to Kohunlich: 42.5 miles by paved road (:56).

2. Chetumal to Kohunlich: 42.7 miles by paved road (:55).

Getting There

1. From Xpuhil head east on Highway 186 to the cutoff for Kohunlich. The cutoff is on the east edge of the town of Francisco Villa and is marked with a sign. Turn right at the cutoff and proceed to the site.

2. From Chetumal head west on Highway 186 to the cutoff and turn left to the site.

There is no food or drink at Kohunlich. Allow 2 hours for a visit.

Buses pass through Francisco Villa but do not run to Kohunlich.

XULHÁ

(shool-hah; derivation: Maya for "The End of the Water")

Location:
    Southern Quintana Roo.
Map: 5 (p. 245)

The Site

The site of Xulhá is well named, as it lies at the south end of Bacalar Lagoon. Structure 1, the largest reported at the site, is the feature of interest, although four dozen other buildings have been recorded. Structure 1 is modest in size and consists of a platform and remains of the lower walls of a two-room building on top. The most interesting part of the structure is its three-member base molding, the middle part of which is recessed from the upper and lower sections, and is unusual. This part, measuring about a foot high, has decorations in stone and stucco, forming a sort of frieze.

Parts of the sculptural decorations are gone, but they may have encircled the structure originally. Motifs include serpents with prominent heads and entwined bodies, geometric designs, and mat symbols. At one time the lower part of a seated human figure, framed with a border of incised designs, was visible. Unhappily, that has been obliterated. Some of the decorations are on colonnettes, while others are on flat stones; the depth of the relief varies from low to high.

There is a stairway on the east side of the building, and the frieze that remains is on that side, so the morning is the best time to photograph the structure.

East side of Structure 1, Xulhá.

Recent History

The main published source of information about the frieze at Xulhá is a detailed article by Karl Herbert Mayer that appeared in 1987. He reports that Structure 1 was exposed by road builders around 1975. Salvage work was then undertaken by Pablo Mayer Guala, who also recovered some ceramics dating to the Early Classic period. Others of Protoclassic date were reported by Duncan Pring in 1977.

In a stylistic analysis of the frieze, Karl Mayer finds it most similar to the one at Tulum on Structure 55, with a known Late Postclassic date. For this reason he tentatively dates the frieze at Xulhá to the same period.

Peter J. Schmidt photographed the sculptural decorations in 1978, and at that time the seated figure within the border was intact except for the head. In 1980 the upper part of the figure was destroyed. Karl Mayer published three of Schmidt's earlier photographs in his detailed article.

In 1981 George F. Andrews recorded the architecture at Xulhá and gave his information to Mayer, who visited the site the following year. Mayer published a brief note about the structure in 1985 and his more detailed study in 1987.

Connection

Chetumal to Xulha: 15.7 miles by paved road (:20).

Getting There

Head west on Highway 186 from Chetumal to the junction with Highway 307, then turn right on Highway 307 to Xulhá. Structure 1 is on the left side of the highway, on the front lawn of the Instituto de Investigaciones Agrícolas (Institute of Agricultural Investigations), and you can see it from the highway behind a barbed wire fence. The gate to the institute is open during working hours. If it is closed when you arrive, a guard on duty will allow you to enter and visit the structure.

The best way to reach Xulhá is in your own vehicle, but you could get a taxi in Chetumal to take you there. Allow 20 minutes to see and photograph Structure 1. The nearest restaurants are in Bacalar and Chetumal.

★
LIMONES

*(lee-moh-nehs; derivation: Spanish for "lemons,"
and the name of the modern town)*

Location:
    Southern Quintana Roo.
Map: 5 (p. 245)

The Site

The structure at Limones is a pyramid with remains of a temple on top. The pyramid rises in terraces, its base is rectangular, and there is a stairway on the west side. According to Karl Herbert Mayer, the structure is over 10 meters (32.8 feet) high. Although the structure has not been excavated, the style of the terracing may indicate a Classic-period date. Since I first mentioned this structure in 1982, it was cleared and later became overgrown with weeds. At one time there was a trail to the top; there still is one that encircles the base.

Recent History

The pyramid at Limones has been visible for many years to anyone driving past, but it apparently was not listed in a register of archaeological sites in Quintana Roo until 1984. Mayer published a short note on the site in 1988.

Connections

1. Chetumal to Limones: 55.8 miles by paved road (1:05).

2. Felipe Carrillo Puerto to Limones: 39.2 miles by paved road (:47).

Getting There

1. Head west from Chetumal on Highway 186 to the junction with Highway 307, then turn north to reach Limones. The structure is on the south end of Limones, on the east side of the highway, and just a few feet from it; it is next to a large water tower that is easy to spot. If you are passing by, it is worth a few minutes to see and photograph the structure. Cold drinks are available in the town.

2. If you are starting from Felipe Carrillo Puerto, head south on Highway 307 to Limones.

SECTION 6, PART 1

• • • •

NORTHERN QUINTANA ROO
(MAINLAND)

Masks on the southwest corner of the Temple of the Frescoes (Structure 16), Tulum. Late Postclassic period.

GENERAL INFORMATION FOR SECTION 6, PART 1

> **Point of Reference:**
> Cancún, Quintana Roo.
> **Maps:** 6 and 6A

Cancún City is the "connection" for most of the sites in this section, and mileages given to the sites are from the north part of the city at the junction of Highways 180 and 307. The Convention Center on Isla Cancún is the "connection" for sites on Isla Cancún, and mileages are given from there.

Cancún, a completely planned vacation resort, was developed in the 1970s after it was selected by computer analysis a few years earlier as the best place on the coast of Mexico to develop one. It has continued to grow, and the number of hotels on Isla Cancún today is mind-boggling, and more are under construction.

Isla Cancún is an island only in the strictest sense. It is connected to the mainland by road at the north and south ends, where you cross bridges that you hardly notice. It is perhaps better thought of as a land spit that juts into the Caribbean, backed by a lagoon. The main thoroughfare looping Isla Cancún is Paseo Kukulcán. Cancún City is the support facility on the mainland at the north end of Isla Cancún.

Generally, Isla Cancún and Cancún City are both simply referred to as Cancún. That designation will be used here when the area of the two is intended. A distinction will be made between them when one or the other is a point of reference.

Isla Cancún is the most expensive place in Mexico, though rates for all of northern Quintana Roo, including Cozumel, are higher than other parts of the peninsula. The large deluxe hotels are on Isla Cancún, while more modest facilities can be found in Cancún City. Most hotels have seasonal rates. The high season is from around mid-December through mid-April, and the rates drop about 30 percent for the rest of the year.

For your money you get luxurious accommodations; beautifully crystalline, azure seas; miles of soft, white sand beaches; and all manner of water sports, including snorkeling, scuba diving, sailing, water skiing, parasailing, jetskiing, windsurfing, and deep-sea fishing. There is a golf course, and most hotels have tennis courts and, of course, swimming pools. There are day cruises around Isla Cancún and to Isla Mujeres. Cancún also provides easy access to many archaeological sites.

There are innumerable restaurants of varying types on Isla Cancún and in Cancún City, and discos for those interested in nightlife.

There are shopping centers and individual shops all over. El Parián is one of the largest centers. It is located near the Convention Center, near the northeast corner of Isla Cancún. Plaza Caracol, another shopping center, is a short distance to the west of El Parián. Both sell fine jewelery, fashion sportswear, leather goods, porcelain, handicrafts, and uncountable other items.

In Cancún City, the Ki-Hiuic artisans market sells reasonably priced handicrafts from all over Mexico. It is on Avenida Tulum (the main north-south avenue in the city), a little to the north of the junction with Paseo Kukulcán, as it leaves the north end of Isla Cancún.

The above are only a few of the many shopping possibilities, and complimentary booklets at the hotels will list others.

The Cancún International Airport is on the mainland, near the south entrance to Isla Cancún, and flights arrive from various cities in the United States (some daily). There are also flights from Mérida, Cozumel, Mexico City, and cities in Central America.

Car rentals are available at the airport, through the large hotels, and at agencies in Cancún City. Several types of vehicles are offered.

Cancún is also connected by bus to all parts of the peninsula, and there is local bus service along Paseo Kukulcán on Isla Cancún that connects with Cancún City. Taxis can be found all over Cancún.

You can also drive to Cancún from the United States (six days from Brownsville, Texas, with good stopovers along the way).

There are travel agencies at the large hotels and in Cancún City. Tours go to Tulum and Xelha, and to Chichén Itzá, and others can be arranged.

FERRIES TO ISLA MUJERES AND COZUMEL: Both islands can be reached by ferry, using Cancún as a point of departure. In all cases the ferry schedules should be verified locally, as they change frequently.

To reach Isla Mujeres there are two choices. A passenger ferry from Puerto Juárez leaves seven or eight times a day, and the trip takes less than an hour. A car ferry from Punta Sam leaves several times a day, and the trip takes about 30 minutes. If you take the car ferry, line up in the parking area near the pier, and go into the office building to buy your ticket. They go on sale 30 minutes before departure. The cost will depend on the size of your vehicle and the number of passengers, but is nominal in any case. The same procedure is followed when you leave Isla Mujeres.

There are also two ferries to Cozumel. The car ferry leaves Puerto Morelos, and the schedule changes daily. Arrive at the dock, get in line (smaller vehicles are lined up separately from large trucks), and wait until the office begins to sell tickets. Have your license plate number available. This ferry is often crowded, and there is no way to avoid a long wait. There is one departure daily, generally in the morning. Some people leave their vehicles in line the night before. The trip takes three to four hours, depending on the condition of the sea.

A more civilized way to reach Cozumel is to take one of the passenger ferries from Playa del Carmen. In addition to the regular ferry, which takes about 1¼ hours, there is a catamaran water jet that makes the crossing in 30 to 40 minutes (although a sign says 20 minutes). Tickets for the catamaran are sold at a booth on the plaza of Playa del Carmen and can be purchased in advance.

The catamaran is air-conditioned and costs a bit more than the regular ferry, but in either case the cost is nominal. Tickets for both the catamaran and the regular ferry are sold near the dock.

There is a parking lot in Playa del Carmen near the plaza where you can safely leave your vehicle when you go to Cozumel. Fees are reasonable.

OTHER STOPOVERS: The north part of the east coast of Quintana Roo is being developed along with Cancún, and many of the hotels also have seasonal rates. There are a number of places to stay, ranging from modest to excellent, between Cancún and Tulum. Most are a short distance east of Highway 307, and signs point out the cutoffs to some of them. The signs also indicate whether there are rooms and/or camping areas.

Heading south from Cancún, some of the best accommodations are at Playa del Carmen, Puerto Aventuras (12.6 miles south of Playa del Carmen), and Akumal. There are a few modest facilities near Tulum, and a good hotel at Cobá. Most of the hotels serve food, and there are a number of restaurants along Highway 307 and at beach-front places just off the highway. There are also restaurants at the ruins of Xcaret and Xelha.

GAS STATIONS: There are gas stations in and on the outskirts of Cancún City and along the highways to the west and south. The distances given below are mileages *between* gas stops. To the west on Highway 180 there are stations at the following places: Xcan (59.6 miles), Chemax (21.4 miles), and Valladolid (17.9 miles).

Going south from Cancún City on Highway 307, there are gas stations at Puerto Morelos, Playa del Carmen, Tulum, and Felipe Carrillo Puerto.

GUIDES: A guide is not necessary to reach any of the sites covered in this section, except possibly one structure at Tancah. See "Tancah" for details. At Tulum, however, you will need a guide to reach the two structures that lie outside the wall. See "Tulum" for details.

★
PUNTA LAGUNA

(poon-tah lah-goo-nah; derivation: Spanish for "Lagoon Point,"
also the name of a nearby settlement)

Location:
   North-central Quintana Roo.
Map: 6 (p. 302)

The Site

Punta Laguna is a site with East Coast–style structures, even though it is about 30 miles inland from the coast. The site includes bases of pyramids, small platforms, and remains of domestic architecture, according to Fernando Cortés de Brasdefer. The feature of interest for the visitor is a typical, small East Coast–style temple that sits atop a fair-size platform.

The one-room temple is partly standing. Its single doorway is intact and faces west, and the temple rests on the west side of the platform. Another couple of temples of the same type are reported, but we only saw the one. Cortés de Brasdefer says, "The ceramics date for the most part from the Postclassic and only rarely from the Classic period." This relates well to the Postclassic style of the architecture.

There are wide, well-kept trails at Punta Laguna. As you are shown around, you will see a group of spider monkeys cavorting in the trees above a small lagoon. This endangered species is reported to sleep in a nearby cave at night.

The jungle around Punta Laguna is home to a variety of birds, including a rare black-and-white owl, so the area can be enjoyed by nature lovers as well as those whose interest is archaeological. You might as well enjoy both.

Recent History

Punta Laguna has been known at least since 1984, when it is briefly mentioned in *Mexicon.* In a 1988 issue of the same journal, Cortés de Brasdefer, director of the Quintana Roo Regional Center of INAH, described the site along with others in Quintana Roo.

Connection

Cancún City to Punta Laguna: 70.8 miles by paved road (1:51).

Getting There

Head west on Highway 180 to Nuevo Xcan (54.5 miles). Turn left at the sign for Cobá and proceed to the village of Punta Laguna (marked with a sign). (This road later connects with the cutoff for Cobá and eventually joins Highway 307 near Tulum.)

Serapio Canul, who is mainly responsible for maintaining the trails at Punta Laguna and protecting the buildings, lives on the left (east) side of the road. Ask for him, and he or his young son will show you around the site, which is on the west side of the road. You can drive in a short distance from the road and park. Having your own vehicle is the best way to reach Punta Laguna. Although buses do pass by, you would have a long wait for the next one.

The temple described above is about a five-minute walk from where you park, but you are taken to this area last on a tour that lasts about 45 minutes.

Have a wide-angle lens for shots of the temple and a telephoto lens for the wildlife. Have cold drinks in your vehicle.

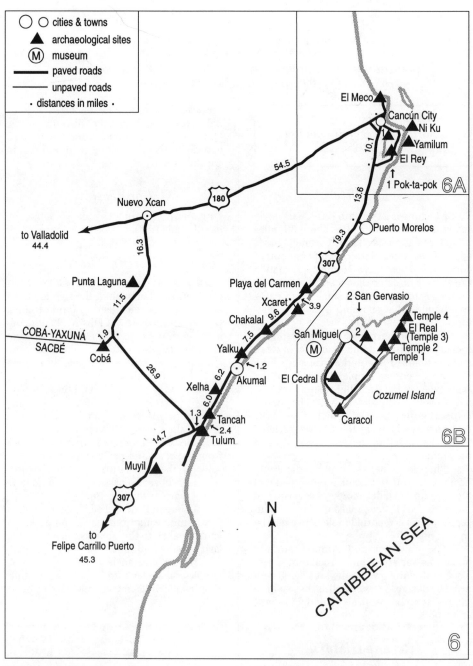

cities & towns
archaeological sites
Ⓜ **museum**
paved roads
unpaved roads
· **distances in miles** ·

El Meco

Cancún City
Ni Ku
Yamilum
El Rey

54.5

180

10.1

1 Pok-ta-pok   **6A**

Nuevo Xcan

13.6

to Valladolid
44.4

16.3

19.3

Puerto Morelos

307

Punta Laguna

11.5

Playa del Carmen

2 San Gervasio

Xcaret
3.9
9.6

Chakalal

Temple 4
El Real
(Temple 3)
Temple 2
Temple 1

COBÁ-YAXUNÁ
SACBÉ

1.9

7.5

Yalku

San Miguel
Ⓜ

2

Cobá

26.9

1.2
Akumal

El Cedral

Cozumel Island

Xelha

6.2
6.0

1.3

Tancah
2.4
Tulum

Caracol

Muyil

14.7

307

Northern Quintana Roo

6B

to
Felipe Carrillo Puerto
45.3

N

CARIBBEAN SEA

6

★ ★ ★
COBÁ

(koh-bah; derivation: Maya for "Ruffled Waters")

Location:
    North-central Quintana Roo.
Map: 6

The Site

Cobá is actually a number of separated sites that go collectively under the one name. Overall, it is a huge site, as you will realize when you walk from one area to another. During Late Classic times Cobá was the largest and most important site of the northeastern Yucatán Peninsula and had an area of dense population of 27 square miles.

Cobá proper is designated Group B and is located between Lakes Cobá and Macanxoc. Nohoch Mul is Group C, and Macanxoc, with its many stelae, is Group A. Group D has a ball court with carved monuments and the Conjunto las Pinturas. Other small ruins in the area have their own names, and all the structures are located amid five small lakes, a rare feature in northern Yucatán.

In the area of Cobá (all groups included), 45 *sacbeob* are now known, more than at any other Maya site. The *sacbeob* connect various parts of the site, and some short ones connect buildings within a group. Some actually go through a portion of one of the lakes (which may have been smaller when the *sacbeob* were built). Some *sacbeob* lead to more distant sites. By far the most impressive is the one that goes due west for an astounding 62 miles, to connect with the minor site of Yaxuná. This is the longest known *sacbé* in the Maya area, and it varies in height from 2 feet to 8 feet where it crosses swampy areas; its average width is 32 feet. (See "Cobá-Yaxuná Sacbé" in Section 1 for details on one place to see it.) The walls of the *sacbé* are roughly dressed stone, and the bed is composed of boulders topped with small stones laid in cement. A stucco or cement layer formed the surface, though it is not badly disintegrated.

A five-ton stone roller was found on the *sacbé* and at one time was thought to have been used in connection with the road's construction (to compact the surface into a hard layer). Now, this interpretation seems to be in question. There is reason to believe that the Cobá-Yaxuná Sacbé continued past Cobá and connected with Xcaret on the Caribbean Coast and that it then branched south to the Tancah-Tulum area, but so far these connecting *sacbeob* have not been found.

Whether Maya *sacbeob* in general, and this one in particular, were used for ceremonial or commercial purposes or both remains a debated point. At any rate, since the Mayas lacked beasts of burden and wheeled vehicles, we can be sure that only foot traffic traversed these ancient roads.

Unfortunately, most of the structures at Cobá are poorly preserved, but excavation and restoration of a few have made their appearances clearer.

The easily followed main trail at the site leaves from the parking area and goes all the way to the Nohoch Mul (about 1.2 miles away). Along the way, there are side trails to the other groups of interest. The first side trail is marked for Groupo Cobá (Group B), and it heads to the right.

Group B is the largest architectural assemblage at Cobá, and the Iglesia (Structure I) is the most imposing in this group. It is a nine-tiered pyramid, with slightly rounded corners and a broad stairway on the west side. There are a few remains of a temple on top. Other rooms may be seen flanking the stairway at the lower level, and you can enter those on the north side. The structure has been excavated and partly restored. Structure A, a large platform, abuts the bottom of the stairway of Structure I on the west and is approached by an even broader, though shorter, stairway. At the rear of the platform there is a low enclosure housing the eroded Stela 11. Both the Iglesia and Stela 11 date to the Late Classic period.

The Iglesia (Structure I of Group B), west side, Cobá. Late Classic period. Note Stela 11 at the lower left.

Farther along the main trail you come to another side trail on the right, marked for the Conjunto las Pinturas. Before reaching that group, you come to yet another side trail on the right that goes to Macanxoc (about 0.6 mile from this last junction). Macanxoc is noted for its stelae; the buildings in this group are greatly ruined. The stelae are whole (or have been restored), but all are fairly eroded. Some are on platforms, and Stela 4 is partly encased by the fallen stairway of one of the larger structures at Macanxoc; all the stelae are protected by thatch shelters.

Stela 1 has one of the longest hieroglyphic stela texts known, with 313 glyph blocks on the front, back, and sides, and records dates from A.D. 653 to 672. Both the front and back of the stela portray a standing figure holding a ceremonial bar, and below the main figures are bound captives. Joyce Marcus believes the same personage is depicted on both sides and that it is a queen of Cobá who is portrayed. Most of the other stelae at Macanxoc are carved on only one side, and dates from 613 to 672 have been deciphered on them. The date 613, on Stela 6 is the earliest deciphered at Cobá.

From Macanxoc, return the way you came and take a right at the junction with the trail to the Conjunto las Pinturas, which you passed on your way to Macanxoc.

The main feature at the Conjunto las Pinturas is the Templo las Pinturas, a small one-room temple sitting atop a stepped pyramid. The temple has a doorway on the west side, with a column of drum-shaped stones in the middle. This structure dates to the Postclassic period, and the architectural style is similar to the Postclassic temples at Tulum and along the coast. Remnants of stucco adhere to the area above the doorway, and some remains of painting are found there, giving the temple (and group) its name. There is also a single doorway on each of the north and south sides; from the one on the north you get a gorgeous view of the Nohoch Mul in the distance.

The pyramidal base supporting the temple has a western stair that faces the remains of other Postclassic structures. There are low walls, columns of drum-shaped stones, and, at the base of the stairway, a one-room building that houses the bottom portion of an eroded stela. The Conjunto las Pinturas has been cleared and partly restored. From this area, return to the main trail and turn right.

On both sides of the main trail you will see large rubble mounds, the remains of some of the other buildings of Group D. Just past one of these mounds, an unmarked and easily missed side trail (on the right and sometimes overgrown) leads a short distance to the greatly ruined ball court of Group D and its three carved monuments. One of the monuments is Stela 30, with a standing personage and 13 glyph blocks. The glyphs are eroded, and no date has been deciphered, but according to George E. Stuart, Stela 30 seems to correspond to an early period, perhaps around A.D. 500–550. A large squarish stone called Lapida C shows a standing figure who seems to be wearing ball game atire, holding a crosslike scepter. The figure is accompanied by a dozen glyphs on the front of the monument and delicately incised glyphs on the edges.

The third monument is rectangular and portrays a bound captive with a beard who

Templo las Pinturas, west side, in Group D (Conjunto las Pinturas), Cobá. Postclassic period.

is accompanied by two glyphs, perhaps recording his name. The glyphs on both these last monuments are eroded and undeciphered, but Stuart believes these monuments date to the same period as the nearby Stela 30. You will need a wide-angle lens to photograph these monuments.

Continue now along the main trail to the Nohoch Mul Group, with its massive temple pyramid of the same name. On the way to the pyramid the trail passes the excavated and consolidated Structure X. This structure rests on a platform with a broad stairway on the west and remains of a two-room building on top. There are five doorways separated by piers, and the lower walls of the structure are standing.

The most interesting feature of Structure X, however, is Stela 20, which stands at ground level, in a niche in the center of the stairway. Stela 20 dates to A.D. 780 and is the

latest recorded monument at Cobá; it also has an interesting history. The lower parts of this broken stela were discoverd in 1930 by Sir J. Eric S. Thompson and other members of the Carnegie Expedition who were working at Cobá. Though fairly well preserved, these parts of the stela did not carry a date, and though a search for the upper, dated portion of the stela was made, it was not found. In 1975 Domingo Falcón, the caretaker of Cobá, found part of a carved stela while clearing an area on the south side of Structure X during work at the site. At first this was believed to be a previously unknown stela, but later it was realized that this was the dated upper portion of Stela 20 that had been searched for forty-five years earlier. The stela is the best preserved at the site, and it has been restored and protected by a thatch shelter. The main figure on Stela 20 is holding a ceremonial bar and stands

Lapida C, portraying a figure possibly wearing ball game attire and holding a crosslike scepter, Group D, Cobá. Possibly Early Classic period.

atop the backs of two bound captives, while two more are kneeling at the sides.

A short distance to the north is the pyramid called Nohoch Mul, a name given the structure by Thompson, which in Maya means "Great Mound." This was the name used for the structure by one of Thompson's Maya guides. The pyramidal base of the Nohoch Mul is about 82 feet high, and the temple of top adds about another 20 feet to the structure; it is the tallest pre-Columbian structure in the northeastern part of the Yucatán Peninsula. Its pyramidal base is terraced in seven sections, and there is a 39-foot-wide stairway that ascends the south side to a well-preserved temple with an intact roof. The temple lies at the rear of the top platform of the pyramid and has a single doorway and one room. There were originally three niches in the upper wall zone of the temple; the one on the west has been destroyed. The two remaining niches contain depictions of the diving god—or descending god— also found at Tulum and Sayil. The figure in the central niche bears some remnants of paint.

According to Ralph L. Roys, the modern Yucatecan Mayas believe in bee gods, who appear in the story of creation. They further believe that these gods dwell at Cobá. This, plus the fact that the diving position of the figures is the same as the one found in the apiculture section of the *Codex Madrid,* leads to Roys's belief that the deity represented is a bee god.

The pyramidal base of the Nohoch Mul dates to the Late Classic period; the temple on top is Late Postclassic and is the best preserved structure at Cobá. According to Stuart, it is possible that the upper part of the pyramid was constructed when the temple on top was added, and that at this time the rooms found on the lower levels (flanking the stairway) were built.

The southeast corner of the pyramid and the stairway have been partly restored, but it is a long and tiring climb to the top. It is worth the effort, though, to see the temple and niche figures, and for views of the area.

Ceramic studies indicate that Cobá was occupied from around A.D. 100 through most of the Late Postclassic period and that its peak of construction was during the Late Classic. Forty-five stelae (almost all Late Classic) are known from Cobá, and 34 of these are covered, making Cobá the site with the most known stelae in the northern Yucatán Peninsula.

There were apparently close ties between Cobá and Maya centers to the south in the Petén of Guatemala during the Classic period, and Cobá's architecture at this time "is very much in the Petén style, as are the polychrome ceramics of the period," according to Anthony P. Andrews. The stela cult at Cobá is also in the Petén tradition, as is the style of the stelae, one special point of simi-

Nohoch Mul, south side, Group C, Cobá. Late Classic and Late Postclassic periods.

larity being the depiction of captives. This motif is much more prevalent in the south, although three stelae at Edzna and one from Dzilám González near the north coast of Yucatán also show this subject matter.

Later in Cobá's history, when there were commercial ties to the Puuc cities to the west, the stela cult came to an end. Cobá seems to have declined toward the end of the Terminal Classic period and during the Early Postclassic, and monumental architectural construction ceased. Neighboring sites at the ends of some of Cobá's *sacbeob* were abandoned, and the remaining population clustered near the lakes at the site's center.

Sometime after A.D. 1200, and for a good part of the Late Postclassic, there was a resurgence at Cobá, with new construction and new ceramic traditions. Classic period buildings were repaired, and on some, Late Postclassic structures were erected, the prime example being the temple atop the Nohoch Mul.

Recent History

The name Cobá appears in the *Chilam Balam de Chumayel,* a chronicle of ancient Maya history and prophecy written in the eigh-

teenth century (in Maya but using the Spanish alphabet). It is probable that the Cobá mentioned is the site covered here, so this may well be its original name.

The first modern mention of Cobá was by John Lloyd Stephens in 1843. He learned of the site from a priest in Chemax, but unfortunately Stephens was unable to visit the site. The priest (who had never visited the site himself) was recording information about "objects of curiosity and interest" from the area under his jurisdiction, by government order. Stephens copied the priest's notes, which included the location of Cobá, its setting on several lakes, a description of some of the architecture, and the existence and direction of the main *saché,* all of which was fairly accurate. With regard to the *saché,* the priest's notes said that "some aver that it goes in the direction of Chichén Itzá," as indeed it does. Yaxuná is just 13 miles southwest of Chichén Itzá.

In 1886 two Yucatecan intellectuals— J. P. Contreras and D. Elizade—made a brief reconnaissance of Cobá and produced a short description and four rather fanciful drawings. In 1891 Teobert Maler visited the site and photographed the temple atop the Nohoch Mul.

In early 1926 Thomas Gann briefly visited the site and reported it to Sylvanus G. Morley, Thompson, and others who were working at Chichén Itzá. (All were unaware of Maler's previous visit.) Later in 1926 Morley and Thompson visited the site, as did Alfred V. Kidder and Jean Charlot, who made drawings of the sculpture. They were accompanied by local Mayas who showed them additional sites in the area. Thompson returned in 1930 with his bride and H. E. D. Pollock for further study of Cobá, and in 1932 Thompson, Pollock, and Charlot published a preliminary study of the site, including a map.

In 1934 Alfonso Villa Rojas published his work on the *sacbé* that goes to Yaxuná, of which he measured the entire length. In 1937 E. Wyllys Andrews IV recorded new groups at Cobá, new *sacbeob,* and a stela.

In the 1970s and 1980s numerous projects by a host of scholars were undertaken at Cobá, and these were sponsored by the Southeast Regional Center of INAH (under the direction of Norberto González Crespo during the early years) and the National Geographic Society. This work included ceramic studies, study of the *sacbeob,* clearing and consolidation of some of the structures, copying of the paintings, and study of some habitational units. Some of the principal investigators were Antonio Benavides Castillo, Fernando Robles Castellanos, William J. Folan, and George E. Stuart.

Connections

1. Cancún City to Cobá (via Nuevo Xcan): 84.2 miles by paved road (2:08).

2. Cancún City to Cobá (via Tulum): 109.9 miles by paved road (2:16).

Getting There

1. From Cancún take Highway 180 west to Nuevo Xcan and turn left. This junction for Cobá is marked with a sign. Follow this road for 27.8 miles, and then take the final right cutoff to Cobá.

Note: If you take this route, you will pass Punta Laguna. See that section for details.

2. From Cancún head south on Highway 307 to the cutoff for Cobá (81.1 miles). The cutoff is marked with a sign and is on the right. From the junction go to the final cutoff for Cobá, and then left to the site. If you are starting from any of the stopovers south of Cancún, the second route is better.

There is a hotel at Cobá (one of the Archaeological Villas run by Club Med) with a restaurant. The rooms are small, well designed, and air-conditioned. There is a swimming pool, bar, gift shop, and library. There are also a couple of small restaurants near the site.

Visiting Cobá can be exhausting because of the distances that you must walk. To see all the areas described above you will have to walk about 5 miles (from the parking area and back).

Guides: Though you can reach most of the interesting areas of Cobá on your own, you will need a guide to get to the carved monuments in the Group D ball court. Guides are available at the entrance to the site, and you may find one who is bilingual.

Allow 4 hours to visit the site, which will give you enough time to climb the major structures. Because of the time involved and the fact that it is almost always extremely hot at Cobá, you may want to consider staying at the nearby hotel the night before and getting an early start in the morning. In any case, carry a canteen of water with you to the site, and wear a sun hat.

Cobá can be reached by private car and on tours from Cancún. Buses go to Cobá, but the service is uncertain.

EL MECO

(ehl meh-*koh; derivation: by tradition of the region,*
the nickname of a local resident in the nineteenth century)

Location:

Northeastern Quintana Roo.

Maps: 6 (p. 302) and 6A (p. 310)

The Site

The main structure at El Meco is El Castillo, or Structure 1-a. It sits in a plaza that is surrounded by other buildings. El Castillo is a five-tiered pyramid with a temple on top. It faces east, and there is a stairway on that side, bordered by *alfardas*. With its temple, only part of which is standing, the structure is 41 feet high, the tallest on the north part of the east coast of the Yucatán Peninsula. At one time the structure was painted white by the Mexican government, and it was used as a landmark by boats plying the nearby waters.

The entrance to the temple atop El Castillo had a triple doorway supported by two round columns. The roof of the temple is completely gone but may have been vaulted.

At the base of the east side of El Castillo are two other buildings. The larger one on the north is Structure 1-c, and it also has two columns in the doorway. Its roof is also gone, but it has been determined that it was of beam-and-mortar construction. The better-preserved, smaller building on the south is Structure 1-b, and it has a single doorway, a simple molding above it, and a partly intact roof. The roof is supported by a stepped vault, and the structure rests on a low platform. It was constructed after the main pyramid.

Of special interest at the base of El Castillo, and extending from the *alfardas,* are stone and stucco serpent heads. The one on the north is fairly well preserved. This feature is found in other areas of the northern part of the Yucatán Peninsula—at Tulum, Chichén Itzá, and Mayapán—and it dates to the Postclassic period.

As is often found in Maya architecture, El Castillo was built over an earlier structure, but even this one is of Postclassic date.

Structure 2 shares the plaza with El Castillo, and it lies a few feet in front of (east of) El Castillo's stairway. Structure 2 is a small rectangular platform with stairs on the east and west sides and no evidence of a structure on top. There are other structures bordering the south, east, and north sides of the plaza, where remains of lower walls and columns are found. In Structure 7 (on the south) there is a fragment of a sculpture in the wall, and we were told it represented an animal.

On the east side of the plaza and facing west is Structure 6. This is a 6-foot-high platform with a western stair, bordered by *alfardas.* There are remains of low walls on top, as well as columns, which were once part of the three doorways of the temple. On either side at the base of the stair are the remains of two small shrines. At the bottom of the *alfardas* there were originally serpent heads, but only fragments of these were found during recent excavations at the site.

There are some other structures at El Meco, but nothing of real interest for the visitor.

There is ceramic evidence for the occupation of El Meco in the Early Classic period (A.D. 250–600). At that time it was probably a small village of fishermen under the cultural influence of larger centers in the interior. The site then seems to have been abandoned until about 1000–1100.

During the Late Postclassic period (A.D. 1200–1500) El Meco reached its peak, and during that time it was a major site on the northeast coast. All of the architecture at the site dates to this time.

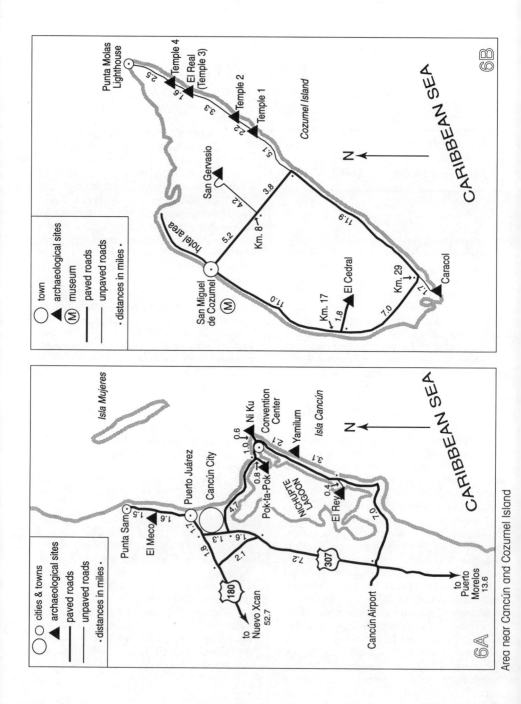

6A

town ◯
cities & towns ◯◯
archaeological sites ▲
museum Ⓜ
paved roads ▬▬▬
unpaved roads ▬▬
· distances in miles ·

Isla Mujeres

Punta Sam
El Meco
Puerto Juárez
Cancún City
1.5
1.6
1.1
1.7
1.8
2.1
1.3
1.6
4.7
0.8
1.0
0.6
Ni Ku
Pok-ta-Pok
Convention Center
2.1
Yamilum
3.1
Isla Cancún
NICHUPTE LAGOON
El Rey
0.4
1.0

180
to Nuevo Xcan 52.7

7.2
307

Cancún Airport

to Puerto Morelos 13.6

N ←

CARIBBEAN SEA

6B

town ◯
archaeological sites ▲
museum Ⓜ
paved roads ▬▬▬
unpaved roads ▬▬
· distances in miles ·

Punta Molas Lighthouse
2.5
Temple 4
1.6
El Real (Temple 3)
3.3
Temple 2
2.2
Temple 1
5.1
Cozumel Island

San Gervasio
4.2
3.8
Km. 8
5.2
hotel area

San Miguel de Cozumel
Ⓜ

11.0
Km. 17
1.8
El Cedral
7.0
11.9
Km. 29
1.7
Caracol

N ←

CARIBBEAN SEA

Area near Cancún and Cozumel Island

El Castillo (Structure 1-a), east side, El Meco. Late Postclassic period.

Structure 1-b, El Meco.
Late Postclassic period.

Sculpture fragment in Structure 7, El Meco. Late Postclassic period.

Recent History

The first report on El Meco was that of Augustus Le Plongeon in 1877. Le Plongeon and his wife, Alice, briefly visited the site, and he gave a general description of the plaza and the pyramid. At that time the site was called El Meco locally. It is possible that El Meco is the ancient Belma, where the troops of Francisco de Montejo the elder spent two months in 1528.

Teobert Maler visited El Meco in 1891, and he described, photographed, and drew El Castillo. He also recorded the serpent heads and was the first to observe that there was an inner structure at El Castillo. This work was published by Gerdt Kutscher in 1971.

Others who recorded El Meco were William H. Holmes, in 1895, who discovered the serpent heads at Structure 6, and two English travelers, Channing Arnold and Frederick J. T. Frost, who visited El Meco around 1907 or 1908.

This was followed by the monumental work of Samuel K. Lothrop for the Carnegie Institution of Washington (CIW). His work focused on Tulum, but it also included many east coast sites as well. Lothrop was accompanied by Thomas Gann in 1918. Lothrop's work was published in 1924 and was the major publication on El Meco to that time.

In the same year Gann published a brief description of the site.

In 1954 William T. Sanders conducted the first stratigraphic test pitting at the site. He concluded, from the analysis of the ceramics he recovered, that El Meco was at its peak during the Postclassic period. This was verified by later studies, and Holmes and Lothrop had reached the same conclusion on the basis of the architecture. The CIW sponsored Sanders's work and published it in 1954, 1955, and 1960.

In 1977 Anthony P. Andrews and Fernando Robles Castellanos conducted excavations at El Meco, under the coordination of Norberto Ganzález Crespo. This included clearing and consolidation of El Castillo, which was in imminent danger of collapse, as well as work on other structures. Participants in the project included Peter J. Schmidt and Rocío González de la Mata.

Ceramics from seven test pits were collected and analyzed, confirming the work of Sanders, and faunal remains were gathered. This work was conducted for INAH, who published the results in 1986.

Some time after Lothrop's work and before that of Andrews and Robles Castellanos, the west part of El Castillo was dynamited, probably to loosen the stone so it could be used in modern construction.

The El Meco Project begun in 1977 was continued in 1979 and 1980 under the supervision of González de la Mata and Elia del Carmen Trejo Alvarado. A report was issued in 1981.

Connection

Cancún City to El Meco: 3.3 miles by paved road (:08).

Getting There

Head east on Highway 180 to Puerto Juárez, then follow the road as it heads north to El Meco.

The site is shortly before Kilometer 3

on the road between Puerto Juárez and the Punta Sam ferry dock. It is on the left side of the road.

Try to visit El Meco in the morning, when El Castillo is well lighted. A wide-angle lens is useful, as the site has become overgrown.

You can reach El Meco by private car or taxi from Cancún. Allow 30 minutes for a visit. There is no food or drink at the site, but there are a couple of restaurants nearby.

POK-TA-POK

*(pohk-tah-*pohk; *derivation: name of the ancient Maya ball game)*

Location:
Northeast part of Isla Cancún, Quintana Roo.
Maps: 6 (p. 302) and 6A (p. 310)

The Site

There are two small structures at Pok-ta-Pok on the golf course of the same name. The one you reach first is composed of a low platform with remains of a low wall and columns on top. There is also one section of wall that rises to almost its original height, and part of a simple, three-member molding can be seen there.

The next structure is a couple of hundred feet away; it is smaller and not as well preserved, and it too, rests on a low platform. Only the lower walls are standing, but a section at the single doorway (on the west) is a

Remains of the columned structure at Pok-ta-Pok. Late Postclassic period.

bit higher than the rest. Remnants of a stair ascend the platform in front of the doorway. Inside the structure on the east are remains of what may have been an altar.

Both structures are of Late Postclassic date and were probably built around A.D. 1300–1400. Construction is typical of east coast sites of that period.

Recent History

In 1975–1976 the Cancún Project was undertaken by the Southeast Regional Center of INAH, directed by Norberto González Crespo, and several sites on Isla Cancún were studied and partly consolidated, including Pok-ta-Pok. The site is briefly mentioned by Ernesto Vargas Pacheco in 1978 and by Anthony P. Andrews in 1986.

Connection

Isla Cancún to Pok-ta-Pok: 1.8 miles by paved road (:04).

Getting There

From the convention center on Isla Cancún head west on Paseo Kukulcán to the cutoff for the Pok-ta-Pok Golf Course. Turn left and proceed to the clubhouse to get permission to visit the ruins. Then cross a small bridge and follow the road to the first structure that is visible from it. Continue a bit farther to the second structure, then proceed following the road as it loops around, and rejoin the road on which you came in.

Allow 15 minutes to see both structures.

NI KU
(nee koo; *derivation: Maya for "Temple on the Point")*
(PUNTA CANCÚN)
(poon-tah kahn-koon; Punta is Spanish for "point")

Location:
Northeast corner of Isla Cancún, Quintana Roo.
Maps: 6 (p. 302) and 6A (p. 310)

The Site

There are a few remains of a small temple here. It was originally a rectangular structure, but today only the north, east, and part of the west wall are standing. On the northeast corner you can see two parts of a cornice molding, and below this, a large crack in the wall.

Since there is no doorway on the east, the entrance must have been on the west, in the area where the wall has fallen. The roof is also gone, but it was probably of beam-and-

mortar construction. The structure dates to the Late Postclassic period and most likely was built between A.D. 1300 and 1400. The construction is typical of east coast architecture from that time.

Recent History

At the end of his travels in Yucatán in 1842, John Lloyd Stephens reported sighting stone structures along the coast of Cancún, and one of these may have been Ni Ku.

In 1975–1976 the Cancún Project was undertaken by the Southeast Regional Center of INAH, directed by Norberto González Crespo, and several sites on Isla Cancún were studied, including Ni Ku. The site is briefly mentioned by Ernesto Vargas Pacheco in 1978 and by Anthony P. Andrews in 1986.

Connection

Isla Cancún to Ni Ku: 0.6 mile by paved road (:01).

Getting There

From the Convention Center on Isla Cancún take the street that goes northeast to the Camino Real Hotel. Ni Ku is on the grounds of the hotel, which is at the extreme northeast corner of Isla Cancún.

Hotel personnel will direct you through a courtyard and walkway, to, and through, the east section of guest rooms. They sometimes find it hard to believe that this is what you came to see, but if you persevere, explaining that it is a *small*, ruined structure that you want to see, they will help you.

Small temple, from the northeast, Ni Ku. Late Postclassic period.

The structure is just a few feet to the east of the guest rooms. Allow 5 minutes to see it.

★
YAMILUM

(yah-mee-loom; derivation: Maya for "hilly land")

Location:
  Northeast part of Isla
  Cancún, Quintana Roo.
Maps: 6 (p. 302) and 6A (p. 310)

The Site

The two structures at Yamilum sit atop the highest rise of land on Isla Cancún, giving the site its name. The views from here are superb; the structures are easy to reach and are definitely worth a look.

The main structure is a fair-size temple, resting on a platform with a low stair on the west side. There are two cylindrical columns on top of the west side of the platform, and they were once part of a triple doorway that formed the entrance to the structure. The columns are standing, as is the jambstone on the south, but much of the west wall has fallen.

The north and south walls are better preserved, and large cornerstones are incorporated into the construction. These walls have a two-member medial molding and a simple, rectangular cornice molding, above which is a cornice of stones laid vertically. Except at the northeast corner, there are only a few courses of stone remaining of the east wall.

On the floor of the structure, near the center of the east wall, is a small, stone-and-stucco construction that may have been an altar.

On a level lower than the main structure, and almost abutting it on the east, is a smaller temple. It rests on its own platform and has a narrow doorway opening to the east. On the back (west side) remains of a two-member medial molding can be seen. This is best observed from inside the east side of the main structure.

To the east of the lower structure is a modern retaining wall of stone; below is a beautiful white-sand beach.

The main structure at Yamilum, from the southwest. Late Postclassic period.

The two structures at Yamilum date to the Late Postclassic period (A.D. 1200–1500), and their architecture is typical of east coast sites from that time. Though the roofs are gone on both structures, it is believed they were of beam-and-mortar construction.

Recent History

At the end of his travels in Yucatán in 1842, John Lloyd Stephens reported sighting stone structures along the coast of Cancún, and one of these may have been Yamilum.

In 1911 George P. Howe described Yamilum under the name Tamul. In 1975–1976 the Cancún Project was undertaken by the Southeast Regional Center of INAH, directed by Norberto González Crespo, and several sites on Isla Cancún were studied, including Yamilum. The site is briefly mentioned by Ernesto Vargas Pacheco in 1978 and by Anthony P. Andrews in 1986.

Connection

Isla Cancún to Yamilum: 2.1 miles by paved road (:04).

Getting There

From the convention center on Isla Cancún head south on Paseo Kukulcán. Yamilum is just north of the Sheraton Hotel, and access is through hotel grounds. Go to the hotel lobby, and an employee will direct you to the pool area, from which you can see and reach the main temple.

You will want to have sunglasses and perhaps a sun hat. A wide-angle lens is useful to get overall shots of the main structure.

Allow 20 minutes to see and photograph both structures, and perhaps a few more to enjoy to view.

EL REY

(ehl rehee; *derivation: Spanish for "the King" [see text])*

Location:
Southeastern part of Isla
Cancún, Quintana Roo.
Maps: 6 (p. 302) and 6A (p. 310)

The Site

El Rey is the most important site on Isla Cancún. Its name comes from a stone-and-stucco sculpture of a human head that was found at the site. All of the sites on Cancún have been given Maya names, so El Rey is also called Kinich Ahau-Bonil. The site is principally composed of two plazas surrounded by buildings and platforms. The structures and the surrounding areas are cleared, and you can see from one area to another, so getting around is easy.

As you enter the site, you come first to Plaza II, and trails lead to the more interesting structures. The architecture of some of the structures is similar, the buildings varying only in size and minor details. They are composed of rectangular platforms with vertical walls and stairways with *alfardas*. The lower walls and columns of the buildings on top are standing, and at the rear of the main rooms are altars. Other structures are simply platforms.

To the south of Plaza II is the Principal Plaza, or Plaza I, the most interesting part of the site. The Principal Plaza is bordered on the north by the L-shaped Structure 1 (a platform with columns) and, next to it on the east, by Structure 2. Structure 2 is a three-tiered pyramid with part of the lower walls of a temple on top; its maximum height is 18 feet. Originally there was direct access between the two plazas, but when Structure 2 was constructed, it blocked this route.

Bordering the east side of the Principal Plaza is a platform with three structures on top. Structure 3-B, in the center, is the best preserved at El Rey, and it has two doorways

on the west, facing the plaza. The doorjambs and lintels are recessed, and the lower wall of the structure slopes inward. The upper wall zone has a slight outward batter, and it overhangs the lower zone. Above the upper wall zone is a simple, rectangular three-member molding, the middle part of which is recessed. Above this is a cornice made of vertical stones. There was a niche (now mostly fallen) in the cornice, in the center of the building, and it is believed that the sculpture called El Rey was once in position in the niche.

Structure 3-B has two long rooms, one behind the other, and the front room has a stepped vault. The medial wall of the building has three doorways, and they are staggered with the two on the front wall, so that from the front you cannot see into the rear room. The back wall of the rear room is fallen except for the lowest part, but there are remains of three small rectangular altars set into its base. The structure was originally painted with various motifs, but only small fragments remain today.

Structure 3-A lies to the north of 3-B. Though not as well preserved, there are two columns at the entrance, two more on the interior of the main room, and a smaller room at the rear containing a small altar. The roof of the structure is gone. Structure 3-C, to the south of 3-B, is the smallest of the group and almost totally destroyed, but it had a doorway facing the plaza, like the other two structures that share the platform.

On the south side of the Principal Plaza is Structure 4, the largest of the explored platforms at El Rey; it is 115 feet long, east to west, rises in two low tiers, and has a stairway facing the plaza. There are remains of low walls and 18 columns on top. Within the Principal Plaza is Structure 5, a group of three small platforms joining each other, with little remaining of the rooms on top. This structure was built in two or three stages, and the platforms on the ends were constructed using stones from other structures.

Structure 3-B, from the northwest, El Rey. Late Postclassic period.

All of the structural remains at El Rey date to around A.D. 1300–1400 in the Late Postclassic period.

Recent History

During the late nineteenth century and early twentieth century several authors visited and recorded El Rey under a variety of names. It is possible that Augustus and Alice Le Plongeon spent the night there in 1876. Later the site was mentioned by William H. Holmes, Channing Arnold, and Frederick J. T. Frost. Raymond E. Merwin also visited El Rey, but his work, recorded in 1913–1914, remains unpublished.

Expeditions in the area sponsored by the Carnegie Institution of Washington were reported by Samuel K. Lothrop in 1924, and El Rey was included. In 1954 William T. Sanders conducted the first excavations at the site; his ceramic studies indicate the dates for the site.

The first extensive work at El Rey was undertaken in 1975 and 1976 by INAH; it included excavation and consolidation and was reported by Pablo Mayer Guala and Ernesto Vargas Pacheco in 1977 and 1978.

Connection

Isla Cancún to El Rey: 5.2 miles by paved road (:08), then 0.4 mile by dirt road (:03).

Getting There

From the Convention Center on Isla Cancún, head south on Paseo Kukulcán to a little past Kilometer 17, to the cutoff for El Rey (marked with a sign). Turn right and proceed to the site. Bilingual guides are available. Allow 45 minutes for a visit, and wear a sun hat.

★ ★
PLAYA DEL CARMEN
(plah-yah dehl kahr-mehn; derivation: Spanish for "Beach of the Villa")

Original Name:
Xamanhá, Maya for
"North Water."
Location:
Northeastern Quintana Roo.
Map: 6 (p. 302)

The Site

There are several groups of structures at Playa del Carmen, lettered A through G, and they are now surrounded by the modern town and the condominiums of Villas Playacar (developed in the 1980s). As you enter the town, and just before the plaza, you will see a sign for Playacar painted on a wall. Turn right as the sign indicates and follow the road as it turns to the left. This brings you to a gate with a guard. Tell him you wish to see the ruins, and you will be allowed to enter.

The groups on Playacar's grounds are C, D, and E, and you come to them in that order. Group C is 0.2 mile from the gate, and the groups are separated by about the same distance. After the last structure it is 0.2 mile to a turnaround at the end of the road. You can drive to all the structures, and all are on the right side of the road and visible from it.

The first structure you reach is one of the largest and best preserved (C-1); it rests on a platform with a stairway on the east. There are two rooms; the outer one encloses an inner shrine on three sides. There are two columns at the main entrance, one of which is complete, and remains of painting on the inset panel above the doorway to the inner shrine. The structure is mostly intact except for part of its back wall and a part of the front wall above the doorway. There are remains of both medial and cornice moldings in this vaulted structure. There are a few remains of a couple of other buildings nearby.

A short distance south is a mostly fallen building; what remains appears to be an inner shrine with its front wall partly intact. There are two standing columns in front of the wall, which may have been the entrance to the building. This structure also faces east and rests on a platform, as does the next one.

The next structure (part of Group D) has a standing front wall and an interior shrine. There is an altar in the shrine, on which is a small vertical stone.

The last structure (part of Group E) is unusual in that its basal platform is huge and quite a bit higher than those supporting the other structures described. Some massive cut stones form part of the platform, and this too is an unusual feature in the area. There are remains of a typical East Coast–style temple on top.

Return now to the Playacar gate and go on to the town plaza and park. Two blocks south of the plaza is a military compound surrounded by a fence, and just beyond are the two structures of Group B. Ask at the compound for permission to cross it to get a clear view of the temples (you actually cannot get *to* the temples). The structures share a platform and are at right angles to each other. Structure I is greatly fallen, but its interior shrine is standing. Structure II is larger and better preserved, with two columns in its front (west) doorway still supporting a wooden lintel. Part of its interior shrine is standing, though the back wall of the building has collapsed. Both structures of Group B are vaulted.

Now go two blocks north of the plaza and turn right for half a block. This brings you to Group A, next to La Ruina campground. Structure I is well preserved, with a single room facing east and medial and cornice moldings that are mostly intact. At one time this building was used for curing tobacco. It shares a platform with Structure II, of which only the lower part of the walls remain. Structure I is vaulted, but since the debris of Structure II has been removed, "it

Structure C-1, east side, Playa del Carmen. Late Postclassic period.

is impossible to tell whether it had a masonry roof," according to Anthony P. Andrews.

Groups F and G are north of Group A, but I have not seen them and do not know if they have standing architecture.

Recent History

Xamanhá was a point of embarcation for Cozumel in ancient Maya times, just as the modern town of Playa del Carmen is today. Francisco de Montejo the elder camped at Xamanhá with his men in 1528. The meaning of the name (North Water) may suggest that Xamanhá was a northern outpost of Xcaret, the other point of embarcation for Cozumel. There is little to note about Xamanhá afterward; it may have been abandoned during the seventeenth century.

In the early twentieth century Sylvanus G. Morley, Thomas Gann, and Samuel K. Lothrop visited the site, and on Lothrop's map, published in 1924, the name Playa del Carmen is used. It seems that it was in the late 1970s or early 1980s that it was definitely determined that Xamanhá and Playa del Carmen were the same place.

A reconnaissance of the Quintana Roo coast was carried out by William T. Sanders, and Playa del Carmen was included. He published his results in 1955.

In 1972 Andrews and Davis A. Gilder recorded structures at the site, and Andrews returned in 1973 with Arthur G. Miller and completed the site map, which was published in 1975 by the Middle American Research Institute of Tulane University. Additional studies were published in 1981 by Rocío González de la Mata and Elia del Carmen Trejo Alvarado, and by this time additional structures had been located.

The structures at Playa del Carmen

were excavated and consolidated by the Southeast Regional Center of INAH.

While studies indicate the presence of Late Preclassic ceramics at Playa del Carmen and evidence of a Classic and Early Postclassic occupation, the temple structures are all of Late Postclassic date and typical of the East Coast style.

Connection

Cancún City to Playa del Carmen (plaza): 43.6 miles by paved road (:57).

Getting There

Head south on Highway 307 to the cutoff for Playa del Carmen (43.0 miles), which is marked with a sign. Turn left and drive 0.6 mile to the center of town.

A bus can drop you off in Playa del Carmen if you do not have your own vehicle. Allow 1 hour to visit the structures described above.

XCARET

(shkah-reht; derivation: perhaps a native corruption of the Spanish word caleta, *"inlet")*

Original Name:
   Pole, possibly meaning "place of trade" in Maya.
Location:
   Northeastern Quintana Roo.
Map: 6 (p. 302)

The Site

Xcaret is one of the larger sites on the east coast of Quintana Roo, with several groups of structures reported in the core area, and others up and down the coast. The part of the site visitors see today are Groups B and A and, from a distance, the single small temple of Group K.

As you enter the site, you come first to Group B, with large platforms surrounding a plaza and a small platform with an eastern stair in the center. There is no standing architecture atop the platforms, and it is believed that most of them supported perishable structures.

A new wide walkway leads from there to Group A, and it points directly to Structures V and VI, which together form a twin-temple pyramid that is the dominant architectural assemblage of the group. The two temples share a platform that is over 10 feet high, and two stairways, one in front of each temple, give access to the structures. The twin temples are not totally intact, but they have been partly restored. Both have simple geometric designs in the remaining upper wall zones, and there are simple moldings above and below.

The remaining structures of Group A cluster near the twin temples, producing an informal courtyard. All the structures in the group have one room with a single doorway and an inset panel above it. There are remains of paint in some of the panels. Some of the structures had vaulted roofs, while in others beam-and-mortar construction was used. All of the temples are typical Postclassic East Coast style, and most rest on low platforms. One has a higher platform but few remains of an upper structure. The largest and most northerly has two stucco bird heads flanking the doorway.

A few feet from Group A a path leads to a cenote and another to a lovely *caleta* that is a nice place for a swim. There is a restaurant at the *caleta*.

When you return to Group A and are heading back to the parking area, take a detour to the left and go toward the sea. You will see a delightful cove and, beyond it, the

Structure A-VI, west side, Xcaret. Late Postclassic period.

one building of Group K. A telephoto lens will be useful here. To the left you can see a newly constructed breakwater that forms a harbor for small craft.

Recent History

Xcaret is the ancient Maya port of Pole, which was of strategic importance in Postclassic times. It was the main port of embarcation for Cozumel (Xamanhá, or Playa del Carmen, was another), and Pole's *caleta* afforded a protected harbor. Religious architecture dominates the site core and "underscores its importance as a ceremonial center," according to Anthony P. Andrews. It is also believed to have been prominent in trading.

Francisco de Montejo the elder camped at Pole in 1528, and the men he left behind when he moved on to the north were killed by the local inhabitants.

There are a few mentions of the site in the latter part of the sixteenth century and early seventeenth century, and a Spanish chapel was built in what is now called Group G, though little of it remains today. Pole is shown on some later maps, but the archaeological discovery of the site under the name Xcaret is credited to the Mason-Spinden Expedition of 1926, and the site was reported by Gregory Mason in that and following years. Xcaret is mentioned in the literature in the 1950s and 1960s, and a major study of the remains was published in 1975 by the Middle American Research Institute of Tulane University. The authors were E. Wyllys Andrews IV and Anthony P. Andrews.

Ceramic studies indicate that Xcaret was occupied beginning in the Late Preclassic period, but the great majority of sherds date to the Late Postclassic, as does the architecture.

In 1990 Groups A and B were nicely cleared and consolidated.

Connection

Cancún City to Xcaret: 46.9 miles by paved road (1:00), then 1.0 mile by rock road (:06).

Getting There

Head south on Highway 307 to the cutoff for Xcaret (marked with a sign). Turn left onto the rock road and continue to the site. You can park near Group G. There are rest rooms, a ticket office, and cold drinks.

Having your own vehicle is the recommended way to reach the site. Allow 40 minutes to see the ruins and the *caleta*.

★
CHAKALAL

*(chah-kah-*lahl; *derivation: possibly "Red Arrow" or "Red Cane" in Maya)*

Location:
   Northeastern Quintana Roo.
Map: 6 (p. 302)

The Site

One of the best-preserved ancient Maya structures on the east coast is the lovely, fair-sized Late Postclassic Caleta Temple at Chakalal. It has one room, a single doorway facing east, and simple medial and cornice moldings, all of which is intact. The roof is vaulted, and there are remains of paintings on the interior walls. They depict a serpent (difficult to make out) and a jaguar (easier to see) and both positive and negative painted hands. The structure sits on the edge of a beautiful *caleta* and is easy to photograph from several vantage points.

There are four other groups of structures at Chakalal, referred to as Chakalal Inland, but none of the structures are as well preserved as the Caleta Temple.

Recent History

In 1926 the Mason-Spinden Expedition discovered the ruins of Chakalal, and Herbert J. Spinden made sketches of the Caleta Temple and two of the inland structures. He recorded the paintings in the Caleta Temple, and these were published in 1927 by Gregory Mason, along with his own photographs.

Other photographs of the temple were published by William T. Sanders in 1955 and Michel Peissel in 1963. In 1975 E. Wyllys Andrews IV and Anthony P. Andrews published a description, plans, and photographs of both the Caleta Temple and the inland groups. Their work was carried out under the research program of the Middle American Research Institute of Tulane University.

Connection

Cancún City to Chakalal: 56.5 miles by paved road (1:12), then 0.4 mile of good rock road (:02).

Caleta Temple, from the southeast, Chakalal. Late Postclassic period.

Getting There

Head south on Highway 307 to the cutoff for Chakalal. The cutoff is not marked, but it is near the Kilometer 90 marker and 0.8 mile south of the entrance to Puerto Aventuras. Allow 15 minutes to see the Caleta Temple.

There is no food or drink at Chakalal, but both are available at Puerto Aventuras.

Note: If you are staying at Puerto Aventuras, you can reach the Caleta Temple directly from their grounds, without returning to the highway. Just follow the signs.

★
YALKU

*(yahl-*koo; *derivation: possibly "Forehead of God" or "Sayings of God" in Maya)*

Location:
    Northeastern Quintana Roo.
Map: 6 (p. 302)

The Site

There is a one-room shrine a little over 4 feet tall at Yalku. It is partly surrounded by a circular wall, to which it is connected at the rear. Both the shrine and the wall are constructed of crude masonry, although the shrine and its vaulted roof are well preserved. There is a small altar in the rear of the shrine that once supported a stucco idol, which has been destroyed. The shrine and wall are built on bedrock, without any platform.

Recent History

The shrine described above was discovered in the early 1950s by Loring M. Hewen, and it was recorded by E. Wyllys Andrews IV in 1955. Andrews IV and Anthony P. Andrews

Small shrine and enclosure, Yalku. Late Postclassic period.

---

reported the structure in 1975, in a Middle American Research Institute publication. They commented that it is "one of the most unusual structures on the central coast."

Another shrine in the vicinity was found by William T. Sanders in 1954, and he reported it the following year.

Connection

Cancún City to Yalku: 64.0 miles by paved road (1:20), 0.4 mile by good rock road (:02), then about 50 yards on foot (:20).

Total from Cancún to Yalku: 64.4 miles (1:42).

Getting There

Head south on Highway 307 to the Yalku cut-off (unmarked but exactly opposite Rancho San Miguel, a plant nursery). Turn left to reach the *caleta* at Yalku, where you can park. The *caleta* has a small northern extension at the parking area. Follow this extension to its end and continue northeast for about 50 yards to the shrine. A compass will help. The walk is over limestone bedrock, loose boulders, and vegetation, and there is no definite trail, so boots would be best; you should wear a sun hat. The vegetation in this area is mostly low, but you cannot see the shrine until you are almost there. With care, you will not get lost.

Allow 10 minutes to see and photograph the shrine, a little extra if you decide on a swim at the *caleta* when you return to it. There is no food or drink at Yalku.

★ ★
XELHA
(shehl-hah; derivation: Maya for "Opening of Water")

Original Name:
　　Xala, a variation of Xelha.
Location:
　　Northeastern Quintana Roo.
Map:　6 (p. 302)

The Site

There are three groups of structures in the main part of Xelha on the west side of Highway 307, and a small shrine at Xelha Caleta on the east side of the highway. When you enter the main part of the site, follow the trail as it curves around to the Palace Group. There are two architectural assemblages here; the one closest to the trail is the Mercado ("Market"), and just beyond is the Palacio ("Palace").

The remains of both are platforms with the lower walls of structures on top. In one area is a group of stone discs that may once have formed a column.

A trail from the side of the Mercado leads to a structure called the Pájaros ("Birds"). (This structure is actually right on the highway, but access is from the interior of the site.) On the way to the Pájaros the trail passes a group of small structures named for Samuel K. Lothrop, an early investigator of the site.

The Pájaros was partly destroyed when Highway 307 was cut through, but what remains has been consolidated. The structure is composed of a platform with remains of rooms on top. The most interesting feature is the medial wall, which has murals on both sides. On the north side of the wall are two rectangular panels bordered in red, with depictions of birds—also mostly red—within the panels. This mural gives the structure its name.

On the back (south) side of the medial wall another mural was discovered in the early 1980s. A Teotihuacán warrior in full regalia is depicted on the right, in red, yellow, and blue paint. To the left are three wide

Structure at the Mercado, from the northwest, Xelha. Late Postclassic period.

vertical red stripes, and beyond is part of a checkerboard pattern in red and yellow, with X's drawn in some of the squares (actually rectangles). Stepped vaults roofed the structure, and parts of these are intact.

The Pájaros (Structure 26-Sub) was later encased in another construction. The earlier Structure 26-Sub is Early Classic, according to Fernando Robles Castellanos, although Arthur G. Miller believes it was not constructed before A.D. 770. In any case, it is still one of the earliest structures at Xelha and along the east coast of Quintana Roo.

Settlement-pattern data and ceramic studies indicate that the predominant period of occupation was during Classic times, although the site's beginnings were in the Late Preclassic, and it continued through the Late Postclassic. Xelha is next to the "largest natural harbor on the east coast," according to Anthony P. Andrews, and Robles Castellanos believes that from around A.D. 600 to 1200, Xelha was a great commercial port.

Return to the Mercado and the trail on which you entered the site, and continue along it to the Group of the Casa del Jaguar ("House of the Jaguar"). Partway there someone will offer to show you the rest of the way, and you pass a lovely cenote before reaching this group. The group is composed of several small structures informally arranged around a plaza, the largest of which is the Casa del Jaguar.

This structure faces south and gets its name from a painting of a jaguar (difficult to see) in a position of the descending god found at Tulum. This mural is found on the outside wall of the inner shrine (east side) of the structure and can be photographed through a doorway in the outer wall of the building. All the doorways of the structure are blocked by wooden poles, but you can get photos in between. According to Miller, the descending jaguar is the seventh layer of painted stucco, of a total of 27 layers, found on the inside of the building. Miller believes

Casa del Jaguar, south side, Xelha. Possibly Late Postclassic period.

that the structure was not built all at one time.

The Casa del Jaguar has two intact columns on the front facade, and all of its interior walls were painted. There are inset panels above the doorways to the interior shrine; in one area, above the panel, are remains of red handprints.

Two other structures in this group are of interest. One is a small shrine with remnants of a simple molding, and the other is larger and partly fallen and rests atop a low platform approached by a stairway on the north. Both buildings are Late Postclassic—and photogenic—while the other structures in this group are mostly rubble. The Group of the Casa del Jaguar was connected to the Mercado by a *sacbé* in ancient times, and another led from the former in the opposite direction. Perhaps this is the beginning of the long-sought-for *sacbé* connecting Xelha to Cobá, but this has not yet been demonstrated. Scholars believe that Xelha was the main port for Cobá, and they believe that a *sacbé* probably connected the two sites.

You now leave the ruins on the west side of the highway and head north to the cutoff for Xelha Caleta. When you leave the entrance building at Xelha Caleta, take the trail that goes on the far side of the lagoon, and you will pass the remains of the small shrine.

Recent History

Xelha was discovered as an archaeological site during reconnaissance projects sponsored by the Carnegie Institution of Washington (CIW) carried out between 1910 and 1922 and published by Lothrop in 1924. In 1955 William T. Sanders, also working for CIW, published ceramic studies and reported new buildings at Xelha.

Underwater studies were conducted by the Exploration and Water Sports Club of Mexico (CEDAM) in 1960, and an underwater altar was found at Xelha Caleta. In 1973 the small *caleta* shrine was recorded by Andrews. Miller undertook an extensive study of the murals in the Tancah-Tulum area, and Xelha was included in his 1982 publication.

Major work at Xelha was conducted in the 1980s by the Southeast Regional Center of INAH, with the support of the Fideicomiso Caleta de Xelha y del Caribe, and many structures were cleared, excavated, and consolidated. The work was coordinated by Norberto González Crespo, director of the Southeast Regional Center; participating archaeologists were Pablo Mayer Guala, Antonio Benavides Castillo, and Ricardo Velázquez Valadéz.

Connection

Cancún City to Xelha (west side of the highway): 71.4 miles by paved road (1:30), then 100 yards of rock road to the parking area.

Getting There

Head south on Highway 307 to the entrance to the site (marked with a sign), turn right on the rock road, and proceed to the parking area. Wear a sun hat and allow 1¼ hours for a visit. There is a small restaurant at the site.

The cutoff for Xelha Caleta—on the east side of the highway—is 0.3 mile north of the cutoff for the ruins on the west side, and it too is marked with a sign. When you approach from Cancún, you will come to the cutoff for the *caleta* first, but I recommend going on to the main part of the site first and returning to the *caleta* later.

There are shops and restaurants at Xelha Caleta. While the *caleta* is as lovely as ever, it has lost some of its serenity because of the influx of visitors. Swimming and snorkeling are allowed in certain areas of the *caleta*.

Xelha Caleta can be reached by bus tours from Cancún.

★
TANCAH

(tahn-kah; derivation: Maya for "He Who Lives in the Center of Town")

Original Name:
Xamanzamá, "North Zamá," possibly Zamá or Tzamá (see "Tulum").
Location:
Northeastern Quintana Roo.
Map: 6 (p. 302)

The Site

The site of Tancah is cut in two by Highway 307. A number of structures and platforms are reported, two of which are of interest to the visitor, but only one is easily accessible. Structure 12 is a few feet east of the highway and has been consolidated. It consists of a pyramidal base rising in three tiers with a one-room temple on top. There are fragments of a mural inside and a few remains of a roof comb above. Access to the temple is by a stairway on the east side of the base.

Arthur G. Miller dates Structure 12 to what he terms the Terminal Classic/Early Postclassic (A.D. 770–1200). He states that he sees "no perceptible change in the murals and architecture of the region during this time."

Near Structure 12, a little farther from the highway, are several overgrown mounds, and some have a few remains of standing architecture.

Across the highway from Structure 12 and about 150 feet from it is Structure 44. This building faces west and has two long rooms, one behind the other. The rear room has only part of its back wall standing, but the medial and front walls of the structure are better preserved. Three doorways enter the front room, two of which are intact, and the vault in this area is in place. There are a few remains of a simple three-member cornice molding between the doorways and of inset panels immediately above the doorways.

The most interesting features at Structure 44 are remains of paintings on the west side of the medial wall. They are on either side of the center doorway. On the upper right (as you face the doorway) is a depiction of God E, the corn god, with a cleft head, and below is God C. On the left side of the doorway is another figure that is more difficult to discern, a running or dancing human who wears an iguana- or alligator-head costume that streams behind him. All three figures are Middle Postclassic style (A.D. 1200–

1400), according to Miller. He believes that the paintings date to the middle part of the period (ca. 1350).

Structure 44 has been consolidated and rests on a low platform that also supports the totally destroyed Structure 45 (to the south) and the lower remains of the small shrinelike Structure 43 (to the west). The platform itself (Structure 42) was built over several times, and burials from earlier periods were found. The earliest layer of the platform, built upon bedrock, dates to the Late Preclassic period, and burials from the Early Classic (the earliest found) were encountered in the next level.

Other structures at Tancah were erected during the Late Postclassic period, and in Early Colonial times a Spanish chapel was built.

Recent History

On their way to Tulum in 1842, John Lloyd Stephens and Frederick Catherwood stopped at the ranch of Tancah and were led to the remains of ancient buildings in a milpa. Stephens described the structures there as "all small and delapidated." Juan José Gálvez, credited with the modern discovery of Tulum, also visited Tancah somewhat before Stephens, but attention was first brought to both sites by the latter in 1843.

In 1924 Samuel K. Lothrop reported on Tulum and other east coast sites, including Tancah, as did William T. Sanders in 1955. Miller's analysis of the mural painting and architecture at Tancah was published in 1982.

Connection

Cancún City to Tancah: 77.4 miles by paved road (1:38).

Mural in Structure 44 depicting God E, the corn god (top), and God C (bottom), Tancah. Probably Late Postclassic period.

Getting There

Head south on Highway 307 to Tancah (unmarked). It is 6.0 miles south of the cutoff for the ruins of Xelha (west side of the highway) and 2.4 miles north of the cutoff for the ruins of Tulum.

You can park on the east side of the road near Structure 12. Reaching Structure 44 can be a bit iffy. Sometimes a trail to the structure is open; most often the trail is overgrown and you will not be able to get there without a guide and machete. Try to find a guide at Tulum who knows the way.

Allow 10 minutes to see Structure 12 and another 30 minutes for Structure 44, plus the time to have your guide cut a trail to it. There is no food or drink at Tancah.

★ ★ ★ ★
TULUM

*(too-*loom; *derivation: Maya for "wall" or*
"fortification"; by extension, "fortress")

Original Name:
Zamá (Tzamá), Maya
for "City of the Dawn."
Location:
Northeastern Quintana Roo.
Map: 6 (p. 302)

The Site

One of the most impressive features of Tulum is its exquisite setting. It is perched on a cliff above the turquoise waters of the Caribbean and is surrounded on three sides be a wall.

It was long thought that the wall was a defensive feature, and perhaps it was, though E. Wyllys Andrews IV makes the point that the construction may have been more symbolic than tactically defensive. The wall has five entrances, one of which is used today as access to the site, and it encloses about 16 acres. It averages 18 feet thick and 9 to 15 feet high. Michael D. Coe suggests that no more than 500 to 600 people lived within the enclosure, but Tulum is thought to have been an important trading center. The wall dates to A.D. 1200–1450, and the structures are all Postclassic in date. In some cases visible structures cover earlier ones, but even those are of late date. For example, there is an earlier temple beneath El Castillo, the tallest and apparently the most important structure at the site.

One puzzling factor at Tulum was the discovery of Stela 1, dated to A.D. 564, since moved to the British Museum by Thomas Gann. This date is several hundred years earlier than the structures at the site, and that much earlier than the ceramic evidence would indicate. It was long postulated that the stela was moved to Tulum from some other site. Andrews feels that it is almost certain that it came from the nearby site of of

Tancah, whose history goes back to the Classic period. Arthur G. Miller believes that the stela probably came from Tancah but maintains that Cobá should also be considered a strong possibility.

Another notable feature at Tulum is the mural paintings, especially in the Temple of the Frescoes (Structure 16). There are striking similarities with the Mixtec codices from the Mexican highlands (Santa Rita in Belize had similar murals), but the themes are clearly Maya. The style has been called the Late Postclassic International Style by Donald Robertson. The Tulum murals are quite different from the Classic Maya murals at Bonampak and Chacmultún, and from the Early Postclassic paintings at Chichén Itzá.

Miller, who studied the murals in the Tancah-Tulum region, says that the murals in Structure 16 (and in the small Temple of the Descending God, Structure 5) are the "finest example of mural painting in the region and stylistically unrelated to the earlier paintings." He dates the murals in both structures to after A.D. 1400.

The Late Postclassic style of architecture found at Tulum and most other east coast sites is quite different from earlier Classic traditions. There was a pronounced degradation in the building arts in the Postclassic period. Ceremonial centers were less extensive in area, and individual structures were smaller. Some truly miniature temples just a few feet high are found at Tulum, Xelha, and other east coast sites.

Stone cutting was poorly developed, and thick coats of stucco were relied upon to cover rough masonry. "The vault, so long a standard form of roofing, was largely replaced by the beam-and-masonry roof," according to H. E. D. Pollock. Stucco was extensively used for decorative elements.

Since almost everything of interest is enclosed within the wall, and since the site is rather small and well cleared, no special

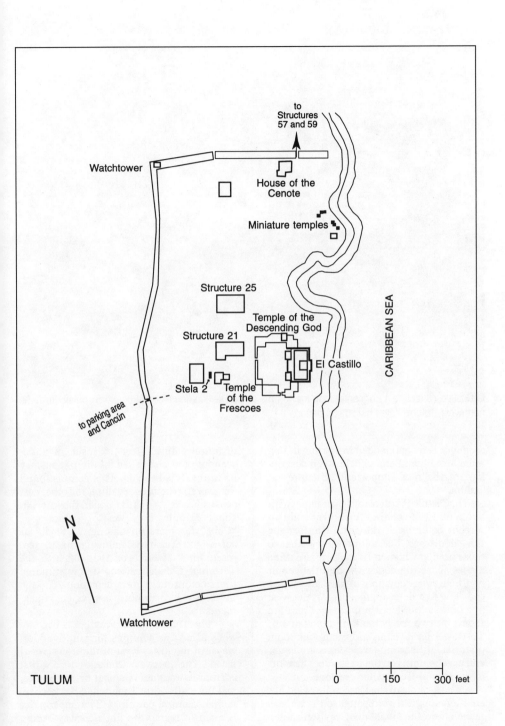

to
Structures
57 and 59

Watchtower

House of the
Cenote

Miniature temples

CARIBBEAN SEA

Structure 25

Temple of the
Descending God

Structure 21

El Castillo

Stela 2   Temple
of the
Frescoes

to parking area
and Cancún

N

Watchtower

TULUM

0   150   300 feet

El Castillo (Structure 1) at center, and the Temple of the Descending God (Structure 5) at left, from the northwest, Tulum. Late Postclassic period.

sequence is recommended in visiting it. Just roam around and enjoy. Below is a description of the most important structures at Tulum.

El Castillo (Structure 1) is a temple with two rooms (one behind the other) and two serpent columns at the entrance, forming three doorways. The columns are similar to those used at Chichén Itzá. There are three niches above the doorways, and the center one houses a depiction of the descending god. The temple is approached on the west by a stairway bordered by *alfardas*. There are rooms on two levels flanking the stairway. The lower-level rooms are small, one-room oratories; the second-level rooms are larger and have columns on the west side. The roofs of the second-level rooms are gone.

The Temple of the Descending God has an interesting outward batter to the walls, a niche above the single doorway with a depiction of the descending god, and remains of mural paintings on the inside. The descending god, also called the diving god, may be in reality a bee god. This deity is found on several structures at Tulum and other east coast sites, as well as at Cobá in the interior, about 25 miles northwest of Tulum. (See "Cobá" for more on this deity.) Sayil, far across the Yucatán Peninsula, has a representation of this god that dates to the Terminal Classic period—a few hundred years before the Tulum depiction. The figure is part human but has winglike attachments.

The Temple of the Frescoes is two stories and has four columns, forming five doorways, in the lower level of the front (west) facade. The doorways lead to a corridor that surrounds an inner chamber on three sides, and the walls of the inner chamber have remains of mural paintings. The upper story is a single room with one doorway. Above the doorways (of both levels and the inner

Temple of the Descending God (Structure 5), from the southwest, Tulum. Late Postclassic period.

chamber) are niches with remains of sculptures; seated figures and the diving god are represented. There are also two interesting masks on the western corners of the first story. The structure was built in a couple of stages.

The doorways in the lower story of the Temple of the Frescoes and the one in the Temple of the Descending God are blocked by poles, but you can get photographs of the murals through the openings. You are not allowed to use flash. The badly eroded Stela 2 has been reerected on a small platform in front of the Temple of the Frescoes.

Other buildings of interest are Structure 25, noted for its excellent depiction of the diving god in a niche above the central doorway of the inner chamber, and Structure 21, with X-shaped crossbars in its small exterior windows.

The many other structures inside the wall, including the watchtowers on the wall, are also worth visiting. Tulum is a most pho-togenic site, and no special photographic problems are encountered. Since most of the interesting structures face west, the afternoon is the best time for photography.

There are two other well-preserved structures at Tulum, located outside the wall along the coast, north of the main part of the site. They perhaps are older than most of the structures in the main part of Tulum, though some authorities believe they were constructed during the Late Postclassic period along with most of the rest of the site. Reaching them entails a rather rough walk over limestone outcrops and loose boulders and through spots with thick vegetation.

Closest to the wall is Structure 57, a one-room shrine. Its walls and roof are intact, and its single doorway faces inland. From the top of the building you can get some nice overall views of the main part of the site. This structure is approximately 0.3 mile from the north wall.

Temple of the Frescoes (Structure 16), with Stela 2 in front, from the northwest, Tulum. Late Postclassic period.

Another 0.3 mile farther north is Structure 59, which is more interesting. It is a one-room building with remains of a roof comb, the only one reported from Tulum. The roof comb is made of slablike stones placed at an angle, which leaves triangular-shaped openings. Parts of two levels of the roof comb remain in place and rise from the center of the roof. It is thought that perhaps a third level existed at one time.

Recent History

In 1518 an expedition led by Juan de Grijalva sailed along part of the east coast of the Yucatán Peninsula and spotted a town that was likened to Seville. Many authorities believe this was Zamá (Tzamá), reported in the Spanish chronicles of the sixteenth century, which we know today as Tulum. Miller believes that Zamá was more likely Tancah,

2.5 miles north, because of details in the documents. In any case it seems that Zamá, mentioned in the early Spanish records, was in the Tulum-Tancah area.

There is little to note about Tulum until the nineteenth century, when credit for its discovery is said to go to one Juan José Gálvez. As with many other ruined cities, Tulum was first made known to the world at large by John Lloyd Stephens and Frederick Catherwood. The account of their visit and illustrations of the structures were published in 1843, and they were the first to clear and explore the site.

Stephens reported a fragmented stela (Stela 1), and in 1910 George P. Howe deciphered the date and buried the fragments for protection. Sylvanus G. Morley was unable to find the fragments on his first visit to Tulum in 1913 but later learned their location from Howe. In 1916 Morley returned to

Detail of the murals on the interior of the Temple of the Frescoes (Structure 16), Tulum. Late Postclassic period.

Tulum, found the fragments, and confirmed Howe's interpretation of the date. Morley and his personnel also cleared and photographed the site, traced some of the murals, and gathered information for a map. The Carnegie Institution of Washington underwrote these trips and continued to support work at Tulum for the next few years. Samuel K. Lothrop reported the data from the later expeditions in 1924.

In 1938 and the following years, Miguel Ángel Fernández studied the site, restored some of the murals, and consolidated some of the buildings. In 1955 William T. Sanders, working for the Carnegie Institution, reported on a reconnaissance of northern Quintana Roo, and in 1960 he presented his study of the ceramics of the area, including Tulum. Miller's work on the mural painting in the Tancah-Tulum region appeared in 1982.

Before the opening of Highway 307 in 1972, Tulum was almost inaccessible to visitors; by 1989, because of the development of Cancún, it had become *the* most visited Maya site.

Connection

Cancún City to Tulum: 80.4 miles by paved road (1:43).

Getting There

Head south on Highway 307 to the cutoff for Tulum (79.8 miles), which is marked with a sign. Turn left and go on to the site. You can reach Tulum by private car or taxi or on conducted tours from Cancún, and a bus can drop you off there.

Guides are available at Tulum. While

Detail of the mask at the southwest corner of the Temple of the Frescoes (Structure 16), Tulum. Late Postclassic period.

you do not need one to get around the main part of the site, you *must* have one to get to the structures north of the wall. Ask at the ticket office and wear boots and a sun hat if you plan to attempt this trek.

Allow 2 hours to see the structures within the wall and another hour to walk to and see the buildings outside the wall. There are small restaurants and stands selling cold drinks at the site.

Temple with the roof comb (Structure 59), outside the wall, from the southeast, Tulum. Probably Late Post-classic period.

★ ★
MUYIL
(moo-yeel; derivation: Maya for "Place of Rabbits")
(CHUNYAXCHÉ)
(choon-yahsh-cheh)

Location:
   Northeastern Quintana Roo.
Map: 6 (p. 302)

The Site

Muyil is sometimes called Chunyaxché, a Maya compound meaning "Trunk of the Green Tree (Ceiba)." Although the names are sometimes used interchangeably, the preferred name today for the archaeological site is Muyil, while Chunyaxché properly refers to the settlement nearby. Muyil is one of the largest sites on the east coast of Quintana Roo and is located at the northern end of the Sian Ka'an Biosphere Reserve. The site has an internal *saché* system; according to Walter

R. T. Witschey and Elia del Carmen Trejo Alvarado of the Proyecto Chunyaxché, Muyil was occupied from around A.D. 1 through 1550.

As you enter the site, you come first to the Entrance Plaza Group. This is near the highway, and the dirt trail to the site passes right by it. This area consists of many structures, six of which are accessible to the visitor (to the right of the path). There are tall pyramidal mounds around a plaza, and though the mounds are mostly rubble, some facing stones and remains of a stairway can be seen.

The mounds date to the Classic period, and in this group three or four construction phases are evident. There is also a one-story building (Structure 6) at ground level that has remains of standing architecture, including two doorway columns. This structure is Postclassic. The earliest ceramics at Muyil date to the Late Preclassic period and were found near this plaza, but there are no known architectural remains from this period. Witschey believes that the earliest settlement at Muyil was in the area of the Entrance Plaza Group.

From the plaza, walk along the path to the small ticket office and continue to the east to the Castillo. This is a pyramidal base with remains of a temple on top; it reaches a height of 52 feet and is the tallest structure at Muyil or any of the east coast sites. The temple faces west and has remains of three narrow doorways and a unique round turretlike construction. On the lower west side of the pyramidal base are remains of an inset stairway with *alfardas* on each side. The base of the Castillo originally rose in terraces that have since collapsed; it was constructed during the Terminal Classic period. There are remains of a narrow stairway near the top of the base that may have been a later addition. The temple itself may be Postclassic, but this is uncertain. Climbing the pyramid is prohibited, as the structure is fragile (especially since the rains of Hurricane Gilbert in 1988, which caused part of the structure to collapse).

The Castillo is connected to other structures by *sacbeob* going east and west, and Sacbé 1, heading east, has been cleared. The system of *sacbeob* runs for 0.3 mile, and they apparently were constructed at different times (from the Classic to the Postclassic periods) because their construction technologies are quite different.

From the Castillo, a trail leads in a northerly direction for a couple of hundred yards to Temple 8, one of the best-preserved structures at Muyil. It has been cleared and consolidated and consists of a pyramidal base, or platform, rising in terraces, with a temple on top. The temple (approached by a stairway on the north side of the base) has two pillars in the main doorway and corbeled vaults inside. The front part of the roof of the temple has collapsed, but its back is mostly intact and has a simple medial molding. An inner shrine enclosed on three sides by the outer room is reached through a low doorway with an inset panel above it. The temple is Postclassic and typical East Coast style.

Within the base of the structure is another temple (not open to visitors), possibly of Late Classic date, that is similar in size to the upper temple. Below this is a natural cave about one acre in size. Traces of geometric frescoes remain on both upper and lower structures.

The area around Temple 8 is enclosed by a wall forming a ceremonial precinct, and large residential mounds were found to the north, east, and west.

During the Classic period Muyil was influenced by sites in the Petén, and this is seen most notably in the architecutre of the lower part of the Castillo. Muyil also had connections with the major site of Cobá, 27 miles to the northwest, and was a link in a trade route that went around the Yucatán Peninsula from the coast of Campeche to the Gulf of Honduras.

In the Postclassic period there is ceramic evidence of contact between Muyil and Chichén Itzá. It was during this period that most of the ceremonial architecture at Muyil was built, and the time when the site had its greatest population.

Recent History

In 1679, in the *Relación de Tzamá* (a questionnaire about the Tulum area filled out for the king of Spain), a river named Muyil is mentioned, although the site itself is not. The river referred to is actually the channel or canal between the site and the sea.

The archaeological discovery of Muyil is credited to the Mason-Spinden Expedition of 1926, and the site was reported by Gregory Mason in that and subsequent years. Mason and Herbert J. Spinden named the site.

Michel Peissel visited Muyil in 1958 on this walk down the Quintana Roo coast and returned for a longer stay in 1961 to explore the site further. In 1963 he published the first map of Muyil in *The Lost World of Quintana Roo.*

The site was mapped by Witschey and Trejo Alvarado during 1987, 1988, and 1989, and ceramic studies were undertaken

The Castillo, west side, Muyil. The base dates to the Terminal Classic period; the temple on top may be of Postclassic date.

Temple 8, north side, Muyil. Post-classic period.

as part of the Proyecto Chunyaxché. The work was sponsored by the Middle American Research Institute of Tulane University and the Quintana Roo Regional Center of INAH. In 1988 two new *sacbeob* were discovered, remains of additional residential architecture were recorded, and three new sites in the area were visited. During the 1990 field season Temple 8 was cleared and consolidated, and the natural cave below it was explored. A survey transect, three quarters of a mile long, was cut going west from the Castillo, and extensive field walls and house mounds were found.

Muyil is connected to the Caribbean Sea by a series of lagoons, a canal, and a natural waterway, but so far no port facilities have been located at the site. Work at Muyil is expected to continue.

Connection

Cancún City to Muyil: 95.8 miles by paved road (2:01).

Getting There

Head south on Highway 307 to the cutoff for Muyil (marked with a sign saying Chunyaxché). The cutoff is 16.0 miles (:20) south of the cutoff for the Tulum ruins. Turn left at the junction and park. From here you are in sight of the Entrance Plaza Group.

You can reach Muyil in your own vehicle, by taxi from Tulum Pueblo or Tulum ruins, or by bus. There is no food or drink at the site, but 2 miles north there is a restaurant on the highway, at the junction for the village of Pino Suárez. Allow 1¼ hours to visit Muyil.

SECTION 6, PART 2

• • • •

NORTHERN QUINTANA ROO (COZUMEL)

West facade of Structure 1, Caracol. Late Postclassic period.

GENERAL INFORMATION FOR SECTION 6, PART 2

Point of Reference:
San Miguel de Cozumel,
Quintana Roo.
Maps: 6 and 6B

Mileages given to the sites in this section are from the Main Plaza in San Miguel de Cozumel.

San Miguel de Cozumel is the only town on the island, but all amenities can be found there. Most of the larger deluxe hotels are north of town, a few are to the south, and all are on the west coast of the island. There are more-modest facilities in the town itself.

There are plenty of restaurants to choose from, and they serve a variety of foods, though seafood is prominent. Las Palmeras, on the *malecón* across from the passenger ferry dock, is an old favorite. Their *ceviche de caracol* is one of the best. This speciality of northern Quintana Roo is sea conch, marinated in lime juice, and served cold with tomatoes, onions, and chili peppers, accompanied by crackers.

Another restaurant, often overlooked by visitors but popular locally, is Santiago's. The food is excellent, and the management is accommodating. It is on the corner of Avenida 15 Sur and Calle Dr. Adolfo Rosada Salas, four blocks from the plaza.

You can fly to Cozumel from Playa del Carmen, Cancún, or Mérida, and from some cities in the United States. You can also reach the island by ferry from two points on the mainland. See "General Information for Section 6, Part 1" for details.

Large cruise ships frequently stop at Cozumel, and their passengers are ferried to town for the day. At these times the area becomes quite crowded.

There are car rental agencies in town and through a couple of the large hotels. Motorscooters (Motos) are also available, but this mode of transportation is not recommended *unless* you are familiar with operating them beforehand. It is all too common to see a tourist on crutches and with bandaged legs who has taken a spill from a Moto.

Avenida Benito Juárez is the main dividing street running east-west in San Miguel de Cozumel; when it leaves town, it becomes the Transverse Highway heading to the east coast. On corners where there are no stoplights, streets running north-south (paralleling the coast) have the right of way over those running east-west (going inland).

Bus service is confined to the town, but taxis can be hired for a tour of the island outlying points of interest. Make price arrangements ahead. Some can be hired by the day. There are conducted tours to the ruins of San Gervasio through travel agencies in town and some of the hotels.

Cozumel is an important center for scuba diving, partly because of the proximity of Palancar Reef off the southwest corner of the island. There are many dive shops in town, and instructions are available from some, as are trips to various diving sites.

In the best tropical fashion, Cozumel (except for restaurants) adheres to a siesta at midday, from 1:00 P.M. until 5:00 P.M.

There is a multitude of shops in town selling a wide array of items, including designer sportswear, gold, silver, black coral and shell jewelry, leather goods, onyx, and handicrafts from all over Mexico—and the ubiquitous T-shirts. There are even stuffed frogs playing guitars.

Of special appeal to those interested in archaeology are the off-set lithographs of Maya temples by Gordon M. Gilchrist. These are high-quality, limited-edition prints, produced from Gilchrist's original drawings and paintings. They are printed on fine paper and come with a certificate of authentication. His renditions of the "Temple of Ix Chel" at San Gervasio and of "Caracol" are superb.

His wife, Jennifer, also an artist, produces stunning serigraphs with Maya motifs. Their work is available at Studio One, Avenida 25 Sur, no. 981. Gordon Gilchrist's prints are also available at two shops on the *malecón*: Cinco Soles (4 blocks north of the

Main Plaza on the corner of Calle 8 Norte) and Mi Casa Es Tu Casa (3½ blocks south of the Main Plaza).

OTHER STOPOVERS: The only other possible stopover on Cozumel, outside of the town and the main hotel area, is an extremely modest motel at Punta Morena that has spartan accommodations. It is on the east coast of the island, 1.6 miles south of the Transverse Highway, and there is also a restaurant. This is perhaps best used as a good place to enjoy a cold beer while watching the sea on the rocky, windward side of the island, in complete tranquility.

GAS STATION: The only gas station on Cozumel is in town at the corner of Avenida Benito Juárez and Avenida 30. There is also a good icehouse on Benito Juárez, one block east of the gas station.

GUIDES: A guide is not necessary to reach any of the sites covered on Cozumel.

★ ★

MUSEUM OF THE ISLAND OF COZUMEL
(COZUMEL MUSEUM, SAN MIGUEL DE COZUMEL)

The Cozumel Museum was opened in 1987 in a lovely building on the *malecón,* 2½ blocks north of the Main Plaza, in the town of San Miguel de Cozumel. There are four salas (exhibition halls) on two floors, as well as a restoration facility, workshop area, and library. The museum is open Sunday through Friday from 10:00 A.M. to 6:00 P.M. (and until 7:00 P.M. in the summer) and Saturday from 1:00 to 6:00 P.M. Photography is permitted, but flash is not.

Sala I, on the first floor, deals with the geology and environment of Cozumel, and there is a large diorama. Sala II also has a diorama, and coral formations are covered in detail. Diagrams are presented in Spanish and English.

Sala III (second floor) houses the archaeological specimens. There is a doorway column carved with a figure of Ix Chel (the goddess of the moon, women, and childbirth) giving birth. The column comes from Miramar, a

Carved doorway column from Miramar (Cozumel), on display in the Cozumel Museum. Late Postclassic period.

site in the hotel area north of town that is now destroyed. Cozumel was a place of pilgrimage for Ix Chel. Also in Sala III are several tenoned serpent heads, a beautiful small jade Olmec head, and a delightful model of Caracol, a shrine on the south tip of the island. Other displays include ceramic specimens and carved stone panels and columns (mostly fairly eroded).

Also the second floor is Sala IV, which deals with the recent history of Cozumel. Displays include photographs and machinery.

The museum is well designed and arranged. Lighting is adequate for viewing the collection but poor for photography. Fast film and a fast lens will help.

On the outside of the museum are some carved but eroded stone monuments that are easier to photograph. Allow an hour to view the collection.

★ ★
SAN GERVASIO

(sahn hehr-vahs-eeoh; derivation: Spanish for "Saint Gervase")

Location:
North-central part of the Island of Cozumel, Quintana Roo.
Maps: 6 (p. 302) and 6B (p. 310)

The Site

San Gervasio is the largest site on Cozumel and is now the most visited one as well. Until the 1980s the site was inaccessible to visitors. It is clearly the most interesting ruin on the island and is a very good two-star site. There are seven numbered groups at the site, but only the area around Groups I, II, and III has been cleared. Some of the architecture in this area has been consolidated.

The trails used today follow the paths of ancient Maya *sacbeob,* of which there are four in this area. The vegetation around the trails and structures has been thinned, so you can generally see from one area to the next. Happily, many small trees were left to provide shade, and this gives the site an informal, parklike ambience.

As you enter the site, you come first to Group III, where there are three structures of interest; two of these border the west and north sides of a plaza. On the west side, facing east, is Structure 27-a, with a stairway on the east side. According to David A. Gregory, who was part of the team that surveyed the site, "Structure 27-a is a modified *talud-tablero* type of platform, with two C-shaped benches on top." A burial vault, reportedly looted in modern times, is found in the southern bench.

Structure 25-a is on the north side of the plaza and faces south. It is the most complex masonary structure at San Gervasio, with an inner shrine that has remains of paintings and red handprints. The shrine is enclosed by a larger structure that has two columns in the doorway. In front of this is an open area with side walls and four piers on the south that formed the main entrance to Structure 25-a.

Just in front of the doorway to the inner shrine, a large tomb was discovered that had been looted in ancient times. It was originally covered with a huge capstone. Another interesting discovery made during excavation was a stone carving of a sea turtle with a piece of jade embedded in a hole in its back. This was found in the rubble that filled the inner shrine.

A short distance to the east of Structure 25-a, and visible from it, is a small oratory with an inner shrine (Structure 24-a). A large stone lintel spans the doorway to the shrine, and there are two columns at the main entrance of the structure. The whole sits on a low platform, and the structure faces west. Along the trail back to structure 25-a,

Structure 31, a stepped portal vault, San Gervasio. Late Postclassic period.

you will see (on the right) the opening to a chultun that is just to the east of the structure.

From Structure 25-a head west on a *saché*, then right on a connecting one, to reach Group II. This group is an elite residential unit, and three of its structures share the same low platform. There are remains of low walls and standing columns in this area.

From the northwest edge of this group you can see Structure 31 to the west, and you can walk directly there without returning to the *saché* you took to get to Group II. Structure 31 is a portal vault that straddles a *saché* that heads northeast toward the east coast of Cozumel. Part of the vault is intact, and it is stepped from the spring line to the capstone. The plaster surface of the *saché* is partly intact in the area under the vault.

From the vault, follow the *saché* to the northeast until you reach another structure sitting in the middle of the *saché*. (You cannot see the structure from the vault.) This is one of the gems of San Gervasio and is called Nonah, the Temple of Ix Chel, or Structure 32-a. The structure sits on a round platform with access stairs on the east and west sides that lead to east and west doorways of this small but charming building. Structure 32-a

is believed to have been a shrine, and it has direct access from the *saché* in either direction. The structure has been nicely consolidated, and there are remnants of paint on it. Sitting in its small clearing with tropical vegetation around it, the building is most photogenic.

Return along the *saché* the way you came, go through the portal vault, and continue a bit farther to Group I. This group is made up of several buildings surrounding a plaza, and another structure in the center of it. As you reach the entrance, the *saché* you are on joins another at Structure 7-a, on the northeast corner of the group. Structure 7-a has eight round columns standing on a platform, and there are a few remains of lower walls.

Structure 8, on the north side of the plaza, is a long low platform, originally plastered, but with no evidence of a permanent structure on top.

On the northwest corner of the plaza is Structure 4-a, a two-room vaulted building with its medial wall and parts of its side walls intact. It is approached by a stairway on the east. Structure 4-b lies to the south of Structure 4-a, and they share a common platform. Structure 4-b was also vaulted, and there are remains of painting on the medial

Nonah (Structure 32-a), San Gervasio. Late Postclassic period.

wall. It likewise is approached by a stairway on the east.

To the south of Structure 4-b is Structure 5-a, an L-shaped building that borders the southwest corner of the plaza. There are many columns here, standing atop a platform that has a stairway on the east side. On the south side of the plaza, between Structures 5-a and 6-a, is another *saché* that heads south.

There is little remaining of Structure 6-a, which rests on a lower extension of the platform that supports Structures 6-b and 6-c. During excavations, however, a mass burial with more than 50 individuals was discovered directly in front of the structure. The tomb was crudely constructed and "seemed simply to have been dug into the support platform and hastily filled in with large rubble without being plastered over," according to Gregory. He further says that the presence of several Spanish beads found in the grave has as one possible explanation that the mass burial was due to the smallpox epidemic that struck Cozumel in 1542.

Of Structure 6-b only some lower walls and columns remain, plus a stairway leading east to the top of the platform. A little more of Structure 6-c is intact. The medial wall is standing in part, as are two columns that

formed the main entrance to the structure. There is a stairway on the west side of the platform; adjacent to the south is a niche in the platform that probably once held an idol or *incensario*.

Now head to the center of the plaza for a look at Structure 10, a small platform encasing an earlier structure with a stairway on the east. From here you leave the plaza and head east on the *saché* that enters Group I; follow it straight ahead to Group III. From there turn right to exit the site.

All of the structures described above date to the Late Postclassic period, though earlier remains are found in other parts of San Gervasio. Group IV dates to the Early Postclassic period, as does one of the structures in Group VI. Group VI also produced the earliest ceramics from San Gervasio, possibly dating to the Late Preclassic period. Of major interest in Group VI was the discovery of an Olmec jade pendant found in a burial crypt, along with several Early Classic bowls and jade and shell beads.

Recent History

It is not certain who published the first report on San Gervasio. It may have been Channing Arnold and Frederick J. T. Frost in 1909, who described a site that may have been what we know today as San Gervasio. An informal account by Prince William of Sweden in 1922 included a site on the interior of Cozumel that may have been San Gervasio.

The first definite report of San Gervasio seems to be that of Alberto Escalona Ramos in 1946. He surveyed numerous sites on the east coast of Quintana Roo and on Cozumel, including Nonah and San Gervasio. In 1955 William T. Sanders reported on San Gervasio among many other sites.

In 1975 a preliminary report of the 1972–1973 season at Cozumel was published by the Peabody Museum of Harvard University. This was part of the Cozumel Project, which included the participation of staff from the University of Arizona and other universities. Editors for the report were Jeremy A. Sabloff and William L. Rathje. Included in it is a description of San Gervasio by Gregory and two maps of the site. This is a major source of information on San Gervasio.

The Southeast Regional Center of INAH carried out a program of surveying, excavation, and consolidation between 1980 and 1982.

Also in the early 1980s a direct road to San Gervasio from the Transverse Highway was built, and in the late 1980s it was improved, making access easier.

Connection

San Miguel de Cozumel to San Gervasio: 5.2 miles by paved road (:09), then 4.2 miles by fair, surfaced road (:15).

Getting There

From San Miguel de Cozumel head southeast on the Transverse Highway to a little past Kilometer 8, to the junction for San Gervasio (marked with a sign). Turn left and follow the road to the site.

Bilingual guides are available at the entrance to the site. If you wish to tour the site on your own, you can buy a site plan for San Gervasio in town ahead of time.

You can reach the site in your own vehicle, on conducted tours, or by taxi from town.

Cold drinks are available near the ticket office at the entrance to the site.

If you want to try to visit any of the outlying groups, make arrangements with a guide at the entrance. They may know how to get there.

Allow 1 hour to see Groups I, II, and III.

Note: There is an extra charge to bring a video camera into the site.

★
EL CEDRAL
*(ehl seh-*drahl*; derivation: Spanish for "Cedar Grove")*

Location:
Southwestern part of the Island of Cozumel, Quintana Roo.
Maps: 6 (p. 302) and 6B (p. 310)

The Site

El Cedral is reported to be a dispersed site with three plaza groups, a number of structures, and the remains of two vaults, similar to the portal vaults at Kabáh and Uxmal. Unhappily, because of stone robbing, only one structure is of interest for the visitor today. This is Structure Ia, which has two rooms, one behind the other, with vaults that are mostly intact. Little of the exterior fac-

Structure Ia, northwest side, El Cedral. Terminal Classic or Early Postclassic period.

ing stone remains, but because of the work of Miguel Ángel Fernández published in 1945, we know that originally there were three-member medial and cornice moldings. A resoration drawing of the structure by Daniel Schavelzon shows the moldings. Roots of a tree have partly encapsulated the structure and penetrated the inside of the rear room.

Structure Ia dates to the Terminal Classic or Early Postclassic period and was used as a jail for the town of El Cedral for many years beginning in 1935. For this reason it is called the Cárcel locally. The single doorway of the structure faces northwest and was altered in modern times and framed with wood. Structure Ia rests on a platform about three feet high and was once connected by a *saché* to another building.

Behind Structure Ia to the east are the destroyed remains of Structure II.

Recent History

The first detailed report on El Cedral was that published by William H. Holmes in 1895–1897, followed many years later by the work of Fernández. Both included drawings of the best-preserved portal vault. El Cedral is mentioned by Jeremy A. Sabloff and William L. Rathje in 1975, and by David Freidel and Sabloff in 1984. Schavelzon's description, photographs, plan, and elevation of Structure Ia appeared in 1985.

Connection

San Miguel de Cozumel to El Cedral: 12.8 miles by paved road (:28).

Getting There

Head south from San Miguel de Cozumel to a little past Kilometer 17 and the cutoff for El Cedral (marked with a sign). Turn left and follow the road to the village of El Cedral. Structure Ia is next to a modern church of similar size, and both face a sheltered plaza area in the center of town. Some of the village children will offer to show you around.

Allow 15 minutes for a visit. Cold drinks are available in the village.

★
CARACOL
(kah-rah-kohl)
(TUMBA DE CARACOL)
*(toom-bah deh kah-rah-kohl; derivation: Spanish for
"snail" (sea conch) and "Tumba de," Spanish for "Tomb of")*

Location:

Southern tip of the Island of
Cozumel, Quintana Roo.

Maps: 6 (p. 302) and 6B (p. 310)

The Site

The small Structure 1 at Caracol is an absolute gem; its diminutive size actually adds to its charm. It is easy to reach, very photogenic, and even though it is rated only one star, it is highly recommended to all visitors.

The structure was built in two phases, though both were during the Late Postclassic period. Structure 1 sits on a low platform and faces west, so the afternoon is the best time to photograph it. The single doorway and the central part of the west facade are part of the first construction stage. Later, a larger but similar structure was built, encasing the earlier one on the north, east, and south sides and forming a sort of gallery around it. The junction of these two stages is quite apparent on the west side.

The earlier structure has a simple medial molding and a two-member cornice molding. The newer addition has a three-member cornice molding.

There are doorways on all four sides, and those on the north and south are off-center in the outer structure, but they align with the north and south doorways of the inner structure. A stepped vault forms the ceiling of the inner structure, and a half vault was used in the ceiling of the addition.

On the roof, above the inner structure, there is a rectangular base that also has openings on all four sides, and this supports a hollow dome, or cupola, in the form of a sea conch shell. The top of the cupola is missing, but the lower part is intact and is embedded with rows of real conch shells. It is reported that the shells sound in the wind, and it may be that the structure was related to a cult to the wind or to the Maya god Kukulcán, who is a wind god in one of his aspects. It is these shells—and perhaps the shape of the cupola—that give the structure its name.

There are remains of red paint above the opening of the base of the cupola on the west side and above the doorway to the structure on the east side.

A few feet to the northeast of Structure 1 are the remains of Structure 2, a small, one-room building. All that is left are some of the lower parts of walls.

Recent History

Caracol was discovered by archaeologist Miguel Ángel Fernández, who was one of a number of Mexican scholars participating in the Expedición Científica Mexicana in 1937. He reported the site in 1945 under the name Islote Celaráin. At the time of his visit the entire cupola of Structure 1 was intact.

William T. Sanders conducted ceramic studies in Quintana Roo, and they included Caracol, which he called Punta Islote. He reported his findings in 1955.

The site was given its current name by the directors of the Harvard University Cozumel Project, Jeremy A. Sabloff and William L. Rathje, who published a preliminary report of their fieldwork in 1975.

In 1979 Structure 1 was restored by the Southeast Regional Center of INAH, and in 1985 architect Daniel Schavelzon, of the University of Buenos Aires, published a detailed report on the structure.

Structure 1, west side, Caracol. Late Postclassic period.

Connection

San Miguel de Cozumel to Caracol: 18.0 miles by paved road (:37), then 1.7 miles by fair sand road (:09).

Getting There

From San Miguel de Cozumel head south along the west coast of Cozumel and then east to Kilometer 29. Take the sand road to the right to Caracol, which lies immediately to the left of the road.

You can also get to the cutoff at Kilometer 29 by going around the other way (20.9 miles by paved road), in about the same time (:38). In this case, take the Transverse Highway from San Miguel de Cozumel and head southeast to the east coast. Turn right and follow the east coast to Kilometer 29, then take the sand road to the site.

Allow 20 minutes to see and photograph Caracol, and wear a sun hat. There is no food or drink at the site.

A NOTE ON FOUR EAST COAST TEMPLES (COZUMEL)

> **Maps:** 6 (p. 302) and 6B (p. 310)

There are four Maya temples adjacent to the dirt road that runs along the east coast of Cozumel between the Transverse Highway and the Punta Molas lighthouse on the north tip of the island. The temples are all fairly easy to spot. I am sure of the name of only one of these, so they will simply be listed in the order that you reach them. All the structures date to the Late Postclassic period.

From San Miguel de Cozumel, take the Transverse Highway (paved) toward the east coast for 9.0 miles (:15). Near the end of this highway you will see a dirt cutoff on your left. Distances given to the temples are from the junction of the Transverse Highway and the dirt road. All four temples lie to the east of the road, between it and the sea. Although other structures have been reported near the road, the four described here are the only ones we were able to find.

The first part of the dirt road is actually fairly decent hard-packed sand. Then there is a about a mile of very rough limestone outcrops. At this point you have reached Temple 1. From there to Temple 2 is also pretty bad, but after that it is a bit smoother.

Allow 3½ hours from the time you leave the Transverse Highway until you return. This will give you ample time to see all four temples and the lighthouse. A high-clearance vehicle is needed for this trip. There is no food or drink available along the dirt road.

Note: In 1988 Hurricane Gilbert hit Cozumel and washed out part of the dirt road (between the Transverse Highway and El Real), and it was reported to be unrepaired in 1991. Check locally before you attempt to take this road, and keep in mind that the road conditions, distances, and times given below may be somewhat different after the road is repaired.

★
TEMPLE 1

This is a one-room structure, with a single doorway facing the sea. The walls are mostly intact, but the roof has collapsed into the interior of the temple. There is a stone-lined opening in the ground in front of the temple that looked like a small chultun.

Temple 1 is 5.1 miles (:25) from the junction, and about 40 feet from the dirt road. It is situated in a cleared area, and you can drive right to it.

TEMPLE 2

Only the rear wall and part of one side wall of this structure remain standing. The rest has collapsed toward the sea. It appears to have been a simple one-room structure.

Temple 2 lies about 50 feet from the dirt road, from which only the top part of the structure is visible. It is 7.3 miles (:38) from the junction, and 2.2 miles (:13) from Temple 1.

EL REAL (TEMPLE 3)

*(ehl reh-*ahl; *derivation: Spanish for "the Royal" or "the Magnificent")*

El Real, also called Castillo El Real, is the most interesting, best preserved, and largest of the east coast temples. It has two rooms, one behind the other with an interior connection, and a single exterior doorway facing the sea. Its roof has a stepped vault, and there are a few remnants of paint on the inset lintel above the exterior doorway. The temple sits on top of a platform with rounded corners on the east side, though the middle part of the east side of the platform has fallen—reportedly dynamited many years ago.

The structure has a simple, rectangular medial molding, and the cornice molding has a similar course, topped by a cornice of vertical stones. The building is intact except for a large vertical crack above the exterior doorway and two holes in the rear wall, one of which affords the best access to the interior of the building.

El Real lies about 100 feet from the dirt road and is harder to spot than the others because of intervening vegetation. The stopping place is 10.6 miles (:54) from the junction, and 3.3 miles (:16) from Temple 2. As the dirt road crosses a cattle guard, look to the right to see El Real.

El Real (Temple 3), east side. Late Postclassic period.

TEMPLE 4

The front of this small structure is over-grown, but it appears that there was a single doorway facing the sea and that the temple had only one room. The roof has collapsed, but from the debris it appears to have been of beam-and-mortar construction. Most of the walls are intact.

Temple 4 is about 30 feet from the dirt road, and its back is cleared and easily visible. It is 12.2 miles (1:02) from the junction, and 1.6 miles (:08) from El Real.

About 2.5 miles (:08) past Temple 4 you come to the end of the road at the Punta Molas lighthouse, which is rather photogenic.

GLOSSARY

aguada: A clay-filled, low-lying area that collects water from rain and runoff. It is an important water source in some areas.

alfardas: In architecture, raised, sloping side sections that border stairways; balustrades.

apron molding: In architecture, a sloped facing that overhangs an inset, vertical section; it is found on the bases of pyramidal structures. Prevalent in the Southern Maya lowlands, it appears occasionally on the Yucatán Peninsula, where it generally dates to the Early Classic period.

Atlantes (also *Atlantean Figures* and *Telemones*): Statues of men used as supporting columns for roofs and altars. They are found at Chichén Itzá and are from the Postclassic period.

caleta: A protected bay or cove; it is especially good for swimming.

Ce Acatl Topiltzin Quetzalcóatl: A Toltec priest-king and culture hero, the legendary founder of Tula. He added the name of the deity Quetzalcóatl to his own name and promoted its worship.

ceiba: A huge tree sacred to the ancient Mayas and found in the tropical rain forest.

cenote: A natural well, formed when the top surface of limestone collapses, exposing the water below.

Chac (Chaac): The Maya rain god.

Chac mask(s): In architecture, the popular designation for stone mosaic masks with curved or curled snouts, often covered with stucco. They are found in frontal view on facades and on exterior angles on the corners of buildings, sometimes stacked one above the other. Some authorities believe that some (or all) of these masks represent not Chac but Itzamná or other deities.

Chac Mool: The statue of a figure in a recumbent pose, holding a receptacle on its abdomen. It is found at Chichén Itzá and some east coast sites on the Yucatán Peninsula, and at Tula and other sites in central Mexico.

champa: A thatched-roof shelter without walls that is supported by poles.

Chenes style: A Maya Late Classic architectural style found at such sites as Hochob and Dzibilnocac and characterized by doorways surrounded by a single monster mask, with the doorway serving as the mouth. Facades of multichambered structures are often divided into three parts, and the center part either projects or recedes from the rest of the facade. *See also* Río Bec style.

chiclero: A man who bleeds the zapote tree for its latex, which, when refined, forms the base for chewing gum. The raw product is known as chicle.

chultun: An underground bottle-shaped storage area with a plastered surface, used originally to store water or food.

Classic Puuc Colonnette style: A Maya architectural style characterized by three- or four-member medial and cornice moldings and three-member base moldings, with colonnettes in the middle (or one of the middle) parts. Upper wall zones are decorated with columns, often banded, in continuous rows or in groups, separated by plain stones. Lower walls are made of finely cut veneer stones and are often plain but may include facade columns. Round columns with square capitals are found in some doorways. Roof combs are rare. This style is dated to A.D. 770–830 by George F. Andrews. *See also* Early Puuc style; Classic Puuc Mosaic style.

Classic Puuc Mosaic style: A Maya architectural style characterized by highly decorative upper wall zones, with geometric designs and masks made of stone mosaics. Columns are also used, some of which are banded. Base moldings are generally in three parts, with colonnettes or other decoration in the middle part. Medial and cornice moldings have three or more parts with various decorations in the middle (or one of the middle) parts. Lower walls are made of finely cut veneer stones and are often plain but may have inset columns or other decorations. Some doorways have round columns with square capitals. Roof combs are rare. This style is dated to A.D. 830–1000 by George F. Andrews. See also Early Puuc style; Classic Puuc Colonnette style.

codex (plural, codices): Painted books from pre-Columbian or, in some cases, early post-Columbian dates. They are made of deerskin or bark paper and are folded like a screen.

corbeled vault: The prevalent type of roofing used in Classic Maya structures. The vault is built up from the tops of vertical walls, and each layer of stone or brick juts past the one below. When the sides of the vault approach each other closely enough, a capstone is added to bridge the remaining gap.

Early Puuc style: A Maya architectural style characterized by a simple rectangular medial molding that often rises, or breaks, above the doorways. The base molding is generally a single rectangular course. Roof combs rise above the front or middle wall on some structures and are often perforated with vertical, rectangular slots and decorated with stucco sculptures. This style is dated to A.D. 670–770 by George F. Andrews. See also Classic Puuc Colonnette style; Classic Puuc Mosaic style.

East Coast style: A Maya Late Postclassic architectural style found on the east coast of the Yucatán Peninsula, at some inland sites, and on the offshore islands. Tulum is the principal site with architecture in this style, which is characterized by relatively small to very small structures made of poorly cut stone, covered with thick coats of stucco. Some structures are vaulted, but many have beam-and-mortar roofs. There is often a recessed panel above the doorways, and the insides

of some of the structures are covered with paintings. Decorative exterior elements are often made of stucco, and moldings are generally simple. Some structures have columns in the doorways and niches above with sculpture in stucco.

ejido: A tract of land owned (and generally farmed) communally.

emblem glyph: A glyph (generally in three parts) whose main sign refers either to a dynastic name or to a place name.

glyphs (also hieroglyphs): The form of ancient Maya writing, which includes both pictographic and ideographic elements; some glyphs have phonetic value.

Goodman-Martínez-Thompson correlation (also GMT correlation): A correlation between the Maya and Christian calendars proposed by Goodman, Martínez, and Thompson. This correlation equates the Maya long-count date of 11.16.0.0.0. to A.D. 1539. This correlation is generally, though not universally, accepted.

hieroglyphs: See glyphs.

huipil: A straight-sided slipover garment with embroidered neckline and hem, worn by Maya women.

INAH: Instituto Nacional de Antropología e Historia (National Institute of Anthropology and History), the Mexican government agency that is responsible for the care of the ancient archaeological sites. It also sponsors excavations and publishes reports as well as guides to the major sites.

incensario: A receptacle for burning incense that is generally made of clay and often highly decorated.

Initial Series (also Long Count date): A method of recording dates in the Maya calendar. It represents the total number of days that have elapsed from a mythical starting point, calculated at 3114 B.C., according to the GMT correlation.

Introducing Glyph: A glyph found at the beginning of an Initial Series date, with a variable element that is the name glyph of the deity who is the patron of the month on which the date ends.

Itzamná: The supreme Maya deity; the heavenly monster-god and creator-god.

Ix Chel: The Maya goddess of the moon, women, and childbirth.

Kinich-Ahau: The Yucatec name for the sun god; a manifestation of Itzamná.

Kinich-Kakmo: A manifestation of Kinich-Ahau.

Kukulcán: The Maya name for the central-Mexican deity Quetzalcóatl.

malecón: Literally a seawall or breakwater along the shore: by extension, the designation for a roadway that follows the shore.

mano: *See* metate.

Maya blue: A durable blue pigment composed of a clay mineral (attapulgite) and blue indigo dye. It was used by the ancient Mayas in painting murals and decorating pottery.

Mesoamerica: The areas of Mexico and Central America where high civilizations arose in pre-Columbian times. It includes parts of western and eastern Mexico; all of central and southern Mexico and the Yucatán Peninsula; all of Guatemala, Belize, and El Salvador; western Honduras; and part of the Pacific Coast areas of Nicaragua and Costa Rica.

metate: A trough-shaped stone used for grinding foodstuffs, generally corn (maize), and accompanied by a cylindrical hand stone (mano).

milpa: A plot of land cultivated by slash-and-burn agriculture, most often used for growing corn (maize).

palace-type structures (also *range-type structures*): Multichambered structures built on low platforms, rather than on tall pyramidal bases. They were probably mostly residential or used for administrative purposes rather than for religious ceremonies.

Putun: A Chontal Maya group known as traders. They occupied eastern Tabasco and southern Campeche.

Puuc style: A Maya architectural style named for the Puuc Hills of Yucatán. It is found at Uxmal, Kabáh, Sayil, Labná, and numerous nearby sites. *See also* Early Puuc style; Classic Puuc Colonnette style; Classic Puuc Mosaic style.

Quetzalcóatl: The major deity of central Mexico: the feathered serpent. He brought knowledge of agriculture, arts, and science.

Río Bec style: A Maya Late Classic architectural style found at such sites as Group B at Río Bec and Xpuhil. It is characterized by tall towers with non-functional stairways and simulated temples on top, joined by a lower range of rooms. Facades are sometimes decorated with monster-mouth doorways, like those on Chenes-style buildings. *See* Chenes style.

roof comb: In architecture, a stone superstructure built on the roof of a structure to give additional height and grandeur. The combs are sometimes perforated and are generally decorated.

saché (plural in Maya, *sacheob*): Literally, "White Road." An ancient Maya road or causeway made of rough-stone blocks topped with crushed stone and then plastered.

stela (plural, *stelae*): A freestanding monolithic stone monument, either plain or carved on one or more sides. Especially prevalent in the Maya area, it is often accompanied by a drum-shaped altar.

stepped fret: A design composed of a squared spiral and a step element.

talud-tablero: In architecture, a sloping lower section, or *talus (talud),* topped by a vertical rectangular, recessed panel *(tablero).*

Tlaloc: The rain god of central Mexico. He also has a lesser-known aspect as a war or warrior god.

tzompantli: A skull rack where heads of sacrificial victims were placed. It was also a platform with depictions of carved skulls on its sides and is from the Postclassic period.

zapote (also *sapote* and *sapodilla*): An extremely hard wood found in the lowland Maya area, often used for lintels in pre-Columbian buildings.

SELECTED READINGS

Andrews, Anthony P., and Robles Castellanos, Fernando
1986 *Excavaciones arqueológicas en El Meco, Quintana Roo, 1977.* México, D.F.: Instituto Nacional de Antropología e Historia.
Andrews, E. Wyllys, IV, and Andrews, Anthony P.
1975 *A Preliminary Study of the Ruins of Xcaret, Quintana Roo, Mexico, with Notes on Other Archaeological Remains on the Central East Coast of the Yucatan Peninsula.* Middle American Research Institute, Publication 40. New Orleans: Tulane University.
Andrews, E. Wyllys, IV, and Andrews, E. Wyllys, V
1980 *Excavations at Dzibilchaltun, Yucatan, Mexico.* Middle American Research Institute, Publication 48. New Orleans: Tulane University.
Andrews, George F.
1975 *Maya Cities: Placemaking and Urbanization.* Norman: University of Oklahoma Press.
1985 Chenes-Puuc Architecture: Chronology and Cultural Interaction. In *Arquitectura y arqueología: Metodologías en la chronología de Yucatán.* CEMCA Études Mésoaméricaines, Série II, 8. México, D.F.
1985 Early Puuc Architecture: Buildings with "Broken" Medial Moldings. *Cuadernos de arquitectura mesoamericana,* 5. México, D.F.: Universidad Nacional Autónoma de México.
1986 *Los estilos arquitectónicos del Puuc: Una nueva apreciación.* México, D.F.: Instituto Nacional de Antropología e Historia.
1987 Architecture at Kohunlich, Quintana Roo: A Preliminary Report. *Cuadernos de arquitectura mesoamericana,* 10. México, D.F.: Universidad Nacional Autónoma de México.
Andrews, George F.; Gendrop, Paul; Rivera, Víctor; Siller, Juan Antonio; and Villalobos, Alejandro
1985 Reconocimiento arquitectónico en la región de Río Bec, Campeche, Marzo 1985. Consideraciones generales. *Cuadernos de arquitectura mesoamericana,* 5. México, D.F.: Universidad Nacional Autónoma de México.
1987 Reconocimiento arquitectónico en la región de los Chenes, Marzo 1986. Consideraciones generales. *Cuadernos de arquitectura mesoamericana,* 10. México, D.F.: Universidad Nacional Autónoma de México.
Bricker, Victoria Reifler, and Sabloff, Jeremy A., eds.
1981 *Supplement to the Handbook of the Middle American Indians.* Vol. 1. Austin: University of Texas Press.
Carrasco Vargas, Ramón, and Boucher, Sylviane
1985 Nuevas perspectivas para la cronología y el estudio de la región central de Yucatán. In *Arquitectura y arqueología: Metodologías en la cronología de Yucatán,* CEMCA Études Mésoaméricaines, Série II, 8. México, D.F.
Coe, Michael D.
1966 *The Maya.* New York: Frederick A. Praeger. Rev. ed. London: Thames and Hudson, 1980.
Covarrubias, Miguel
1957 *Indian Art of Mexico and Central America.* New York: Alfred A. Knopf.
Díaz del Castillo, Bernal
1956 *The Discovery and Conquest of Mexico.* Translated by A. P. Maudslay, edited by Génaro García. New York: Farrar, Straus and Giroux. 6th printing, 1972.
Dunning, Nicholas P.
1990 *Prehistoric Settlement Patterns of the Puuc Region, Yucatan, Mexico.* Ph.D. dissertation, University of Minnesota. Ann Arbor, Mich.: University Microfilms International.

Ferguson, William M., with Royce, John Q.
1977   *Maya Ruins of Mexico in Color.* Norman: University of Oklahoma Press.
Ferguson, William M.; Rohn, Arthur H.; and Royce, John Q.
1990   *Mesoamerica's Ancient Cities.* Niwot: University Press of Colorado.
Garrett, Wilbur E.
1989   La Ruta Maya. *National Geographic,* vol. 176, no. 4. Washington, D.C.
Garza Tarazona de González, Silvia, and Kurjack, Edward
1980   *Atlas arqueológico del estado de Yucatán.* México, D.F.: Instituto Nacional de Antro-
        pología e Historia.
Gendrop, Paul
1987   Nuevas consideracions en torno a los estilos Río Bec y Chenes. *Cuadernos de
        arquitectura mesoamericana,* 10. México, D.F.: Universidad Nacional Autónoma de
        México.
Hunter, C. Bruce
1974   *A Guide to Ancient Maya Ruins.* Norman: University of Oklahoma Press. Rev. ed.
        1986.
Kelly, Joyce
1982   *The Complete Visitor's Guide to Mesoamerican Ruins.* Norman: University of Okla-
        homa Press.
Kowalski, Jeff Karl
1987   *The House of the Governor: A Maya Palace of Uxmal, Yucatan, Mexico.* Norman:
        University of Oklahoma Press.
Lothrop, Samuel K.
1924   *Tulum: An Archaeological Study of the East Coast of Yucatan.* Carnegie Institution
        of Washington, Publication 335. Washington, D.C.
Maler, Teobert
1895   Yukatekische Forschungen. *Globus,* 68. Braunschweig, Germany.
1902   Yukatekische Forschungen. *Globus,* 82. Braunschweig, Germany.
N.d.   *Península Yucatán.* 3 vols.
Maudslay, Alfred P.
1889–   *Archaeology.* Biologia Centrali Americana. 5 vols. London. Facsimile ed. New York:
1902   Milpatron Publishing, 1974.
Mercer, Henry C.
1896   *The Hill Caves of Yucatan: A Search for Evidence of Man's Antiquity in the Caverns of
        Central America.* Philadelphia: Lippincott. Reprint. Introduction by Sir J. Eric S.
        Thompson. Norman: University of Oklahoma Press, 1975.
Miller, Arthur G.
1982   *On the Edge of the Sea: Mural Painting at Tancah-Tulum, Quintana Roo, Mexico.*
        Washington, D.C.: Dumbarton Oaks.
Morley, Sylvanus G.
1946   *The Ancient Maya.* 2d ed., revised by George W. Brainerd, 1956. 4th ed., revised by
        Robert J. Sharer. Stanford, Calif.: Stanford University Press, 1983.
Piña Chan, Román
1985   *Cultura y ciudades mayas de Campeche.* Edited by Luis Gutiérrez Muñoz. México,
        D.F.: Editora del Sureste.
———, and Stuart, George E.
1983   *Arte maya: Selva y mar.* Edited by Luis Gutiérrez Muñoz. México, D.F.: Editora del
        Sureste.
Pollock, H. E. D.
1970   Architectural Notes on Some Chenes Ruins. In *Monographs and Papers in Maya
        Archaeology,* edited by W. R. Bullard, Jr. Papers of the Peabody Museum, vol. 61.
        Cambridge, Mass.: Harvard University.

1980   *The Puuc: An Architectural Survey of the Hill Country of Yucatan and Northern Campeche, Mexico.* Memoirs of the Peabody Museum, vol. 19. Cambridge, Mass.: Harvard University.

Proskouriakoff, Tatiana
1946   *An Album of Maya Architecture.* Washington, D.C.: Carnegie Institution of Washington. Reprint. Norman: University of Oklahoma Press, 1963.
1950   *A Study of Classic Maya Sculpture.* Carnegie Institution of Washington, Publication 593. Washington, D.C.

Ruppert, Karl, and Denison, John H., Jr.
1943   *Archaeological Reconnaissance in Campeche, Quintana Roo, and Peten.* Carnegie Institution of Washington, Publication 543. Washington, D.C.

Sabloff, Jeremy A., and Rathje, William L., eds.
1975   *A Study of Changing Pre-Columbian Commercial Systems: The 1972–1973 Seasons at Cozumel, Mexico.* Monographs of the Peabody Museum, no. 3. Cambridge, Mass.: Harvard University.

Scholes, France V., and Roys, Ralph L.
1968   *Maya Chontal Indians of Acalan-Tixchel: A Contribution to the History and Ethnography of the Yucatan Peninsula.* Norman: University of Oklahoma Press.

Spinden, Herbert J.
1913   *A Study of Maya Art.* Cambridge, Mass.: Peabody Museum, Harvard University. Reprint. New York: Dover Publications, 1975.

Stephens, John Lloyd
1843   *Incidents of Travel in Yucatán.* 2 vols. New York. Reprint. Norman: University of Oklahoma Press, 1962.

Thompson, Sir J. Eric S.
1954   *The Rise and Fall of Maya Civilization.* Norman: University of Oklahoma Press. 2d ed. 1966.

von Euw, Eric
1977   *Corpus of Maya Hieroglyphic Inscriptions: Pixoy, Tzum, Itzimte.* Vol. 4, part 1. Cambridge, Mass.: Peabody Museum, Harvard University.

Wauchope, Robert, ed.
1965   *Handbook of the Middle American Indians.* Vols. 2 and 3. Austin: University of Texas Press.

Witchey, Walter R. T.
1988   Recent Investigations at the Maya Inland Port City of Muyil (Chunyaxche), Quintana Roo, Mexico. *Mexicon,* vol. 10, no. 6. Berlin.

INDEX